Shopping Spaces and the Urban Landscape in Early Modern Amsterdam, 1550–1850

Shopping Spaces and the Urban Landscape in Early Modern Amsterdam, 1550–1850

Clé Lesger

Routledge
Taylor & Francis Group
LONDON AND NEW YORK

This edition was produced with financial support from:
The Amsterdam University Fund
De Gijselaar-Hintzen Fonds
The Faculty of Humanities, University of Amsterdam
The Professor van Winter Foundation

AMSTERDAMS UNIVERSITEITSFONDS

UNIVERSITEIT VAN AMSTERDAM
Faculteit der Geesteswetenschappen

De Gijselaar-Hintzenfonds

First published as: Clé Lesger, *Het winkellandschap van Amsterdam. Stedelijke structuur en winkelbedrijf in de vroeg-moderne en moderne tijd, 1550–2000* (Hilversum: Verloren, 2013).

Translation: Vivien Collingwood

First published in 2020 by Amsterdam University Press Ltd.

Published 2025 by Routledge
4 Park Square, Milton Park, Abingdon, Oxon OX14 4RN
605 Third Avenue, New York, NY 10158

Routledge is an imprint of the Taylor & Francis Group, an informa business

ISBN: 9789463720625 (hbk)
ISBN: 9781041186083 (pbk)
ISBN: 9781003703693 (ebk)
NUR 685

Cover illustration: Second-hand shop in Amsterdam, sixteenth century. Hortensius, *Het boeck van den oproer der weder-dooperen*; BC/UvA, 2 C 18.

Cover design: Kok Korpershoek

DOI: 10.5117/9789463720625

In memory of my parents, who were both shopkeepers and the children of shopkeepers.

Table of contents

Preface

This book is based on a more extensive Dutch-language study of the retail trade in Amsterdam between 1550 and 2000, which was published by Verloren publishers in 2013.[1] I am grateful to Thys VerLoren van Themaat for granting permission for the early modern part of the study to be published here in English. When producing the English-language edition, I benefitted from the expertise and advice of Inge van der Bijl at Amsterdam University Press and from Vivien Collingwood's translation skills. This English-language edition would not have been possible without the support of four funding institutions, and it is with pleasure that I mention the financial contributions from—in alphabetical order—the Amsterdam University Fund, the De Gijselaar-Hintzen Fonds, the Faculty of Humanities of the University of Amsterdam and the Professor van Winter Foundation.

The research that underlies this book is based on a very considerable quantity of archival material, and I would like to thank the employees of the Amsterdam City Archives for their contribution to this project. This consisted not only of lugging around large quantities of records and helping me to find yet more archival material, but also of the trouble they have taken over the years to digitize many thousands of images and make them available via the image archive (*Beeldbank*). In this study, these images form an important source of information on the exterior and interior of shops. I also looked for visual material elsewhere, and in doing so I benefitted, among others, from the expertise and suggestions of Mrs Miekie Donner, who managed the collection of the Royal Antiquarian Society of the Netherlands (het Koninklijk Oudheidkundig Genootschap). I am also grateful to the late Dr Henk Zantkuijl, who provided detailed answers to my numerous questions about front steps, *pothuizen* and display cases in Amsterdam, and who also put me on the track of relevant prints and architectural drawings. Finally, colleagues, students and former students informed me when they came across images that might be of interest to the research. Without mentioning specific names, I am extremely grateful to them all. I should add that I am aware of the limits of visual material when reconstructing the material life of the past, and that is precisely why the results of the image-based research were constantly tested against what was recorded in written sources on shops.

For the analysis of patterns of accessibility in Amsterdam's urban grid—to be discussed in the chapters to come—the Bartlett Faculty of the Built Environment at University College London generously made computer software available. I am pleased to mention that it was Dr Marlous L. Craane, at that time a doctoral candidate at Tilburg University, who informed me of the existence of the software in question. She also advised and assisted me during my initial attempts to analyze the Dutch material from this perspective.

It would not have been possible to conduct the research without the skilled and helpful staff and excellent collection of the University of Amsterdam's library. In the University Library, one seldom fails to find a title contained in some exotic journal or book, and when it comes to cartographic material on Amsterdam, the Library nearly always comes up with the goods. The History Department of the

1 Lesger, Clé, *Het winkellandschap van Amsterdam. Stedelijke structuur en winkelbedrijf in de vroegmoderne en moderne tijd, 1550-2000* (Hilversum 2013).

University of Amsterdam facilitated this study by twice granting me an exemption from teaching, by never complaining about the large numbers of copies and prints that were made as part of the research, and by providing me with office supplies in all shapes and sizes. I am grateful for the collegial atmosphere that I have enjoyed there over the years. Once I had a text, this collegiality was also expressed in the willingness shown by my now former colleagues, Dr Boudien de Vries and Prof. Piet de Rooy, to read and comment on the Dutch manuscript. Their remarks and suggestions contributed to the final result and saved me from making several blunders. During the research, my former colleague Prof. Jan Hein Furnée proved to have a similar interest in the history of shopping and the retail trade, and I have fond memories of our joint efforts in this field.

I would once again like to thank all those, named and unnamed, who contributed to the creation of this book, and I hope that I have done justice to their efforts with the end result. In line with established academic practice, but no less sincere for that, I should like to conclude this preface by stating that any errors in this work are the responsibility of the author alone.

Clé Lesger,

Haarlem/Amsterdam, 2019

Introduction

Watching the hordes of people spilling out of Amsterdam Central Station into the city's shopping streets on a Saturday or Sunday, it is hard to imagine that just a few decades ago these same streets were beset by a lack of occupancy and decline. The affected streets included not only Kalverstraat and Nieuwendijk, the city's best-known shopping streets, but also streets in old working-class areas such as the Jordaan. In the 1960s, one shop after another closed. Some retailers packed up and left for the new districts that had been built on the city's periphery after the Second World War. Others abandoned entrepreneurship for wage employment, singing the praises of fixed working hours and holiday pay, whilst older shopkeepers muddled through until a redevelopment grant or old-age pension allowed them to shut up shop for good. In that same period, the sun shone on the freshly painted apartment blocks in new districts, and the shops there enjoyed a brisk trade. Nowadays, the situation is very different. Particularly on the edges of what are no longer such new districts, shops have almost disappeared altogether, the vacant retail spaces filled by offices, physiotherapy practices and other service providers. By contrast, today the shoppers are back in force in Kalverstraat and Nieuwendijk, and these streets have the highest rents in the Netherlands. As a result of gentrification, even streets in what were once run-down working-class neighbourhoods are now experiencing a thriving retail trade and the high shop rents that come with this.

It was recent changes in the retail landscape such as these that initially fuelled my interest in the early modern history of shops and shopping. Shops—and retail trade in general—have played a much more important role in our towns and cities than the relatively small amount of attention paid to this phenomenon by Dutch historians would suggest. In a strictly economic sense, shops and markets are the final link in the chain connecting producers to consumers. They are where people purchase the things that they are unable or unwilling to produce themselves, thereby profiting from the expertise, skills and also, in many cases, lower wages of producers located both near and far. We should add that what they select from the offering is not accidental but a reflection of their personality and sometimes, too, the impression they wish to create. This applies both to clothing and shoes and to the objects with which they surround themselves at home and the food they eat.

There is also a spatial aspect to the economic, social and cultural dimensions of retail trade, and it is on this aspect that I shall focus in this study; and this is hardly surprising, given that we are looking at retail trade. A whole series of factors plays a role in the successful exploitation of a shop, but ultimately it is via a shop's location that goods are made available to the consumer.[1] Ghosh and McLafferty put it thus: 'prices can be matched, services can be extended and improved, merchandise may be duplicated, and promotion can be imitated, but a retailer's locational advantages are difficult to assail or neutralize'.[2]

1 This only changed in the recent past with the introduction of mail-order companies and Internet shopping.

2 As cited in Van Duren, *De dynamiek van het constante,* p. 72.

Lesger, C., *Shopping Spaces and the Urban Landscape in Early Modern Amsterdam, 1550–1850.*
Taylor & Francis Group, 2020
DOI: 10.5117/9789463720625_INTRO

The aim of this study is thus not only to tell the history of shopping spaces in early modern Amsterdam but also to understand the location patterns in retail trade. I am interested in questions such as: where were shops located in early modern Amsterdam, why were they located there in particular, and which factors caused shopkeepers to change their location behaviour? The obvious answer to these questions is that shopkeepers based their businesses where they expected to find customers, and that they either ceased to trade or moved their shops when customers stayed away. Whilst all of this is undeniably true and many shopkeepers have experienced this firsthand, in order to get a better understanding of the underlying dynamics, we need to examine the spatial purchasing behaviour of consumers in more depth. In this study, I shall argue that the spatial structure of towns and cities—that is to say, the pattern of streets, squares, canals and alleyways—has a dominant influence on the movement of consumers through the urban landscape and thereby on the attractiveness of certain locations for retail trade, too. Disasters aside, as fundamental changes to the structure of the urban grid occur during periods of urban expansion and the restructuring of the urban landscape, in the following chapters we shall pay considerable attention to the spatial development of Amsterdam in our attempt to understand the relationship between the city as a physical structure and its functioning as an economic space.

The urban retail landscape has more than two dimensions, however, which means that our analysis should not be limited to studying location patterns in two-dimensional space. After all, it is particularly in the external appearance and interior design of shops and shop premises that the retail landscape presents itself to consumers, and these aspects therefore make an important contribution to a city's atmosphere and vitality. Nowadays, it tends to take large-scale shop vacancies to make us realize how iconic the shop has been in the urban landscape, but the situation in the past was no different. Shop windows and displays in front of the façade functioned like small exhibitions, as shopkeepers attempted to lure customers with their more or less refined presentations. In early modern Amsterdam, shops and shopping districts also had distinct appearances and characters. In this way, they sent out a message to potential customers and played a role in the complex game of appearance and behaviour with which people present themselves to the world.

Shops fulfil such functions almost cursorily, and until recently their presence in the urban landscape was so self-evident that we seldom reflected on it. It is perhaps for this reason that retail trade has largely eluded the attention of Dutch historians to date.[3] The Netherlands lacks the studies that geographers and historians have devoted to retail trade in other parts of the world, especially in the Anglo-Saxon world. Many of these studies are rooted in policy. The dramatic decline in many American inner cities in the second half of the twentieth century was also reflected in the shrinking of the central retail facilities—a predicament that called out, as it were, for studies that

3 Notable exceptions are Furnée, 'Om te winkelen'; Furnée, 'Winkeletalages als moderne massamedia'; Steegen, *Kleinhandel en stedelijke ontwikkeling*; De Nijs, *Op zoek naar de verdwenen middenstand*; Van den Heuvel, *Women and Entrepreneurship*; and Furnée, '"Our Living Museum of Nouveautés"'. Less recent are studies on large-scale shopping businesses like Miellet, *Honderd jaar grootwinkelbedrijf*; Miellet, 'Immigratie van katholieke Westfalers'; Hondelink, 'Vroom en Dreesmann'; and Jager, *Arm en rijk*. In Flanders, research into the retail trade is more extensive. See the historiographic overviews in Blondé et al., 'Retail Circuits', and Van Damme, *Verleiden en verkopen*.

analyzed and explained the process itself and its underlying causes. The urban crisis in the Netherlands never reached the scale witnessed in the US, and to a great extent, the inner cities have been spared large-scale interventions in the urban fabric. Perhaps it is for this reason that less need has been felt in the Netherlands for reflection and documentation.

In the United Kingdom, which finds itself between mainland Europe and the US—and more than just in the geographical sense—it was likewise the problems of the inner cities that undoubtedly stimulated academic interest in retail trade. But the history of retail was also studied within the broad framework of the Industrial Revolution and the modernization of British society, particularly in the nineteenth century. It will come as no surprise that older studies drew a direct link between these dramatic changes and the development of the modern retail sector. Much less attention was paid by these studies to retail trade in the early modern era, which was often seen as traditional and underdeveloped. Some were even of the opinion that prior to around 1800, shops—defined as fixed sales outlets for goods that are not produced on-site—did not exist, or hardly existed. It was thought that retail trade largely overlapped with market trading at that time.[4] In recent decades, this account of a process of modernization covering almost every aspect of society and a sharp break between the early modern and modern periods has proved untenable in many respects.[5] Likewise, in research on British retail trade and consumption patterns, it has become clear that things that were once described as typically 'modern' were less novel than they initially appeared. In many respects, it seems to have been a case of evolution rather than revolution.[6]

The direct relationship that was initially assumed to exist between developments in the retail sector and the changes set in motion by the Industrial Revolution not only reflected the modernization perspective that was dominant at the time but was also a matter of a lack of sources. For the period prior to around 1800, we lack many of the sources, mainly quantitative, that have formed the basis for research into nineteenth- and twentieth-century retail trade. This hampered the comparison with the early modern period, and for some, this evidently led to the conclusion that the lack of source material was an indication that the phenomenon under study simply did not exist at that time. But as well as the near-compelling logic of the modernization perspective and the limitations of early modern source material, there was also a third factor at play. With the exception of London, British towns in the early modern period were relatively small and not especially populous. In 1650, London had around 400,000 inhabitants, making it Europe's second most populous city after Paris. Edinburgh, the second-largest city in the British Isles, was home to just 35,000 inhabitants, and Bristol and Norwich tied in third place with no more than 20,000 inhabitants. The other towns were even smaller. A century later, the population of London had grown to 675,000, and Dublin (90,000 inhabitants) and Cork (58,000 inhabitants) had assumed second and third place. But most British towns never had more than 20,000 inhabitants, and many had far fewer.[7]

4 See for example Jefferys, *Retail Trading in Britain*. Willan, *The Inland Trade* is one of the first studies in which the myth of an underdeveloped early modern retail trade was challenged. Also important in this respect is Mui and Mui, *Shops and Shopkeeping*.

5 Compare De Vries, 'The Industrial Revolution and the Industrious Revolution'.

6 See among others Glennie, 'Consumption, Consumerism and Urban Form', p. 933 ff, and Stobart, *Spend, Spend, Spend!*

7 Population figures for European cities in De Vries, *European Urbanization*, appendix 1, and also in Bairoch, Batou and Chèvre, *La population des villes Européennes*.

Given these population numbers, it was hardly possible for a highly developed and spatially differentiated retail system to emerge.[8] This would only happen when the existing towns expanded considerably in the nineteenth century, and new industrial towns penetrated the highest echelons of the urban hierarchy. From this perspective, it is perhaps unsurprising that the development of retail trade has largely been seen as a nineteenth- and twentieth-century phenomenon.

In the present study, I shall examine the development of shops and shopping over a long period (from around 1550 to 1850) in a city whose size did not preclude beforehand the emergence of a differentiated retail system: the city of Amsterdam. From the late sixteenth century, Amsterdam enjoyed a period of unprecedented economic and demographic growth, and around the mid-seventeenth century, it was one of the five largest cities in Europe. A century later, its growth would lag behind that of front-runners such as London and Paris, but with around 230,000 inhabitants, Amsterdam was always a member of the select group of very large early modern cities. And it would remain so, even after a prolonged period of stagnation and decline that began in the mid-eighteenth century and was reversed only in the second half of the nineteenth century. Moreover, the long view that is taken here allows us to trace continuities and discontinuities that would otherwise remain hidden.

In order to avoid misunderstandings, it is useful to reflect briefly on a number of concepts. In a book about shopping spaces, we need to consider, first and foremost, the concept of the shop. The term is used here to describe a fixed location for the sale of consumer goods that are not produced or consumed on-site. A number of activities are thereby excluded from this definition; they include market trade, for example, and the trade plied by the many itinerant sellers who passed through the city until well into the twentieth century.[9] The same is true of the workshops run by artisans who sold the fruit of their labour directly to consumers. In a study with a particular focus on location patterns, it makes sense to exclude itinerant trade. Artisan trade also deserves a separate study, as artisans have to consider many factors when making location decisions, not just accessibility, which is so crucial to shops. When the term 'retail trade' is used in the following chapters, I am thus referring to shops as they are defined here. That is not to say that Amsterdam's markets will be disregarded altogether; they come into the picture when their presence affected the location behaviour of shopkeepers and the spatial purchasing behaviour of consumers.

The goods sold in shops can be divided into numerous categories, but studies on the location of shops usually distinguish between daily necessities ('convenience goods') and durable goods ('shopping goods'), on the grounds that these categories generate contrasting location patterns. In the next chapter, we will focus in more detail on the theory of shop location patterns. The composition of the convenience and shopping goods categories is explained at greater length in the appendix.

Finally, a brief word on the topography of the city. To avoid the reader losing his/her way in the many streets and neighbourhoods that inevitably come up for discussion, I have included a large number of maps on which the

8 Glennie, 'Consumption, Consumerism and Urban Form', p. 944 for a similar argument. For location patterns in small cities, see Wild and Shaw, 'Trends in Urban Retailing', figure 2, and Blondé, *Een economie met verschillende snelheden,* figures 3.8 and 3.10.

9 I do pay attention to market trade and itinerant sellers in my upcoming chapter in *A Cultural History of Shopping in the Age of Enlightenment* (*1650–1820*) (London: Bloomsbury).

Figure 1: The urban area of Amsterdam, end of the sixteenth century.

topographical indications described in the text have been marked where necessary.[10] Aside from this, it should be noted that in this study the terms 'the medieval city' or 'city centre' are used to refer to the area of Amsterdam encircled by the waters of the Singel, Kloveniersburgwal and Geldersekade canals and the open harbour front to the north, which is nowadays separated from the IJ by Amsterdam Central Station (see Figure 1). By the 'early modern city' I mean the crescent-shaped urban area (including the city centre) that was established after the large urban expansions of the seventeenth century, encircled by the Singelgracht canal (not to be confused with the Singel). Strictly speaking, the Plantage neighbourhood also formed part of the early modern city, but no residential homes were built there until the mid-nineteenth century (see Figure 2).

With the Plantage, though, we have already drifted far from the era in which our study of shops and shopping in Amsterdam begins. In the next chapter, we therefore turn

10 Since the urban grid and street names in Amsterdam have survived the passage of time relatively unchanged, the streets mentioned in the text can also be found on modern maps and on the Internet.

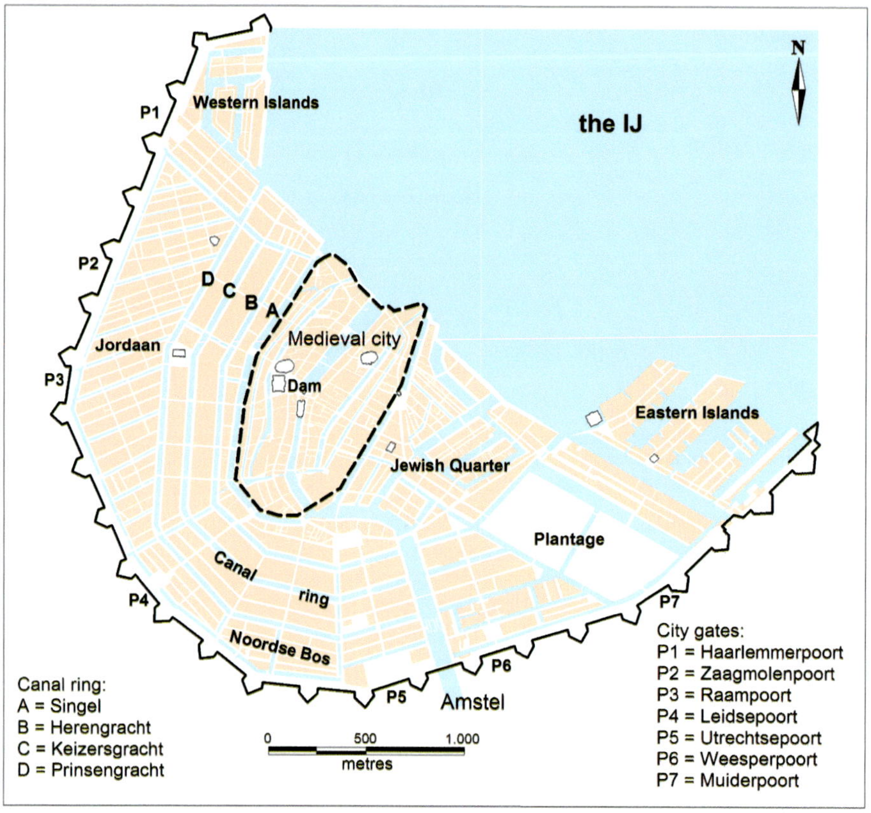

Figure 2: The urban area of Amsterdam, ca. 1665 to the mid-nineteenth century.

back to the sixteenth century. We shall also consider some of the theory of the location of shops in the urban landscape, including a method that allows us to measure the accessibility of streets and street segments within the larger whole of the urban grid. The foundations are thereby laid for an analysis in which general location principles are linked to the morphological specificity of Amsterdam in the early modern era.

1. Shops, markets and the urban landscape in sixteenth-century Amsterdam

Abstract:
Chapter one explores modern retail location theory in order to provide the tools with which to research and interpret the location patterns of shops in early modern Amsterdam. The spatial analysis clearly reveals that, already in the second half of the sixteenth century, consumer durables were sold in real shopping streets, while suppliers of daily necessities were dispersed over the city. In these years, the display and sale of goods took place almost exclusively in front of the shopkeeper's door or in the window, where both goods and customers were protected from the weather by a canopy extended from the wooden façade.

Keywords: location theory, shopping streets, shop fronts, outdoor sales

In the course of the sixteenth century—the starting point of this study—Amsterdam already had a history of retail trade dating back several centuries. Little is known about shops in this period, but we are able to establish some rough outlines. These form the background to the situation in the sixteenth century, when the source material allows us to sketch a picture of shops and shopping in Amsterdam for the first time.

Historical background

With the construction of a dam on the Amstel river in the thirteenth century, a number of pre-urban sites on both sides of the river were connected, transforming the nature of the young settlement. The dam acted as a barrier to shipping between the catchment basin of the Amstel and the external waters of the IJ and Zuiderzee, meaning that goods had to be transferred. Carters and porters were needed for this, but trans-shipment points such as these were also typically places where artisans and merchants made a living; for when the vessels came to a temporary halt and people came together, there was business to be done.[1] There would also have been fishermen and fish traders at the settlement on the Amstel and the IJ, of course, and there would have been farmers, too, although the settlement's low-lying position in a marshy river delta made the surroundings rather unsuitable for farming.

1 For the earliest history of Amsterdam, see especially Gawronski, 'Ontstaan uit een storm'; Jayasena, 'Amsterdam 1200–1300'; Speet, 'Een kleine nederzetting in het veen'; and Kaptein, 'Poort van Holland'. Comparable developments could also be found elsewhere along the coasts of the Zuiderzee (see Lesger, *Hoorn als stedelijk* knooppunt, chapter 2 and the literature cited there).

Lesger, C., *Shopping Spaces and the Urban Landscape in Early Modern Amsterdam, 1550–1850*.
Taylor & Francis Group, 2020
DOI: 10.5117/9789463720625_CH01

Although the settlement is unlikely to have had more than ca. 1,000 inhabitants in 1300, it undoubtedly had an urban character.[2] This is evident from the statute with which Guy of Avesnes, the Bishop of Utrecht, granted Amsterdam a certain degree of independence around 1300. It is also shown by the market law granted to the town: the right to hold daily, weekly and annual markets. At these markets, the citizens of Amsterdam and folk from the vicinity would buy daily necessities that they did not produce in their own households as well as goods imported from more distant regions. It is at these markets in the still-young city that we come across the earliest traces of Amsterdam's retail trade.[3]

Shops in the modern sense of the word—that is to say, fixed business locations where customers purchased goods that were not manufactured on-site—did not yet exist in this early period. The number of consumers in the town and the surrounding countryside was still too small for this, and the economy was not yet sufficiently developed. It is not possible to ascertain when the first shops were established in Amsterdam, as the medieval archival material is simply too scarce and fragmentary. However, we do know the sources from which the first shops developed.[4] First and foremost, there was the sale of second-hand goods. Due to the long lifespan and high price of woollen cloth, clothing played a particularly important role in the second-hand circuit in medieval and early modern times. The men and women who sold second-hand merchandise from fixed locations rather than from market stalls or from door to door can be seen as shopkeepers. After all, they traded in goods that were not produced on-site and were based in a room in a house, somewhere in town. A second source for the development of shops was that of artisan sellers. Particularly in the earliest period, an important role was played by producers who sold directly to consumers. When the size of demand grew and consumers started to desire a wider variety of wares, some artisans evidently extended their ranges by adding products they had not produced themselves but had purchased elsewhere or had had someone else produce for them. It was then but a small step to a situation in which they exclusively sold goods made by others—a step that marked the transition from artisan seller to retailer. Incidentally, these artisan sellers did not disappear from the picture altogether but have continued operating in some trades until the present day. Well-known examples include gold- and silversmiths and artisan furniture-makers in the luxury and exclusive segment of the market. Finally, shops also had their roots in the sale of goods that were not produced in the surroundings but had to be imported from elsewhere, including wine, subtropical fruits, spices, fine textiles such as silk, and other high-quality industrial products. If these were supplied to customers from a fixed location, this could be described as a shop.

It is impossible for us to say even approximately what kinds of consumer purchases took place before the sixteenth century (and for many years afterwards) in shops and what were made at markets and from artisans, street traders and others. We do know for certain, though, that there were shops in sixteenth-century Amsterdam. For example, in the assessment register of the *Capitale Impositie* of 1585, a tax to raise funds to break the Spanish siege of Antwerp, we come across sixteen second-hand dealers, male and female.[5] We also come across

2 The population figure for 1300 in Kaptein, 'Poort van Holland', p. 110.

3 For the early history of retailing in Bruges and London, see Stabel, 'From the Market to the Shop' and Keene, 'Sites of Desire'.

4 Stobart, *Spend, Spend, Spend!*, p. 31.

5 Van Dillen, *Amsterdam in 1585*, p. xxxix.

a number of second-hand dealers in Amsterdam's sixteenth-century *poorterboeken* (burgher registers).[6] But these sellers of old clothes and used household goods were not the only people who ran shops. The *poorterboeken* also mention considerable numbers of *wantsnijders*, who sold fabric by the yard to consumers, often from a dedicated room at home.[7] In addition, both the *poorterboeken* and the register for the *Capitale Impositie* make mention of many *kramers* (non-itinerant sellers). The latter sold a wide range of wares, including many products that were not manufactured in the city itself. A by-law of 1476 stipulated that members of the *kramersgilde* (*kramers'* guild) were only allowed to display and sell their wares indoors.[8] Not only does this tell us that they were also active elsewhere in the city, but it is also clear that selling from a fixed location was by no means a new phenomenon in the fifteenth century and—depending on the level of compliance with the by-law—may even have been common practice for *kramers* in the sixteenth century.[9]

In summary, we have been able to establish that shops in sixteenth-century Amsterdam were run by a mixed company that included *wantsnijders*, *kramers*, second-hand dealers, and also pharmacists and grocers. There were also goods on sale at the daily, weekly and yearly markets, of course, and artisan sellers and street traders also played a role in Amsterdam's retail trade, but they do not fall within the definition of the shop used in this study.

The location of retail activities: Theory

If we want to build a picture of the spatial distribution of shops over the city and the considerations made by shopkeepers that underlie this pattern, it is useful to reflect on some general observations on location patterns in retail trade. These can aid the researcher in getting to grips with the source material, and they can also be helpful when interpreting research findings. Modern research is often based on two concepts that we owe to the work of economists and geographers in pre-war Germany: those of 'range' and 'threshold value'.[10] A product's range is the maximum distance that the consumer is prepared to travel in order to buy it. The maximum distance will obviously vary from product to product. In the case of goods that are relatively cheap and purchased frequently, consumers will not usually be prepared to travel long distances, but in the case of goods that are expensive and bought only occasionally, people are prepared to travel a long way. This is because for the latter type of

6 I used a digital file of the *poorterboeken* available at the Amsterdam City Archives (Stadsarchief Amsterdam = SAA).

7 For example, around the mid-sixteenth century, some *wantsnijders* were found in Warmoesstraat (Van der Leeuw-Kistemaker, *Wonen en werken in de Warmoesstraat*, p. 33).

8 Breen, *Rechtsbronnen der stad Amsterdam*, pp. 111–112, and see also Van Nierop, 'De handeldrijvende middenstand', p. 195.

9 On Mondays, (weekly market) *kramers* were exempt from the obligation to sell exclusively from their own home.

10 I am thinking in particular of Walter Christaller (1893–1969) and August Lösch (1906–1945). The concepts of range and threshold value (and the associated location theories) are dealt with in almost all handbooks on economic geography. See for instance Lloyd and Dicken, *Location in Space* and Buursink, *Stad en ruimte*. As a matter of fact, both concepts have been developed in the context of theories about the location of economic activities at regional and supra-regional levels. It was not until around 1960 that they were also used in research into the location patterns of the retailing industry within cities (Kivell and Shaw, 'The Study of Retail Location', p. 109).

goods, the travel costs weigh much less heavily in the total acquisition cost (i.e., the purchase price plus the travel costs) than for a convenience item such as bread. The threshold value is the minimum market that is needed to keep a business—in this case, a shop—running. If demand drops below the threshold value, it is no longer possible for an entrepreneur to offer the product in this specific location in an economically viable way.[11]

The above implies that there is a tension between the location preferences of the retailer and the wishes of the consumer. For the shopkeeper, the most attractive location is the geographical heart of a place. That is because, leaving aside disruptive factors, this location is by definition the most accessible to the largest number of consumers. By contrast, for the consumer, the ideal situation is to have shops in one's immediate surroundings. In small towns with relatively short distances between the periphery and the centre, this tension will not be very large, and shops selling all kinds of goods will indeed cluster in the centre. Historically, the centre was also the place where the market square or the most important market street was usually located. Around 1800, traces of the old situation were still clearly manifest in the Yorkshire towns studied by Wild and Shaw.[12]

When towns expand over time, the distances to the centre become so great that they are no longer acceptable for all kinds of goods. The latent tension between the location advantages for the retailer (centre) and the consumer's desire to minimize the travel time and the distance to the shop then becomes stark, and a new balance is only achieved when new retail businesses are established outside the centre. This decentralization of the retail system does not apply to the entire range of goods for sale, however; in the light of the above, it will be clear that mostly sellers of goods with a small range will establish businesses outside the centre, close to the consumer.[13] This is because consumers buy these goods frequently and in considerable quantities, meaning that the disadvantages of a large distance weigh heavily.

For costly goods that are purchased less frequently, the centre remains the obvious location. This is because these goods have a high threshold value and require a large market area, one that sometimes even extends far beyond the town or city. In practice, this leads to clusters of shops in town centres selling similar goods. Unlike for shops selling convenience goods, such clustering is an advantage, not a disadvantage, for when buying consumer durables such as these—including clothing, shoes and jewellery—the consumer likes to compare what is for sale in different shops in terms of price, quality and appearance. It is no coincidence that such goods are also known as 'shopping goods' or 'comparison goods'. By establishing themselves in close proximity to one another, these shops magnify their appeal to the public and generate more turnover than they could have done in isolation.[14]

In addition to easy access from all parts of the city and the benefits of proximity to similar shops, however, there are also other advantages associated with a central location. One factor that is critically important when selling consumer durables is that the centre is not only easily

11 The terms usually refer to goods and services, but I will not address the location of services in this study.

12 Wild and Shaw, 'Trends in Urban Retailing', in particular the maps of Hull, York, Leeds, Beverly and Wakefield in figure 2.

13 They thereby aim for a monopoly position in a geographically limited part of the market.

14 Nelson speaks in this context of 'cumulative attraction' (Nelson, *The Selection of Retail Locations*, chapter 7). See also Kivell and Shaw, 'The Study of Retail Location', p. 127; Buursink, *Stad en ruimte*, p. 178; and Hotelling, 'Stability in Competition'.

accessible for the townspeople themselves but also for consumers from the surrounding region. This is because the city centre tends to be a hub for inter-local connections and transport services. Indeed, some highly specialized shops would be unable to survive without demand from the surrounding area. Finally, it should be emphasized that the concentration of shops in an area of limited size makes it possible for consumers to purchase a series of goods in one go. With 'multiple purchase trips' such as these, the travel costs are spread over a number of products, meaning that more money is left over for purchasing goods—a situation that benefits both the consumer and the retailer.[15]

Where we find shops in a town or city has everything to do with the accessibility of locations. The British geographers Davies and Bennison distinguish between:

1. general accessibility: 'the need to be central to a surrounding consumer body';
2. arterial accessibility: 'the need to be aligned alongside a major access route'; and
3. special accessibility: 'the need to occupy areas exhibiting prestige, historical affiliations or some particular environmental attribute'.[16]

The principle of general accessibility was raised above when addressing the distinction between daily necessities and consumer durables, because for shops that sell consumer durables, it is all about (general) accessibility to the population of the whole city and possibly also the surrounding area. For shops selling daily necessities, it is all about (general) accessibility to consumers in the part of the city where they are based.

The principle of arterial accessibility is based on the desire of retailers to intercept passers-by. Nelson describes this as 'accessibility to people moving about or gathering together on errands other than shopping'.[17] In a spatial sense, we should picture arterial accessibility in terms of rows of shops along important access roads and through-roads; this is why they are described as 'ribbons' in the literature. In smaller towns, these ribbons largely coincide with access roads to the centre, whereas in larger towns, shopping ribbons also develop along the major traffic axes within neighbourhoods. The third form of accessibility, 'special accessibility', refers to the clustering of shops in areas with specific characteristics, such as the presence of an affluent clientele, important public buildings, or the presence of a popular daily or weekly market.

Davies combines in a graphic model these three forms of accessibility and the location preferences of retailers that are associated with them.[18] What was described above as 'general accessibility' is represented spatially as a series of concentric zones around the city or town centre, where accessibility is greatest (Figure 1.1A). This is also where many suppliers of durable goods and highly specialized shops are located. As the distance to the centre grows, the offering becomes narrower, with the typical offering on the periphery of the city consisting of food, beverages and tobacco.[19] 'Arterial accessibility' is shown as a number of radials that transect the town from the centre

15 Jones and Simmons, *The Retail Environment*, p. 119.

16 Davies and Bennison, 'Retailing in the City Centre', p. 271, and see also Davies, 'Structural Models'. The authors base this classification on the following, among others: Nelson, *The Selection of Retail Locations*; Berry, *Commercial Structure and Commercial Blight*, and Simmons, *The Changing Pattern of Retail Location.*

17 Nelson, *The Selection of Retail Locations*, p. 45.

18 Davies, 'Structural Models', figure 9.

19 These are also sold in the city centre, of course, but there they do not play a defining role in the retail landscape.

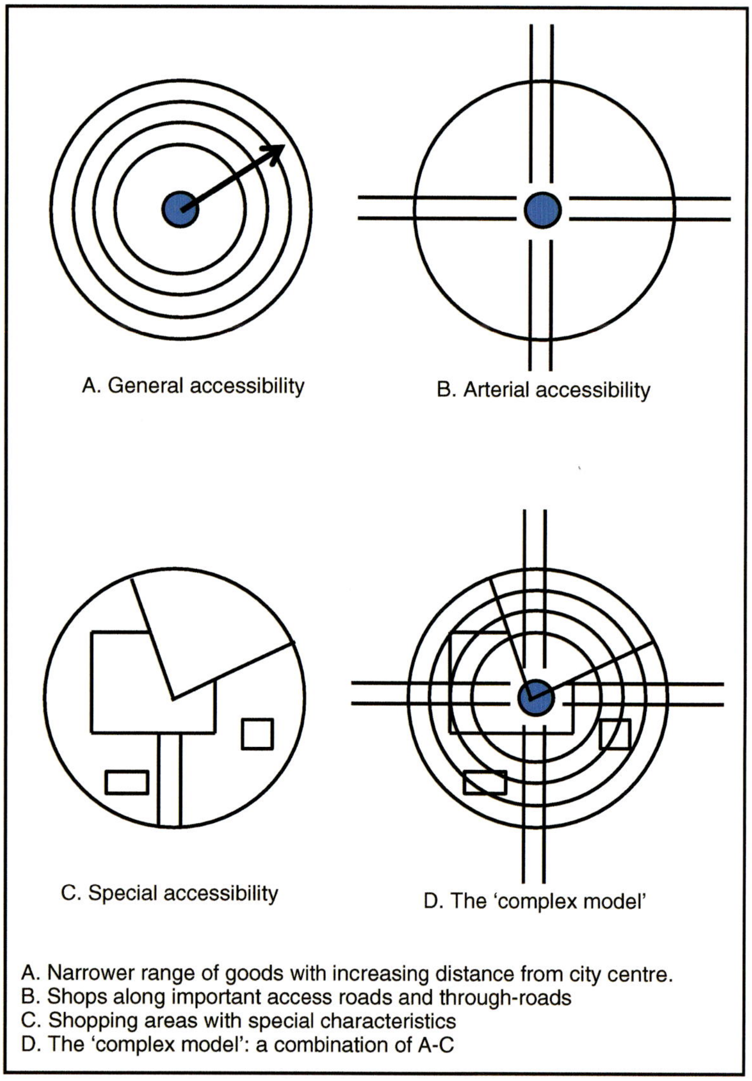

Figure 1.1: The spatial reflection of location preferences and the complex model.

and establish connections with the suburbs and the surrounding region (Figure 1.1B). With 'special accessibility', the town or city districts contain shops with specific qualities that are often linked to the prosperity of the inhabitants of these districts, and there are also much less extensive clusters of retailers selling similar merchandise (Figure 1.1C).

In what Davies calls the 'complex model', the spatial models that correspond to these three forms of accessibility are projected on top of one other, as it were, creating a model that consists of a combination of concentric, radial and clustered location patterns (Figure 1.1D). It is this combining of location patterns that allows for differentiation within each of the separate models, preventing the complex model from becoming so far removed from reality that it no longer enhances our understanding of the spatial structure of retail trade. Variation will emerge within the zones of the concentric model, for example, because in some places they are intersected by radial shopping streets, and in other places they fall in urban districts with prosperous residents or, by contrast, consumers with less spending power.[20]

In this study, the complex model and the theoretical considerations underlying it will be used as tools for ordering and understanding the confusing reality of retail locations in Amsterdam. The model offers insufficient insight into one important aspect, however: as a tool for analyzing and interpreting shop location patterns, it is remarkably vague when it comes to the question of the factors that shape what one might consider to be the core of the model—accessibility. Only years later would Davies and Bennison point to the significance of the urban grid as a determinant of location patterns.[21] And indeed, a location's accessibility is determined by the likelihood of a person visiting this location, and this, in turn, is largely dependent upon the structure of the urban grid. This was also the argument made by a group of researchers led by Bill Hillier of the Unit for Architectural Studies at University College London. From the 1970s onwards, they maintained in a long series of publications that the street pattern in a town—the 'urban grid'—is largely responsible for patterns of movement through the town and thereby for the accessibility of locations.[22]

At first glance, this claim might seem counterintuitive. We tend to assume that the location of offices, schools—and also markets and shops, of course—'steers' the traffic flows in a town. This would seem obvious, because they function as a destination for countless town-dwellers as well as for people who come to the town from elsewhere to work, study and shop. But the question is why are these facilities in these specific locations rather than elsewhere? And the answer to this question—according to the London-based researchers—is that these locations are on streets with a high density of traffic, which, in turn, is dependent on the position of these streets within the urban grid as a whole.[23] For within that grid, not all streets (or street segments) are equal; some are much more accessible than others.

The technique developed by this research group, known as Space Syntax Analysis, allows one to establish, based on a street map, the degree of accessibility of every street and every street segment.[24] Counts of numbers of passers-by in a series of streets have shown a high degree of correlation with the degree of accessibility found on the basis of street maps. The physical structure of the urban grid evidently exercises an independent influence on the accessibility of locations, on the resulting size of traffic flows, and also, by means of the latter, on the attractiveness of locations for shops. This is because retailers prefer to establish shops in

20 For a correct interpretation of the model, it is important to emphasize that it relates to situations in which the free market drives the location behaviour of retailers (Davies and Bennison, 'Retailing in the City Centre', p. 271). When this condition is met, empirical research broadly confirms the validity of the model (Brown, 'The Complex Model', p. 5).

21 Davies and Bennison, 'Retailing in the city centre', p. 271.

22 I would like to thank Marlous Craane of Tilburg University who introduced me to this line of research.

23 The following is mainly based on Hillier, 'Cities as Movement Economies'; Hillier et al., 'Natural Movement', and Hillier and Hanson, *The Social Logic of Space*.

24 In practice, a set of intersecting line segments is drawn that includes all open and public spaces (streets, squares) in the city and therefore all possible routes through the city. Next, it is determined for each line segment how many line segments it is removed from all other line segments in the area under investigation. For the use of Space Syntax Analysis in research into modern Dutch cities, see Read, *Function of Urban PATTERN*.

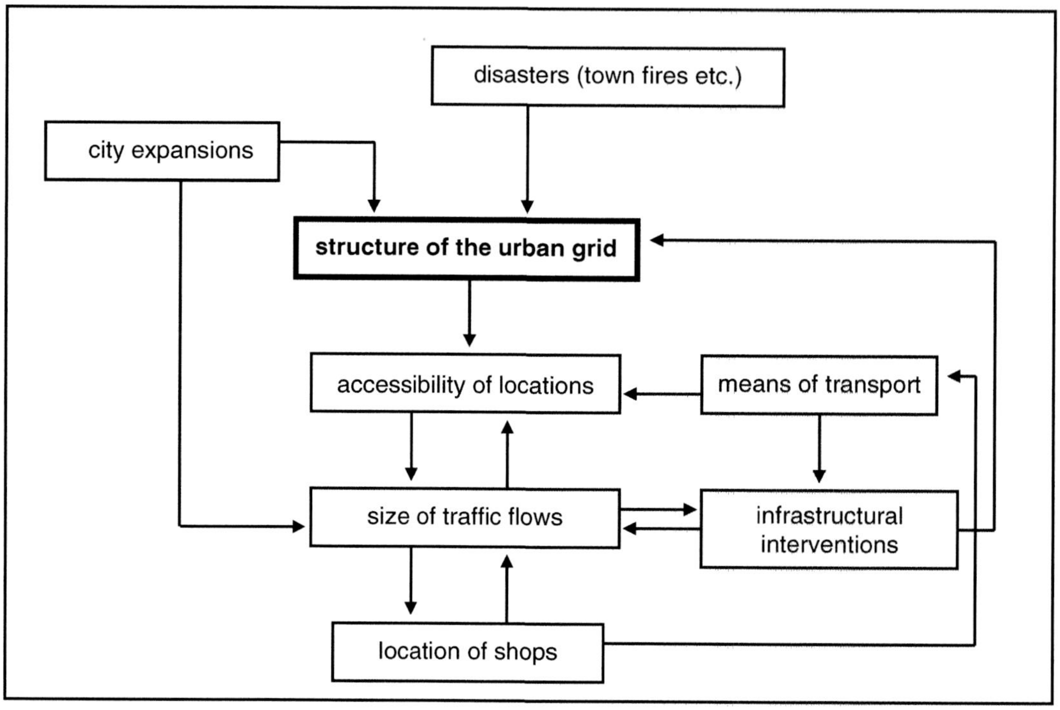

Figure 1.2: The relationship between the structure of the urban grid and the location of shops.

places that attract many passers-by, thanks to their position in the urban grid.[25]

This is shown in Figure 1.2, which also shows that once shops and other activities are established in a particular location, they reinforce the size of the traffic flows and the attractiveness of streets with a high degree of accessibility; whilst conversely, a lack of crowd pullers can cause low traffic flows in streets with a low degree of accessibility to decrease even further.[26] The diagram also shows that the structure of the urban grid is not unchanging. Radical changes usually occur after disasters such as town fires, exploding gunpowder depots or bombardment, but in this respect, Amsterdam survived intact for the long period between the mid-sixteenth century and the beginning of the twenty-first century. City expansions and infrastructural interventions did have a major influence on the structure of the urban grid, however; both also had a direct impact on the size of traffic flows in the city and thus on the attractiveness of certain locations to shopkeepers. Finally, the diagram shows that the type of transport (across water, across land, public or private) and the available means of transport affect both the accessibility of locations and the size of traffic-related interventions and other infrastructural adjustments.

With this diagram, we have made the step from an abstract complex model to specific local circumstances. After all, the urban grid varies from town to town, and is itself mainly a product of local circumstances and developments. What I shall call the 'local context' in this study covers much more than has been

25 Hillier, 'Cities as Movement Economies', p. 47, speaks of *natural movement*: '[...] the proportion of movement on each line that is determined by the structure of the urban grid itself rather than by the presence of specific attractors or magnets'.

26 Hillier et al., 'Natural Movement', pp. 31–32.

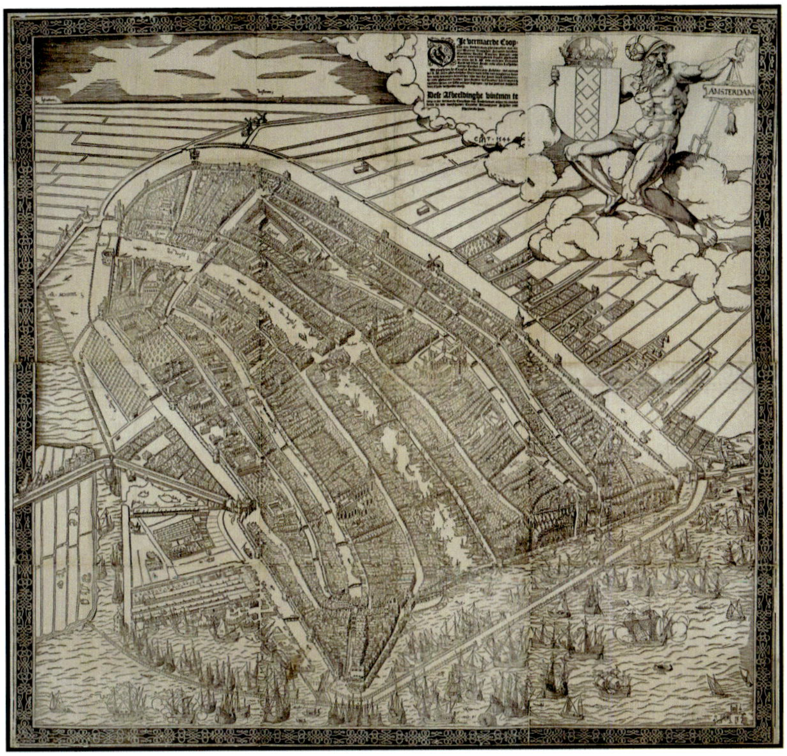

Figure 1.3: Amsterdam in the mid-sixteenth century (north at the bottom).

included in this diagram; it also includes institutions such as guilds, the distribution of income groups across the city, political relations, views on what constitutes the ideal city, and laws and regulations pertaining to retail trade. In short, the conclusion of this section is that, in practice, the interaction between general location principles and local context shaped shop location patterns in Amsterdam.

The urban landscape of Amsterdam in the sixteenth century

In order to make fruitful use of the tools discussed above, we need to sketch an impression of the urban landscape of Amsterdam as it had developed in the late Middle Ages and sixteenth century.[27] It is thus time to return to the empirical context and to Amsterdam. A map from 1544, made by Cornelis Anthonisz, gives an impression of Amsterdam in the mid-sixteenth century (Figure 1.3). It is a large-format woodcut showing a highly detailed representation of the city in bird's-eye-view.[28] The map features a beautiful image of Neptune

27 Conzen defines the urban landscape as follows: 'Die Stadlandschaft ist der an die Erdoberfläche geknüpfte morphologische Ausdruck des Stadtlebens in seiner lokalen Eigenart und in seinem historischen Zeitablauf' (Conzen, 'Zur Morphologie der englischen Stadt', p. 1).
28 For the context in which the map was made, see Colijn, 'Amsterdamse graanhandel'. An inventory of maps of Amsterdam produced up to the mid-nineteenth century is in Hameleers, *Kaarten van Amsterdam*.

and the city's arms in the top right-hand corner and a great many ships on the river IJ, but what interests us is the city centre. This roughly followed the shape of a capital letter 'H', with the 'legs' of the letter formed by the old river dikes: Warmoesstraat and Nes on the eastern side of the city and Nieuwendijk and Kalverstraat in the west.[29] These were connected by the square known today as Dam Square, but at that time it was shaped very differently and was home to very different buildings. On the eastern side of the river Amstel, the axis of Warmoesstraat-Nes was linked to Zeedijk and provided access—via Zeedijk and the St Antoniespoort—to the Antoniesdijk and the road in the direction of the region known as the Gooi. In the south, though, Nes stopped dead at the water of the Grimburgwal canal, providing access only to the religious houses and grounds that were ubiquitous in this area.[30] By contrast, the Nieuwendijk-Kalverstraat axis functioned as an important thoroughfare. On the southern side of the city, one could leave the city via the Regulierspoort and travel along the bank of the Amstel in the direction of Utrecht, whilst the road in the direction of Sloten ran via Heiligeweg and the Heiligewegpoort. To the north, Nieuwendijk provided a connection to the dike-road to Haarlem, via the Haarlemmerpoort. For a town such as Amsterdam, built on swampy peatland, it is hardly surprising that the oldest streets were constructed on the dikes that protected the residents and lower-lying land from the river water of the Amstel and the waters of the Zuiderzee and the IJ.

Let us reflect a little longer on what is immediately recognizable from the map as the heart of the city: the dam on the Amstel, then known as the Middeldam, and the adjacent square that is marked on the map as *die Plaets* ('the square'). In the thirteenth century, the dam on the Amstel created a link between four pre-urban settlements on both sides of the river, thereby laying the foundations for what, over time, would develop into a true city. The Middeldam was elevated, as it was constructed over two arched locks that had to be tall enough to allow inland river vessels through. During the sixteenth century, only the larger of the two, the Oostersluis, retained this function, whilst the Westersluis was transformed into a culvert.[31] The map by Cornelis Anthonisz clearly shows that the Middeldam, with the exception of the Oostersluis, had houses built upon it—not unlike the bridges in Florence, Venice, Paris and elsewhere (Figure 1.4). The square on the northern side of the Middeldam was the fish market, which could be stocked easily from the waters of the Damrak, Amsterdam's inner harbour. Close to the Middeldam, there was an open space between the buildings on the western bank of the Amstel river; this was the city's central public square, and one of the few such squares in Amsterdam. It does not seem to have been very large, and the surface level was also very uneven. In the west, the Plaets ran to the slope of the river embankment (Nieuwendijk-Kalverstraat); in the east, it sloped upwards to the arched locks; and in the north and south, it sloped downwards to the waters of the Damrak and Rokin, respectively.[32]

It was there that the secular government of Amsterdam had its seat and presented itself to the world.[33] It did so in what, by 1544,

29 Ter Gouw, *Geschiedenis van Amsterdam*, II, p. 303.
30 Ter Gouw, *Geschiedenis van Amsterdam*, V, p. 38 and chapter 2 for a detailed discussion of the map by Cornelis Anthonisz.
31 Breen, 'Topografische geschiedenis van den Dam', p. 104, and see also Ter Gouw, *Geschiedenis van Amsterdam,* II, pp. 302–303.
32 Ter Gouw, *Geschiedenis van Amsterdam,* II, pp. 302–303.
33 For the spatial developments in this part of the city, see Engel and Gramsbergen, 'Het eerste beursgebouw', pp. 57–87.

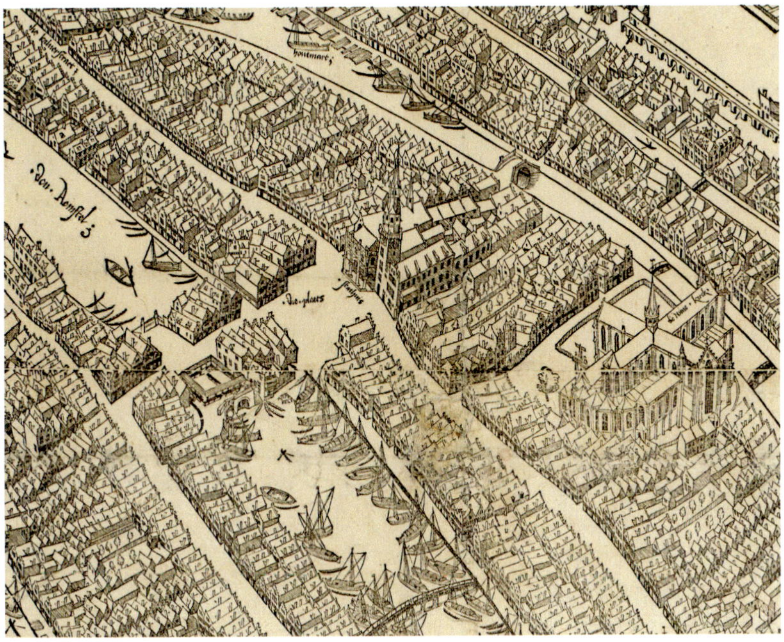

Figure 1.4: The Plaets and surroundings (north at the bottom), 1544.

had become a complex of buildings: the actual city hall lay furthest to the north; the tribunal, where justice was administered, was next door; and south of this was the former St Elisabeths Gasthuis hospital, which contained a meeting room that was named *die nyewe zale* ('the new hall') in 1501.[34] The Plaets was also the economic heart of the city; it was where the daily, weekly and yearly markets were traditionally held, and where the weighing house (*Waag*) was located, at the top of Nieuwendijk. No wonder, then, that there was an urgent lack of space in this central square. The city government responded with two kinds of measures: by dispersing the markets to the streets and canals surrounding the Plaets and enlarging the square by purchasing and demolishing houses. Judging from the frequency of these measures, the pressure on the available space only seems to have increased in the final quarter of the fifteenth century. A series of adjustments was made in the course of the sixteenth century and in the following centuries. No other part of Amsterdam was modified as frequently or as radically as the Plaets and its surroundings, something that also explains why today's Dam Square in no way resembles the situation shown on the bird's-eye-view map of 1544.

In the period that Cornelis Anthonisz drew his map, the Amstel had long been narrower than it once was. When Amsterdam had been a new settlement, the river's waters had lapped the base of the dikes. Only much later, when the city's population grew, was a wide strip of land filled in on either side of the river to create space for housing and economic activities. On the eastern side of the Damrak, this space was used to build a row of houses backing directly onto the water, which made them perfect for storage. On the western side, not only were houses built but also a broad quay known as '*Op 't Water*'. Until 1526, however, the quay did not run the full length of the Damrak but only

34 Breen, 'Topografische geschiedenis van den Dam', pp. 108–113.

from the IJ to Zoutsteeg (roughly as far as the southernmost bridge). As a result, the houses between Zoutsteeg and the Plaets backed directly onto the water, like those on the other side. The extension of the quay was undertaken 'for the convenience of the sailing and travelling man, for storage and transferral'.[35]

South of the Dam, too, there were initially no continuous quays after the filling-in and construction had taken place. On the eastern side of Rokin, the religious houses backed directly onto the water, and the quay was limited to a small section following on from the Middeldam. Nor was there a quay along the full length of the western side. A construction plan was agreed by the city government in 1527 but, as the map by Cornelis Anthonisz clearly shows, the quay was interrupted half-way along Rokin by a series of houses built right up to the water.[36] It should be emphasized that until the sixteenth century, there was no alternative traffic route to the old dike-roads in the heart of the city. Only after 1526 could the Plaets also be reached from the IJ via Op 't Water, and even today, there is no quay on the eastern side of the Damrak. Continuous quays were only built on both sides of Rokin at the end of the sixteenth century.[37]

Filling in land on the bed of the Amstel did not solve Amsterdam's space problem, however, and the city also expanded outwards over the centuries. From the bird's-eye-view map, we can see that Amsterdam was built in multiple rounds of construction.[38] The Burgwallen mark the line of the old defensive canals of Amsterdam. The Voorburgwallen were dug in the second quarter of the fourteenth century, and the Achterburgwallen date from around 1380. Several decades later, around 1425, another city expansion took place. This created a significant amount of space, largely on the eastern and southern sides of the city. The canal that encircled the city of Amsterdam was now formed by the line of canals that are today known as Singel, Kloveniersburgwal and Geldersekade. There was no city wall as of yet, but due to the expansionism of the Kingdom of Burgundy, to which Holland had belonged since 1433, there was a threat of conflict with Utrecht and Gelre. In the 1480s, a wall was built around Amsterdam on three sides; only on the harbour front, which was protected by a double row of stakes in the IJ, was there no wall. Life in Amsterdam would take place within these walls until the end of the sixteenth century. We can also see the wall clearly on the map by Cornelis Anthonisz. It was a five-to-six-metre-high construction with brick arches, topped by a walkway. There were semi-circular or square defence towers at regular intervals, and one could enter the city via the three above-mentioned main gates (Haarlemmerpoort, Reguliersspoort and St Antoniespoort) and two smaller ones (Heiligewegpoort and Jan Roodenpoort).[39] Beyond the city walls on the eastern side of the city lay the Lastage, an area that was home to shipbuilding, rope-making and other industries, as well as the frames on which woollen cloth was stretched and dried.

35 '[T]ot gerijflijckheit van den varende ende verkerende man, tot enen opslach ende ofslach' (Ibidem, p. 118). *Ofslach* is probably used here in the sense of transhipment.

36 Ibidem, pp. 117–118. The absence of a continuous quay along the Rokin can also be clearly seen on the map by Jacob van Deventer from around 1560. This map lacks the details of the map by Cornelis Anthonisz, but the infrastructure has received particular attention. For the situation around 1425, see Ter Gouw, *Geschiedenis van Amsterdam*, II, p. 302.

37 See the map of Amsterdam made and published by Pieter Bast in 1597.

38 Speet, 'Verstening, verdichting en vergroting'.

39 Ter Gouw, *Geschiedenis van Amsterdam*, V, p. 41 and the map by Cornelis Anthonisz.

Figure 1.5: Shop locations in Amsterdam, 1585.

There was no longer any room in the city for all these activities. A similar situation existed in the environs to the west of the city. Industries were located there, too, and just outside the Haarlemmerpoort a small residential neighbourhood even developed, known as the Vissersbuurt or 'fishing neighbourhood' (see Figure 1.5 for the location of the gates and the main streets).[40]

40 The presence of houses and industries outside the city walls gave rise to a long series of problems in the sixteenth century (Brouwer Ancher and Breen, 'De doleantie', and Taverne, *In 't land van belofte,* chapter 4).

The location of shops in the urban landscape

Now that we have an impression of the topography of Amsterdam in the mid-sixteenth century, we are ready to address the question of the location of shops in the urban landscape. Answering this question puts great demands on the source material, because we want to know as accurately as possible where shops were established. Based on the city's by-laws, we are able to say several things about the location of markets, but to date we know next to nothing about the shop location pattern. One source, however, does give a good impression for the year 1585: the above-mentioned register of the *Capitale Impositie*, a tax meant to generate the financial means needed for the relief of Antwerp, which had been besieged in 1585 by the troops of Alexander Farnese, Duke of Parma.[41] The States of Holland stipulated the sum to be paid by the towns of Holland, including Amsterdam, which the city government could divide amongst the residents at its discretion. In total, almost 3,000 households contributed to the tax. They formed the wealthier share of the total population of Amsterdam, which at that time was home to more than 30,000 people, or around 7,000 to 8,000 households.[42] The register is of great value to this research, as Van Dillen succeeded in using a range of sources to discover the professions of almost 1,400 taxpayers. Moreover, the register follows the walking route that the tax collectors took through the city, meaning that we can roughly pinpoint the residences of the taxpayers. One drawback of the source is the lack of less wealthy households, as these would undoubtedly have included a number of shopkeepers.[43] When determining the location of Amsterdam's main shopping streets in 1585, though, this drawback weighs less heavily, as property was expensive in those streets, and thus few poorer shopkeepers would have been based there.

Which professional groups one selects has a significant impact on the results. As this research focused on shopkeepers, craftsmen were not included, nor were people who were exclusively (or almost exclusively) engaged in overseas trade. Not all merchants belonged to this latter group; as I shall explain below, many merchants also sold directly to consumers at this time. It would make little sense to exclude them on the grounds that they engaged in wholesale as well as retail trade. With the exception of traders in raw materials (such as corn traders, wood traders and flax traders), I therefore included merchants in specific trades in the analysis. Among them were a considerable number of drapers, silk traders, dairy merchants and wine merchants. Finally, groups such as *kramers*, *wantsnijders*, second-hand dealers and bakers were also included among Amsterdam's shopkeepers.[44]

Figure 1.5 shows the situation as it was in 1585, but without the area added by the so-called *Eerste Uitleg* or 'first expansion' of 1578–1586, which brought the Lastage and the area between Singel and what would later become Herengracht within the city's walls. This can be justified on the grounds that when the register for the *Capitale Impositie* was drawn up, no retailers were yet registered in this new ring around the medieval city.[45] The quays on both sides of Rokin had been extended by then; however, demolition had created more space on the Plaets, and a new weighing house had been built that came into use in 1566. The latter continued to be used until 1808, when the beautiful gothic building was demolished on the orders of King Louis Napoleon.[46]

41 Van Dillen, *Amsterdam in 1585*.

42 The number of persons per household is found in Van der Woude, 'Demografische ontwikkeling', table 21. See for estimates of the population size of Amsterdam: Nusteling, *Welvaart en werkgelegenheid*, appendix 1.1, and Van Dillen, *Amsterdam in 1585*, p. xxxi.

43 Dudok van Heel, 'Waar waren de Amsterdamse katholieken', pp. 42–47. Van Heel claims that Catholics are also underrepresented in the register.

44 I am aware of the fact that bakers are sometimes considered as artisan sellers. Because bread is a daily necessity and because the Amsterdam bakers almost exclusively sold bread from the baker's house, they are included here among Amsterdam shopkeepers.

45 Van Dillen, *Amsterdam in 1585*, p. xxxi.

46 Breen, 'Topografische geschiedenis van den Dam', pp. 131–132.

Table 1.1 Location of cloth-sellers, silk-cloth sellers and second-hand dealers, 1585

	drapers		silk merchants		second-hand dealers	
Nieuwendijk	38	54.3%	3	17.6%	0	0.0%
Warmoesstraat	10	14.3%	11	64.8%	0	0.0%
Kalverstraat	4	5.7%	0	0.0%	0	0.0%
Nes	1	1.4%	0	0.0%	1	6.3%
St. Jansstraat	0	0.0%	0	0.0%	10	62.4%
elsewhere	17	24.3%	3	17.6%	5	31.3%
total	70	100.0%	17	100.0%	16	100.0%

Source: Calculated on the basis of Van Dillen, *Amsterdam in 1585*.

Even a cursory examination of Figure 1.5 clearly reveals that the era in which shops were clustered around the central market square had come to an end. Although there can be no doubt that the Plaets and the adjacent Middeldam—which we shall refer to jointly as 'the Dam'—was an important site for shops, it was not the only one. The shops were spread throughout the city.[47] What is clear, though, is that they were not evenly dispersed. There was a strong concentration of shops in the northern half of the city, roughly from the area around the Dam and Halsteeg to the waters of the IJ. Not all of this area's many canals, streets and alleyways were equally popular. Shops were mainly located on the Dam and Nieuwendijk and on Gasthuissteeg, Warmoesstraat, St Jansstraat, Pijlsteeg, Halsteeg and, to some extent, also on Damrak. There was also some clustering in the southern part of the city, where shops were much scarcer; Kalverstraat and, to a lesser degree, Nes were important locations.

Following common practice in modern research, I made a distinction between suppliers of daily necessities (convenience goods) and suppliers of consumer durables (shopping goods). As explained above, these have different location preferences. Shopkeepers who sell daily necessities are usually located close to their customers and therefore spread throughout the city. For consumer durables, which are purchased less frequently, the distance to the shop plays a less significant role, and we would thus expect to see a concentration of similar shops. These expectations are largely confirmed by Figure 1.5. Suppliers of daily necessities did indeed show a relatively high degree of dispersal and were even to be found on the periphery of the city. By contrast, shops selling durable goods were heavily concentrated on a few axes: Nieuwendijk, Warmoesstraat and St Jansstraat. The picture becomes even sharper when we focus our attention on the key textile industry, particularly on suppliers of fabric and used clothing (see Table 1.1).

Now it turns out that the trend towards clustering in the consumer durables sector was even stronger than one would have expected based on Figure 1.5. More than 54 per cent of all drapers registered in the *Capitale Impositie* were located on Nieuwendijk, the silk

47 It should be emphasized that the shop locations on the map are not exact. Although we can roughly reconstruct the route that the tax collectors took through the city, it is not always clear which side of the street they were on. See also Kam, *Waar was dat huis in de Warmoesstraat*, p. 439.

merchants were mainly based on Warmoesstraat (almost 65 per cent), and second-hand dealers mainly on St Jansstraat, a small street linking Warmoesstraat to Oudezijds Voorburgwal.[48] And whilst the drapers were relatively spread out over Nieuwendijk—which is hardly surprising, given their numbers—nine of the eleven silk merchants were based at the northern end of Warmoesstraat, between the Oude Kerk and Oudezijds Armsteeg. The concentration is highly consistent with what the theory tells us about suppliers of consumer durables. Setting up shop in close proximity to others would have been more attractive to potential clients, as it gave them more choice, and would have generated more turnover for shopkeepers than they could have achieved in an isolated location.

Suppliers of daily necessities, by contrast, were not located in one or a few streets but were dispersed over the city, and they did profit from having an isolated location. Bakers are a good example. Customers would not have wanted to travel great distances for bread, and they did not usually make a detailed comparison of the price and quality of bread in a series of shops. Only if there were grain shortages and bread was scarce would it be useful to compare the offering, but the city government fixed the price, weight and composition of bread in such circumstances, meaning that the offering remained more or less homogeneous. The fact that there were nevertheless clusters of bakers in several places makes it clear that whilst the patterns we have found are consistent with the findings of modern research on retail location preferences, our analysis should not end there. We need to look in more depth at the context in which location decisions were made. It was argued above that the structure of the network of canals, streets and alleyways in a city has a near-decisive influence on the course of traffic flows and hence on the accessibility and attractiveness of locations, too. Many years ago, Ter Gouw wrote: 'The composition of the streets and canals forms the framework of the city';[49] and it is to that framework that we shall now turn.

The structure of Amsterdam's urban grid and the accessibility of streets and canals can be analyzed effectively using Space Syntax Analysis, as described above.[50] More specifically, we are concerned with a technique known as 'segment analysis' whereby—as the name suggests—streets are divided into segments between intersecting streets (street corners).[51] For each segment, it is then determined how easy it is to reach all of the other street segments within a certain radius.[52] The results of the analysis of the urban grid in 1585 are summarized in Figure 1.6. Warm colours indicate a high degree of accessibility and cool colours a

48 The percentage of drapers on Nieuwendijk becomes even higher if we also include the shops that were located just around the corner in Kapelsteeg and St. Nicolaasstraat. For second-hand dealers in Amsterdam, see Van Eeghen, 'Uitdraagster 't zij man of vrouw', and Van Wijngaarden, 'Barber Jacobs'.

49 Ter Gouw, *Geschiedenis van Amsterdam*, V, p. 97.

50 I have used UCL Depthmap, versie 8.15.00c (University College London, Bartlett School of Graduate Studies), and I gratefully acknowledge their permission to use this computer programme.

51 The computer programme does not use streets but street segments as a unit of measurement, because in the first case, long streets with many side streets would have a disproportionate influence on the analysis. In fact, the length of the street segments is also corrected for.

52 According to Hillier, the results of this *segment angular analysis* are very similar to the way in which people actually move through the urban landscape. The figure presents *Normalized Mean Depth* at a radius of 200 metres. See also Hillier, 'Using Depthmap'.

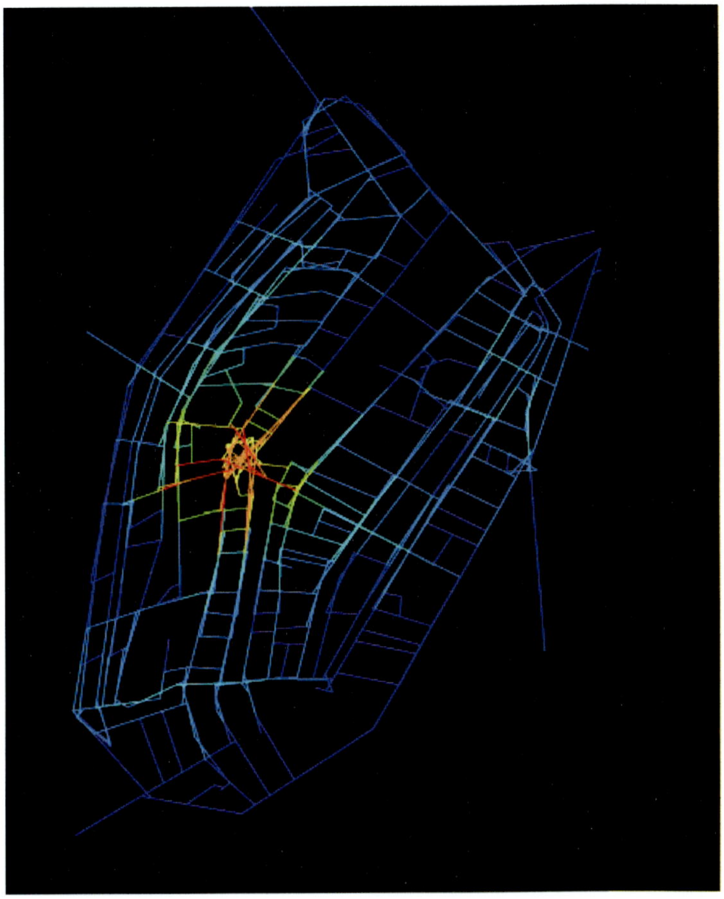

Figure 1.6: Amsterdam 1585: to-movement potential.

low degree. On the map, the degree of accessibility ranges from red (high), through orange, yellow and green to blue (low).

A glance at the map clearly shows that the degree of accessibility varied significantly from street segment to street segment, and that segments with a high level of accessibility were not dispersed throughout the city but clearly clustered on and around the Dam. We know from the above that the Dam formed the heart of the city and was its central market square, but even in the absence of any historical context, a strictly geometrical analysis of Amsterdam's urban grid would confirm that the Dam was the place that could be accessed most easily from all other locations in the city and thus formed the heart of Amsterdam in a topographical sense, too. The streets that fanned out from the Dam in all directions were likewise some of the city's most accessible streets and street segments. On the whole, the further one moved away from the Dam, the less accessible the street segments became. That was also true of what we described above as the main axes on both sides of the Amstel (Nieuwendijk-Kalverstraat and Warmoesstraat-Nes).

In Space Syntax Analysis, the accessibility of a street segment from all other segments within a certain radius is known as 'integration or to-movement potential'. A technique

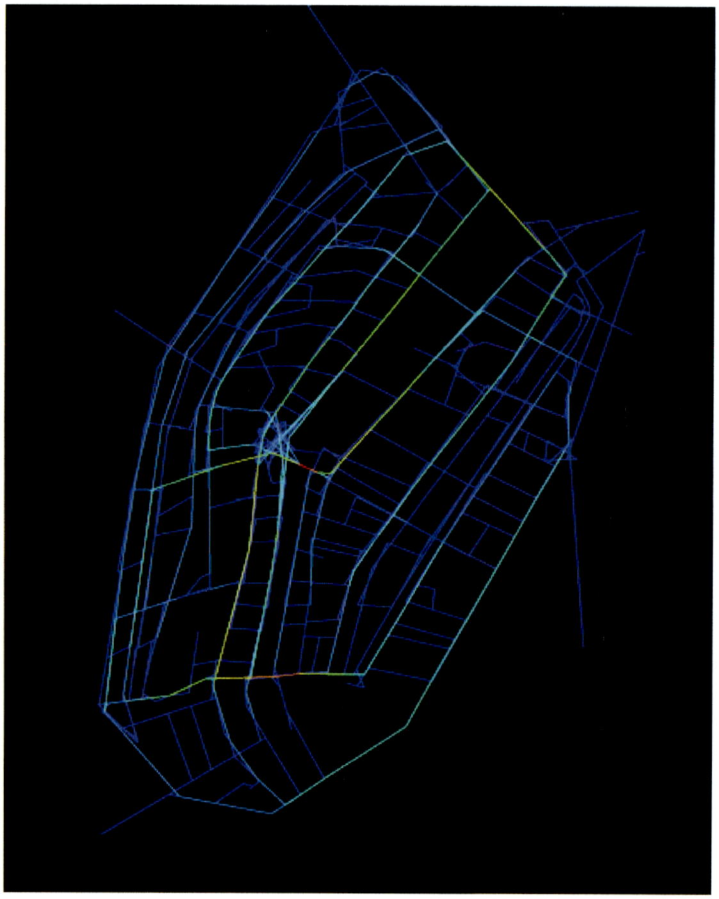

Figure 1.7: Amsterdam 1585: through-movement potential.

has also been developed that measures 'through-movement potential': the degree to which each street segment forms part of the shortest routes between all possible pairs of segments in the urban grid.[53] This value is also known as 'choice' because it is a representation of the route that people choose when they want to move from one place in a city to another. Through-movement potential gives a good indication of the key through-routes in a city. These are shown on the map in Figure 1.7. It will come as no surprise that many segments have been assigned low values,[54] indicating that they did not form part of through-routes. Relatively high values have been assigned to Damrak, Warmoesstraat and Nieuwendijk north of the Dam, and Kalverstraat and the western side of Rokin south of the Dam. The eastern side of Rokin and Nes had little through-movement potential, the three east-west connections more so. The route along the banks of the IJ across the Nieuwe Brug ('new bridge') was the most northerly of these east-west connections; a second axis ran through

53 Shortest routes are defined as routes with as few sharp turns as possible (*least angle routes*).

54 The figure presents *Choice* with a radius *n*, meaning that all street segments are involved in the analysis.

the heart of the city from today's Damstraat, via the Dam, to today's Paleisstraat; and a third connection lay on the southern side of the city, where the Langebrug ('long bridge') linked Langebrugsteeg in the east to Taksteeg in the west.

By revealing hidden patterns of accessibility in Amsterdam's urban grid, Space Syntax Analysis indicates where we might expect to find shops if the urban grid were the only factor affecting the location behaviour of retailers. If we compare the maps showing the accessibility of Amsterdam's streets with the actual distribution of shops in 1585, we cannot but conclude that there is a large degree of overlap. The locations preferred by retailers were indeed mainly on streets that were found to be easy to access from all parts of the city (the Dam and surroundings) and along streets that formed important through-routes (the axes on both sides of the Amstel river and several east-west connections).

The implications of this finding are significant. The notion that accessibility is critically important to the success or failure of a retail enterprise is probably as old as retail trade itself, and it is an idea that we also encounter in Nelson's work and Davies' complex model. What underlies accessibility is seldom made explicit, however, let alone investigated. As a result, one can get the impression that it is the location of public buildings and other prominent landmarks in a city that shapes urban traffic flows and thereby generates patterns of accessibility. This turns out to be a misconception; rather, it is the 'bare' pattern of streets, canals and squares that shapes traffic flows to a significant extent and thereby organizes urban space in terms of accessibility. Accessibility within the urban grid, in turn, makes some locations more attractive than others as sites for shops and public buildings. To exaggerate somewhat: the Dam did not become the heart of the city because shops, markets and public buildings were located there; instead, these activities were located there because the Dam was the focal point in Amsterdam's network of streets and traffic flows.

This does not mean, however, that the local context can simply be reduced to the structure of the urban grid; the degree to which the latter could affect the distribution pattern of shops was dependent on a number of other local factors. One key factor was the natural condition of the ground. Amsterdam was built in a river delta, and in this low-lying area, the river dikes were traditionally the most important traffic connections, something that does not come over sufficiently in the analysis of the 'bare' urban grid. This explains why Haarlemmerdijk, Nieuwendijk and the southern end of Kalverstraat come out of the analysis of through-movement potential less prominently than one would expect. The Haarlemmerdijk-Nieuwendijk-Dam-Kalverstraat route was certainly the most attractive through-route. It had few sharp turns and there were no significant height differences. The situation for the Damrak-Dam-Rokin axis was different. There, vehicles would have had to contend with height differences at the locks on the Dam, and by Spui and on Damrak there was also the nuisance of flooding at high tide.

Local factors other than the structure of the urban grid are also key to understanding the contrast between the northern and southern halves of the city. On the map showing through-movement potential, we can see little difference between the two halves; Kalverstraat alone has a remarkably strong position as a through-route. When we look at the distribution of shops, the picture is very different. This is striking, because Kalverstraat would appear to be a classic example of a 'major access route'; in other words, a street that is perfect for intercepting passers-by, in this case people travelling to and from the city centre. Despite this, there were few shops. This undoubtedly had to do with the presence of the cattle market, which meant that the southern end of Kalverstraat was regularly soiled with manure, making it almost impossible for consumers to take a peaceful look at what was for sale in the shops. As a result, hardly any shops selling durable goods—for which comparison of the offering is important—were located there (see Figure 1.5).

But there was even more going on. The commercial heart of the city lay unmistakably in the north, on both sides of the inner harbour and by the IJ. In the analysis of the urban grid, these masses of water appear to be barriers, but this was only partly true. For a harbour city such as Amsterdam, the waters of the IJ and Damrak were also a wide entranceway that brought the city into contact with the world beyond the city walls. People from the countryside of North Holland reached the city by crossing the IJ, as did visitors from more distant cities and regions. It was precisely due to the proximity of the inner harbour and the IJ that the northern part of the city was home to the wealthy commercial elite at this time. They lived in Warmoesstraat for many years, preferably on the western side, where merchants used the buildings backing onto the water of the Damrak for storage. A commodities exchange was held on the eastern side of the Nieuwe Brug in those years, and when the weather was bad, people would shelter under the canopies of the houses at the northern end of Warmoesstraat.[55] The presence of a wealthy clientele, the arrival of many visitors from across the IJ *and* the fact that two of the city's three main gates provided a connection to the northern outskirts of the city meant that this part of the city, particularly the old dike-roads that led to the Dam (Nieuwendijk and Warmoesstraat), was by far the most suitable location for shops.

Finally, the regulations issued by the city government also shaped the retail landscape that emerged on the basis of general location principles and Amsterdam's urban grid. When it came to retail trade, the government was anything but aloof in the early modern era. A series of by-laws announced provisions on the permissible width of displays by doorways, the quality of the merchandise on sale, and competition from market traders and street-sellers. The location of shops was not subject to rules, however; the renting or acquisition of retail space was governed by the laws of supply and demand, and potential retailers could set up shop where they expected the highest turnover for a certain cost level. Despite this, the government did exercise an important indirect influence on shop location patterns. By issuing mandatory prescriptions on where certain markets could be held and by relocating markets, the government influenced the direction of pedestrian flows through the city. Since it is not evident beforehand that this influence was consistent with the effect of the urban grid on traffic flows, let us therefore take a closer look at the location of markets in Amsterdam around 1585.

Figure 1.8 clearly shows that the markets were spread across the city, with a clear cluster on the Dam, Damrak and Nieuwezijds Voorburgwal, lying to the west of the Dam.[56] These were almost exclusively markets selling

55 See Lesger, *Rise of the Amsterdam Market*, pp. 243–249, for the Amsterdam merchants at the end of the sixteenth century, and Van der Leeuw-Kistemaker, *Wonen en werken in de Warmoesstraat* for a detailed analysis of the residents of the Warmoesstraat around the middle of the sixteenth century.

56 Figure 1.8 is based on information in Van Dillen, *Amsterdam in 1585*; Ter Gouw, *Geschiedenis van Amsterdam*, V, pp. 429–434; Kistemaker, 'De Amsterdamse markten', and Noordkerk, *Handvesten ofte* privilegiën, p. 1667.

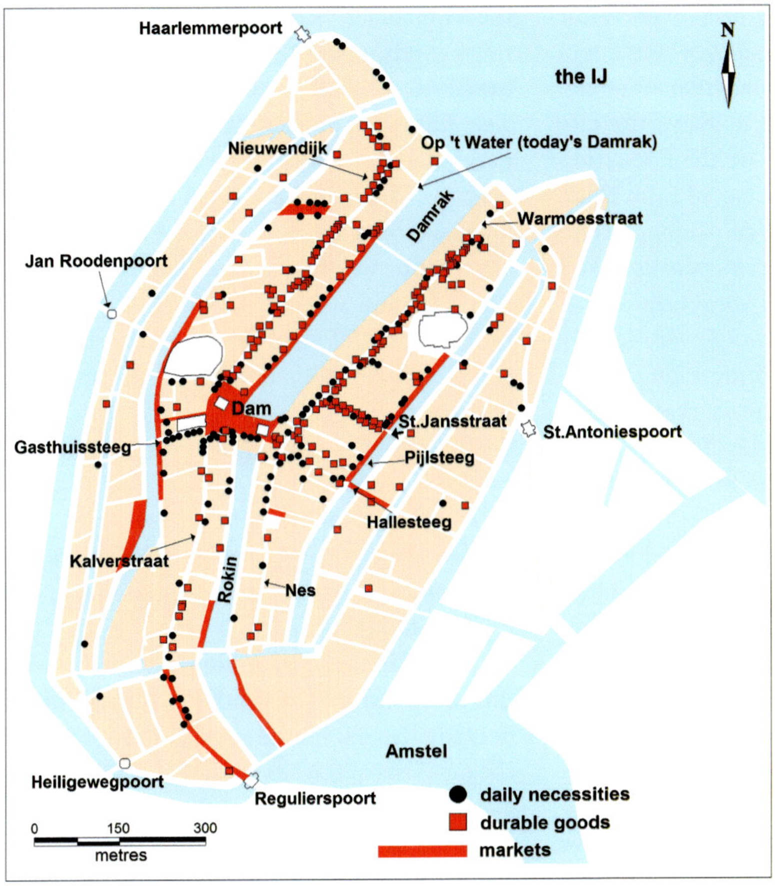

Figure 1.8: Markets and shops in Amsterdam, ca. 1585.

foodstuffs such as fish, butter, cheese, fruit and vegetables. Located on the eastern side of the Dam were the markets on Oudezijds Voorburgwal for grain, peas, beer and yarn. The nearby Oude Hoogstraat and the bridge over Oudezijds Voorburgwal functioned as a pig market, and Kalverstraat between Spui and the Regulierspoort was the site of the cattle market. Sheep and calves were traditionally traded on the Dam. The sale of meat, which for health reasons was subject to strict controls, took place in the *vleeshal* (meat market). Until 1582, this was located in Waagsteeg by the city hall, but due to the lack of space in this busy part of the town, the meat market was moved in that year to the former Pieterskapel (Chapel of St Peter) on Nes. The sellers of *coocte spijse*, prepared foods such as sausages, also moved there. The markets for building materials and peat were located on Rokin, in the southern part of the city, and on the eastern side of Nieuwezijds Voorburgwal, somewhat on the periphery of the city.

When we compare the distribution of markets with the to-movement potential shown in Figure 1.6, it is clear that the markets on and around the Dam, on the nearby part of Nieuwezijds Voorburgwal, on Oudezijds Voorburgwal and on the Damrak enjoyed a high degree of accessibility. The location of many markets along canals and quays was undoubtedly related to the fact that it was much more efficient to move merchandise over water than through the relatively narrow streets of Amsterdam. But it also appears that when determining the site of these markets, the city government took account of their location relative to the crowded streets and the Dam. Thus, it will have been no coincidence that, with the exception of the grain, pea, beer and yarn markets on Oudezijds Voorburgwal, the markets in the heart of the city were largely consumer markets. Located more on the periphery of the city were the markets selling goods that were purchased less frequently, or markets that mainly supplied wholesalers and butchers (livestock markets).

All in all, it seems unlikely that the location of markets exercised a significant and independent influence on the retail landscape of Amsterdam in the final quarter of the sixteenth century. After all, the consumer markets were located in places where, based on their location in the urban grid, we would already expect to see relatively large flows of pedestrians. The presence of markets would undoubtedly have reinforced the retail function of the approach streets, though; retailers set up shop in these streets in order to intercept passers-by and thereby benefit from what is known in the literature as linear accessibility.

Although the sixteenth-century source material does not allow for a very refined analysis, it will have become clear that the three forms of accessibility introduced in this chapter also shaped the retail landscape of Amsterdam in 1585. When considering general accessibility, we made a distinction between daily necessities and durable goods. As one would expect from the theory, suppliers of foodstuffs such as bread were dispersed quite widely over what was then still a relatively small city. When it came to cheap but frequently purchased and relatively homogeneous goods such as these, the shopkeepers would draw customers from the immediate vicinity. The situation for durable goods was different, and here we would expect to see a concentration of shops selling a similar range of goods. As durable goods are purchased much less frequently than daily necessities, it would have been very important for retailers to secure a location in the part of the city that was most accessible to consumers. This situation was also evident in 1585, with the clustering of shops on and near the Dam, along Nieuwendijk and Kalverstraat and in St Jansstraat.

The presence of many shops selling similar goods on what were in essence radial streets clearly shows that even in those years, Amsterdam's central square, the Dam, lacked sufficient capacity to accommodate all of the trade in durable goods. The shops in this sector fanned out, as it were, along the streets with the most turnover potential, and not coincidentally these were the radials that connected the outskirts of the city to the Dam. As a result, general and linear accessibility overlapped on these major access roads. Nor is it possible, in a spatial sense, to distinguish special accessibility from other forms of accessibility in a city of Amsterdam's size in 1585. Warmoesstraat, with its prosperous merchants and administrators, and the Dam, the site of the city's important public buildings, partly derived their significance as retail areas from these special 'attractions', but at the same time, Warmoesstraat was also an important approach route to the Dam (linear accessibility) *and* formed part of the central retail system (general accessibility). The Dam, meanwhile, lacked the linear character of the other shopping streets but showed a combination of general and special accessibility. Davies' complex model thus helps us to distinguish analytically between the three forms of accessibility, but when we consider actual practice in sixteenth-century Amsterdam, it is clear that the spatial patterns associated with this distinction overlapped with and merged into one another.[57]

Streets, houses and shops

The spatial distribution of shops in 1585 and the clustering of providers of shopping goods, especially on Nieuwendijk and Warmoesstraat, suggest that something resembling shopping streets existed at this time. But what exactly were these streets and shops like? In order to get a good impression of the retail landscape of Amsterdam, we cannot limit ourselves to the two-dimensional world of maps, but we need to try to sketch a picture of the third dimension. This is no simple task for the late Middle Ages and the sixteenth century, because hardly any images have survived from this period. Nor can the unsurpassed bird's-eye-view map by Cornelis Anthonisz help us in this respect. Anthonisz may have drawn the houses and especially public buildings in great detail, and he also paid careful attention to the ships on the IJ and the timber yards on the IJ and Nieuwezijds Voorburgwal, but we see no traces of life in the street, the crowds on the Plaets, or the front steps and canopies of the houses. We thus need to reconstruct this aspect of reality in a different way.

Perhaps we should start at the most basic level of all, that of street paving. In medieval Amsterdam, paving was not considered a governmental task; every house-owner was expected to take responsibility for paving the stretch of road in front of their own home. This custom probably dated back to the time when dikes such as the later Nieuwendijk and Warmoesstraat were constructed on private land. This remained the property of the owner, of course, who was in turn liable for the maintenance of the dike itself and the road that ran along it. As long as these roads were merely access roads, the situation changed little, but when traffic began to roll along them, the city government intervened.[58] The latter checked whether the compulsory maintenance had actually been carried out and monitored the state of the roads, as shown by the repeated bans on 'stones protruding from the street'. Stones could not be left to protrude, according to a by-law of 1484, even if they were *not* used for throwing at people or smashing windowpanes.[59]

The result of this private liability for maintenance was a colourful mix of stone cobbles and brick paving, and by the sixteenth century, this was no longer considered desirable. The year 1524 saw the appointment of a paviour, who would henceforth pave the streets in a uniform manner and charge the owners of adjacent houses for the work.[60] This system evidently gave rise to multiple problems and ultimately proved unsatisfactory, for in 1556 the city government decided that the main thoroughfares and the streets where the procession of the Miracle of Amsterdam was held were to be paved at the city's expense. The owners of the houses would be charged a street tax, which would also cover the maintenance of the paving.[61] At the end of the sixteenth century, in 1593, this system was expanded to cover 'all through-roads and alleyways where two sledges can pass'.[62]

57 That is also something that Davies and Bennison themselves pointed out (Davies and Bennison, 'Retailing in the City Centre', p. 271).

58 Donath, 'De rechtstoestand van de stoepen', pp. 70–71, and also Zantkuijl, *Bouwen in Amsterdam*, p. 22.

59 Breen, *Rechtsbronnen der stad Amsterdam*, pp. 148, 197 and 442. See also Noordkerk, *Handvesten ofte privilegiën*, pp. 732, 983 and 995.

60 Ter Gouw, *Geschiedenis van Amsterdam*, V, p. 243.

61 Ibidem, pp. 243–244.

62 '[A]lle doorgaende Straten ende Stegen, daer twee sleden elck anderen konnen wijcken'

The problem of overdue maintenance on major traffic axes thereby became less urgent, but one can hardly imagine that the early modern streets were really comfortable. In order for the many cart horses that spent their days lugging carts and sledges to get a grip on the road surface, the cobblestones were not laid flat but had pointed tops. Little wonder, then, that in the sixteenth century, corn hauliers and other labourers laid planks in the street 'so that they might do their work with greater ease'.[63] What is more, the road surface was pitted with drains that carried away household waste water and rain water. According to sixteenth-century by-laws, every house-owner was explicitly forbidden from covering these drains with stone slabs or brick arching for more than seven feet. The open section, which could be covered with a wooden plank, was used for cleaning the drain. This was no doubt essential, but the presence of half-open drains, some of which cut across the streets, can hardly have improved the negotiability of the streets.[64]

Judging from the by-laws, the streets were an unholy mess. In the absence of a proper drainage system, for instance, the occupants of upstairs apartments threw their waste water out of the window. The streets were also soiled with the 'muck and other filth' discarded by young and old. Many people even relieved themselves in the street, eschewing the privies that the city had built by the city walls, bridges and elsewhere. Nor was the Plaets in front of the city hall spared, as shown by a by-law of 1581, whereby a fine of twenty stivers was to be imposed on anyone, young or old, who relieved themselves in front of the building.[65]

Contrary to the impression given by Cornelis Anthonisz's map, the streets and squares of the city would have been littered with building materials and commodities. The detailed building regulations of 1565 included a ban on leaving wood, iron, barrels or other items on bridges, locks, quays or elsewhere. It was forbidden to stack or leave wood that had been brought from outside of town in the street, and instead it had to be 'lugged or carried to the timber-yards'. One was evidently allowed to use one's own front step for storage, though, because the 61st article of the by-law threatened a fine of one *Carolusgulden* for every time a resident left barrels, *pijpen* (a kind of cask) 'or any other goods or things' anywhere but on their front step.[66] In particular, the Plaets, the city's central but rather cramped market square, must have been packed with all imaginable commodities and building materials. In 1581, burghers and outsiders were exhorted not to leave any sacks (hops, wool, feathers), casks (flax, hemp, lime, mead), bales (skins), jars, pots, pans or 'all other such goods' on the Plaets for longer than one night, and lead could not be left overnight at all.[67]

These were undoubtedly attempts to prevent the limited space on the Plaets from being used for storage, but clutter on the streets also represented a significant danger for residents at night, for the city was then pitch-dark. There was no street lighting in the city until well into the seventeenth century; the only light at night was that of the lanterns carried by nocturnal wanderers and the lanterns that

(Noordkerk, *Handvesten ofte privilegiën*, p. 731). In transport, not only carts and wagons were used but also sledges that were pulled over the pavement on iron runners. To reduce friction, the gliders were lubricated with a greasy cloth.

63 '[O]mme daer over te gemackelijcker hare werck te doen' (Ibidem, p. 984).

64 Ibidem, pp. 979 and 1668, and also Breen, 'De verordeningen op het bouwen', pp. 122 and 137.

65 Noordkerk, *Handvesten ofte privilegiën*, pp. 735 and 1668.

66 Ibidem, p. 984.

67 Ibidem, p. 1668.

landlords were required to hang above their doors in the dark winter months. After the curfew sounded at nine o'clock in the evening, the landlords were allowed to extinguish the lights, and near-total darkness settled over the city. After this, all that remained was the occasional devotional lamp by an image of a saint, but even this custom came to an end with the *Alteratie* ('Alteration') of 1578, when the Catholic city government was deposed and Calvinists took control of the city.[68]

No wonder, then, that as late as 1670 the city government expressly determined that no timber or other building materials were to be left in the street. Moreover, it was customary for bricklayers and hodmen to leave lime vats in the middle of the street, 'causing many accidents in the evenings and early hours.' Henceforth, these vats had to be placed on the front steps of houses and, in the case of houses on canals and ramparts, on the edge of the quay wall beyond the line of trees.[69] Quaysides such as these were used by individuals for all kinds of illegal constructions; in 1581, these included privies, booths, sheds and other *timmeragien* (buildings). Those that had not been built with the express permission of the city government had to be demolished.[70] We do not know how many people were in the streets, but Amsterdam was certainly crowded. In 1585, around 30,000 people were living in a city no larger than the area encircled by the Singel, Kloveniersburgwal and Geldersekade canals. Moreover, all of these people spent much of the day outside, where it was light and where urban life took place.

Now that we have an impression of the streets, let us turn our attention to the houses that made up the city landscape and accommodated the shops. Much about these houses had changed over the course of time. In medieval Amsterdam, there were hardly any large stone houses, because the soil conditions made building in stone an extremely costly affair. Even the stone parish churches on Oude and Nieuwe Zijde had wooden vaulting in order to reduce weight and pressure on the foundations. On the peat moors of Holland, an area that included Amsterdam, houses were built by constructing a timber frame that was finished with wattle and daub or wooden panelling.[71] In this early period, roofs were covered with reeds—a logical solution given that reeds were a ubiquitous and cheap raw material in the low-lying countryside. The interior of the old townhouses consisted of a large room with a freestanding hearth. Chimneys did not yet exist, and the smoke was let out of the roof through a smoke-hatch. This form of heating was entirely adequate so long as there was no wish to construct an attic floor across the whole area of the house, as this prevented the smoke from clearing and risked the floor above the hearth catching fire. Following what was customary in large stone houses elsewhere in the country, the open hearth was therefore moved to the side wall, which was now partially built in stone. This made it possible to construct an attic floor and the smoke was carried off through a pipe. We know from statute books that such pipes were still made out of wood in the second half of the fourteenth century, but due to the risk of fire, in 1531 it became mandatory for chimneys to be built out of stone. The fear of fire was not exaggerated: in 1421 and 1452, large parts of Amsterdam were reduced to ashes,

68 Van Dillen, *Bronnen bedrijfsleven en gildewezen,* I, nr. 429 (by-law from 1556), and Ter Gouw, *Geschiedenis van Amsterdam,* I, pp. 381–382. For street lighting, see also Zahn Jr., *De geschiedenis der verlichting.*

69 Noordkerk, *Handvesten ofte privilegiën,* p. 989.

70 Ibidem, p. 1668.

71 The following is mainly based on Meischke, *Het Nederlandse woonhuis*; Zantkuijl, *Bouwen in Amsterdam,* and Meischke et al., *Huizen in Nederland.*

and countless smaller fires also ravaged the city. No wonder, then, that a by-law of 31 May 1452, eight days after the last large fire, proclaimed that 'no new houses may be built unless they have stone walls and a solid roof.'[72] But it took a long time for Amsterdam's housing stock to be converted into stone, and there were repeated demands for solid roofs and stone side walls until well into the sixteenth century.

The practice of building side walls in stone had been adopted long before the city fires of the fifteenth century, with the introduction of brick foundations as a base for the timber frame. This represented a great improvement on the previous situation, when the upright posts of the timber frame had rested on separate stone foundation blocks. Brick foundations were less prone to subsidence and also dispersed the weight of the building over a larger area. Moreover, building the foundations in stone opened up the possibility of including a basement or cellar, and in practice this meant that a storey was added to the house. In the second half of the fourteenth century, this type of house—with a ground floor, attic and possibly also a basement or cellar—was common and remained so for many years.[73] On Cornelis Anthonisz's map from 1544, a large proportion of the houses in Amsterdam have been built in this way. The side walls of houses were also increasingly built of stone in order to limit the risk of fire spreading. Around the mid-sixteenth century, these stone fire walls were increasingly used as supporting walls, and the traditional timber frame slowly became a thing of the past.[74]

The one aspect of the sixteenth-century townhouse that still resembled the old timbered townhouse was the façade, for Amsterdam's city government never ruled that the façade had to be made of stone. From the same bird's-eye-view map by Cornelis Anthonisz, we can see that in the mid-sixteenth century, a great many houses in Amsterdam still had timber façades.[75] The city's appearance was thus completely different from the city we know today. Amsterdam was a sea of relatively small houses, many with timbered façades, above which towered the tall stone constructions of monumental public buildings such as the Oude Kerk and the Nieuwe Kerk. The map of 1544 also captures this aspect of the city in beautiful, if somewhat exaggerated, fashion (see Figure 1.9).

From the mid-sixteenth century, when pressure on the available space in the city increased and people started to build house foundations by driving long wooden piles into the layers of sand underlying the peat, the cityscape changed and Amsterdam's townhouses grew in height and volume. The façades of the houses changed, too. The all-timber façade slowly disappeared from the cityscape, to be replaced in many cases with what could be described as a timber-and-stone façade.[76] This consisted of a high wooden façade of the kind typically seen on shopfronts, topped by a thin stone façade.[77] It was the most common variant of the Amsterdam townhouse and even today, it can be found throughout the old city in more or less garbled forms. The major advantage of the timber façade—and also the reason why it persisted for so long—was the amount of light that it

72 '[N]yemant geen nye huyzen en moet tijmmeren, anders dan mit stenen wanten ende mit harden dake' (Breen, 'De verordeningen op het bouwen', p. 112).

73 Zantkuijl, *Bouwen in Amsterdam*, pp. 30–31.

74 Ibidem, p. 39, and see also Van Tussenbroek, 'Voor de grote uitleg'.

75 Zantkuijl, *Bouwen in Amsterdam*, p. 66.

76 Meischke, *Het Nederlandse woonhuis*, p. 120.

77 Façades made entirely of wood were still being built in considerable numbers in the relatively poor Jordaan district, which formed part of the seventeenth-century urban expansions.

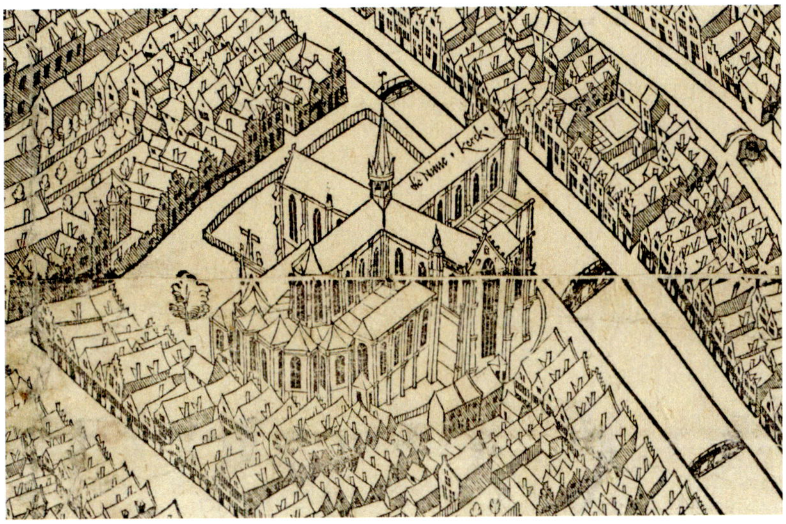

Figure 1.9: The Nieuwe Kerk and surroundings (north at the bottom), 1544.

let in. A wooden construction was much better suited to the inclusion of many high windows than heavier constructions in brick. As we shall see below, this same high façade and the generous amount of light it let in provided the perfect setting for shops.

Over time, what had originally been a single living and working space was divided into a number of rooms, each with a specific function. This development began when the open hearth was replaced by a hearth with a chimney flue. Now most of the smoke and soot was carried away from the house, creating, according to Zantkuijl, a 'completely different living atmosphere'.[78] More attention could now be paid to decorating one's home, for example by painting the woodwork and introducing fine fabrics. This change not only added to the comfort of living, it also strengthened the presentational character of the house and its furnishings. The disadvantage of having a chimney that drew was that this caused draughts. To counter this, part of the large room was partitioned off in order to tend the fire there, and this back room was known as the *binnenhaert* or *binnenhaard* (inner hearth). And with the introduction of this inner room, a distinction emerged between the inside and the outside, between the occupant's private space and public space. In the unheated front room, the *voorhuis*, contact with the outside world continued to be important. The *voorhuis* was the place where the private and public spheres met, as it were, and it was also where the occupant managed a shop or practised a craft.

The *voorhuis* retained the relatively high ceiling (4 to 5 metres) that had been typical of such townhouses before they were divided into separate rooms. By contrast, at the back of the house in the *binnenhaard*, the process of functional separation and refinement continued, and the kitchen was separated from the living space. Sometimes the kitchen was moved to the very back of the *binnenhaard* and separated off with a wall, but in Amsterdam it was more common to split the *binnenhaard* horizontally, as lowering the ceiling of the *binnenhaard* allowed one to make optimal use of the warmth from the fire. The space above, which got some warmth from the chimney flue, was

78 Zantkuijl, *Bouwen in Amsterdam*, p. 82.

ideal for a bedroom, but over time it became a living room and was given its own fireplace and chimney. The room that had previously been the *binnenhaard*—which, due to the presence of the fire, had served as both a kitchen and a living space—was now mainly used as a kitchen. As the residential and presentational function of the mezzanine floor became increasingly important, there was a need for more height. If this proved lacking in what had been the *binnenhaard*, the floor beyond the *voorhuis* was lowered and part of the kitchen came to lie below ground-level. A whole host of variations was possible on this basic configuration. In an urban context where land was scarce and expensive, adding extra storeys was the obvious option, and there was space for a basement under the *voorhuis*, as the foundation walls were already deep. On the street-side, such basements were often rented out separately as storage cellars, residential basements or shop spaces, and thus required a separate entrance. And this brings us to the front step.

The front step, not to be confused with the pavement, was one of the most characteristic elements of the medieval and early modern urban landscape and played a major role in the history of the shop. Cornelis Anthonisz did not include front steps in his bird's-eye-view map of 1544, but that is not because they were not there. On the contrary, every house had its own front step, which was used by the occupants at their own discretion.[79] Viewed from the street, the front step was a transitional zone to the *voorhuis*, where the public domain became the private domain of the interior. Viewed from the house, the front step was the most public part of a property; the place where the worlds of occupant and passer-by met and where contact with the public domain was most direct. As we shall see, this meant that the front step was ideally suited to the display of merchandise and trading. The private nature of the front step was also recognized by the city government; not the line of the façade, but the gutter in front of the step was the border that determined where the private domain of the home-owner ended and the public domain of the road began.

What did these front steps look like? Front steps and everything that was on, below and above them have disappeared so completely from most streets in the centre of Amsterdam that it is difficult to imagine what they were like. We get a first impression when we look at what remains of front steps today on the main canals in the part of the city that was built in the seventeenth century. Here, the façade hardly ever lies directly on the public highway, but on a strip of land paved with stone and sometimes edged with railings. The step provides access to the property but has no additional function. A solitary canal-house occupant sitting on their front step makes a somewhat lost impression, subject to the stares of passers-by and the exhaust fumes of motorized vehicles. Over time, we have become accustomed to a strict separation between inside and outside, and the diffuse, transitional zone of the front step is somehow at odds with this. In fact, it was only in traditional working-class neighbourhoods that this strict division did not develop, at least not until the 1950s and 1960s. In these neighbourhoods, people would still use the pavement like the front step of early modern times, as it were: to expand the household outside, in front of the door.

In pictures, what one invariably sees on the front step is a bench; and perhaps this is the most obvious use of such a space. You can put a bench there and observe the hustle and bustle of the street whilst remaining at a slight distance from it. In the panel entitled 'Feeding the hungry' by the Master of Alkmaar, from around

79 For front steps, see Boeken, *Amsterdamse stoepen*; Brouwer, *Stoepen, stoeppalen, stoephekken*, and Rouwhorst, 'Oog voor detail: stoepen'.

Figure 1.10: Front step and bench, early sixteenth century.

1504, the essential nature of the front step is captured in the foreground (Figure 1.10). The front step is marked out with paving and the low wall of the public road. A woman stands on the step holding a basket of bread, which a man is distributing to the needy gathered next to (but not on) the step.[80] The low wall is topped with a wooden plank and can thus

80 Christ is standing among them. He looks the spectator straight in the eye, as if to remind them of their duty to do good works.

serve as a seat. But there was more to the front step than benches.

As more and more of Amsterdam's townhouses had basements, and the basements under the now-raised *voorhuis* were rented out as separate living or working spaces, the entrance to the house came to be on and in the front step. In many cases, this would consist of a few steps leading up to the front door, and a basement door with a staircase going down to a basement lying (partially) below ground level. It was relatively unusual to have a ground-floor *voorhuis* and a basement completely below ground level in medieval and early modern Amsterdam, as the high ground-water level did not allow for deep cellars. The opposite did exist, however: in order to optimize use of the basement space, the floor of the *voorhuis* was raised until it came to lie a metre or more above ground level. One would then enter the house via a stone staircase, next to which was the cellar door. In a picture after a drawing by Anthonie van Beerstraten, we see a row of houses on Rokin dating from the second half of the sixteenth century, and we can clearly see the stone staircases and cellar entrances (Figure 1.11). Elsewhere in the city, in less prosperous neighbourhoods, wooden stairs rather than stone steps were used to access the *voorhuis*.[81] Given that the city was pitch-dark at night, however, an open trapdoor brought the risk of life-threatening falls. Gates and fences were therefore built around the basement entrances—these were constructions that consisted of wooden partitions on both sides of the opening and a flat cover above.[82]

But the potential uses of the front step were not yet exhausted. The narrow strip of land in front of the house—and also along the side of the house, in the case of a corner house—was also used for the construction of annexes known as *pothuizen*. The history of the *pothuis* in Amsterdam dates back to the Middle Ages. The phenomenon is thought to have originated in the practice of digging rainwater tanks in the street, directly in front of the façade. By building over these, rainwater could be drawn from the well from inside the house, via the basement. For this reason, it is thought that the term was originally *puthuis* ('well-house'), not *pothuis*.[83] The residents of Amsterdam soon realized that these outbuildings could be put to a great many other uses. Some installed a privy there, others used the *pothuis* to extend the basement or to improve the incidence of light. If the basement was not rented out, it was not necessary to have a separate *pothuis* entrance. Just like the basement, however, the *pothuis* and the combination of *pothuis* and basement was ideal for rental, and its location on the edge of the front step made it perfect for retail and artisan activities. We know that many *pothuizen* in Amsterdam were used by cobblers in the seventeenth and eighteenth centuries, but we do not know whether this was already the case in the sixteenth century. It seems very likely, though, that wares were already being sold from *pothuizen* at that time. As far as the first half of the seventeenth century is concerned, there can be no doubt about it: a by-law of 1642 prescribed that bacon and cheese had to be displayed *in* the *pothuis* and not *in front of*

81 See for instance Boeken, *Amsterdamse stoepen*, pp. 37, 46–47, and Vriese, 'Stoepen', figures 2 and 3.
82 Vriese, 'Stoepen'.

83 The name *pothuis* only came into being later when *pothuizen* were added to the sidewalls of corner houses to expand the kitchen. Then one could actually put pots and pans in the *pothuis* and the term *puthuis* gradually felt into disuse (Rouwhorst, 'Oog voor detail: pothuizen'). I owe a lot to the late Mr. H.J. Zantkuijl (Gemeentelijk Bureau voor Monumentenzorg) for his patient explanation of things that can be seen on prints and which I found difficult to interpret at first.

Figure 1.11: Front steps and cellar entrances on Rokin in the sixteenth century.

the *pothuis* on the public highway.[84] For those who ran a shop in the *voorhuis*, the roof of the *pothuis* often functioned as a display space for merchandise – a display window *avant la lettre*. Sixteenth-century images of *pothuizen* are very rare, but an anonymous print in Olfert Dappers' *Historische beschryving der stadt Amsterdam* (*Historical description of the city of Amsterdam*) does show a stone house on Kalverstraat close to the Dam, built in 1594, complete with *pothuis*, folded-down lower shutters and a trap door with a wooden fence (also by the neighbouring house) that protected the entrance to the basement (Figure 1.12).

The print also shows a large canopy, and canopies such as these likewise belonged to the space in front of the house that was defined by the front step. We know that canopies were already in use in medieval Amsterdam, because the city's oldest statute book, a summary of the laws applying in 1413, included a prescription on coating reed-covered canopies with loam.[85] The same statute book set a minimum height and maximum depth for canopies and included a ban on placing wooden partitions on canopies or on the sides of canopies; the latter, no doubt, because this would have obstructed the view and light of neighbouring properties, although the aim may also have been to prevent house-owners from building up their front steps and incorporating them into their houses.[86] The very common incidence of canopies on medieval houses was related to the lack of drainpipes. For those houses that had gutters, water was drained off onto the street via drainpipes

84 Rouwhorst, 'Oog voor detail: pothuizen', and also Vriese, 'Pothuizen'.

85 Ter Gouw, *Geschiedenis van Amsterdam*, II, p. 340.

86 Breen, *Rechtsbronnen der stad Amsterdam*, p. 14, and Van Lennep and Ter Gouw, *De uithangteekens*, p. 44.

Figure 1.12: Front step, *pothuis* and cellar entrance on the Dam, ca. 1660.

protruding from the façade. The canopy thus protected the entrance of the house from the falling water. Unlike in Figure 1.12, medieval canopies took the form of downwards-sloping roofs. This shape remained dominant until the end of the sixteenth century and can also be made out from the few sixteenth-century images that we have of Amsterdam and from copies of sixteenth-century originals. The latter category includes the prints from *Het boek van den oproer der weder-dooperen* (*The book of the Anabaptist riot*), a Dutch translation, published in 1614, of the original work in Latin by Lambertus Hortensius. In the print, we see Anabaptists running, swords drawn, past a row of houses with canopies in Amsterdam (Figure 1.13).[87]

Sloping canopies are also clearly visible in a sixteenth-century picture of the cheese and butter market on the Dam (Figure 1.14). This image, the oldest view of the Dam, was produced ca. 1590. As well as a number of women wearing traditional hooded cloaks, in the background we can see the familiar downwards-sloping canopies, and on the left in the foreground a canopy that was modern for this time, sloping downwards from the front edge to the façade.[88] The advantage of this latter construction was that the canopy could be secured to a lower point on the timber façade, allowing taller windows to be placed above the canopy and thereby letting more light into the *voorhuis*.[89]

87 Hortensius, *Het boeck van den oproer der weder-dooperen*. More on these prints in Carasso-Kok, *Geschiedenis van Amsterdam*, I, pp. 346–348.

88 Pontanus, *Rerum et urbis Amstelodamensium historia*, and see also Carasso-Kok, *Geschiedenis van Amsterdam*, I, p. 94.

89 For canopies, see Meischke, *Het Nederlandse woonhuis*, pp. 122–123, and Waal, 'Oude winkelluyfels'.

Figure 1.13: Houses in Amsterdam with canopies, sixteenth century.

What is more, with this design, rainwater and gutter water no longer ran off the front of the canopy but was collected on the façade and drained off via a drainpipe. Not only was this pleasant for occupants and passers-by, but the wide canopy also provided ample shelter for the customers of shops in the *voorhuizen* and the merchandise displayed on the front step. Finally, the broad edge of the modern canopy was the perfect place for an inscription providing information about the nature of the trade and the name of the shopkeeper or house. There was also space on the canopy itself for images or signs with the same function.

Identifying the house, the trade done there or the occupant was also exactly what signboards did. Although we rarely come across them in bird's-eye-view maps and prints, they were certainly there, even in large numbers. For the sixteenth century, Van Lennep and Ter Gouw have identified many dozens of house names, some of which would have been depicted on façades or canopy edges and some on signboards that were fixed to the timber façade or even to the

Figure 1.14: Houses with canopies on the Dam, ca. 1590.

edge of the canopy.[90] In 1544, for example, there was a house behind the Nieuwe Kerk with the board or sign *'de Schrijvende Hant* [The Writing Hand]'; this was where Cornelis Anthonisz ran his shop and sold his bird's-eye-view map. In Cornelis Anthonisz's case, there was a relatively close relationship between the signboard and his profession, but that was not always the case. After all, the primary function was to identify the house and the occupant; something that was essential at a time when there were no house numbers and patronymics were common. Without the addition *'in 't Paradijs* [in paradise]', for example, how could one know that this was indeed the Claes Jacobsz who was a city father and married to the foundress of the orphanage? For the same reason, Franz Hendricksz's residence was identified with the addition *'in de Wildeman* [in the wild man]', Claes Dircksz's with the addition *'in de Drie Koningen* [in the three Kings]', and so on.

No wonder, then, that in 1542, the city fathers issued a ban on changing the boards or other signs by houses,[91] as this would cause

90 Van Lennep and Ter Gouw, *De uithangteekens*, chapter 5.

91 Ter Gouw, *Geschiedenis van Amsterdam*, V, pp. 52–53.

great confusion and uncertainty. The problem was partly overcome by putting *gevelstenen* (plaques) on the stone façades, which left the owners free to use the signboards for advertising purposes. The question remains as to whether this advertising on the signboards always referred directly to the activities of the shopkeeper or craftsman. Many signboards depicted biblical scenes or proverbs, animals' names, place names, and other things that were completely unrelated to the trade practised in the house. To nevertheless make it clear to passers-by what was for sale, shopkeepers and craftsmen used the shutters and *pothuizen* to display their goods, and they also hung merchandise from the canopy. Moreover, there was a tendency to push further and further into the middle of the street in pursuit of customers.

In a long series of by-laws, the city government attempted to tackle this and force residents back to their front steps. A detailed building ordinance of 1565, for example, opened with the declaration that there were many rules regarding 'buildings, the building line, front steps, canopies, signboards, window-shutters and doors', but these were not being complied with, leading to 'great inconvenience, disorder and inequalities'.[92] The extensive thirtieth article of the by-law prescribed a maximum width of the front step for each of the city's alleyways and narrow streets, where the traffic was most disrupted. According to the ordinance, the size of the front step should also determine the depth of the *pothuizen* and the size of the window-shutters, signboards and canopies.[93] In a series of alleyways, there was even a total ban on front steps, *pothuizen*, canopies and signboards, but residents were allowed 'a foot of window-space'; in other words, the lower shutters of the windows in which shopkeepers displayed their wares could protrude from the façade, when folded open, for about 28 centimetres. On the Damrak, the Burgwallen and along major thoroughfares, the width of the front step and everything that was on, underneath or above it was prescribed as seven-quarters of a yard; that is, around 1.2 metres. In the alleyways and narrow streets in particular, this by-law would have remained a dead letter. The government hardly helped in this regard, because in 1594 it allowed deeper canopies in a number of alleyways than had been permitted in 1565, and it also determined that existing signboards could remain even if they protruded beyond the canopies.[94]

It was these densely built, crowded and messy streets that were home to Amsterdam's shops, and they, in turn, also contributed to the vibrant streetlife that can be reconstructed from the statute books but that we seldom encounter in contemporary images.

When we consider the few sources that do relate to shops, one conclusion is clear: the display and sale of goods took place almost exclusively out of doors. This was obviously true of markets and street trading, of course, but it was also true of shops, which were run in front of the owner's door or in the window. At any rate, this is what we can conclude from the city of Amsterdam's oldest statute book, a codification of the laws that applied in 1413. This, among other things, established and confirmed that fruit sellers were only allowed to sell their wares 'in front of their own houses, where they live', and the butcher should

92 '[O]p 't stuck van de Timmeragien, Royinge van Straten, Stoepen, Luyffenen, uyt hangende Borden, op-geslagen Veynsteren, ende op-hangende Deuren' [...] 'groote inconvenienten, disordre ende ongelijckheyden' (Noordkerk, *Handvesten ofte privilegiën*, p. 979).

93 Ibidem, pp. 981–982.

94 Ibidem, p. 991.

display his meat 'in his window'.[95] But this also remained the custom for many years. In 1505, sellers of cheese, apples, brandy and other goods were forbidden from displaying wares for sale on the Plaets, as this should be done 'in their windows or not at all'.[96] Several years later, in 1511, the city government's statute book referred to 'troubling times' and fears that the Lord in Heaven was angered. On the Friday before Easter, a procession would thus be held and followed humbly by all, and 'there should be no setting of wares or trading outside the house' before the procession was over.[97] Only very occasionally did the by-laws make mention of indoor sales, but these, too, took place with 'open windows'.[98]

During this period, shop sales were very similar to market trading and took place in the street in broad daylight. Sales in a confined space may have been regarded with a certain suspicion. After all, agreements might be made at the expense of the community, or the customer might be ripped off by the seller. The latter danger was very real, because the shop premises were often dimly lit or half-dark. Indeed, a by-law from around 1500 notes irregularities in the houses of '*kramers* and flax-sellers' and of those in related industries: lighter Cologne weights were being used in these houses in place of the prescribed Troy weights, meaning that buyers were being put at a disadvantage. In the past, it had already been decreed that larger consignments should not be weighed indoors.[99]

I know of just one print that gives an impression of the exterior of a shop in Amsterdam in the sixteenth century. It is one of the images from the above-mentioned book on the Anabaptist riot, images that were most likely based on paintings made for the city hall in the sixteenth century by the painter Barend Dircksz (? – after 1557). On the print in question, we see Anabaptists selling clothing and jewellery to a shopkeeper (Figure 1.15). The latter is trading in a townhouse of a type typical of Amsterdam at that time, with a timber façade and sloping canopy. The goods are displayed in the windows, no doubt on the horizontally folded-down lower shutters. Indeed, this is what we should imagine when by-laws refer to 'in the window'. Merchandise—in this case, clothing—is hanging from the canopy, which immediately tells us that it is a shop.

The shopkeeper himself is not in the *voorhuis* behind the well-stocked *veynsteren* but on the front step, in front of his house. There, he has placed a heavy wooden table with thick side panels, and he is negotiating with one of the Anabaptists. The table is probably what is described in the sources as a *thoochbanck* or *toonbank* (a counter) in modern Dutch.[100] The *thoochbanck* has been placed under the canopy in the space that would (later?) become known as the *slag* (plot or lot).[101] No wares are displayed on the table; these would have been in the window, where they were also better protected from the rain and the dirt of the street. The counter was where the seller

95 '[E]en ygelijc voir sijns selves huyse, dair hy in woent.' [...] 'op sijn veynster' (Breen, *Rechtsbronnen der stad Amsterdam*, pp. 23–24). See also Van Nierop, 'De handeldrijvende middenstand', pp. 193–195.
96 '[O]p heuren veynsteren ende anders nyet' (Breen, *Rechtsbronnen der stad Amsterdam*, p. 423).
97 '[G]heen waer oft coopmanscap buyten huyse [...] setten oft doen setten' (Breen, *Rechtsbronnen der stad Amsterdam*, pp. 490–491).
98 '[O]penen veynsteren' (Ibidem, p. 430).
99 Ibidem, pp. 66 and 290, and Ter Gouw, *Geschiedenis van Amsterdam*, III, pp. 266–267. For views on fair trade in late Medieval cities, see De Kerf, *De juiste prijs*.
100 Ter Gouw, *Geschiedenis van Amsterdam*, V, p. 239.
101 Waal, 'Oude winkelluyfels', p. 341.

Figure 1.15: Second-hand shop in Amsterdam, sixteenth century.

could display the goods that had sparked the customer's interest, whereby the seller would extol their virtues and the customer would assess their quality and appearance. The price and payment conditions were also negotiated at the counter. This particular print does not show the sale of goods to the consumer but the shopkeeper himself purchasing goods. It is clear from the clothes on the canopy that this is a second-hand shop. The mistress of the house also seems to be playing a prominent role in purchasing goods. From the register of the *Capitale Impositie*, we know that this was not unusual in 1585; of the sixteen second-hand shops recorded in the register, six were run by women.

All in all, the print confirms what has already become clear from the statute books and historical buildings research. The house, the timber façade with its canopy, the wares displayed in the windows and the use of the front step as a shopping space: this is how we should imagine the shop in sixteenth-century Amsterdam. The situation would have been similar in the *cassen*, the small booths or lean-tos that were found in relatively large numbers by churches, by houses on the Dam and on the Oude Brug. *Cassen* were hired out to shopkeepers by the city and churches, and, unsurprisingly, they were located in some of the most attractive locations in the city. As retail trade largely took place in the façade (windows) and on the front step, their small size would hardly have been a problem. After all, customers would not normally have stepped inside but would have made their selection, asked questions and made purchases in the semi-public domain of the front step.

What we lack from this print is the context of the shopping streets where much retail trade took place. Whilst there were certainly shops that served people in the immediate vicinity with food and durable goods from isolated locations, research on the register of the *Capitale Impositie* clearly reveals that there were already real shopping streets in 1585. The Dam, Nieuwendijk and Warmoesstraat are the most obvious examples. I have been unable to find any pictures of these shopping streets in the sixteenth century, but they must have been crowded and noisy. Their location in the network of Amsterdam's streets, alleyways and canals made them very accessible, and this would have drawn shopkeepers, who in turn would have made the streets even more attractive. The ordinance setting out the rights and obligations of members of the *kramers'* guild even refers to a situation in which a number of guild members lived in the same house. In this case, they were not permitted to 'put their shop wares in front of or above each other's displays'.[102] This extremely intensive use of the available space would have been a feature of the main shopping streets in particular and reinforces the impression of densely packed streets where people made their way past numerous shops and displays. Until the end of the sixteenth century, houses where shops were run were indistinguishable from ordinary residential homes,[103] but because retail trade largely took place in the windows and in front of the façade, no contemporary would have had any doubts as to the location of the shops or the nature of the goods sold there.

102 '[N]iet boven malcandere toegen noch deen voir den andere mijt hoere goeden' (Breen, *Rechtsbronnen der stad Amsterdam*, p. 112). Meischke et al., *Huizen in Nederland*, p. 22, refer to shops (*winkels*) on the upper floors of houses in Warmoesstraat. However, these were probably not retail facilities but workshops of tailors, hat makers and others (information kindly provided by P.T.E.E. Rosenberg, co-author of the book).

103 Meischke, *Het Nederlandse woonhuis*, p. 122.

2. Changing distribution systems: differentiation and specialization in early modern Amsterdam

Abstract:
This chapter charts the evolution of the extensive distribution system connecting producers and consumers. From the middle of the sixteenth until the second half of the seventeenth century, the size of the Amsterdam market increased sharply, and so did the wealth of the urban elites. These changes gave rise to an expanding trade sector and to differentiation and job specialization within the distribution system. The modernity of the distribution system that emerged in Amsterdam was expressed in the presence of specialized wholesalers and retailers, who together guaranteed a wide and varied range of goods in the city. At the same time, the division between wholesale and retail was not as stark as it would become much later.

Keywords: distribution system, differentiation, specialization

Retail trade is not a self-standing phenomenon but forms part of an extensive distribution system connecting producers and consumers. Shopkeepers play a role in this distribution system, but they are not alone in doing so. In this chapter, we take a closer look at the different links in what is sometimes the long chain along which goods are driven, from producers all the way to the households where they are used and ultimately consumed. This also gives us an opportunity to distinguish more precisely than we have until now between retailers and other suppliers of consumer goods. But let us begin at the beginning and consider the question of what exactly is meant by distributive trade and when the need arises in society for the services of middlemen.

Distribution systems in the US and England

In economies where there is still little division of labour, the roles of producer and consumer tend to overlap. Households mainly produce for their own needs, and only a small part of that which is produced is exchanged or handed over to secular or religious authorities in tax or as a fee for services rendered. Consumers' needs are limited and not particularly varied—which is also necessary, because there are few means for purchasing goods that are not produced in the household or the immediate vicinity. But when the division of labour starts to play a larger role, relations with the outside world become more intensive and the

Lesger, C., *Shopping Spaces and the Urban Landscape in Early Modern Amsterdam, 1550–1850.*
Taylor & Francis Group, 2020
DOI: 10.5117/9789463720625_CH02

demand for goods becomes greater and more varied, then the situation changes. The household and the immediate vicinity are no longer able to deliver all the desired goods at the time the consumer requires them. The gap between the producer and the consumer thus becomes wider—so much so in the case of some goods that direct relations between the two are no longer possible.

If the needs of the consumer go beyond the goods that can be produced in the immediate vicinity at a given time, then a second problem arises. Due to irregularities in production and transport, many goods cannot be supplied in even quantities over the year but are subject to strong fluctuations. Harvest products such as fruit are a well-known example, but in the pre-industrial age, industrial products were also subject to distinct seasonal fluctuations.[1] In order to have enough goods at all times, the consumer therefore had to lay down a significant amount of stock at home. It stands to reason that this was not an appealing option; private households rarely had the space or the money to build up large stocks. Problems of distance and time such as these thus paved the way for distributive trade.[2] The function of distributive trade is to drive the flow of goods in the direction of the consumer, the aim thereby being to bridge this gap in distance and time. By means of a whole series of activities including purchasing, storing, selecting and selling, middlemen ensure that the 'right goods are in the right place at the right time and in the right quantities'.[3]

The retailer forms the final link in what is sometimes the long chain connecting producers to consumers. In order to gain a good understanding of retail trade, it is thus essential to pay some attention to the other links, all the more so because in the past, retail trade was often combined with functions that were related to other links in the chain. What were these links, and how did they help to move the flow of goods in the direction of the consumer?

When describing the different links and functions in the early modern distribution system, it is useful to consult studies on the development of the distribution system in the United States in the first half of the nineteenth century.[4] This comparison is less strange than it might first appear. Around 1800, the US was a sparsely populated country with a relatively undeveloped economy. With its small domestic market, poor transport and communication facilities and workforce dominated by farmers and artisans, its distribution system could hardly be described as complex.[5] This changed in the following decades, and precisely because these developments took place so late in the US, they are relatively well documented. The ports on the East Coast were the major trading centres at the beginning of the nineteenth century. It was there that the main importers and shipping merchants who had their own fleets of trading vessels were based. Whilst the shipping merchants engaged almost exclusively in import

1 This of course had to do with the organic origin of many raw materials, shorter working hours in winter and problems with transport during wet and/or cold seasons.

2 Vance puts it as follows: 'Once local self-sufficiency is limited, there is no longer the automatic adjustment of production and demand, either in location or in timing, so that there have to be *agents of trade* seeking to rationalize the flow of goods from producer to consumer' (Vance Jr., *The Merchant's World*, p. 104).

3 Ter Hart and Tates, *De Amsterdamse groothandel*, p. 15. See also Bucklin, *Competition and Evolution*; Haccoû, *De groothandel*; Van Muiswinkel, *Handel, markt en beurs*; Mahieu, *De distributie*, and Polak, 'De taak van den tusschenhandel'.

4 Jones, *Middlemen in the Domestic Trade*; Bucklin, *Competition and Evolution*, and Vance Jr., *The Merchant's World*.

5 Jones, *Middlemen in the Domestic Trade*, p. 9.

and export trade, the importers sold to retailers and also directly to consumers. Most of these merchants were relatively unspecialized when it came to regions and products. This was also understandable, because the size of demand in the American hinterland was relatively small and did not allow for much specialization. Moreover, the merchants were often paid in kind for the goods they imported from overseas.[6]

When the population of the towns on the East Coast and elsewhere in the US grew, tensions arose in this relatively simple distribution system. The volume of imports and exports increased, and it became less and less common for consumers and retailers to buy goods directly from internationally operating trading companies. The latter increasingly focused on imports and exports and tried, by making fast sales, to free up money for the branches of trade where the odds of making a profit appeared greatest at any given time. As a result, it became less viable to keep stocks in order to be able to meet demand from retailers and consumers throughout the year. This particularly affected retailers in the countryside, who would travel to coastal towns just a few times a year to replenish their stocks. They found that the overseas trading companies no longer had the goods that they needed, and they thus turned to the larger retailers in the port cities. A new link in the distribution chain was thereby created: the wholesaler. The wholesaler was positioned, as it were, between the importer and the retailer. He bought relatively large consignments of goods from the importer (or producer) and sold his stock in smaller consignments to the shopkeeper who might want it at any given time. Stockbuilding was thus an essential function of this link in the system.[7]

But stockbuilding was not the wholesaler's only function. Jones argues that at the beginning of the nineteenth century, total demand in the US for certain types of goods (largely textiles) was large enough to allow for specialization among overseas traders. For retailers, this was a mixed blessing. They served a circle of consumers that allowed for very little specialization, and they now had to go to a whole series of importers in order to compile a sufficiently varied package of goods. The wholesalers eased their burden by purchasing from different importers and putting together an appealing assortment for retailers, which they also offered in relatively small consignments.[8] In doing so, they usually limited themselves to one or a few sectors, but within these sectors they offered a wide range.

At the beginning of the nineteenth century—and also long afterwards—the average shop in the US had the character of a general store. After all, outside the big cities many goods were produced at home, and the size of the market was so small that it was not possible for shops to specialize in a particular range of goods. The broad range of the general store is captured nicely by an advert for such a shop in Worcester, a village in Massachusetts. In 1804, this store sold: 'West India goods and groceries, viz: best cognac and Spanish brandy; West India and New England rums; real Holland gin, Madeira wines; flour, molasses, loaf, white, and brown sugar; teas, coffee, chocolate, spices, raisins, copperas, alum; rock and fine salt; dried and pickled fish; glazed China tea sets, crockery and glassware, violins and flutes'.[9] The quantity of stock was often so small that the shops could also be modest in size. Of general stores in St Louis, it has even been written that all the

6 Ibidem, and Bucklin, *Competition and Evolution*, p. 182.

7 Bucklin, *Competition and Evolution*, pp. 187–190.

8 Jones, *Middlemen in the Domestic Trade*, pp. 9–10, 64.

9 Bucklin, *Competition and Evolution*, p. 50.

merchandise—sugar, coffee, blankets, paint, spices, salt, knives, kitchen utensils, fabric and much more—was kept in a big chest that was opened whenever a customer turned up.[10]

For many years in remote and sparsely populated parts of the US, the general store continued to be the most important type of shop, but retailers elsewhere underwent a process of specialization in the nineteenth century. This process was triggered by the enlargement of the market due to population growth and a widening of demand due to the growing size and purchasing power of the middle and upper classes. These affluent customers were no longer satisfied with the limited range in general stores. They desired a broader and deeper range of goods; that is to say, more kinds of goods and, for each kind, a greater variety in terms of price, quality and appearance. Shopkeepers initially responded by broadening and enhancing their product ranges, but they quickly ran into almost insurmountable problems when purchasing, storing, presenting and selling their increasingly voluminous and varied range of goods. In its traditional form, the general store could no longer satisfy the wishes of the consumer. Opportunities now arose for shops offering fewer kinds of goods but with a wide range of each kind in stock. In the period between around 1825 and 1875, there was a proliferation of speciality stores on the East Coast of the US.[11] This was not only because they could respond better to the wishes of consumers but also because specialization brought several benefits that the general store lacked. For example, the speciality store could buy in larger quantities and thereby negotiate lower prices. Moreover, the narrower range made it possible to build up expertise in the products and suppliers, and this could also lead to better conditions and lower prices when purchasing goods. As a result of all of this, the prices in speciality stores were usually lower than those in general stores, which increased the size of the market.[12] But speciality stores competed with general stores not only on price; at a time when there were still no branded goods, consumers appreciated the specialist's detailed knowledge of his wares.

The distribution system in the US that we have described above can be represented in a diagram (see Figure 2.1).[13] On the right, we see distributive trade in the interior, with the now-familiar chains of importer-wholesaler-retailer-consumer. On the left, we see the overseas producers and the collecting traders who assembled the goods and prepared them for export.[14] The diagram clearly reveals the rationale for the very existence of intermediary traders: in the final analysis, it was based on the fact that middlemen were able to bridge distance and time more efficiently, and thus more cheaply, than direct contact between producers and consumers. In theory, it would be possible for all of the producers on the left-hand side of the diagram to sell to all of the consumers on the right-hand side, but this would be inefficient. On an annual basis, the number of transactions would be much too large and transport

10 Jones, *Middlemen in the Domestic Trade*, p. 44. In these years, retailers were not solely dependent on shop sales for their income, but they also bought agricultural surpluses which were then sent to merchants in the port cities (Jones, *Middlemen in the Domestic Trade*, pp. 45–46).

11 Bucklin, *Competition and Evolution*, pp. 51–55.

12 Jones, *Middlemen in the Domestic Trade*, pp. 48–49.

13 The figure is based on Van Muiswinkel, *Handel, markt en beurs*, p. 48.

14 See for the following Polak, 'Taak van den tusschenhandel', pp. 7–16; Mahieu, *De distributie*, pp. 23–28; Van Muiswinkel, *Handel, markt en beurs*, pp. 18–20, and Ter Hart and Tates, *Amsterdamse groothandel*, pp. 11–16.

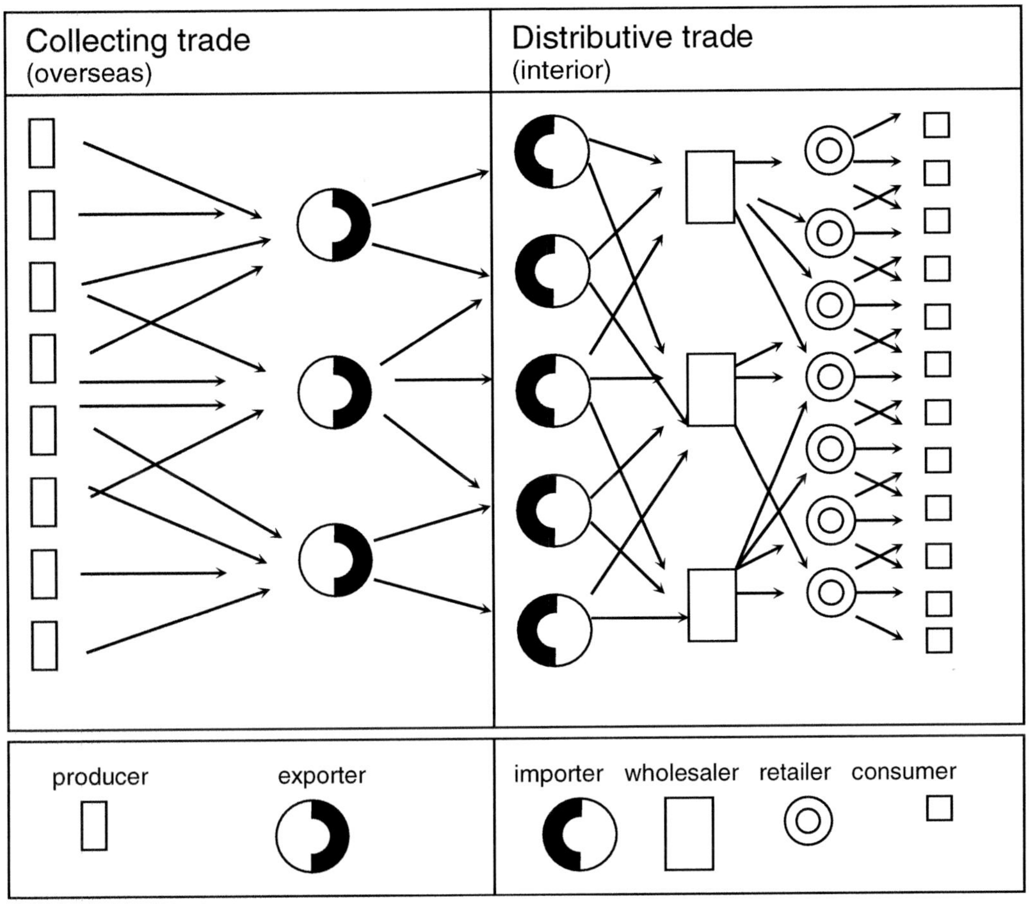

Figure 2.1: The distribution system in diagrammatic form.

prohibitively expensive. Such problems were the *raison d'être* of collecting traders, who assembled the supply of various products and ensured they were sent to the importers. After all, the concentration of commodities among a limited number of trading firms delivered major cost-savings on storage and transport. Similar cost-savings were made in distributive trade. Any consumer could obtain goods directly from any importer, but the involvement of the wholesaler and the retailer allowed for a significant reduction in the number of transactions and the costs of storage and transport. Distributive trade thus existed by the grace of the economies of scale it generated.

Let us now briefly restate the changes that the American distribution system underwent in the first half of the nineteenth century, what caused them, and what this can tell us about the distribution system in Europe at a much earlier time. With respect to the changes in the distribution system, it is clear that there was very little job specialization in the US around 1800. Merchants in the coastal towns not only engaged in the import and export trade but also sold to shopkeepers and even directly to consumers. This situation came to an end when the merchants involved in overseas trade started to limit their activities to imports and exports, whereupon a new group of middlemen—wholesalers—took their place in the distribution chain. These wholesalers tended to specialize in particular sectors. Changes also took place within the retail trade, due to the rise of the speciality store in consumer sales, which supplemented and replaced the traditional general store. In short, distributive trade in the US underwent a process of differentiation and specialization, while at the same time the number of companies engaged in distributive trade grew.

From the above, we can infer a number of explanations for the numerical growth in distributive trade and the division of what was initially a relatively undifferentiated distribution system into a series of more or less specialized functions. In very general terms, Jones describes changing economic circumstances as a consequence of the increasing division of labour.[15] More specifically, two factors in particular appear to be important: the size of the market and the composition of the market. When it comes to the size of the market (the volume of demand), not only does the growth of the population play a major role but also its spatial distribution. After all, even if the total population does not grow, the concentration of people in towns generates a large urban market, which in turn facilitates and promotes differentiation and specialization. Rising purchasing power and falling transport costs have a similar effect on the volume of demand and the degree of differentiation and specialization; in the former case, very directly, in the latter case, because lower transport costs for producers and middlemen facilitate lower retail prices, allowing consumers to buy more products and new groups of potential consumers to emerge.

With regard to the composition of demand, we need to consider the purchasing behaviour of the different layers in the population, the consumer preferences of the higher and highest income groups being especially important. The latter were prepared to pay over the odds in order to purchase consumer goods that through their price, appearance and exclusivity, could express their (desired) social position and ambitions.[16] It was demand from these wealthy and status-conscious consumers that led to the enhancing of shop ranges and that promoted the rise of speciality stores.

Studies on the structure and evolution of the distribution system in early modern Europe are thin on the ground. One exception is Westerfield's study, published back in 1915, on distributive trade in England in the period between 1660 and 1760.[17] He noted a similar tendency towards specialization and differentiation, which began in some parts of the country long before 1660. Until the early seventeenth century, according to Westerfield, the travelling merchant was still a well-established figure in England's overseas trade, and the combination of merchant-shipmaster was also common. This picture changed in the course of the seventeenth century, as merchants increasingly ran their trade from their offices and drew on the services of specialized freighters and agents abroad.[18] For the overseas merchant, the seventeenth century seems to have been a time of increasing specialization by product and region.

The differentiation within distributive trade also shows significant parallels with later trade in the US. Contact with other countries was maintained by importers and exporters, whilst domestic trade lay in the hands of tradesmen. Some of the latter were engaged in what we

15 Jones, *Middlemen in the Domestic Trade*, p. 68.

16 For consumer preferences among the higher and highest income groups, see the classic studies by Veblen (*The Theory of the Leisure Class*) and Bourdieu (*Distinction*).

17 Westerfield, *Middlemen in English business*.

18 Ibidem, pp. 329–333.

called 'collecting trade' above: driving the produce of the British industrial and agricultural sectors in the direction of exporters. Others focused on distribution and moved goods in the direction of the consumer, and this latter group included both wholesalers and retailers. Wholesale and retail were often combined in practice, and here, too, we note significant parallels with the situation in the US in the nineteenth century. The same was true of the development of retail trade. In the US, the general store continued to be a stalwart of remote and sparsely populated regions, but on the East Coast between 1825 and 1875, there was a massive expansion in the number of speciality stores. In England, shops selling a broad, general range of goods were also common, but as early as 1632, London had a large number of speciality shops. In that year, a visit to London by a group of people from the provinces was described as follows: 'Now when they were brought into Cheapside, there with great Wonder they beheld the Shops of the Goldsmiths; and on the other Side, the wealthy Mercers, whose Shops shined with all Sorts of coloured Silkes; in Watling-street they viewed the great Number of Drapers; in Saint Martins, Shoemakers; at Saint Nicholas Church, the Flesh Shambles; at the End of the Old Change, the Fish-mongers; in Candleweeke-street, the Weavers'.[19]

Westerfield describes in summary a long term process of increasing differentiation in distributive trade.[20] Tasks that had once been carried out by one individual or firm were divided among a large number of specialized professionals. At the same time, distributive trade developed a more sedentary character. Examples include the merchant who made orders and traded from his office and the shopkeeper who sold goods to his customers from a fixed location. The main force behind these changes, in Westerfield's view, was the size of the market. This grew as a result of population growth, population density, rising prosperity, general progress in communication and transport, and the commercialization of society.[21] Although Westerfield puts less emphasis on growing income differences and the resulting differentiation in demand, it is clear that the distribution system in England, as far as its composition, historical development and underlying causality were concerned, showed considerable similarities with that in the US. The main difference was the period in which the process of differentiation and growth in distributive trade took place, and this had everything to do with the fact that the underlying changes in the size and composition of the market took place at different times.

Distributive trade and distribution in Amsterdam

Now that we have a better understanding of the factors that played a key role in the early development of distribution systems, it is time to return to Amsterdam. What might we expect to find with regard to changes in distributive trade in the early modern era, and are these expectations confirmed by the available source material? In order to get an impression of the size of the market and the changes that occurred within it, it is useful to focus our attention on the demographic development of both the city itself and the larger area of which it was part.

Table 2.1 clearly shows that the population of Amsterdam grew rapidly in the sixteenth and seventeenth centuries. Amsterdam expanded

19 Ibidem, pp. 342–344 for general stores.
20 Ibidem, pp. 409–410.
21 Ibidem, pp. 368–369 and 409.

Table 2.1 Population of Amsterdam, Holland and the Netherlands (absolute figures in thousands and index), 1500–1800

	1500	1550	1600	1650	1700	1750	1800
Amsterdam	14	30	65	175	230	235	203
Holland excl. Amsterdam	236	320	510	625	600	548	587
Holland total	250	350	575	800	830	783	790
the Netherlands excl. Holland	700	900	925	1100	1070	1117	1310
the Netherlands total	950	1250	1500	1900	1900	1900	2100
indexcijfers 1500 = 100							
Amsterdam	100	214	464	1250	1643	1679	1450
Holland excl. Amsterdam	100	136	216	265	254	232	249
the Netherlands excl. Holland	100	129	132	157	153	160	187
the Netherlands total	100	132	158	200	200	200	221

Sources: Figures for Amsterdam in: De Vries, *European Urbanization*, appendix 1 and Van Leeuwen and Oeppen, 'Reconstructing the Demographic Regime of Amsterdam', table 9. Figures for Holland and the Netherlands in: Klep, 'Urban Decline in Brabant', table 13.4 and Van der Woude, 'Demografische ontwikkeling', 134.

from being a relatively small city of 10,000 to 14,000 inhabitants in 1500 into a metropolis of around 230,000 inhabitants in 1700. Amsterdam was then the third-largest city north of the Alps, after Paris and London.[22] The size of the local market therefore expanded rapidly. This expansion—as shown in the table—was most rapid in the period between the mid-sixteenth and mid-seventeenth centuries. From censuses of new burghers, we know that the growth that began in the 1550s came to a halt in the 1570s. The population only began to truly explode from 1578, when the city switched its loyalty from the Spanish King to the rebels in the Dutch War of Independence.[23] The majority of the growth in the period between 1550 and 1650 was thus realized in the much shorter period from 1578, despite a series of devastating plague epidemics that mainly affected the city in the first half of the seventeenth century.[24]

But the growth was not limited to Amsterdam; the population also grew elsewhere in the Province of Holland, and the same was true of the other parts of the Netherlands. The growth there was much less spectacular, but again, the population increase was most pronounced in the period between 1550 and 1650. In the eighteenth century, the growth in Amsterdam and Holland came to an end, but beyond Holland this same period was one of demographic expansion.

The degree to which population growth in the Province of Holland and the rest of the Netherlands contributed to the size of Amsterdam's market was dependent on the level of commercialization in these regions and the intensity of communication and transport links. That the degree of market orientation can vary considerably from region to region is an established phenomenon and has been confirmed in research by Van Bavel.[25] Holland, Utrecht, the riverine parts of Gelderland and the coastal regions of Friesland and Groningen are all

22 De Vries, *European Urbanization*, appendix 1.

23 Van Dillen, *Bronnen bedrijfsleven en gildewezen*, I, table 1.

24 Noordegraaf and Valk, *De gave Gods*, appendices 2 and 3.

25 Van Bavel, *Manors and markets*.

examples of regions with market-oriented economies. By contrast, the levels of commercialization were much lower in Drenthe, the Veluwe and large parts of North Brabant. The latter were also regions where the population density in the countryside was very low in the mid-sixteenth century, and there were few cities of any size.[26] In the second half of the sixteenth century and during most of the seventeenth century, this picture remained largely the same. It was only in the eighteenth century that the population of regions such as North Brabant, Limburg and Twente grew (sometimes very strongly), becoming more market-oriented than in the past.[27] Although we should be cautious, given the level of commercialization, when drawing a direct link between population development and market size, that link was certainly there in the sixteenth and seventeenth centuries. After all, the population grew in the most commercialized parts of the country: Holland, those parts of Utrecht, Gelderland and Brabant bordering Holland, and the coastal regions of Friesland and Groningen.

This link was conditional upon good communication and transport links between Amsterdam and these market-oriented areas, a condition that was amply met. The geographical location of Amsterdam and the abundance of water in the Netherlands played a major role in this. Holland, in particular, whose population and economy experienced rapid growth, could easily be accessed from Amsterdam via the many inland waterways and across the Zuiderzee. The Zuiderzee also provided access to the Gooi area, parts of Utrecht, regions in the north of the country, and the towns on the eastern flank of the Zuiderzee and on the IJssel. No wonder, then, that Amsterdam had traditionally been an important centre for trade with these nearby areas.[28]

That is not to say, though, that optimal accessibility was thereby guaranteed. Although the conditions for this were present, for many years the organization of inland shipping had been far from ideal, as inland shipping was akin to tramp shipping. In practice, this meant a lack of fixed departure times, fixed rates and fixed routes.[29] Bargemasters therefore had a tendency to remain on shore until the ship was fully loaded, and there was also a temptation, both prior to departure and during the journey, to exchange freight in order to create the most efficient route. This was frustrating for merchants and charterers because it left them in great uncertainty as to the time of departure and the whereabouts of the goods. In the first half of the sixteenth century, regular line services were introduced in Holland, and this institutional reform finally brought an end to the uncertainty. The regulations agreed by the city governments stipulated fixed departure times, rates and routes. In order to prevent bargemasters from competing for the most favourable departure times and gaps opening up in the schedule, captains had to leave in order and by turn (the origin of the Dutch term *beurtvaart*, '*aan de beurt*' meaning 'taking one's turn'). Finally, checks were performed on the professional competence of the bargemasters and the quality of their vessels, and this, too, reduced the risks of transportation for charterers.

26 See the map in Lesger, *Rise of the Amsterdam Market*, p. 18.
27 Population figures in Van der Woude, 'Demografische ontwikkeling', pp. 128–139.
28 See for instance Ketner, *Handel en scheepvaart*, and idem, 'Amsterdam en de binnenvaart door Holland'.
29 For the following, see Lesger, 'Intraregional Trade'.

From the final decades of the sixteenth century in particular, dozens of regular line services were set up by city authorities.[30] By around 1700, a considerable network of such services had developed. Amsterdam was undoubtedly the most important node—that is to say, the node with the most connections and the connections with the greatest geographical reach.[31] Not coincidentally, the most intensive connections were with regions where the population grew rapidly in the sixteenth and seventeenth centuries and the market played a major role in society. One should note, though, that it was not impossible to reach more peripheral regions from Amsterdam; in many cases, the contact points in the network of regular line services were themselves nodes in more or less extensive transport systems, which were thereby connected with the overarching network with Amsterdam at its centre.[32]

In the densely populated and most commercialized regions of the Netherlands—Holland, the neighbouring part of Utrecht, and the coastal regions of Friesland and Groningen—the regular line system was supplemented with a towing barge network. Whilst the regular line services tended to use the natural infrastructure of rivers and other waterways and transported both passengers and freight, the towing barges were intended exclusively for passengers and the transport of packages and post. They used canals that had been dug especially for this purpose, with draft horses using the towpaths that had been built next to them.[33] The dead-straight towpaths and the passenger barges made for an exceptionally comfortable and efficient transport system, at least for the standards of the time. Like the regular line service, it had a fixed schedule and had the added advantage of not being dependent on wind speed or wind direction. Only when there was a severe frost did the barges get stuck in the ice and the towpaths had to accommodate large numbers of travellers. Jan de Vries has established that the towing barge system was built in two phases: between 1632 and 1647, and between 1656 and 1665. Looking at the map he published, it is clear that Amsterdam lay at the centre of the network in Holland. Moreover, the city had good line-service links with the Friesian cities, which in turn had connections to the towing barge system in Friesland and Groningen.[34] All in all, it is clear that the available means of transport both facilitated and stimulated intensive contact between Amsterdam and the most commercialized parts of the Republic, thereby reinforcing the expectation that population growth in these regions did indeed lead to an increase in the size of Amsterdam's market.

The size of that increase, in turn, partly depended on the purchasing power of the population. If this rose, the size of Amsterdam's market would grow rapidly; if purchasing power fell, then the effect of population growth would be weaker. Research into the long-term development of purchasing power is a field full of pitfalls. This is mainly because we know quite a lot about the income development of men in the construction business but much too little about the incomes of small entrepreneurs, piece workers, women and children.[35] Nor is it easy to trace shifts in consumption

30 Fuchs, *Beurt- en wagenveren*, p. 72.

31 Lesger, 'Intraregional Trade', figures 2 and 3 (also included in Jan de Vries and Ad van der Woude, *The First Modern Economy*, pp. 181–182).

32 See Lesger, 'Intraregional trade', pp. 198–199, for studies on the extensive transport system that connected Zwolle to the east of the Netherlands and the neighbouring Münsterland.

33 De Vries, *Barges and Capitalism*, chapter 3.

34 Ibidem, p. 35.

35 For family incomes and the household economy, see De Vries, *The Industrious Revolution*.

patterns, which can have a major influence on purchasing power calculations.

Despite the limits to the data, the picture presented by De Vries and Van der Woude is relatively well substantiated. For the Western Netherlands, they found a fall in purchasing power that probably started in the late Middle Ages and continued until shortly after the mid-sixteenth century.[36] After this, purchasing power rose, increasing particularly rapidly in the period between 1580 and 1620. The 1620s were very unfavourable due to the high cost of food and beverages, but this was followed by a recovery. This recovery was frequently interrupted, for example when wars led to rising food prices, but the 1680s saw a peak in purchasing power. This was followed by a period of sharp fluctuations in purchasing power until around 1730, after which a decline set in that continued until after 1800. In the mid-sixteenth century, declining purchasing power thus weakened the effect of population growth on the size of the market, but, by contrast, in the era of rapid population growth (1550–1650), the purchasing power of the population of the Western Netherlands also increased. After around 1730, the stagnating or falling population size and the declining purchasing power reinforced one another, and the size of the market was eroded.

Taking all of this into consideration, we can safely conclude that the size of Amsterdam's market grew sharply from the middle of the sixteenth until the second half of the seventeenth century, and that this increase was most pronounced in the years between 1580 and 1650. This conclusion is further reinforced by the fact that this was also the period in which Amsterdam's trade network expanded over an increasingly large part of Europe, and in which contact was made with the non-European world.[37] Although this is not the place to chart Amsterdam's commercial expansion in detail, the observation that Amsterdam's trade and shipping experienced unprecedented growth from around 1580 is beyond dispute. This can be inferred, among other things, from the number of ships that put in at Amsterdam's harbour. In the first half of the 1580s, around 2,000 to 2,300 ships and boats put in at the harbour. When the harbour started charging lastage in the 1640s, there were already around 4,000 ships a year, and in the peak years of 1649 and 1650, this rose to more than 5,000. The actual number must have been much higher because the smallest vessels were exempt from lastage and therefore went unregistered. The contrast with the figures for the 1580s, which include small vessels, is thus greater than would first appear; moreover, the loading capacity of ships had increased substantially since that time.[38]

It is no coincidence that it was precisely during this period that Amsterdam's merchants remarked, with scarcely hidden satisfaction, 'that we, through our actions and cunning during the Twelve Years' Truce, have driven all other nations from the seas, drawn all trade from other countries here and serve all Europe with our ships'.[39] Although these claims were accompanied by a hefty dose of exaggeration, the fact remains that Amsterdam's trade and shipping

36 De Vries and Van der Woude, *The First Modern Economy*, chapter 12, in particular page 627.

37 This is discussed in more detail in Lesger, 'De wereld als horizon'.

38 Lesger, *Rise of the Amsterdam Market*, pp. 91–92.

39 '[D]at wij door onse mesnage ende beslepentheyt geduerende de Treves alle natiën uut het waeter gevaeren, meest alle negotiën uut andere landen hier getrocken en gansch Europa met onse schepen bedient hebben' (Van Dillen, *Van rijkdom en regenten*, p. 20).

Figure 2.2: Ships in front of and behind the row of stakes in Amsterdam's harbour, mid-seventeenth century.

experienced rapid growth that continued until around the middle of the century and that was partly based on conquering foreign markets. Thus, in addition to the increasing size of the local and national market, foreign markets also contributed to growing demand, especially in the last decades of the sixteenth century and in the first half of the seventeenth century.

We can be briefer regarding the composition of this demand. In doing so, we limit ourselves to Amsterdam, because from the end of the sixteenth century this city grew rapidly to become the largest city in the Dutch Republic and a trading centre of international repute. It is precisely here that we would expect to see the rise of a group of extremely prosperous merchants with consumer preferences reflecting their incomes and ambitions.[40] By around the mid-sixteenth century, Amsterdam had already grown into a trade centre of considerable importance. This is clearly shown when between 1543 and 1545, the government imposed a tax on the value of goods that were exported from the Habsburg Netherlands. At that time, Amsterdam was head and shoulders above the other trading centres in Holland, Utrecht and Zeeland.[41] In comparison with other centres, Amsterdam was

40 Within the Dutch Republic, comparable consumption preferences can only be expected at the Stadholder's court and among ambassadors and senior officials in The Hague.

41 Lesger, *Rise of the Amsterdam Market*, pp. 26–28.

also home to considerably more merchants with commercial capital of at least 1,000 guilders. In Middelburg, for example, 27 such merchants were registered; in Vlissingen, 11; in Veere, none; in Goes, 17; in Delft, 29; in Leiden, 6; and in Amsterdam no fewer than 92 individuals.[42]

Despite this, we should not make too much of the capital wealth of Amsterdam's citizens. The bulk of the commercial capital (67 cases) did not rise above 1,500 guilders. Data from estates also confirm that truly large fortunes were still lacking in Amsterdam at this time. In Warmoesstraat, the favourite place of residence of the most prosperous burghers in the mid-sixteenth century, the sums that the occupants left their minor offspring did not normally exceed 10,000 guilders.[43] Because in most cases this concerned the estate of one of the two parents, the total value will usually have been higher than the sum that was registered by the *weeskamer* (the government body that managed such legacies), but this does not alter the fact that the assets of Amsterdam's elite were relatively modest.

This changed after the *Alteratie* of 1578, when the Catholic government was replaced with a Calvinist one and the economy rapidly expanded.[44] In the mid-1580s, Amsterdam's richest citizen, the mayor and merchant Dirck Jansz Graaf, possessed a fortune of around 140,000 guilders, and there were another four or five citizens with fortunes of 100,000 guilders or more. A few decades later, when the wealth tax of 1631 was collected, this number had risen to 97, and a quarter of these individuals (24 taxpayers) had assets of at least 200,000 guilders. The wealthiest of all were the heirs of the immensely rich merchant and mayor Jacob Poppen, who were taxed on 500,000 guilders. They were followed by Guillielmo Bartholotti and Balthasar Coymans, each taxed on a fortune of 400,000 guilders.[45] In fact, they were considerably richer than their fiscal capital would suggest. Jacob Poppen's fortune actually amounted to 920,000 guilders, and Bartholotti left behind 1.2 million guilders on his death. Moreover, each time information from estates is available, the fiscal estimates prove to be too low—often much too low.[46] This implies that the number of people with assets of at least 100,000 guilders in 1631 was larger than suggested above. For 1674, we do have a source that is similar to the tax of 1631; by that year, the number of (fiscal) fortunes of at least 100,000 guilders had risen further to more than 200, with 82 of these fortunes amounting to 200,000 guilders or more.[47]

Even when we allow for inflation, it is clear that a relatively large group of very wealthy individuals emerged in Amsterdam in the late sixteenth century. Notwithstanding the fact that Amsterdam was a Calvinist city, the rich were keen to show the outside world what they were worth (financially, that is) by moving into impressive homes on distinguished canals or streets and living there in fine style. Country estates, carriages, clothing and jewellery were

42 Meilink, 'Gegevens aangaande bedrijfskapitalen', appendix B. For business capital in the fifteenth century, see Posthumus, *De Oosterse handel*, chapter 7.

43 Van der Leeuw-Kistemaker, *Wonen en werken in de Warmoesstraat*, appendix 1. For Warmoesstraat, a total of 19 legacies were found in the archives of the *weeskamer*, of which 14 were worth less than 10,000 guilders.

44 Van Ravesteyn Jr, *Onderzoekingen*, pp. 272–274.

45 Frederiks and Frederiks, *Kohier van den tweehonderdsten penning*, and Van Dillen, *Van rijkdom en regenten*, pp. 310–312.

46 Van Dillen, *Van rijkdom en regenten*, p. 311, and Zandvliet, *De 250 rijksten van de Gouden Eeuw*, p. xi.

47 Zandvliet, *De 250 rijksten van de Gouden Eeuw*, p. xii.

likewise used to show off the owner's status and ambitions. As early as 1614, Minister Trigland, a pastor in the Oude Kerk, criticized this extravagance and taste for opulence, which he believed to have been introduced by immigrants from the Southern Netherlands. He claimed, for example, 'that people have their clothes made from such flimsy fabrics that they can hardly shield their bodies from the cold'. And what did the rich do with their money? 'They must wear all kinds of expensive and strange cuts of clothing: there must be embroidery on the breast, the gold and the pearls must lie thickly, rings must be purchased that cost many hundreds of pounds, expensive meals and banquets must be held.'[48] All in all, there is sufficient evidence to suggest that especially in the final decades of the sixteenth century and the first half of the seventeenth century, not only did the size of Amsterdam's market grow sharply but also the nature of the demand changed. The new rich led a luxurious lifestyle, generating significant demand for high-quality consumer goods that had hardly, if ever, been sold in Amsterdam in the past.

The question that we now need to answer is whether in Amsterdam—like in the US in the nineteenth century or England in the seventeenth century—the growing volume and changing nature of demand gave rise to an expanding trade sector and to differentiation and job specialization within the distribution system. Let us first consider the size of the distribution system. Although there were no periodic censuses of professions in Amsterdam, there can be no doubt that a growing number of people worked in the commodities trade. Between 1586 and 1595, for example, the deeds on the issuing of bans for an intended first marriage recorded 33 people who worked in the commodities trade, but in the periods 1641–1650 and 1691–1700, this rose to 687 and 1,418 people respectively.[49] Thirty-three is undoubtedly an underestimate of the actual number, because in a relatively small city such as Amsterdam in the sixteenth century, it was not considered necessary to record the professions of prominent merchants. After all, such information was already public property. But even if this number were to increase substantially, the strong growth in the commodities trade in the last decades of the sixteenth century and during the seventeenth century would still be indisputable.

This growth is also shown, for instance, by the increasing size of the community of merchants from the Southern Netherlands in Amsterdam. In 1580, there were just 26 individuals in this community, but in 1590 there were 234, in 1600 around 350, and in 1610 around 470.[50] Finally, the growing number of account holders at the Amsterdam exchange bank also points in the same direction. In 1609, the year in which the exchange bank in the city hall

48 '[D]at men zulke lichtvaerdige stoffen neemt om de kleederen van te maken, dat men qualijk zijn lichaem daermede tegen de kouwde kan bedecken' [...] 'Allerley kostelijke ende vremde fatsoenen van kleederen moet men daer van dragen: geborduerde borsten moet men daervan laten maken, 't gouwd ende de paerlen moeten daer wel dik opleggen, ringen van etterlijke hondert ponden moet men daervan koopen, kostelijcke maeltijden ende bandquetten moet men daervan houden' (cited in Briels, *De Zuidnederlandse immigratie*, p. 66). See also Zandvliet, *De 250 rijksten van de Gouden Eeuw*, pp. xxxi-xxxv, and Van Dillen, *Bronnen bedrijfsleven en gildewezen*, I, nr. 1005.

49 SAA, Archief 883 (Collectie Hart) inv. nrs. 223–284. Merchants' servants and merchants' clerks have not been included in the analysis.

50 From that time on, this specific group did not increase further in size (Gelderblom, *Zuid-Nederlandse kooplieden*, appendix 1, table 3 and chapter 5, table 5.1).

opened, 731 merchants opened an account, and from that year onwards, the number of account holders increased almost continuously to more than 2,100 in 1661. This was followed by several decades of stagnation, but in the 1680s the number of account holders grew again, and in 1706 there were no fewer than 2,755.[51] The size of the distribution system therefore grew; but was this accompanied by differentiation and job specialization?

In order to be able to answer this question, we first need to establish when a distribution system with little differentiation was still the norm. According to Van Dillen, this was at the beginning of the sixteenth century: 'It is a fact', writes the author, 'that at the beginning of the century, many merchants were still simultaneously shipmaster and shopkeepers, and that their way of life hardly differed from that of prosperous artisans. Merchants and artisans still belonged to the same families and married amongst themselves.'[52] This is not to say, though, that some merchants had not already abandoned the combination of merchant and shipmaster many years beforehand. Between 1485 and 1490, for example, Simon Reyersz and Reyer Dircsz worked as partners in the Baltic trade, but they delegated the transport to others. Their company already had modern characteristics, whereby one of the partners represented the business in Amsterdam and the other the business in the Baltic. They also had an agent in Lübeck.[53] Despite this, the two men still travelled a great deal, and one could not yet describe this as a fully developed agent system whereby the merchant would act as the linchpin, trading and managing other representatives from his house in Amsterdam.[54]

The question of whether the two partners also engaged in wholesale and retail is not easy to answer. This cannot be deduced from the account book that has survived, but this is not surprising, as the book appears to have been used exclusively for the administration of the joint trade with the Baltic region. If we consider the goods that were transported to Amsterdam, retail would not have been the obvious option, as they were mostly grain and raw materials for industry (ash, pitch, tar, wood and tallow). However, the partners would have acted as wholesalers for manufacturers who processed the raw materials into semi-finished and finished products. Among the commodities that were shipped to the Baltic were products that were suitable for both wholesale and retail sales, in particular woollen cloth, which was recorded in a range of qualities in the accounts of Symon Reyersz and Reyer Dircsz.[55] It is very possible that they sold cloth wholesale in Amsterdam to *kramers* (non-itinerant sellers) and *wantsnijders* (cloth sellers) and retail to consumers. Whatever the case, the two men's accounts confirm that in the decades around 1500 in Amsterdam, trade was still being conducted in relatively simple fashion. What happened to this largely undifferentiated distribution system when, in the course of the sixteenth century and particularly in the years after 1580, the size of Amsterdam's market grew rapidly and demand became more varied?

Table 2.2 contains information about the professions of the many thousands of people who reported that they worked in the commodities trade when registering as *poorters*

51 In 1721, the largest number of account holders (2918) was registered at the Amsterdam exchange bank: Van Dillen, 'Bloeitijd der Amsterdamse Wisselbank', pp. 406–407.
52 Van Dillen, *Amsterdam in 1585*, p. xxii.
53 Posthumus, *De Oosterse handel*, p. 215.
54 Ibidem, pp. 33–35.
55 Ibidem, pp. 230 and 232.

Table 2.2 Number of job titles relating to the commodities trade in Amsterdam's *poorterboeken,* 1541–1811

	1541–1577	1579–1600	1601–1654	1655–1700	1701–1750	1751–1811
merchant / trader	1	1	1	1	2	3
merchant (specialized.)	1	13	7	5	8	37
trader (specialized)	0	1	8	7	3	3
wholesaler	0	0	0	0	0	1
wholesaler (specialized)	0	0	1	0	1	3
koper / buyer (specialized)	15	29	42	90	89	105
verkoper / seller (specialized)	10	23	52	118	94	98
kramer	1	1	1	1	1	1
kramer (specialized)	1	4	7	21	10	9
shopkeeper	0	0	1	2	1	1
shopkeeper (specialized)	0	1	8	32	36	45
job titles total	29	73	128	277	245	306

Sources: SAA, *poorterinschrijvingen* (data file and card index on occupations).

or burghers of Amsterdam. The table contains the numbers of job titles (not the numbers of burghers) found in the *poorterboeken*. One is immediately struck by the fact that in the years before the *Alteratie* (1578), there was only a paltry number of job titles in the commodities trade (29), but that immediately after this, the number quickly grew to a provisional maximum of 277 different job titles in the second half of the seventeenth century.[56] In other words, the distribution system experienced strong differentiation and specialization in the same period that, as we saw above, the size of Amsterdam's market grew rapidly and its nature also changed. In this sense, the material from Amsterdam confirms what was observed above in relation to the US and England.

If we look at the table more closely, we see that the largest numbers of new job titles fall into two categories: namely, the people recorded in the source who worked as buyers or *kopers* (apple buyer, stockings buyer, cloth buyer, tobacco buyer, etc.) and the people who worked as sellers or *verkopers* (bonnet seller, silk seller, etc.).[57] For the time being, let us focus our attention on the former group. Aside from a few fish buyers and cloth buyers, this group hardly appears in the sources prior to 1500. The latter refer almost exclusively to *comans* and *coopluden* (traders, vendors).[58] In other words, this is a job category that emerged in the course of the sixteenth century and that grew in importance at the end of the century. Who were these people? The fact that they were recorded in the source with a job title specifying the nature of their trade makes it clear that they were specialized traders. In the US in the nineteenth century, these specialized traders were the people who occupied the space, as it were, between importers and retailers (see

56 During the eighteenth century, the changes were relatively minor. In the years 1701–1750 and 1751–1811, I counted 245 and 306 job titles in the commodities trade respectively.

57 Male and female professionals are included under the same job title.

58 Compare Van der Leeuw-Kistemaker, *Wonen en werken in de Warmoesstraat*, appendix III; Van der Laan, *Oorkondenboek van Amsterdam*, and De Melker, *Oorkondenboek van Amsterdam: supplement.*

Figure 2.1), and this also seems to have been the case in early modern Amsterdam. In the literature, 'buyers' are normally seen as wholesalers. In a resolution by the Amsterdam city council of 1594, the cloth buyers were also literally described as such: 'laeckencoperen, soe grossiers als uytslyters'; 'cloth buyers, both wholesalers and purveyors'.[59] Thus, the fact that the term *grossier* or 'wholesaler' hardly occurs in Amsterdam's *poorterboeken* is not because this job hardly existed in the distribution system but because wholesalers were described as 'buyers' in everyday life.

In many cases, these buyers also engaged in retail trade, as indicated by the resolution itself, which refers to both 'wholesalers and purveyors'. Nor did the shopkeeping wholesaler disappear from the scene in later years. This is shown, among other things, by a contract that the silk buyer Isaac Vlamingh agreed with an apprentice from Nuremberg, Jeronimus Speugler, in 1636. The contract includes provisions on the trade trips that Speugler had to make for his patron, both at home and abroad. He was also forbidden from breaking the contract prematurely in order to set up his own cloth business or to go into partnership with others. All of these provisions, as well as Speugler's Southern German origins, indicate that Vlamingh was engaged in wholesale trade in cloth. But there was also a shop where Speugler was expected to work. On Sunday mornings at six o'clock, for example, he had to attend the early sermon and then 'return home immediately and spend the whole day minding the shop, serving the folk or customers and ensuring that all is as it should be'.[60] And we know from the division of Maria Cloppenburg's estate on her death in 1688 that she and her husband had not only owned a shop, probably on Nieuwendijk, but that these cloth buyers also had customers in a whole series of towns in the Netherlands and the neighbouring German states. Given the size of the outstanding debts, these were not usually private individuals but shopkeepers and cloth traders.[61]

By selling to retailers, wholesalers performed one of the classic tasks of distributive trade: building up stock. Van Nierop describes these wholesalers as the 'second hand', and this brings us to a long-running debate in Dutch historiography about the organization of early modern trade.[62] In a very influential study published in 1931, Van der Kooy argued that at the time of the Republic, wholesale covered three functions that were performed by three different groups of merchants.[63] According to Van der Kooy, sea traders (*zeehandelaren*) formed the 'first hand'. They usually specialized in trade with certain regions, from which they imported a wide range of products. For the sea trader, it was important to sell these imports as quickly as possible in order to free up capital for new trading activities. Their overseas suppliers would have also pressed them for prompt payment. The sea traders therefore tried to quickly sell the wares they imported to the 'second hand', a

59 Van Dillen, *Bronnen bedrijfsleven en gildewezen*, I, nr. 851, and Van Nierop, 'De handeldrijvende middenstand', p. 200, note 3.

60 '[D]atelijck thuys comen ende den gehelen dagh de winckel bewaeren, de luyden ofte de calanten te bescheyden ende alles naer behooren waer te nemen' (Van Dillen, *Bronnen bedrijfsleven en gildewezen*, III, nr. 244).

61 Elias, *Het geslacht Elias*, pp. 93–94, and SAA, archief notarissen (5075), Notaris Nic.Brouwer, 29 July 1690. The outstanding debts are specified on fol. 498v-501v. For the wholesale function of Amsterdam's cloth buyers, see Van Dillen, *Bronnen bedrijfsleven en gildewezen*, II, nrs. 1070 and 1147.

62 Van Nierop, 'De handeldrijvende middenstand', p. 200.

63 Van der Kooy, *Hollands stapelmarkt*, pp. 16–25.

group of very wealthy merchants who often specialized in particular sectors. They knew the market for their products much better than the sea traders, and their wealth allowed them to maintain large stocks. The second hand thereby formed a buffer between irregular imports into the Amsterdam market and steadier demand from retailers and consumers. In addition, the second hand also took care of sorting the merchandise and compiling consignments in the desired qualities and quantities. Finally, there was a third group of merchants—the 'third hand'—who sold the goods at home and abroad. Just like the first hand, these exporters often specialized in a particular area. In this area, they were familiar with the size and nature of the demand, bought from the 'second hand' and arranged shipping. Because customers often failed to pay on time, the functioning of the third hand was partly dependent on the credit that the merchants from the second hand were prepared to extend to them.

Van der Kooy's work has been subject to fierce criticism, mostly centred on the claim that he based his work on several publications dating from the early nineteenth century, and applied a model based on these to the seventeenth and eighteenth centuries without much debate or empirical testing.[64] For our purposes, it is important to establish whether the merchants recorded in the *poorterboeken* (burgher registers) and elsewhere as 'buyers' did indeed belong to the wealthy 'second hand' described by Van der Kooy and Van Nierop—and this does not appear to have been the case. This can be inferred from an analysis of the *Personele Quotisatie* of 1742, a tax on the wealth of all Amsterdam citizens with an income of at least 600 guilders per annum.[65] This is the only source from the entire early modern period that gives us both the profession and an indication of the wealth and income of a substantial part of the population of Amsterdam. For example, for each taxable person, it was reported whether they had assets of 2,000 guilders or more, assets of 1,000 to 2,000 guilders, or assets worth less than 1,000 guilders. In the source, the first two groups are described as 'capitalist' (*kapitalist*) and 'semi-capitalist' (*halve kapitalist*). The taxpayers' income was also estimated.

Table 2.3 shows information about the wealth and income of the more than 4,400 individuals listed in the *Personele Quotisatie* who worked in the commodities trade. We can see from the table that the specialized traders (*kopers*) by no means belonged to the wealthy 'second hand'. Only 41 per cent of them were taxed on assets of at least 1,000 guilders, and just 14 per cent fell into the 'capitalist' category. The large fortunes were not among the specialized traders but among the sizeable group of people described in the source as *koopman* or *koopvrouw* (male or female merchant). Of this group, 73 per cent possessed a fortune of 1,000 guilders or more, and no fewer than 53 per cent had at least 2,000 guilders. Their incomes also speak volumes. In the case of the specialized *kopers* (buyers), these amounted on average to less than 1,900 guilders a year, and for the merchants, 4,268 guilders. This picture is

64 Westermann, 'Beschouwingen', pp. 97–98, 108; Van Dillen, 'Een eeuw economische en sociale ontwikkeling', pp. 160–161. Research by Klein has shown that the functions distinguished by Van der Kooy did exist as such, but that the associated division between the first, second and third hands was absent in practice. Moreover, the organization of trade in the case of the Trip firm was also much more complex than Van der Kooy's model suggests (Klein, *De Trippen*, pp. 470 and 477, and see also Veluwenkamp, *Ondernemersgedrag*, pp. 24–25). A critique of Van der Kooy's staple market model is also in my *Rise of the Amsterdam Market*, chapter 5.

65 Oldewelt, *Kohier van de Personeele Quotisatie*.

Table 2.3 The capital wealth of merchants and retailers* in the *Personele Quotisatie*, 1742

	less than 1000 gl	1000 to 2000 gl	2000 gl or more	total	average income (gl)	N =
merchant / trader	27%	20%	53%	100%	4268	1087
merchant (specialized.)	43%	29%	29%	100%	1974	21
trader (specialized)	100%	0%	0%	100%	1150	2
wholesaler (specialized)	83%	0%	17%	100%	1333	12
koper / buyer (specialized)	59%	27%	14%	100%	1894	888
verkoper / seller (specialized)	83%	14%	3%	100%	1182	387
kramer (specialized)	75%	25%	0%	100%	1575	4
shopkeeper	100%	0%	0%	100%	700	4
shopkeeper (specialized)	82%	14%	4%	100%	1157	1998
N =	2796	811	796	4403		4403

Source: Oldewelt, *Kohier van de Personeele Quotisatie*.
* Persons with multiple occupations are not included.
** The numbers in the table have been rounded off and therefore do not always add up to 100.

reinforced by additional information from the *Personele Quotisatie*. In the category of merchants, 17 per cent of those taxed had a country estate, whereas among the specialized *kopers* this figure was just 4 per cent.

Thus, as a group, the wealth and capital of the specialized *kopers* lagged far behind that of the individuals described as 'merchants' in 1742. The same was also true of the preceding period. This has been shown by research by Van Dillen into the professions of the highest-taxed individuals as recorded for a wealth tax imposed in 1631. Of the 387 rich individuals whose professions could be traced, no fewer than 253 were merchants (65 per cent), whilst just 64 of them were specialized traders (17 per cent).[66] Rather than being the wealthy linchpin of the distribution system, these specialized *kopers* were wholesalers of relatively modest means. They provided their services to retailers within and beyond the city, they did not eschew retail sales, and they were sometimes even involved in international trade themselves. It was not so much thanks to their wealth but their numbers that they fulfilled an essential buffer function in the distribution system between the irregular supply of goods onto Amsterdam's market and the regular and not inconsiderable demand from individual retailers. It has been wrongly assumed that this key buffer function must have been fulfilled mainly by important merchants—that is to say, distinguished individuals with considerable financial means—but this was evidently not the case.

The increasing differentiation and specialization within Amsterdam's distribution system is not only shown by the rise and rapid growth of the above-mentioned group of specialized *kopers*/wholesalers; Table 2.2 also shows that a similar process took place in retail trade. In the period between 1541 and 1577, there are just ten job titles in the 'sellers' category, but this number rises to a peak of 118 job titles in the second half of the seventeenth century. Before we consider this development in more detail, it is useful to look briefly at the history of retail trade in Amsterdam in the years before information about the professions of those who lived in the city becomes available. In the fourteenth

66 Van Dillen, *Bronnen bedrijfsleven en gildewezen*, II, p. xxxix.

century, the typical retailer was the *merseman* or *mairceman*.[67] Besides this figure, we come across few other kinds of retailers in the sources. The *merseman* did not specialize in a particular trade but sold a whole range of items, mostly of relatively little value and intended for personal or household use. Even before 1400, the term *kramer* (non-itinerant seller) was being used synonymously with *merseman*, and this would become the standard term over time. In the *kramers'* ordinance, a guild statute of 1476, we get an impression of the activities of these retailers. They were engaged in the sale of '*marcerye, cramerye, malgerye en specerye* [haberdashery, pedlars' wares, metalware and spices]'—that is to say, a whole series of what were generally small utensils and items made of textile, metal and wood. But they also sold sugar, candied fruits, semi-tropical fruit, oil, spices and many other things.[68] There was thus hardly any specialization in retail trade.

When Amsterdam's market grew in the sixteenth century, this range became even wider. In 1554, *kramers* were permitted to sell knives and nails; in 1565, also ribbons and serge (woven woollen cloth); and in 1581, they were also allowed to sell tin 'spoons and small (drinking) dishes, each weighing no more than three-quarters of a pound'.[69] But just as the general store in densely populated parts of the US hit the limits of what was marketable for a single business in the nineteenth century, it seems that Amsterdam's *kramers* were no longer able to meet the growing size and differentiation of the demand. The division of what had originally been a very wide range over a large number of specialized retailers is clearly evident from Table 2.2. There, we see that from the final decades of the sixteenth century, in addition to the *kramer*, a series of specialized colleagues appears in the sources; and in the second half of the seventeenth century, there are no fewer than 21 different kinds of *kramers* listed in the *poorterboeken*. But that is not all. Much more spectacular is the increase in the number of specialized job titles among sellers: from ten in the third quarter of the sixteenth century to 118 in the second half of the seventeenth century. Finally, the *poorterboeken* show increasing specialization among shopkeepers. In the period between 1579 and 1600, we find just one single stocking-vendor, but in the first half of the seventeenth century, we already come across eight different specializations; in the second half of the century, 32; and a century later, as many as 45.

One could conclude from Table 2.2 that the sellers, *kramers* and shopkeepers represented different kinds of retail trade, even though they did not specialize by product, but that would be incorrect. Just as the word *merseman* was once replaced by the word *kramer*, the latter, in turn, appears to have been replaced by the word *winkelier* or 'shopkeeper' in the course of the seventeenth century.[70] The interchangeability of the two terms is revealed, among other things, by a long poem about winter in Amsterdam by Six van Chandelier, written in ca. 1650. In this, he wrote of a rainy day:

> The gutters are splashing on the stones,
> And every canopy weeps and cries.
> Every *kramer* with an open façade
> Closes his windows and his shop door.[71]

67 For the following, see Van Nierop, 'De handeldrijvende middenstand', pp. 193–200.
68 Ibidem, p. 195, and the guild statute in Breen, *Rechtsbronnen der stad Amsterdam*, pp. 111–112.
69 '[L]epels en kleyne gedopte schaelkens, 't stuck niet meer wegende ten hoogsten dan drie vierendeel ponts' (Van Nierop, 'De handeldrijvende middenstand', p. 196).
70 Ibidem, p. 198.
71 'De gooten kletsen op 't gesteent, En elke luiffe huilt en weent. Elk kraamer onbeslooten veur, Sloot

Moreover, the many dozens of kinds of specialized sellers that we encounter in the *poorterboeken* are described elsewhere as *winkeliers* or shopkeepers. This is shown most clearly when we compare the terms in the *poorterboeken* with those in the register of the *Personele Quotisatie* of 1742. For the entire eighteenth century, around 130 different job titles are mentioned for *verkopers* (sellers) in the *poorterboeken*, around 15 for *kramers*, and around 55 for *winkeliers* (shopkeepers).[72] In the very accurate registration of professions in the *Personele Quotisatie*, just 10 different job titles for sellers are listed, 2 for *kramers* and no fewer than 113 for shopkeepers.[73] Our conclusion must therefore be that the people who were listed in the *poorterboeken* as sellers and *kramers* were described in the *Personele Quotisatie* with the much more modern term *winkelier* (shopkeeper). *Marskramers* (hawkers) and *venters* (street traders) were not listed in the registers of the *Personele Quotisatie*, but that is hardly surprising, as they would not have reached the threshold of 600 guilders per annum and were therefore exempt from the tax.

However people may have described themselves, it is clear that retail trade underwent a process of specialization and that this process was most manifest in the period that was described above as an era in which the size of the demand in Amsterdam's market increased rapidly and the character of the demand also changed. This was no accident, because analogous to what Bucklin has argued in relation to the rise of speciality stores on the American East Coast in the nineteenth century, we can assume that a few centuries before this in Amsterdam the time was ripe for the rise of speciality shops. There, too, the range offered by *kramers* (comparable to general stores in the US) was gradually no longer able to meet the demand from consumers for more kinds of goods and a greater variety of price, quality, and appearance for every type of merchandise. The *kramers*, sellers and shopkeepers who specialized in particular products may have offered fewer kinds of goods, but they could offer a wide range of every kind. At the time of his bankruptcy in 1644, for example, around 100 qualities of fabric were to be found in the fabric shop of Jacob Herlijn in Warmoesstraat.

Moreover, thanks to this specialization, retailers were able to expand their knowledge of their goods and thereby serve the consumer better when choosing from the ever-expanding range of goods in Amsterdam's market. It is not impossible that this same specialization also allowed them to buy in bulk and negotiate volume discounts from wholesalers and producers. In that case, they would have also competed with the traditional, non-specialized *kramers* on price. What we do know for sure is that Amsterdam's distribution system underwent significant changes, especially from the end of the sixteenth century. The hardly differentiated nature that typified this system in the late Middle Ages and early sixteenth century disappeared, to be succeeded by the development of a relatively modern distribution system in which wholesalers and retailers who specialized in particular products played an important role.[74] It is also clear that the different roles within the

veinsters, en syn winkeldeur.' (Six van Chandelier, ''s Amsterdammers Winter', lines 331–334). I wish to thank prof. dr. E.K. Grootes for drawing my attention to this poem.

72 For the sources, see the caption to Table 2.2.

73 Counted in Oldewelt, *Kohier van de Personeele Quotisatie*.

74 We can make out the same trend towards specialization among Amsterdam's markets, and here, too, the growing volume and changing nature of demand in Amsterdam would have been the main driver of change. For markets, see Kistemaker, 'De Amsterdamse markten'.

distribution system were often played by the same people or firms; thus, we now turn our attention to the wholesalers who kept shops and the retailers who traded wholesale.

Combinations of wholesale and retail

We can get a somewhat better impression of this group in the years around 1742, for then it is possible to search for the names of creditors listed in bankrupt shop estates in the register of the *Personele Quotisatie* (provided that the creditors lived in Amsterdam and met the tax threshold of 600 guilders a year). Among other things, the *Personele Quotisatie* contains information about these creditors' professions, addresses and incomes—details that are hardly ever found in the papers left by bankrupts.[75]

When studying the files on bankrupt shopkeepers, we are immediately struck by the fact that particularly the keepers of small shops purchased much of their stock from large retailers in the same or a related trade. In other words, this latter group indeed acted as wholesalers. Take Adolf Dijkman's grocery shop on Prinsenstraat, for example. When Dijkman went bankrupt in 1744, he had debts for rice purchased from the widow of Gerrit Katers, a grocer on Damrak; for oil and saffron bought from Hendrik Wees, a grocer on Rokin; for coffee bought from Hendrik van Egten, a grocer on Nieuwezijds Voorburgwal; for raisins bought from Marten van der Poel, a grocer on St Antoniesbreestraat; and for groceries (not further specified) purchased from Godfried Fabricius, Clemens Kever and Mathijs Cosijn, grocers on Runstraat, Nieuwendijk and Kalverstraat respectively.[76] With the exception of Godfried Fabricius on the rather undistinguished Runstraat, all of these grocers enjoyed incomes of 1,000 to 2,500 guilders a year. Their location on major shopping streets also makes it clear that these were considerable shops.

The fact that small grocers made many purchases from large retailers in the same sector is also shown by a by-law of 31 January 1729 forbidding commodities brokers from selling small quantities of groceries to 'the small shops and *komenijen* [shops selling bacon, dairy, and dry goods] that have become accustomed to buying their goods from grocers'.[77] The by-law was clearly intended to protect the large grocers' interests on the grounds that they had 'to pay steep rents in order to trade'. This was certainly true, for we know from the *Personele Quotisatie* that rents on the main shopping thoroughfares were indeed high and could easily amount to 500 to 1,000 guilders a year. Perhaps the problem was not as great as the by-law suggests, or perhaps the by-law was unusually effective, but the fact is that in the papers of bankrupt retailers, one comes across debts to fellow grocers but not, or hardly ever, to commodities brokers as far as I can see.

The phenomenon whereby large retailers also sold wholesale to fellow retailers in the same trade was not limited to foods and other daily necessities. When Anna de Graaff, the widow of Alexander van Langenberg, went bankrupt, it turned out that she and her husband had made purchases for their fabric shop

75 The archives of the *Desolate boedelkamer*, where bankruptcies were registered, are discussed in more detail in the following chapters.

76 SAA, Desolate boedelkamer, inv. nr. 746, file 3. For similar cases, see inv. nr. 745, files 7, 37 and 54, and also inv. nr. 746, file 30. In this period, the term grocer no longer refers to internationally operating spice merchants.

77 Noordkerk, *Handvesten ofte privilegiën*, pp. 1073–1074.

on Geldersekade from four wool and damask shops on Warmoesstraat and Nieuwendijk, cloth shops on the same streets, and an English bonnet and hat shop on Nieuwendijk. In the years prior to the bankruptcy of their fabric shop on Hoogstraat, Gerrit van Tij and his wife Dyna Yonkmans purchased wares from seven fabric shops, mainly on Warmoesstraat.[78] Harmanus Krouwel likewise ran up debts for his small porcelain and Delftware shop with Abel Booning, who himself ran a large porcelain shop on Haarlemmerdijk, and with Barent Molter, who managed a porcelain shop on Kloveniersburgwal.[79]

As well as buying from fellow retailers, who thereby also acted as wholesalers, shopkeepers also bought shop wares directly from producers. This was particularly the case for the purchase of sugar, candy and syrup by grocers and *komenijshouders* (sellers of bacon, dairy and dry goods). These purchases were almost invariably made from one of the many sugar refineries in Amsterdam at that time. Nor was it a coincidence that Adolf Dijkman bought starch from the village of Koog aan de Zaan, for it was there that grain—the raw material for starch—was husked, split and ground. Harmanus Krouwel, to give a last example, bought his porcelain and pottery not only from wholesale retailers in Amsterdam but also directly from manufacturing centres such as Harlingen and in particular Delft.

Finally, the creditors included people who were listed in the sources only as 'merchants'. They seem to have acted mainly as wholesalers in coffee, tea, spices and fabric. The use of the term 'merchant' (*koopman*) and the fact that their incomes were almost invariably much higher than those of the wholesaling retailers makes it unlikely that they ran shops or were otherwise engaged in retail. Rather, they were more likely to be nationally and internationally operating merchants, those described in Van der Kooy's study as the 'first hand' and the 'third hand'. In this group, I also include the creditors—mainly based in Leiden—of fabric shopkeepers such as Anna de Graaff and Gerrit van Tij. These suppliers were not weavers but cloth merchants or drapers. They bought the raw materials, had them processed by homeworkers or in workshops (*manufactuur*), and then traded the finished article. Thus, when they supplied directly to shops, they also functioned as wholesalers: the 'second hand' in Van der Kooy's argument.[80]

Sometimes, when the clerk mentioned not only the creditors in a bankruptcy file but also all the debtors, we can see the extent to which retail and wholesale were intertwined in the larger shops. Jan Goris de Visser, for example, was a grocer on Nieuwendijk. Like his fellow grocers, he bought from other grocers, manufacturers and merchants, but in addition to this, De Visser himself also acted as a wholesaler—at least, this is what we can infer from the list of debtors. The latter opens with the observation that 'little can be hoped' of these people, but the administrator of the bankrupt estate nevertheless took the trouble to record their places of residence accurately. And we therefore know that De Visser not only had customers in Amsterdam but also clients in a whole series of towns and villages in North Holland, the Wadden Islands, and even in Friesland and in Elberfeld in Germany.[81] The arrival

78 SAA, Desolate boedelkamer, inv. nr. 851, file 1 for the De Graaff bankruptcy, and inv. nr. 745, file 24 for the Van Tij and Yonkmans bankruptcy. Files concerning bankrupt fabric shops can also be found in inv. nr. 745, file 8, and in inv. nr. 746, files 8, 11, 29 and 40.

79 SAA, Desolate boedelkamer, inv. nr. 745, file 32.

80 For the organization of the Leiden textile industry, see Posthumus, *De Leidsche lakenindustrie,* II, chapter 4.

81 SAA, Desolate boedelkamer, inv. nr. 746, file 30.

of such customers would not have surprised a retailer on Nieuwendijk because intensive contact was maintained with these regions via the Zuiderzee and the IJ. Moreover, Nieuwendijk traditionally formed a key link between Amsterdam's harbour and the city centre around the Dam. Many people who arrived in the city over the IJ would thus have walked along Nieuwendijk and made purchases there. For our purposes, it is significant that the size of the debt carried by some debtors does not indicate private purchases but the laying-in of shop stock or merchandise. This is the case for the debt of 354 guilders owed by Albertus Wijthoven from West-Zaandam and for the 120 guilders still owed by Anna Visser, also from West-Zaandam. Individuals from Uitgeest and Elberfeld also owed large sums, and Arent Anthonisz Smit from Harlingen even owed Jan Goris de Visser 1,384 guilders and 13 stivers. De Visser was not exceptional in having such a wide circle of customers; precisely because Amsterdam was the key node in the domestic transport network, Amsterdam's large shops functioned as wholesalers for retailers in the wider area. Just like the small retailers in the city, these retailers profited from the considerable stocks and wide ranges kept by large shops.

Amsterdam's shopkeepers not only had suppliers in their own city and country but also far beyond the country's borders. We rarely encounter these in the bankruptcy cases discussed above, but in the files of retailers selling luxury items, they are no rarity. *Galanterieën* (fancy goods) are a good example of what are now known as luxury goods. Today, the term *galanterieën* evokes associations with cheap jewellery and knickknacks, but in the early modern period it was used to refer to fashionable items and attractive trinkets. These were available in all price ranges and sold not only in luxury shopping streets such as Kalverstraat but also in backstreets and basement shops. Until his bankruptcy in 1778, Bernardus van Delm ran a fancy goods shop from a basement on Oude Leliestraat, and it will come as no surprise that aside from a single person from Rotterdam, all his suppliers were from Amsterdam.[82] We should be no less surprised that the creditors of Pierre Tauran and his wife, fancy goods retailers in Reguliersdwarsstraat, included many suppliers from Amsterdam. Given that the latter were usually based on Kalverstraat, Nieuwendijk, Rokin and Nes, it is clear that Tauran and his wife bought shop wares from large shops in Amsterdam.[83]

Those who ran large shops also bought from their colleagues in Amsterdam, but not exclusively. When Franciscus Xaverius Schorrer, a fancy goods retailer on Nieuwezijds Voorburgwal, went bankrupt in 1782, he left not only a considerable stock of wares but also over 24,000 guilders of debt. Schorrer owed 20 per cent of this debt to individuals whose place of residence is not listed but who were probably fellow citizens of Amsterdam. The other creditors were located outside of Holland and, aside from a single exception in Den Bosch, also outside the Republic. To business relations in Lyon, Schorrer owed almost 5,300 guilders, 22 per cent of the total debt. Sixteen per cent of the debt was owed to business relations in Paris, over 13 per cent to contacts in Valenciennes, and 11.5 per cent to London. He also had debts in Antwerp and Brussels.[84]

82 SAA, Desolate boedelkamer, inv. nr. 3018.
83 SAA, Desolate boedelkamer, inv. nr. 5091. For the period around 1742, when the register of the *Personele Quotisatie* was drawn up, I was unable to find usable bankruptcies of shops selling luxury items. I therefore used information for later years, but I consequently missed an opportunity to find out more about the professions, addresses and incomes of the people concerned.
84 SAA, Desolate boedelkamer, inv. nr. 3480.

A fellow fancy-goods retailer, Johannes Silo on Kalverstraat by the Dam, left a much less considerable debt of 12,000 guilders, but he, too, owed a large share (86 per cent) of the arrears to foreign creditors. Specifically, these were debts to Paris (39 per cent), London (25 per cent), Lyon (13 per cent) and Como in Italy (9 per cent).[85] Amsterdam's suppliers were presumably able to exercise more pressure on arrears owed to a fellow citizen. Although their actual share is probably underestimated in the list of creditors following bankruptcy as a result, it is abundantly clear that Amsterdam's fancy-goods retailers placed considerable orders abroad. In the file opened after the bankruptcy of François Haram Rilliet and his wife Nanette Françoise Rilliet, the street name of creditors in Paris is mentioned. The Rue St Denis and the Pont Saint Michel come up most frequently, and in those days these were the most important shopping streets in Paris.[86] Combined with the fact that both Schorrer and the Rilliet couple made purchases from a whole series of suppliers in Paris, this suggests that large luxury goods retailers in Amsterdam purchased some of their shop wares from large Parisian retailers. This is hardly surprising because there, of all places, they could expect to find goods that satisfied the tastes of wealthy and fashion-conscious citizens of Amsterdam.

It is clear from the above that in the decades around 1600, a relatively modern distribution system emerged in Amsterdam. This modernity was expressed in the presence of specialized wholesalers and retailers, who together guaranteed a wide and varied range of goods in the city. At the same time, we have observed that in the early modern era, the division between wholesale and retail was not as stark as it would later become. Although combining the two activities might strike us as old-fashioned today, we should not forget that the shopkeeping wholesaler was a common phenomenon in Amsterdam until the early twentieth century and would continue to exist for even longer in the provinces.[87]

85 SAA, Desolate boedelkamer, inv. nr. 3949.

86 SAA, Desolate boedelkamer, inv. nr. 4879 and for shopping streets in eighteenth-century Paris, see Coquery, *Tenir boutique*, chapters 4 and 5, and appendix 1. Foreign creditors are also mentioned in the administration of the bankruptcy of fancy-goods retailers Philippe du Bois (SAA, Desolate boedelkamer, inv. nr. 3100) and Jan Frans Commert (SAA, Desolate boedelkamer, inv. nr. 3993).

87 Elias, *Het geslacht Elias*, p. 83.

3. Shop location patterns in the age of the great urban expansions

Abstract

The lack of space caused by rapid economic and demographic growth, and also the need to bring Amsterdam's defences up to an acceptable level, gave rise to a number of city expansions from the end of the sixteenth century. Nevertheless, the retail function of the medieval heart of Amsterdam remained largely unaffected by the expansions that had multiplied the surface of the city many times. It was especially the elongated shape of the wealthy canal ring that prevented a compact luxury quarter with matching shopping facilities from evolving. The filling-up of the new neighbourhoods and the city centre's unrivalled position as the main shopping area made the radials crowded approach routes and therefore attractive locations for shopkeepers to establish themselves.

Keywords: city expansions, continuity of retail location, canal ring, radial streets

The boom that Amsterdam enjoyed around the mid-sixteenth century was rooted to a large extent in the favourable economic development of the Low Countries in general and the commercial vitality of Antwerp in particular.[1] Antwerp was by far the most important trading centre in the Low Countries at that time. In the period between February and September 1545, the city accounted for almost 75 per cent of registered exports from the Habsburg Netherlands. Amsterdam, the second trading city, trailed far behind with little more than 6 per cent of total exports. This did not mean that Amsterdam's trade was insignificant, though—far from it. The various port and trading cities played specific roles within the larger whole of the Low Countries, and Amsterdam was the place that maintained the most intensive contact with northern and northeastern Europe. These regions were the source of imports of wood, hemp, tar and many other raw materials for industry as well as much of the grain that, when made into bread and beer, was essential for sustaining the population. High-quality industrial products from the Low Countries, large quantities of salt and herring, and spices that were brought to the Low Countries via Portugal and Italy were shipped in the opposite direction.

With the outbreak of the Dutch Revolt against Spanish rule, the Dutch economy was disrupted for a long period, and this also had negative consequences for Amsterdam. It was only in the second half of the 1570s—when

1 For a detailed account of this period and the effect of the Dutch Revolt on the economic development of the Low Countries, see Lesger, *Rise of the Amsterdam Market*, and for the economy of Antwerp: Van der Wee, *The Growth of the Antwerp Market*.

Lesger, C., *Shopping Spaces and the Urban Landscape in Early Modern Amsterdam*, 1550–1850.
Taylor & Francis Group, 2020
DOI: 10.5117/9789463720625_CH03

Holland was no longer on the front line and Amsterdam chose to side with the rebel provinces in the *Alteratie*—that the recovery was able to begin. But after that, things went fast. The strong expansion of Holland's economy, the ongoing war and economic upheaval in the southern part of the Low Countries, the conquest of Antwerp by the Duke of Parma, the subsequent blockade of the Scheldt, and the arrival of large numbers of skilled migrants in the northern Low Countries created opportunities that fell on fertile soil in Amsterdam. In an incredibly short time, the city grew to be the most important harbour and trading city in the Netherlands and far beyond. At this point, we pick up the thread of the first chapter once more.

A period of dynamism and expansion

In early modern cities, there was a close relationship between economic growth and population development. This is because it was the arrival of immigrants, more than the natural increase in the resident population, that caused urban populations to grow. At a time when social facilities for newcomers hardly existed, migrants tended to flow towards places that could provide work and an income. Moreover, being able to eke out a living in a city prevented newcomers from leaving again a short while later. Powerful economic growth therefore attracted large numbers of migrants to Amsterdam, and the city rapidly grew into one of the larger European cities. In 1578, Amsterdam had around 25,000 to 30,000 residents; in 1622, there were already more than 120,000; and around the mid-seventeenth century, there were 160,000 to 175,000 people in Amsterdam.

The rapid growth of the population put huge pressure on the existing housing stock, as is clearly shown by the rents. Between 1580 and 1595, rents almost tripled, causing many to fall into great financial difficulties.[2] In August 1595, the chartered salt measurers (*zoutmeters*) demanded a pay rise because, they wrote, 'as the year ends—they have been unable to put anything aside for illness and old-age, beyond the cost of living and rent, and it is mainly that rent which oppresses them'.[3] Not only the rapidly growing population but also trade, shipping and industry needed more space. Industry found temporary solace by using property that had belonged to religious foundations, but in the long term this was utterly inadequate. Moreover, it was proving difficult to find room for the rapidly growing fleet of ships that put in at Amsterdam's harbour. Finally, not only the lack of space but also the defence of the city played a role in the building activities that flourished from the end of the 1570s.[4] For decades, the Lastage area on the eastern side of the city had lain virtually unprotected from enemy attack, and the owners of land in this 'suburb' had long wanted to bring this area within the city walls. Nor was the old brick city wall, which is visible on the bird's-eye-view map by Cornelis Anthonisz, able to meet the demands of the age any longer. A heavy earthen wall with ditches and bulwarks was needed to withstand modern artillery. The city expansions were thus not only intended to provide space for the population and economic activities, it also had to bring Amsterdam's defences up to an acceptable level. The defensibility of

2 Lesger, *Huur en conjunctuur*, p. 45 and appendix 1.

3 '[H]et jaar omme zijnde – [zij] niet bemercken en connen, dat se eenen stuver vry gelts connen overhouden voor siecte ende ouderdom, boven cost ende huyshuyr, [en het is] voornamelijck die huyshuyr, die hen supplianten, gans onder hout en verdruct' (Van Dillen, *Bronnen bedrijfsleven en gildewezen*, I, p. 522, nr. 870).

4 Burger jr., 'Amsterdam in het einde der zestiende eeuw', and Bakker, 'De zichtbare stad'.

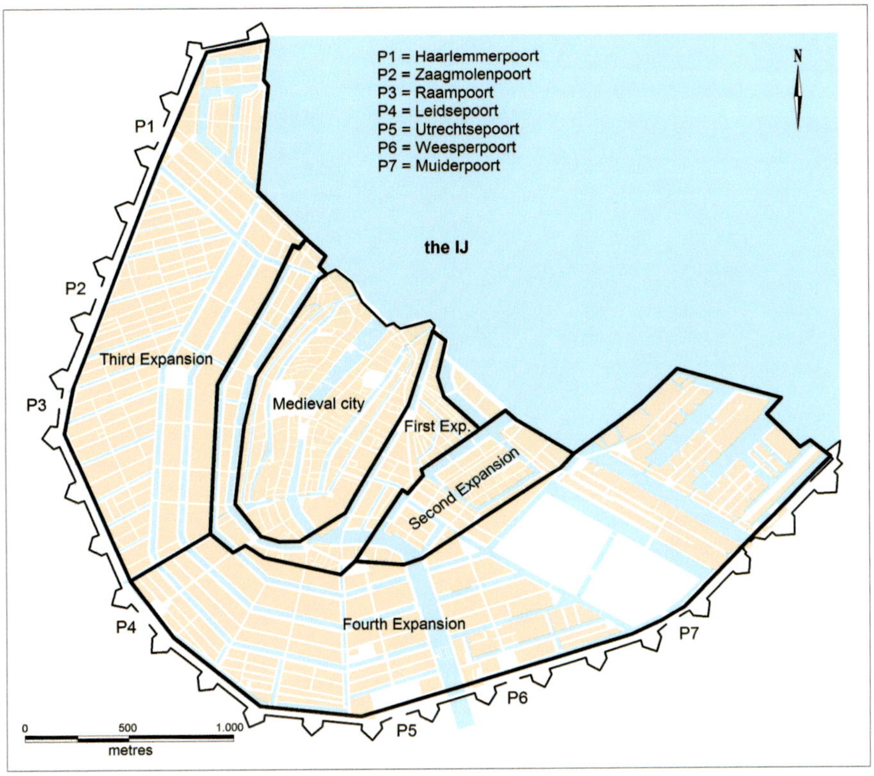

Figure 3.1: City expansions in Amsterdam.

the city seems to have played the main role in the so-called First Expansion (after the *Alteratie*) because, aside from the Lastage, only a relatively small amount of space was gained between 1578 and 1587 (Figure 3.1).

Thus, not many years later, Amsterdam was enlarged again with the Second Expansion (1592–1596); and this time, too, it was mainly land on the eastern side of the city that was brought within the city walls. In 1597, shortly after the completion of the Second Expansion, Pieter Bast made a map of the situation (Figure 3.2). The map gives a good impression of the city in this transitional period: we can still see the old brick city wall running along the inner side of Singel, whilst beyond it a new neighbourhood and city ramparts with bastions have been built. The British traveller Fynes Moryson visited Amsterdam in the same period and described what we can see on Bast's map as 'a wall of stone, higher than the city [and] beyond this wall there is another of earth, and betweene these wals [sic] the new city was plotted out'.[5]

Although the land area of the city would almost double, the First and Second Expansions were by no means extensive enough to accommodate the growing population and the expansion in trade, shipping and industry.[6] Thus, it would not be long before expansion was again on the city government's agenda. The Third and Fourth Expansions that followed in the seventeenth century became the subject of a lengthy discussion

5 Jacobsen Jensen, 'Moryson's reis', p. 223.

6 For the growing size of the city during the expansions, see Bakker, 'De zichtbare stad', note 3.

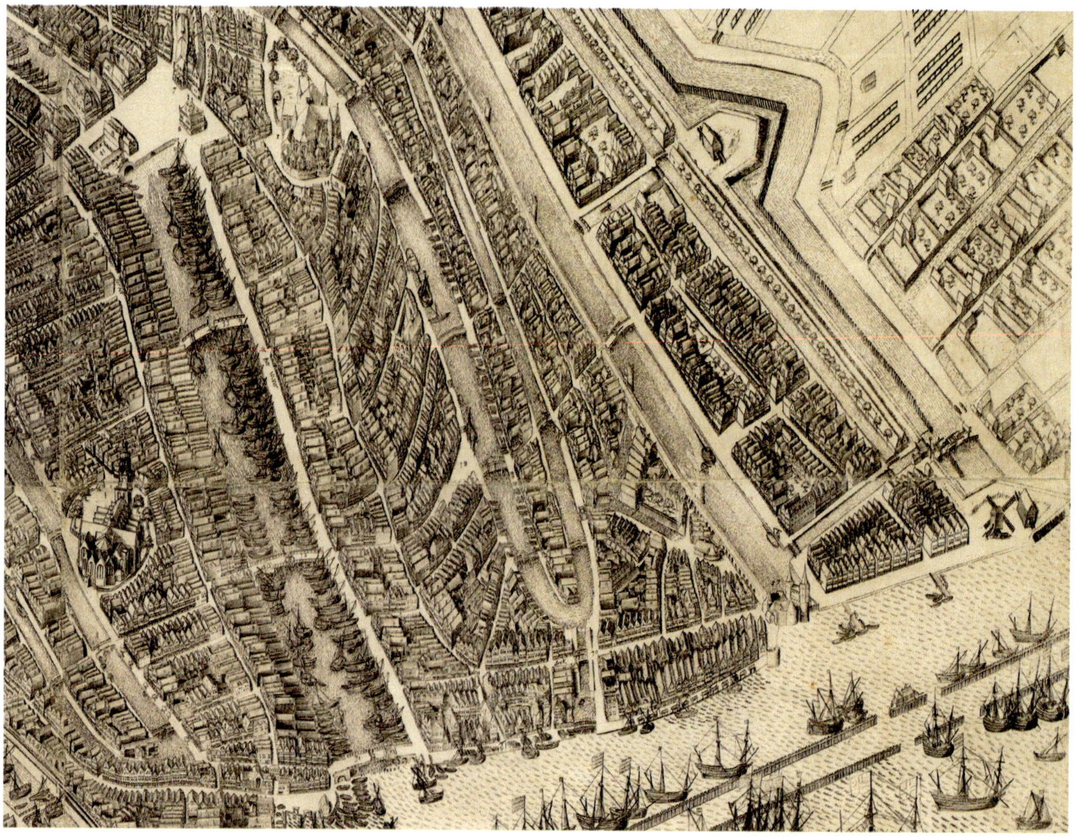

Figure 3.2: The western side of the city in the late sixteenth century (north at the bottom).

among historians. This focused on the question of whether the famous 'half-moon' shape created at the time was based on a masterplan, itself possibly based on the models of 'ideal cities' described and propagated in Italian treatises.[7]

Thanks to a comprehensive and very detailed study by Abrahamse, it has become clear that there was no masterplan behind the entire seventeenth-century city expansion. At the beginning of the century, the city's chief architect (*stadstimmerman*), Hendrick Jacobsz Staets, did admittedly make a map—which has not survived—of an expansion around the whole city, and there are images—which have survived—of the city surrounded by semi-circular fortifications, but none indicate the existence of a masterplan. After all, this would suggest that all of the aspects of the city expansions were analyzed as a coherent whole and processed in an urban plan. Although the seventeenth-century city expansions took shape in an environment where people were undoubtedly aware of Italian treatises on urban planning and the ideal city, Abrahamse makes it clear that it was primarily practical considerations and the specific problems facing the municipal government that determined the actual course of events.[8]

7 Important contributions to this discussion are Jansen, 'De derde vergroting'; Taverne, *In 't land van belofte*, and—most recently—Abrahamse, *Metropolis in the Making*. Chapter 1 of the latter study summarizes the discussion.

8 Abrahamse, *Metropolis in the Making*, chapter 7.

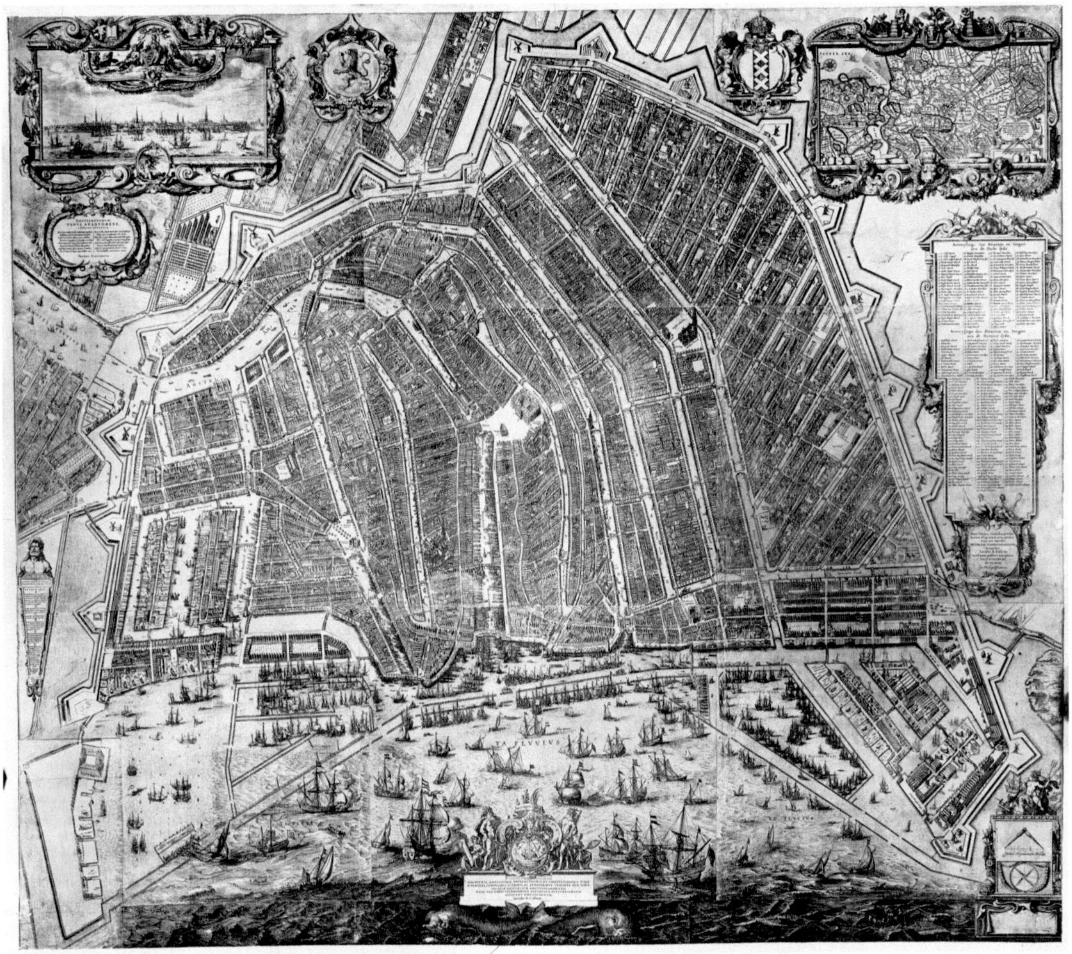

Figure 3.3: Amsterdam after the Third Expansion (north at the bottom).

These specific problems were not very different from those that had been grappled with during the First and Second Expansions. The growing trade, shipping and industrial sectors needed more space in the city itself and on the roads. The flow of newcomers was constantly growing, and partly because of this, suburbs of unprecedented size were emerging beyond the city ramparts. Finally, these expanding suburbs were adding to the concerns about the city's defensibility, as enemy soldiers could potentially entrench themselves there. The fear of siege warfare was not far-fetched, as at this time the outcome of the struggle against Spanish rule was still far from guaranteed. Only once the fighting had ceased for some time, especially after the signing of the Twelve Years' Truce (1609–1621), did the city dare to start building new fortifications.[9] As early as 1609, the States of Holland gave Amsterdam permission to expand the city and expropriate the necessary land and buildings for this purpose.

9 For the following, see ibidem, pp. 41–42, and Bakker, 'De zichtbare stad'.

Early in the following year, Staets presented his plan for an expansion around the whole city, but doubts quickly arose regarding the project's feasibility. The instruments that the city had at its disposal were not well-suited to an operation of this scale. In particular, the fact that former owners of expropriated land had a right to buy it back once it had been reallocated and lay within the new fortifications (the right of preference) gave rise to enormous administrative, financial and practical problems. The financial problems were magnified by the failure of attempts to collect tax owed on the increase in the value of land that had come to lie within the city (amelioration). In order to keep things somewhat manageable, in 1613 the decision was made to limit the expansion to the western part of the city, from the IJ to the location of today's Leidsegracht.[10] There, the city wall would take a sharp bend and rejoin the old wall from the Second Expansion (Figure 3.3). As far as the fortifications were concerned, this created a highly undesirable situation, but the city government clearly preferred this to the risk of spiralling costs and insufficient income.

This modest expansion became known as the Third Expansion, but even though the size of the expansion area was limited, the problems were not over yet. In combination with the right of preference, the redevelopment of the area that had now come to lie within the city ramparts led to administrative chaos and sharply rising costs. Attempts to control the costs and maximize the proceeds of land sales were clearly evident in the end result. For example, in the area to the west of the canal ring—what would later be called the Jordaan—the pre-urban residential axes along paths and ditches were maintained as far as possible in order to limit the costs of expropriating existing buildings and redeveloping the infrastructure. As a consequence, the urban grid in this area did not connect, or hardly connected, with the transverse streets of the canal ring that gave access to the city centre. Little of the area was raised, either, which would result in this densely populated neighbourhood having major problems with water management.

The problems can also be inferred from the spatial organization of the canal ring, however. Cost savings were maximized in those parts of the public space that did not directly serve the living comfort of the canal ring's future residents. As a result, there were wide canals and spacious quays, but the two squares that had been planned were merged to form the rather ungenerously sized Westermarkt, which lay in a virtually inaccessible location.

In fact, Westermarkt was little more than the space in the bend of the canal ring that was left after the rectangular building lots on the canals had been marked out (Figure 3.4). Everything about the way the Third Expansion was carried out makes it clear that it was not based on a detailed urban plan. New streets were still being added even as the lots were being assigned. This happened in the canal ring, for example, where Huidenstraat and Runstraat were fitted in at the last minute, and also in the area between Haarlemmerdijk and Brouwersgracht, where Vinkenstraat was added to bisect what had originally been two very deep lots. Even Noordermarkt and the Noorderkerk did not originally form part of the expansion plan.[11]

10 The decision to expand the city to the west will not have been entirely independent of the fact that members of the city government owned land there (Dudok van Heel, 'Regent Families and Urban Development', p. 129).

11 Abrahamse, *Metropolis in the Making*, chapter 2 ('The Noordermarkt and the Noorderkerk').

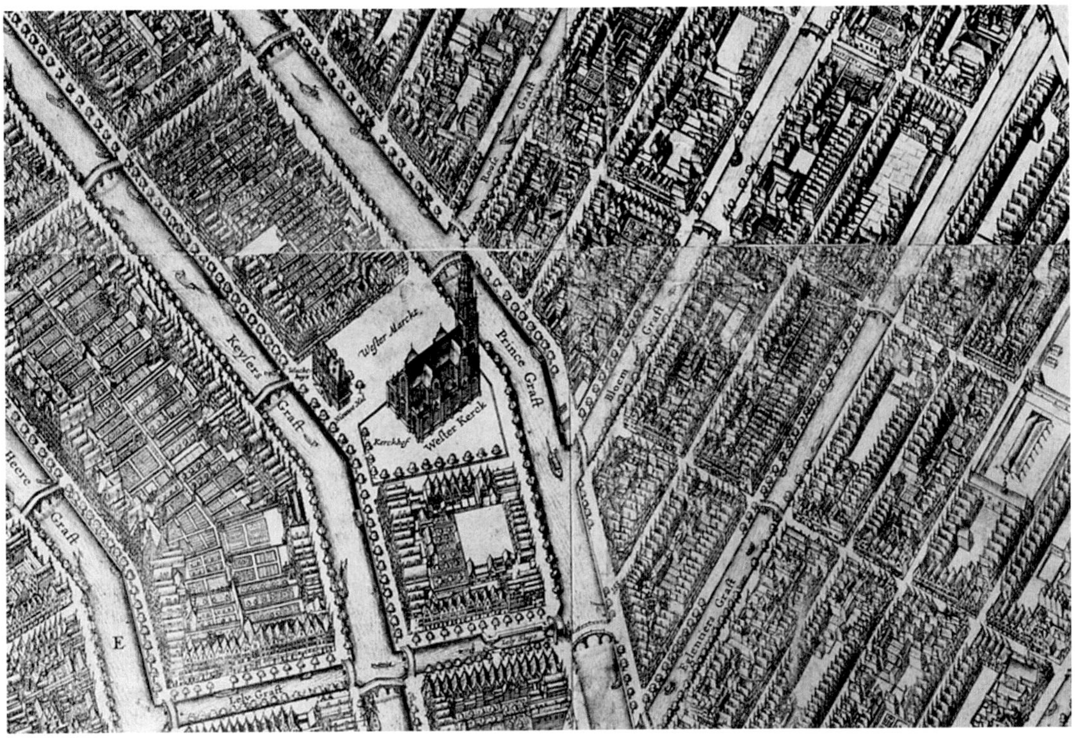

Figure 3.4: The location of the Westermarkt (north at the bottom).

What remains clearly recognizable, despite the financial and administrative problems and the ad hoc nature of many of the decisions, is the city government's vision on the organization of society and urban space. Even in the medieval city, which had developed more or less organically, economic activities and social groups had not been dispersed at random over the urban space, but the Second Expansion of the 1590s had seen the first deliberate attempts to create a spatial division of economic functions and social groups. Some parts of this city expansion were intended for residential functions, others for large-scale industry and harbour-related activities. In the residential areas, there was also differentiation by social class and financial capacity. The streets that led from the new neighbourhoods to the three old city gates, for example, were intended for wealthy citizens. These streets (*breestraten* or 'wide streets') were spacious compared to the streets in the city centre, and artisans who caused noise, smells and fire hazards were kept away. Of these streets, St Antoniesbreestraat on the eastern side of the city was the most attractive for Amsterdam's wealthy citizens. After all, Reguliersbreestraat suffered from the proximity of the livestock market, and on the western side of the city, Haarlemmer(bree)straat competed with the nearby Singel. During his stay in Amsterdam, Fynes Moryson had already noted that along the new side of Singel, which no longer formed part of the defensive works, 'many faire houses were [...] built'.[12] Indeed, the new side of Singel became home to a number of very wealthy citizens of Amsterdam. It was on double lots there that the first

12 Jacobsen Jensen, 'Moryson's reis', p. 223.

large townhouses appeared, such as the house known as the 'Dolphin', built in 1593 and commissioned by the poet and philosopher Hendrick Laurensz Spiegel.[13]

Artisans and those from lower social classes found lodgings in side streets and backstreets. In the Lastage, not far from St Antoniesbreestraat, the narrow Jonkerstraat and Ridderstraat had the character of a working-class neighbourhood. Shortly after the middle of the seventeenth century, Van Domselaer wrote: 'in these two long streets there live such an incredible number of common shipping and artisanal folk, who make their living from the shipyards and shipping, sometimes four families to a house, in the *voorhuis*, *achterhuis*, cellars, front and back rooms'.[14]

With the Third Expansion, this spatial division of economic activities and social groups took place on a much larger scale. From the outset, Herengracht and Keizersgracht were intended for the very affluent residents of Amsterdam. This is shown by the generous size of the building lots, the broad quays and stately canals, but also from the rules that prevented rental housing for lower income groups being built in inner courtyards, or the latter being used for large-scale industrial activities. Once again, craftsmen who disturbed the peace of the residential surroundings were barred by the elite, and the residents' peace was further secured by restricting the amount of traffic on the canals. This was simply achieved by avoiding creating a direct link between Herengracht, Keizersgracht and the external waters of the IJ, and by protecting them from markets and the storage of commodities such as wood. There were locks to the IJ on the outer canals of the canal ring—Singel and Prinsengracht—and these canals functioned as a busy shipping route and marketplace. As a result, Singel inevitably trailed behind Herengracht and Keizersgracht as a luxury living location.

Large-scale industry such as shipbuilding was assigned to special islands (the Western Islands), the space-hungry storage of wood and tar was located mainly on the banks of the IJ, and warehouses were found in large numbers on Brouwersgracht. The middle and lower classes and working folk were assigned to the 'Nieuwe Werk', the area that would later become known as the Jordaan. The lots were much smaller there, the population density much greater, and the cost of living lower. Van Domselaer described the streets in the Nieuwe Werk as 'teeming and bustling with all kinds of artisan folk'.[15] The Jordaan was also the neighbourhood where crafts that were associated with nuisance and fire risk were concentrated. Thus, although the Third Expansion may have been undertaken without a detailed urban plan, it did not lack structure altogether. It clearly reflected the ideas about the organization of the city and society that predominated among the upper classes at the time.

In the first decades of the century, the area created by the expansion was built up, and between about 1625 and 1660, the existing city was built up even further. Nevertheless, the Third Expansion was by no means a definitive solution to the problems facing Amsterdam's government. The population continued to

13 Dudok van Heel, 'Regent Families and Urban Development', pp. 126–128.

14 'In deze twee lange straten, woont tegenwoordig zo grouzamen menichte van gemeen varendt, en handtwerksvolk, 't welk met de scheepstimmerwerven en vaarten, hun kost wint, ja wel vier huys gezinnen zomtijdts in een huys, als in de voorhuyzen, achterhuyzen, kelders, voor, en achterkamers, dat het ongelooffelijk is' (Van Domselaer, *Beschryvinge van Amsterdam,* Book III, p. 239).

15 '[K]rielen en grimmelen van alderley handtwerks volk' (Ibidem, Book III, p. 251).

Figure 3.5: Amsterdam after the Fourth Expansion (north at the bottom).

grow, despite a number of devastating plague epidemics; the expanding industrial, trade and shipping sectors needed more space; and the suburbs continued to grow. Moreover, defending the city remained a problem. On the eastern side, the old wall (dating from the Second Expansion) was severely weakened, and on the western side the connection between the old and new defensive walls was anything but ideal. With the conflict between Amsterdam and Stadholder Willem II and the stadholder's (failed) attack on Amsterdam in 1650, the need to address the city's defences became acute. In the wake of the problems with Willem II, a new fortification plan was agreed, but this was superseded by the outbreak of the First Anglo-Dutch War (1652–1654) and the consequent need to expand the shipbuilding capacity on the eastern side of the city. Some years later, around 1660, the thread was picked up again, and in 1662 the design for the Fourth Expansion was approved by the city fathers.[16]

Unlike the Third Expansion, now there was a masterplan, according to Abrahamse; one 'that was wholly considered and designed in

16 For the Fourth Expansion see Abrahamse, *Metropolis in the Making*, chapter 3; Bakker, 'De zichtbare stad', pp. 37–47, and Jansen, 'De stadsuitbreiding van 1663'.

a functional respect and in relation to traffic, urban planning and water management'.[17] It can be presumed that this was largely a consequence of advances in understanding and the hard lessons learned from the past. Moreover, due to population growth and the accompanying increase in income from excise duties and other taxes, after the mid-seventeenth century the city had larger budgets at its disposal than half a century previously. The new expansion could be approached in a radically different way because the decision was made to expropriate all of the land that lay within the new fortifications and strongly limit the right of preference (the right to buy back land). This meant that the designers could start with a clean sheet, unhindered by private ownership and the existing patterns of paths and ditches in the expansion area. For this reason, the Fourth Expansion did not result in the creation of problematic areas in urban planning terms, such as the Jordaan. Moreover, this time the periphery of the city formed an integral part of the design.

The fact that the Fourth Expansion formed what was almost an organic whole with the previous city expansion, despite the very different approach, was thanks to the incorporation of successful elements from the earlier expansion, especially in the canal ring. Herengracht and Keizersgracht, in particular, were extremely popular among the wealthy elite, meaning that the sale of lots on these canals promised to be a lucrative affair for the city. The broader scope of the design was expressed, among other things, by further boosting the quality of life on these canals by building backstreets (Kerkstraat, Reguliersdwarsstraat, Amstelstraat, Nieuwe Amstelstraat) with space for coach houses and stables and that drew traffic away from the residential canals. The system of radial streets was also perfected: the city paid attention to these streets' transport capacity in order to ensure that traffic flows between the city centre and city gates were as efficient as possible. Leidsestraat, for example, was widened sufficiently to allow three wagons to pass in the traffic lane, and the bridges were made as wide as the street to prevent congestion.[18]

The spatial segregation of economic functions and social groups also continued under the Fourth Expansion. The wealthy lived in the canal ring and by the Amstel, and the middle and lower social classes lived mainly in the area between Prinsengracht and the city ramparts, which was also home to small-scale industries. The lower social classes also lived on the Eastern Islands which, like the Western Islands under the Third Expansion, were intended to provide space for shipbuilding and harbour-related activities.[19] This area was also home to the Admiralty and the Dutch East India Company (VOC). Indeed, the expansion of the harbour was an important driving force behind the city's development, and with the Fourth Expansion, Amsterdam's harbour front was widened from two to over four kilometres.[20]

The Fourth Expansion created lots of space to absorb the population—too much space, as it soon turned out. Although Amsterdam's population continued to grow, for many years the rate of growth was not as spectacular as it had

17 Abrahamse, *Metropolis in the Making*, Conclusion ('The fourth extension: the perfect plan?').

18 Ibidem, 264.

19 A more elaborate discussion of social residential differentiation in preindustrial Amsterdam in Lesger, Van Leeuwen and Vissers, 'Residentiële segregatie'.

20 Quite a contrast with the 600 metres in the period up to 1578. As a result of the Fourth Expansion, the port area became three times larger than it had been during the Third Expansion (Bakker, 'De zichtbare stad', pp. 30 and 43).

been in the first half of the century. The lots on the eastern side of the Amstel thus attracted little interest from buyers. When demand failed to pick up, the city government made the land available to social care institutions, which constructed what were sometimes very extensive buildings there. One such building was the Diaconie Oude Vrouwen Huys ('parish home for elderly ladies', now Hermitage Amsterdam), which was built by the Amstel in 1681 and provided accommodation for around 400 elderly women in need. Even further to the northeast lay a large area that remained undeveloped. After 1680, it was divided up into gardens and henceforth known as the Plantage. Even when Amsterdam's population slowly grew to a maximum of around 230,000 to 240,000 residents, there was no construction allowed in the Plantage. Elsewhere in the city, particularly in poor neighbourhoods such as the Jordaan and the Jewish Quarter, the population density increased and living conditions deteriorated accordingly.

In the old city centre, too, the pressure on available space grew constantly—particularly on the cramped Dam, where every inch of space was in use. The Dam had traditionally been home to economic activities, the city government and spiritual government. In an age of rapid economic expansion and the rising prosperity and power of the city, it is hardly surprising that merchants and administrators desired more space and a more prestigious symbol of their growing importance.

In the first decade of the seventeenth century, when it became clear that Holland would not return to Spanish rule and that the trade boom was not merely a flash in the pan, there was a growing need for a separate building to house the city's commercial activities. Until that time, merchants had held an exchange on the Nieuwe Brug over the Damrak, and in bad weather under the canopies of nearby houses and in church buildings. In 1607, the decision was made to build a commodities exchange. In a sign of the optimism of the age, it was reported that 'no money should be spared in decorating the work'.[21] As a city-centre location was considered desirable, and given that there was little space on the Dam and high land prices made demolition of existing buildings expensive, the decision was made to build over the Amstel river at Rokin. In 1608, the first pile was driven in the construction of a large and fitting merchants' exchange that, like existing exchanges in Antwerp, London and elsewhere, consisted of an open square surrounded by arcades.[22]

This form of double land-use—a square above the waters of the Amstel—was not possible when, several decades later, the city government devised a plan to build a new, larger and more prestigious city hall. The commission ultimately went to the painter and architect Jacob van Campen, and the huge construction was built between 1648 and 1662. To make way for the building, not only the old city hall but also a whole series of houses on the Dam and in adjacent streets were demolished.[23] The Nieuwezijds cemetery next to the Nieuwe Kerk and the Ellendige ('wretched') cemetery, the final resting place of convicted criminals and suicides, were also cleared. The Dam thereby grew to the size that it would maintain until the nineteenth century, and the new city hall towered above the relatively small buildings on the edge of the square.

21 '[T]ot vercieringe van 't werk niet op een cleyntge sou worden gesien' (Breen, 'Topografische geschiedenis van den Dam', p. 145).

22 Engel and Gramsbergen, 'Het eerste beursgebouw'.

23 Breen, 'Topografische geschiedenis van den Dam', pp. 159–163.

For a short time, it seemed the city hall might gain a competitor in the form of a tall tower to be built next to the Nieuwe Kerk.[24] The design was commissioned in 1648, and not much later construction began on the sturdy foundations on which the tower would rest. The construction activities subsequently ceased, however, and the tower was never built. In all likelihood, the political struggle between government factions about the degree of influence wielded by the Reformed Church in the city administration proved fatal for the tower. Nevertheless, in the age of the great city expansions, the Dam changed radically in both size and aspect. Now that it was also home to the merchants' exchange, this square was even more emphatically the heart of the city.

Patterns of accessibility in the enlarged city

In the first chapter, we learned about the importance of the structure of the urban grid for the accessibility of locations in the city and thereby for the structure of the retail landscape. Now that we have a general impression of how the city expansions took place, we can use Space Syntax Analysis to chart with great accuracy the effect of these urban expansions on the accessibility of the streets, canals and squares. Figure 3.6 shows the situation in the mid-seventeenth century.[25] The First, Second and Third Expansions had already taken place and the city had grown much larger, particularly to the west. But, as was the case at the end of the sixteenth century, the Dam and its surroundings were still the most accessible part of the city and thus the ideal place for businesses that served citizens from all over Amsterdam. Although we have identified the high 'to-movement potential' of the Dam and its surroundings purely based on the structure of the urban grid, it will be clear that the presence of buildings such as the city hall, the Exchange, the Nieuwe Kerk and the weighing house was not coincidental and thus further reinforced the Dam's central function.

In comparison with the situation around 1585, the most striking change was the transformation of the former St Antoniespoort into a weighing-house on a square—Nieuwmarkt—that, like the Dam, enjoyed a high degree of accessibility. A new node thus emerged on the eastern side of the medieval city centre. In this square, with its excellent traffic links, the city government established several important markets. The surroundings of the Reguliersspoort on the southern side of the city also enjoyed a relatively high level of accessibility. This area had been brought within the city during the First Expansion of 1578–1587, and around the mid-seventeenth century it became the site of the cattle market that had previously been held at the southern end of Kalverstraat and Reguliersbreestraat.[26] Accessible locations such as these were notably lacking on the western side of the city, where most people lived. The Jordaan, in particular, was a densely populated neighbourhood at this time.

Figure 3.6 gives a good impression of the haphazard nature of the Third Expansion. Westermarkt, the location of the new neighbourhoods' main church as well as a market and weighing house, lay in a difficult-to-access spot in the urban grid. This is hardly surprising

24 Bakker, 'De zichtbare stad', pp. 48–49, and Van Tussenbroek, *De toren van de Gouden Eeuw*.

25 Figure 3.6 is based on a map of the entire infrastructure of roads, canals and squares, and it shows *Normalized Mean Depth* (*to-movement potential*) at a radius of 200 metres.

26 Van Domselaer, *Beschryvinge van Amsterdam*, Book IV, p. 237.

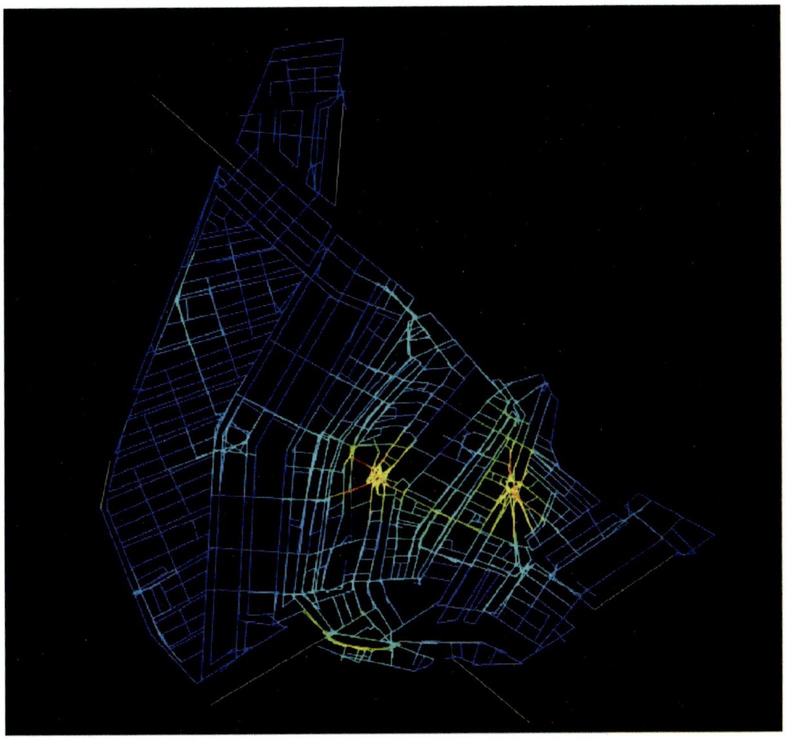

Figure 3.6: Amsterdam ca. 1650: to-movement potential.

because, as we already saw above, the church and market were placed in a bend in the canal ring where an efficient lot pattern could not be realized. Optimization of the land yield in the canal ring, and not accessibility to the population, had weighed most heavily in the location of Westermarkt. But the specific structure of the canal ring—a number of parallel canals intersected by narrow radials that provided a link with the inner city—also reinforced this lack of an easily accessible node for traffic flows, such as that at Nieuwmarkt. And this, as we have seen, was precisely the intention. At the end of the sixteenth century, Amsterdam's economic and political elite sought an alternative to the crowded, noisy and relatively narrow Warmoesstraat. During the First and Second Expansions, this alternative was found on the 'new' side of Singel and Kloveniersburgwal, two canals that had previously encircled the city and that were brought within the city's walls at that time. During the Third Expansion, this concept was implemented on a broader scale. A residential environment was created in the canal ring, consisting of wide, low-traffic canals lined with trees. Crowded market squares and populous approach routes were at odds with this vision.

Like Westermarkt, Noordermarkt was also added to the expansion plan at a late stage—something that is also clearly visible from the map. The market square, home to the church of the Protestant congregation in the northern part of the Jordaan, was very difficult to reach from the city centre and the canal ring, and even from the neighbouring Jordaan. As far as connections and accessibility were concerned, the street network in the Jordaan was nothing short of a disaster. The desire to replicate the existing pattern of paths and ditches as far as possible not only meant that the neighbourhood

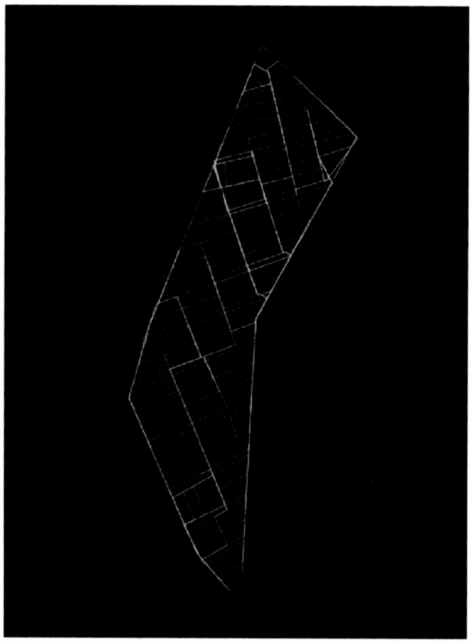

Figure 3.7: The Jordaan ca. 1650: through-movement potential.

was difficult to access from the rest of the city but also that crossing the Jordaan itself was a problem (see Figure 3.7).[27] Sandwiched between Prinsengracht and the city ramparts, the longitudinal streets had virtually no function other than providing access to the adjacent houses. If one wanted to cross the Jordaan, there remained the transverse streets, which had a higher degree of through-movement potential than the longitudinal ones. No transverse street provided a direct north-south link, however, meaning that the traffic had to zigzag its way through the Jordaan from north to south, or vice versa. The only alternative routes were Lijnbaansgracht, along the city ramparts, and Prinsengracht, on the eastern edge of the neighbourhood.

Considering the accessibility patterns generated by the structure of the urban grid, it does not seem an exaggeration to suggest that the extensive city expansions that were undertaken until the mid-seventeenth century did not bring about a genuine change in the retail landscape of Amsterdam. The road network in the canal ring was structured in such a way that it was not possible for a well-connected shopping district to develop there. The only market square in this district lay in a leftover corner, and it also lacked radial streets that linked it directly with the city centre and the rest of the city. The poor accessibility of the Jordaan did not result from the creation of a peaceful and low-traffic residential environment, of course, but the lack of political will and financial resources to overhaul the area. There were insufficient connections between the existing pattern of paths and ditches and the canal ring and city centre, and the traffic connections within the Jordaan were also problematic. Only in the east of the city did a square emerge—Nieuwmarkt—that had good traffic connections from a geographical perspective and that was a potentially attractive location for retail businesses.

A glance at Figure 3.8 reveals that the Fourth Expansion in the second half of the seventeenth century did not really change the accessibility patterns in the city either.[28] Without doubt, the Dam and the surrounding area remained the most accessible part of Amsterdam's street network. Even in the absence of important public buildings, this square would thus have remained the heart of the city for the local population. But it was also easy for people from outside Amsterdam to access the Dam and surroundings, because the IJ and Damrak functioned as an entryway for the large numbers of visitors who arrived in Amsterdam from across the water. To the east of the Dam, Nieuwmarkt continued to come a close second in

27 The figure shows *Choice* (*through-movement potential*) at a radius of 200 metres.

28 The figure shows *Normalized Mean Depth* (*to-movement potential*) at a radius of 400 metres.

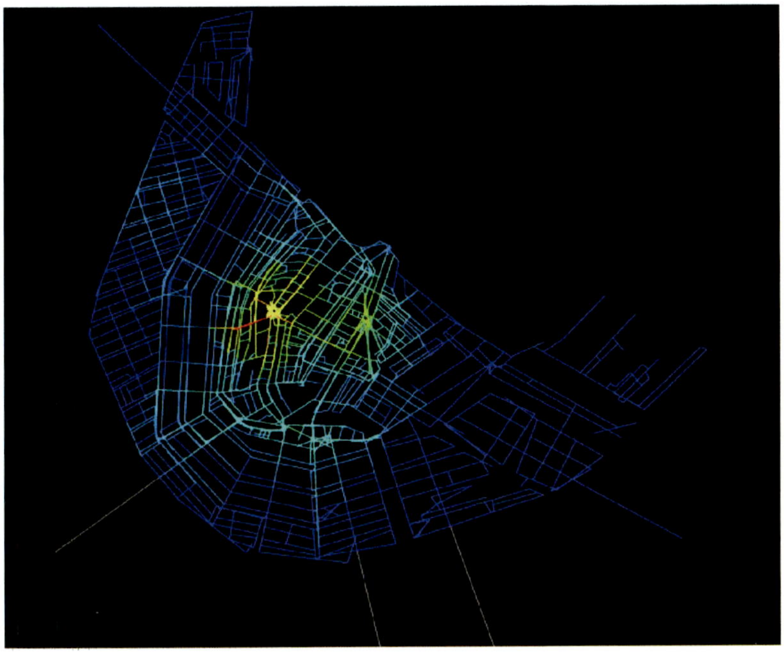

Figure 3.8: Amsterdam ca. 1700: to-movement potential.

terms of accessibility. Nor did much change to the west of the Dam; Westermarkt and Noordermarkt were opened up only a little, if at all, and the same applied to the Jordaan.

We have already observed that prior to the mid-seventeenth century, Reguliersbreestraat and its surroundings—then still the southern border of the city—enjoyed a relatively high degree of accessibility. With the Fourth Expansion, a wide zone consisting of the canal ring and the Noordse Bos was created to the south of Reguliersbreestraat, but the area continued to enjoy easy access. At the end of Reguliersbreestraat, where the livestock market had previously been held, a new market square was built: Reguliersmarkt. The old Regulierspoort, which had lost its function when the city was expanded, was transformed into one of the city's weighing houses. From 1669, the square hosted a market every Monday selling butter, cheese and other dairy products; products that had previously been sold on the Dam.[29] It was not long before Reguliersmarkt was dubbed *Botermarkt* (butter market) by the people of Amsterdam, a name that was changed by decree to 'Rembrandtplein' on 17 May 1876.[30]

Finally, we can see from Figure 3.8 that, with the exception of the radial streets, no well-connected squares and streets were created during the Fourth Expansion. As far as the canal ring was concerned, of course, this was the intention. The construction of the above-mentioned backstreets minimized the traffic there and guaranteed the peace that the neighbourhood's distinguished and wealthy residents evidently valued. The canal ring was expanded

29 Wagenaar, *Amsterdam, in zyne opkomst*, Part IV, p. 417.

30 De Ridder, *Verdwenen straatnamen*, p. 85.

into the area to the east of the Amstel, but the lots proved hard to sell, and mostly social care institutions were located there. Private buildings were mainly to be found on Weesperstraat, a radial street that linked the surroundings of today's Mr. Visserplein with the Weesperpoort and the road to the Gooi area. On the city's northern periphery lay the Eastern Islands, a working area that, like the Western Islands in the Third Expansion, was isolated from the rest of the city and could only be reached by crossing two bridges.

All in all, it will have become clear that the huge expansion of the city in the seventeenth century did not undermine the medieval city centre's position as the most accessible part of the street network. That being said, it is now time to consider the extent to which the accessibility patterns construed on the basis of the street network correspond with the actual distribution of shops in Amsterdam.

Shops in the city centre and the new neighbourhoods

In his eulogy on the 'celebrated commercial city of Amsterdam' of 1597, Cornelius Plancius sang the praises of the city, reporting, among other things, an increase in the number of shops, which he believed were now to be found on every street in the city.[31] Even if Plancius' notion of a shop was broader than ours, there was clearly some exaggeration at work here. We already established in Chapter 1 that there were not, in fact, shops on every street. Shops were mainly to be found on and around the Dam and a number of streets on both sides of the Amstel, with particularly high shop densities in Warmoesstraat and Nieuwendijk. The question that lies at the heart of this section is the extent to which this sixteenth-century retail landscape changed at the time of the great city expansions. Answering this question is by no means simple because we lack sources for the whole of the seventeenth century that are comparable to the register for the *Capitale Impositie*. Nevertheless, we shall attempt to build a more impressionistic picture of the changes that occurred in this century of economic dynamism and urban expansionism.

When one searches for information about shops in seventeenth-century Amsterdam, one is not left completely empty-handed. Information turns up in the most unexpected places, such as in a report on the reception of the French queen-mother Maria de' Medici in Amsterdam in 1638, written in Latin by Caspar Barlaeus and translated into Dutch by Vondel. In this, we read that Maria de' Medici rode in a carriage through the 'populous and commercial' Warmoesstraat. Barlaeus observed of this street that the houses were very expensive, the residences small, and that it was home to goldsmiths, jewellers, coppersmiths, *maeldeniers* (metalsmiths), *Neurenbergiers* (sellers of items that traditionally came from the Nuremberg region), scales makers, *zwaardvegers* (harness and metalsmiths), tinsmiths, linen merchants, sellers of silk and woollen cloth, silk and *passementerie kramers*, wine merchants, *pluimeciers* (feather sellers), hat sellers, ribbon sellers, grocers, dry-salters, pharmacists, 'and every kind of artisan and shopkeeper imaginable'.[32] A few days later, when the ceremonial part of the visit was over, Maria de' Medici travelled through the streets and alleyways in a simpler carriage and 'went into various shops to enquire about the price of wares and porcelain'—behaviour, in Barlaeus' view, befitting 'a trader's wife, not [...] a queen'.

31 Plancius, 'Beschrivinge der loflijcke ende wijtvermaerde coopstede Aemstelredamme', p. 10.

32 Barlaeus, *Medicea Hospes*. I owe thanks to Paul Knevel, who provided me with this reference.

We should not be surprised that Warmoesstraat is mentioned at length in the text, as it had traditionally been the main thoroughfare of Amsterdam. Interestingly, the street's character seems to have changed over time. In the sixteenth century, Warmoesstraat was home to the great merchants and administrative elite of Amsterdam. In Bredero's farce *Klucht van de koe,* published in 1612, Giertje the innkeeper's wife speaks the following lines: 'she has very rich friends, [...] they are among the best in the city, they live in Warmoesstraat'.[33] By 1638, the situation had evidently changed. Barlaeus described the street as commercial and packed with artisans' businesses and shops. Had there really been a change, or was Barlaeus only emphasizing the things that most struck contemporaries? After all, shops tend to catch the eye more than merchants' offices. Thus, we cannot rely on chance finds such as these alone to gain a more detailed view of the retail landscape of Amsterdam. For this reason, I looked for descriptions of streets in a series of city descriptions or urban topographies that were published in the seventeenth century.[34] As the authors and publishers plagiarized each other's work shamelessly and on a large scale, we must take their words with a grain of salt. But a book by Melchior Fokkens, published in 1662 and entitled *Beschrijvinge der wijdt-vermaarde Koop-stadt Amstelredam* (*Description of the far-famed commercial city of Amsterdam*), proved particularly useful. This is mainly because Fokkens provided detailed descriptions of the economic activities in a number of streets, and he did not base these—as far as I can ascertain—on older writings. His observations therefore relate to the years around 1660, when the Third Expansion was completed and the Fourth Expansion was in the pipeline.[35] Another useful volume is the book by the Amsterdam merchant Tobias van Domselaer, published a few years later (1665), which built on Fokkens' work with many of Van Domselaer's own observations.[36] Combining the information from Fokkens and Van Domselaer gives us a rough impression of what, in the first half of the 1660s, were important shopping streets—streets that, according to the authors, were 'commercial' or home to 'respectable shopkeepers'.

Of the city's central square, the Dam, Van Domselaer remarks that the square and its immediate surroundings—that is to say, by the weighing house, the fish market, the Exchange and Beursstraat—were full of 'open shops selling all kinds of wares'.[37] The Exchange played a special role in this respect, for on the upper floor of the building, which could be reached via a broad flight of stone steps, there was a gallery with a large number of *kassen* (booths) that were open all year round. There were no fewer than 123 such booths, which should

33 'Se het hielle rijcke Vrienden, [...] Ja vande beste vande stadt, kijnts, sy wonen inde Warmoesstraet' (Bredero, *Kluchten*).

34 For these city descriptions, see Van der Zande, 'Amsterdamse stadsgeschiedschrijving'; Haitsma Mulier, 'The image of Amsterdam'; Van Melle, 'Waar vindt men uw's gelijk', and Haitsma Mulier, 'De zeventiende-eeuwse stadsbeschrijvingen'.

35 Fokkens mentions the construction of the shipping exchange 'now in the year 1661' (Fokkens, *Beschrijvinge der wijdt-vermaarde koop-stadt Amstelredam*, p. 59).

36 Van Domselaer, *Beschryvinge van Amsterdam*.

37 '[O]pen winkels, van alderley slach van waren'. Fokkens and Van Domselaer, but also Plancius at the end of the sixteenth century, all use the term 'open shop'. This does not mean a booth or stall but a shop that was located in the front part of the house (*voorhuis*). This is in contrast to a shop that was not visible from the street, as was the case for some wholesalers who also sold *en détail*. See Winschooten, *Seeman*, and Marin, *Nederduitsch en Fransch woordenboek*.

be visualized as lockable wooden structures used to sell all kinds of *kramers'* wares, such as knives, gold, silver and silk ribbons, hats, and skillfully turned and cut ivory work. Outside, at street level, the sides of the Exchange were flanked with brick arches that could also be rented as shops, and finally, on the short outer wall, there were shops on both sides of the entrance.[38] Shops thus enjoyed a prominent presence on and around the Dam.

We shall now leave the Dam and follow Fokkens. His detailed description of the 'appearance of the city' is reminiscent of a tour and begins, not coincidentally, at Amsterdam's old inner harbour, the Damrak, and the bridges crossing the water. Having remarked that the Nieuwe Brug teems with sailors (the 'Neptunis hordes'), he focuses his attention on the quay along the Damrak and describes in detail the series of 'large retailers' established door-to-door selling semi-tropical fruits, oil, spices, sugar, almonds and other nuts, pottery, pigments and ironware. In the cellars under the houses, wine and beer were served, and food ('all manner of cooked fare') was sold to thousands of customers every day. The houses had rents of 800 to 1,500 guilders per year, and the cellars cost 400 to 500 guilders to rent, even though they sometimes flooded to the rafters at high water.[39] This was clearly a prime location.

It is evident from the goods that were sold here (pigments, ironware) as well as Fokkens' own description that many wholesalers were established on Damrak. Just as in the sixteenth century, wholesale and retail trade were still intertwined. The term *winkelier* or 'shopkeeper' thus referred not only to retailers but also to shopkeeping wholesalers and wholesaling retailers. The fact that actual sales also took place is evident, among other things, from the remark that Damrak 'constantly sways with thousands of people, for it is always crowded here in the large shops selling all kinds of wares'.[40]

After this, Fokkens describes the whole waterfront, from the Haarlemmerpoort in the west to Kattenburg in the east. He mentions shops only on the Texelse quay, today's Prins Hendrikkade between Damrak and Martelaarsgracht. Some of these sold spices and semi-tropical fruits but, just as on Zeedijk, many specialized in selling to sailors and shipowners. On the Texelse quay, too, the goods on sale included tobacco, liquor, clothing, hats, gunpowder, artillery and many other things. The rents were higher than on Damrak: 1,000 to 2,000 guilders a year, and more if one included the cellars.

After the harbour front, Fokkens discusses the 'principal canals' and 'important streets'. He first discusses the canals in detail, noting that Herengracht and Keizersgracht were home to the wealthiest and most distinguished merchants, and that there were no houses there belonging to shopkeepers with 'open shops'. 'Very rich merchants' lived on Singel, too, but there were also some open-air shops there, close to Spui.[41] Fokkens then addresses the main thoroughfares: Warmoesstraat, Nieuwendijk, Kalverstraat and Nes. From the urban topographies, it is quite evident that Warmoesstraat was the city's main street. Fokkens observes that the wealthiest and most distinguished citizens lived there before the Third Expansion. Van Domselaer is more expansive,

38 Dapper, *Historische beschryving der stadt Amsterdam*, p. 453, and Breen, 'Topografische geschiedenis van den Dam', p. 148.

39 Fokkens, *Beschrijvinge der wijdt-vermaarde koop-stadt Amstelredam*, pp. 60–62.

40 '[Z]wiert het steedts vol menschen by duyzenden, want hier is 't altijdt even drok in de groote winkels met alderhande waren' (Ibidem, p. 60).

41 Fokkens, *Beschrijvinge der wijdt-vermaarde koop-stadt Amstelredam*, p. 76.

adding that the urban elite left Warmoesstraat in order to set up residences on the new canals, so that almost exclusively shopkeepers still lived on Warmoesstraat. 'This street,' writes Van Domselaer, 'is the most expensive in the whole city' because it contains 'so many large, almost priceless shops selling all kinds of silk and silk cloth.'[42] This is evidence of a long-term trend because, as we saw in the first chapter, silk was already one of the main goods sold in shops on Warmoesstraat in 1585. Fokkens likewise mentions the silk shops, but he also reports shops selling wares from the Nuremberg region, buttons, linen and lace, and *Franse winkels* ('French shops') selling fashion accessories, 'everything one could imagine for the gentlemen and ladies'.[43] In the first half of the seventeenth century, this was undoubtedly the most important shopping street in Amsterdam; the street where expensive fabrics, luxury items and fashionable accessories in French taste could be purchased. Thanks to this range of shopping goods, it was also typically a street where people came to window-gaze, not merely to buy.

In combination with Haarlemmerstraat, Nieuwendijk was the longest street in the city, and both authors mention the many large shops. Fokkens offers the most detail. He begins his description with the observation that this street, like Warmoesstraat, was home to many shopkeepers selling fabric (worsted and silk cloth); this had also been the case in 1585. In addition, he mentions 'vast shops' selling stockfish, butter and cheese, and states explicitly that the stockfish sellers were wholesalers—something that would also have been true of the vendors of butter and cheese. Retailers of butter and cheese, known as chandlers or *vettewariërs*, would have been less likely to ply their trade in the 'vast shops' of Nieuwendijk but would have had small shops spread over the city. The rents would also have been prohibitively high. According to Fokkens, these were similar to those on Warmoesstraat: 1,000 to 1,600 guilders a year.[44]

If we rely on the urban topographies by Fokkens and Van Domselaer, shortly after 1660 it was not yet evident that Kalverstraat would become the city's primary shopping street in the future. The rents were considerable, says Fokkens, without going into detail; there were shops selling prints, dry-salts, paint and meat, as well as a few furriers 'offering all kinds of priceless sable muff'.[45] Once again, we find a combination of retailers and typical wholesalers (dry-salts, paint) but also butchers, who undoubtedly established their businesses there in proximity to the oxen and pig market, and some artisans in the luxury segment of the market. The presence alone of 'many meat-sellers' clearly shows that in those days Kalverstraat was not yet in the same league as Warmoesstraat as a shopping street. It was busy, however, in this approach street to the city centre and the Dam. Around 1650, the poet Six van Chandelier referred to 'the crowded Kalverstraat'.[46] Nes, by contrast, was home to a range of high-quality merchandise: silversmiths' shops, hat sellers, 'expensive linen shops' and 'large shops selling French wares [...] full of gold and silver lace, [and] expensive hats [*kastooren*]'. There were also two meat markets and a poultry

42 '[Z]oo veele, by na, onwaerdeerlijke, en sware winkels van alderley zijde, en zijde stoffen gehouden worden' (Van Domselaer, *Beschryvinge van Amsterdam*, Book III, p. 257).

43 '[D]aar al wat men kan bedenkken voor heeren en juffers te koop is' (Fokkens, *Beschrijvinge der wijdt-vermaarde koop-stadt Amstelredam*, p. 92).

44 Ibidem, p. 93.

45 '[M]et allerhande overkostelijkke sabele moffen' (Ibidem, p. 94).

46 '[D]e vollikryke Kalverstraat' (Six van Chandelier, ''s Amsterdammers Winter', line 329).

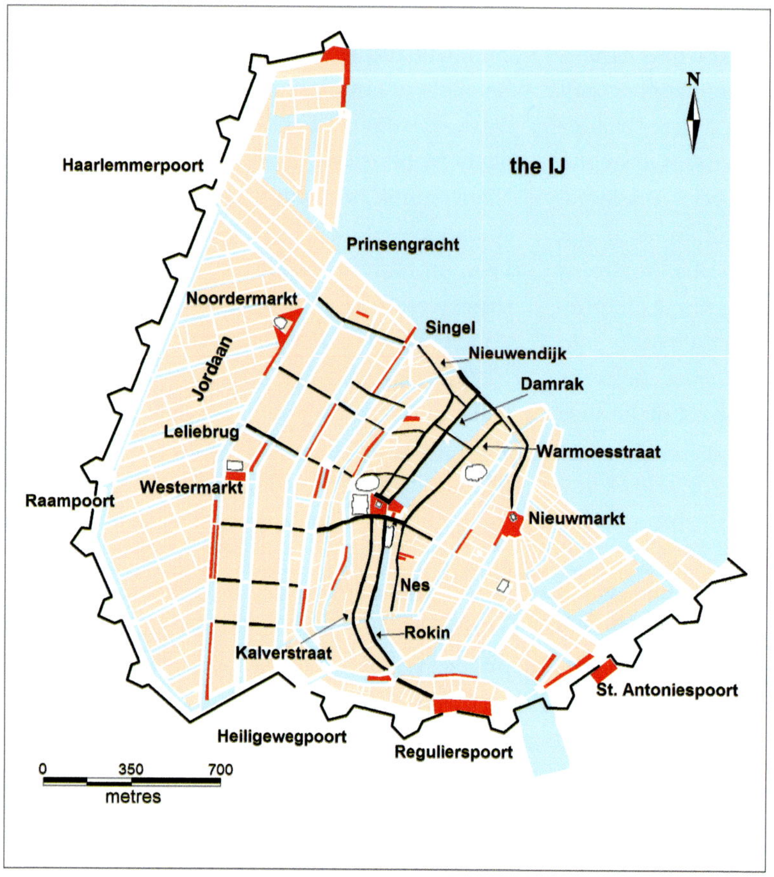

Figure 3.9: Shopping streets (black) and markets (red) around 1660.

market, and, following in their wake, a whole series of food vendors.[47]

The authors of the urban topographies considered Halsteeg, a key connecting street between the Dam and the east of the city, worth mentioning thanks to what was evidently a striking number of shops selling 'all kinds of shoes' and other 'costly wares'—in other words, just like elsewhere in the city centre, a typical specialization in shopping goods and clustering of shops selling similar ranges, allowing the consumer to compare and choose.[48] So close to the Dam and on a major traffic route, we would expect little else. Fokkens and Van Domselaer are less forthcoming about the radial streets to the west of the Dam, the streets and canals that connected the city centre to the western canal ring and the Jordaan. They do mention that many shops were located on these radials, however, and that there were all kinds of wares for sale.[49] An offhand comment by Fokkens reveals

47 '[G]roote France-kramers [...] vol van goude en silvere kanten, kastooren of kostelijke hoeden' (Fokkens, *Beschrijvinge der wijdt-vermaarde koop-stadt Amstelredam*, p. 94, and Van Domselaer, *Beschryvinge van Amsterdam*, Book III, p. 259).

48 Fokkens, *Beschrijvinge der wijdt-vermaarde koop-stadt Amstelredam*, p. 95.

49 Ibidem, p. 96, and Van Domselaer, *Beschryvinge van Amsterdam*, p. 259.

how busy these radials were. In 1656, he writes, the Leliebrug over Prinsengracht at the corner of Leliegracht collapsed, resulting in the deaths of eight to ten people, because 'it is always crowded there with passers-by'.[50] It is obvious that it would always have been very busy on this bridge in particular because it formed part of the route that residents took from beyond the city walls to the centre. They entered the city through the Raampoort and subsequently took Nieuwe Leliestraat, crossed the Leliebrug, and then took a route via Leliegracht, Oude Leliestraat, Torensteeg and Molsteeg to reach the Nieuwe Kerk and the Dam. Many residents of the Jordaan would also have taken this route to the city centre.

In Figure 3.9, the shopping streets mentioned by Fokkens and Van Domselaer are marked on the map.[51] If we compare these shopping streets with the accessibility patterns in Amsterdam's urban grid found using Space Syntax Analysis (Figure 3.6), it is clear that the accessibility of the streets did indeed determine their attractiveness as shop locations to a significant extent. The streets that figured prominently in Fokkens' and Van Domselaer's accounts unmistakeably lay in the heart of the city, where accessibility was greatest, and along the radials that provided access to the Dam and the main shopping thoroughfares. What remains unclear is the situation regarding the provision of shops in the rest of the city. The analysis of the street network suggests concentrations of shops around Nieuwmarkt and at the Regulierspoort, but one would also expect to find shops elsewhere, too.

In order to build up a more comprehensive picture of the retail location patterns, I resorted to the deeds drawn up in Amsterdam upon the issuing of banns for an intended marriage (*akten van ondertrouw*). In the seventeenth century, these deeds contained information about both the profession and the address of the prospective groom.[52] For the years following the publication of the urban topographies by Fokkens and Van Domselaer, there is hardly any other source material available for reconstructing location patterns. For the periods 1601 to 1660 and 1661 to 1700, I took the addresses of tobacco sellers given in banns deeds as representative of suppliers of daily necessities, and of hat sellers, sellers of Nuremberg wares and silk vendors as representative of consumer durables. In order to strengthen the empirical foundations of the distribution pattern of shops selling daily necessities, for the periods 1601 to 1635 and 1661 to 1690, I also took a sample from the more than 2,000 bann deeds of bakers in Amsterdam. The total sample consists of no fewer than 900 deeds, but in a few cases we lack information about the address, the street name is unreadable, or they cannot be placed. At the time the banns were issued, several dozen men were not yet living in the city, which means that we do not have any address details for them.

How realistic is the picture of Amsterdam's retail landscape that can be reconstructed based on the topographical descriptions by Fokkens and Van Domselaer and represented in Figure 3.9? For the periods 1601 to 1660 and 1661 to 1700, we find that 49 and 36 per cent, respectively, of the addresses listed in the banns deeds lay on streets that were characterized by Fokkens and Van Domselaer as

50 '[W]ant 't isser altijdt vol van de voorby gaande lieden' (Fokkens, *Beschrijvinge der wijdt-vermaarde koop-stadt Amstelredam*, p. 90).

51 Ibidem, pp. 59–99, and Van Domselaer, *Beschryvinge van Amsterdam*, Book III, pp. 227, 257–259 and Book IV, 5th chapter (pp. 225–254).

52 Van Nierop, 'De bruidegoms van Amsterdam', and Hart, 'Geschrift en getal'.

Table 3.1 Addresses of prospective bridegrooms working in selected sectors*, 1601–1700

	1601–1660		1661–1700	
Fokkens en Van Domselaer:				
main shopping streets*	78	33%	58	24%
radials	38	16%	29	12%
elsewhere in the city	123	51%	150	63%
total	239	100%	237	100%

Sources: SAA, *ondertrouwregisters* and card index on occupations.
* The selected sectors are tobacconists, hat sellers, silk sellers and sellers of Nuremberg wares. The main shopping streets are the Dam, Nieuwendijk, Kalverstraat, Damrak, Rokin, Warmoesstraat and Nes.
** The numbers in the table have been rounded off and therefore do not always add up to 100.

shopping streets (see Table 3.1). Some caution is advised when interpreting these figures. The retail trades mentioned above represent only part of the total range of shops and, moreover, the unmarried grooms were relatively young men and still at the beginning of their careers. Despite this, it would not be going too far to conclude that the streets mentioned in the urban topographies (see Figure 3.9) did indeed fulfil an important shopping function. For the entire period between 1601 and 1700, Warmoesstraat, Nieuwendijk, Nes, Kalverstraat and Dam were those named most frequently by shopkeepers, and Rokin also scored highly. In other words, Fokkens and Van Domselaer seem to have been correct in emphasizing the retail function of these main shopping streets.[53] The radials mentioned by Fokkens and Van Domselaer were also popular locations, as shown by Table 3.1. This makes it likely that both authors sketched a realistic picture of Amsterdam's retail landscape in the city centre and on the radials of the canal ring, but they also left much unmentioned. What were the locations of the many shops grouped under the header 'elsewhere in the city' in Table 3.1?

Table 3.2 gives an impression of how the selected trades were distributed over the different expansion areas. The category 'unclassifiable' mainly concerns locations on Amsterdam's main canals for which it was not possible to ascertain in which city expansion area the shop was located. In the first period, the number of betrothed tobacco sellers was still very small and can best be disregarded. Once this has been done, it becomes clear that particularly in the years between 1601 and 1660, many of the shops were located in the city centre—the area encircled by Singel, Binnen-Amstel, Kloveniersburgwal and Geldersekade. This was the site of the main shopping thoroughfares and the radials that connected the two sides of the Amstel and provided access to the new neighbourhoods. But shops were also located outside the city centre, in the First and Second Expansion zones. There was a relatively large number of shops on St Antoniesbreestraat, which was connected to Nieuwmarkt, and on Reguliersbreestraat, to the south of the city centre. These are also typically places where a high degree of accessibility was found using Space Syntax Analysis.

In the area created during the Third Expansion, the small number of shops on the main canals confirms what we observed above: that the peaceful and stately appearance of this residential environment for wealthy citizens of

53 Only Damrak is strikingly absent. The descriptions by Fokkens and Van Domselaer make it clear that relatively few textiles and related items were sold there. Damrak is therefore underrepresented in my research into the location of shops on the basis of bann deeds.

Table 3.2 Addresses of prospective bridegrooms working in selected sectors, 1601–1700

	1601–1660			1661–1700		
	bread*	tobacco	durable*	bread	tobacco	durable
city centre						
main shopping street	14%	3%	38%	6%	5%	40%
radial	42%	11%	22%	19%	20%	18%
elsewhere	13%	11%	14%	10%	11%	13%
First/Second Expansion						
radial	8%	14%	5%	6%	11%	4%
elsewhere	4%	14%	4%	7%	17%	2%
Third Expansion						
radial	1%	8%	5%	7%	5%	5%
Jordaan	11%	14%	5%	23%	13%	6%
main canal	3%	5%	3%	1%	0%	4%
elsewhere	1%	8%	1%	4%	1%	0%
Fourth Expansion						
radial				7%	7%	1%
main canal				0%	0%	0%
elsewhere				5%	3%	0%
unclassifiable						
radial	0%	5%	0%	0%	1%	0%
main canal	1%	5%	0%	5%	5%	7%
elsewhere	0%	3%	0%	1%	2%	0%
total	100%	100%	100%	100%	100%	100%
N=	97	37	202	228	103	134

Sources: SAA, *ondertrouwregisters* and card index on occupations.
* Sellers of durable goods include hat sellers, silk sellers and sellers of Nuremberg wares. The main shopping streets are the Dam, Nieuwendijk, Kalverstraat, Damrak, Rokin, Warmoesstraat and Nes. The main canals are Singel, Herengracht, Keizersgracht and Prinsengracht.
** The numbers in the table have been rounded off and therefore do not always add up to 100.

Amsterdam was at odds with the presence of many shops and the hubbub of eager shoppers. These shops were thus mainly located on side streets that were connected to the main canals. Side streets that gave easy access to the Dam were particularly popular. Fokkens also mentions the presence of '*groote winkeliers*' (large shops) in Hartenstraat and Reestraat, streets that led directly to the Dam via Gasthuismolenstegen (now partly Paleisstraat).[54] At the northern end of the canal ring, Brouwersgracht appears most frequently in the banns deeds of retailers in the first half of the century. In 1665, Van Domselaer likewise described Brouwersgracht as one of the connecting streets where 'all kinds of wares' were sold.[55] The banns deeds from the period between 1661 and 1690 reveal that this role was assumed by Haarlemmerstraat and Haarlemmerdijk in the second half of the century. This should not come as a surprise, given that these streets also formed the

54 Fokkens, *Beschrijvinge der wijdt-vermaarde koop-stadt Amstelredam*, p. 96.

55 Van Domselaer, *Beschryvinge van Amsterdam*, Book III, p. 259.

link between Nieuwendijk (and thereby the Dam) and Haarlemmerpoort and the exit road to Haarlem.

The densely populated Jordaan is a neighbourhood that rarely features in urban topographies and other sources, but the banns deeds show that the local residents were not deprived of shops altogether. The analysis of the street network in the Jordaan already revealed that this neighbourhood was isolated from the rest of the city and lacked major traffic thoroughfares. This morphological peculiarity was reflected in the location patterns of shops. In the early years, in particular, there was no hierarchy of shopping streets. Shops were to be found on some seventeen streets, transverse streets and canals, but the numbers for each street differ little and it is not possible to reconstruct walking routes. By the second period, the number of streets in the Jordaan named by prospective grooms had grown to 28, and several clusters of shops now seem to have emerged. In the northern Jordaan, these were in the surroundings of Noordermarkt (Boomstraat, Boomdwarsstraat, Lindenstraat and Lindendwarsstraat), and in the southern Jordaan, these were Lauriergracht and Looiersgracht and the surroundings. Especially in the centre of the Jordaan, however, there was a relatively large number of shops, with Nieuwe Leliestraat standing out in particular. Not coincidentally, as observed above, this was a street where wares were purchased not only by local residents but also by passers-by travelling from the western suburbs to the heart of the city, a route that took them via Nieuwe Leliestraat and the crowded bridge over the Prinsengracht.

Table 3.2 also reaffirms the argument presented in the first chapter regarding the distribution pattern of shops selling daily necessities and shops selling durable goods. For the former category, we would expect to find a relatively even distribution over the urban area, and for the latter, we would expect to find clustering in the most accessible places in the city. Viewed from a historical and morphological perspective, the most accessible locations in Amsterdam were the Dam and the streets running from the Dam on both sides of the river in a northerly and southerly direction. In both 1601–1660 and 1661–1700, around 40 per cent of the betrothed hat sellers, silk retailers and sellers of Nuremberg wares gave these streets as their addresses. In the table, they are summarized under the heading 'durable'. Warmoesstraat and Nieuwendijk were by far the most frequently named streets. This is consistent with the situation at the end of the sixteenth century and with the accounts by Fokkens and Van Domselaer. But we also came across considerable numbers of shops selling durable goods elsewhere in the city, too. Ultimately, for the selected trades, over 70 per cent of sellers of durable goods sold their merchandise to customers in the medieval heart of the city. Although the enormous growth of the population and the large-scale town expansions meant that seventeenth-century Amsterdam was many times larger than it had been at the time of the *Alteratie* of 1578, the centre of the city, and more specifically the traditional shopping thoroughfares, continued to form the heart of Amsterdam's retail system.

That is not to say, however, that consumer durables could not be purchased elsewhere in the city; the table shows that this was indeed the case but that the numbers were not very large. This may have been because it took time for suppliers of durable goods to see the new neighbourhoods as suitable locations, and dispersal over the city thus took some time—and this was indeed the case, to a certain extent. This would explain the very limited supply of consumer durables available in the area created by the fourth and last city expansion. Over the years, the range of goods for sale in this newly built district certainly became more extensive. The figures for the First, Second and Third Expansion areas likewise show that even when the new districts were fully built-up and inhabited, the range of durable goods for sale continued to trail far behind that in the heart of the city. Thus, demand in the new districts evidently did not lead to a larger spatial dispersal of available goods and the core shopping area becoming less attractive.

Nevertheless, this does not tell the whole story. The poor residents of neighbourhoods such as the Jordaan, the Lastage and the slowly emerging Jewish Quarter, in particular, would have had access to other channels to meet the need for durable goods, and such channels certainly existed in the form of markets (see Figure 3.9 for the situation around 1660). One was at Nieuwmarkt, in an easily accessible place in the urban grid, on the edge of the Lastage and close to the Jewish Quarter. Despite a ban by the city government, the weekly Monday market included many stalls selling fabric, lace and second-hand clothing.[56] Market traders also took matters into their own hands at Westermarkt where, without the government's permission but evidently tolerated for many years, traders sold new and second-hand clothing and household goods. At Noordermarkt, on the edge of the Jordaan, the Monday market sold 'almost anything one could imagine', according to Van Domselaer; among other things, he mentions woollen and linen cloth, new and used clothing, books, tools, household goods, pots and other earthenware.[57]

In addition, there were even more specialized weekly markets for chairs (Nieuwezijds Voorburgwal); baskets (Nieuwezijds Voorburgwal); tubs, buckets and other coopers' wares (Singel); pine furniture (Singel); old shoes and clogs (Nieuwezijds Kolk); rags (on the city ramparts by St Antoniespoort) and jugs and glasses imported from Germany (on the square outside St Antoniespoort). Moreover, from the by-laws that regulated trade on Nieuwmarkt and Noordermarkt, we know that retail trade there was not limited to market stalls. The same types of goods that were available on market stalls were also sold from houses, *pothuizen* and cellars. Unlike the market vendors, these shopkeepers were able to ply their trade for the rest of the week as well. One was forbidden from displaying one's wares beyond the *pothuis* and the front step, however, something that was clearly permitted on the Monday market day.[58]

Weekly markets played a key role in the supply of foodstuffs, too, and there was also a series of daily markets selling vegetables and fruit. Moreover, dairy farmers from outside the city were permitted to sell milk from door to door. But bread, an essential foodstuff, and tobacco, which was rapidly growing in popularity, were sold from shops. As mentioned above, I used the location of bakers and tobacco sellers to chart the distribution pattern of shops selling daily necessities. Table 3.2 clearly shows that between 1661 and 1700, suppliers of daily necessities were dispersed over the city much more widely than sellers of consumer durables. No more than around 35 per cent of bakers were located in the city centre, and their numbers were few on the main shopping thoroughfares. That is what we should expect, as these locations were very attractive to suppliers of goods that required an extended

56 For markets in the 1660s, see Van Domselaer, *Beschryvinge van Amsterdam*, Book IV, chapter 5, and Kistemaker, 'De Amsterdamse markten'.

57 Van Domselaer, *Beschryvinge van Amsterdam*, Book IV, p. 242.

58 Ibidem, Book IV, pp. 241–243.

customer base due to their relatively high prices and low purchase frequency. Bread, tobacco and other daily necessities were mostly sold in the immediate surroundings, and it was not necessary to have an expensive location on a main shopping thoroughfare for this kind of merchandise. Bakers and tobacco sellers preferred to set up shop on radial streets, with their high level of accessibility and lower rents. Outside the city centre, too, bakers were to be found in large numbers. The Jordaan, for example, was home to no fewer than 23 per cent of all betrothed bakers and 13 per cent of betrothed tobacco sellers.[59] There were even suppliers of daily necessities to be found in the Fourth Expansion area, too.

In the years between 1601 and 1660, the tobacco sellers showed a similar degree of distribution, but the bakers were still strikingly concentrated in the heart of the city. This may have been a consequence of the fact that the sample covers the period 1601–1635, when the process of spreading out from the city centre was still in full flow. This suggestion is confirmed by a small investigation into the addresses of betrothed bakers in the years between 1655 and 1660. At that time, scarcely one-third of the bakers lived in the city centre and the rest in the expansion areas. Retailers, led by suppliers of daily necessities, slowly permeated the new districts. Thanks to the high purchase frequency of bread and tobacco, the distance to traditional points of sale in the old city was considered too large, and demand emerged in the new neighbourhoods for the services of shopkeeping fellow citizens.

59 The high percentage of bakers in the Jordaan may to some extent reflect the presence of a large ship's biscuit bakery on Anjeliersgracht (Fokkens, *Beschrijvinge der wijdt-vermaarde koop-stadt Amstelredam*, p. 90).

The retail landscape of Amsterdam in the seventeenth century

It is an unfortunate twist of fate that for the century when early modern Amsterdam experienced the strongest population growth and greatest transformation in its urban territory, there are hardly any sources available that offer insight into how the dynamism of the seventeenth century shaped the retail landscape. In this chapter, we therefore had to resort to fragmentary remarks in the urban topographies by Fokkens and Van Domselaer and the equally fragmentary information from Amsterdam's banns registers. Thanks to the availability of cartographical material, and the fact that Amsterdam's urban grid has not changed radically since the seventeenth century, we nevertheless have quite a lot of information about the street network in Amsterdam. Despite the many limits, by combining these sources it is possible to sketch a broad picture of continuity and change in retail location patterns; and it turns out that the degree of continuity was unusually high. At the end of the sixteenth century, the Dam and the river dikes on both sides of the Amstel formed the core of Amsterdam's retail system. A century later this was still the case, even though the appearance of the city was now completely different. In terms of general accessibility, the medieval heart of Amsterdam remained unaffected by the expansions that had multiplied the surface area of the city many times. Underlying this striking continuity was the structure of the street network as it had been shaped by the four city expansions that took place after the *Alteratie*. The most striking, and also—from an international perspective—unique element of these expansions was the development of a pleasant, spacious residential environment for wealthy citizens, forming a wide band around the medieval city.

The impulse for this zone of luxury buildings was already visible during the First Expansion, but only with the Third and Fourth Expansions did the canal ring assume its definitive form.

It was the elongated shape of the canal ring that perpetuated the city centre's role at the heart of Amsterdam's retail landscape. Had this sizeable luxury quarter assumed a compact form, it is very possible that a shopping area would have developed in the immediate surroundings that sold a range of goods tailored to the tastes and purchasing power of the elite. This expression of special accessibility would undoubtedly have led to fierce competition with the shops in the city centre, resulting in a completely different retail landscape. Due to its elongated form, however, the distances within the canal ring were so great that it was not possible for a shopping area to develop that could be accessed easily by all residents. At the same time, the centre was still easily accessible from all parts of the semi-circular canal ring. The wealthy elite thus went to the city centre, as they had always done, to buy consumer durables. And this was another finding of the research: in accordance with modern location theory, providers of consumer durables with low purchase frequency were mainly to be found in locations that were most accessible to the largest number of people. In Amsterdam, these were the Dam and surroundings and the main shopping thoroughfares on both sides of the Amstel. Shops were not absent within the canal ring itself, but they were mainly to be found in the transverse streets that connected the main canals and provided access to the city centre. Although retail facilities did arise there that reflected the wealth of the local residents, they did not really compete with the shops in the heart of the city.[60]

Despite this, the construction of the canal ring did have an impact on the retail landscape in the medieval heart of Amsterdam. As argued above, the construction of the luxurious canal ring drained the elite away from what had once been Amsterdam's most prestigious street: Warmoesstraat. As a result, this street developed into a shopping street *par excellence* in the second quarter of the seventeenth century. It was the street where people came to shop, compare what was on offer, and choose from the countless luxurious fabrics, clothing accessories and fashionable items for sale. In the longer term, however, Warmoesstraat's position as a shopping street was not unassailable. During the First and Second Expansions, it was mainly the eastern side of the city that grew, and it was there, on St Antoniesbreestraat and Kloveniersburgwal, that some of the wealthy upper classes set up home. The very wealthy merchant Jan Poppen had an impressive house built on Kloveniersburgwal in the first decades of the century, for example, and around 1660, the brothers Louis and Hendrick Trip commissioned the construction of an even more grandiose house on the same canal.[61]

For the residents of this eastern part of the city, Warmoesstraat was easily accessible, but in the course of the seventeenth century the living environs of the elite shifted unmistakably towards the canal ring, and thereby to the western and southern sides of the city.[62] From that time onward, Warmoesstraat proved much less favourable. For the residents of the southwestern and very wealthy southern part of the canal ring in particular, Kalverstraat was the most obvious approach route to the heart of the city. By now, the troublesome cattle

60 The supply of luxury items in these transverse streets is documented in Fokkens, *Beschrijvinge der wijdt-vermaarde koop-stadt Amstelredam*, pp. 70–71.

61 Elias, *De vroedschap van Amsterdam*, pp. 286 and 547.

62 For vacancy in St. Antoniesbreestraat, see Dudok van Heel, 'Regent Families and Urban Development', pp. 140.

market had disappeared, and access to Kalverstraat via Heiligeweg also seems to have been 'upgraded'. The small houses there that the city had made available to poor widows and unmarried women were demolished in 1649, and 'respectable dwellings' were built on the northern side of Heiligeweg, according to Van Domselaer. The western side of Kalverstraat, between Heiligeweg and today's Muntplein, was also 'much improved', according to the author.[63] Perhaps it was also due to Kalverstraat's growing significance as a shopping street that the booths (*kassen*) on the upper storey of the Exchange dwindled in popularity. More generally, one can imagine that the relatively dark booths aged quickly and no longer reflected the tastes of the shopping public. When the building was completed in 1611, there had been 123 booths, but by 1669, lack of interest had caused this to fall to 43; and at the end of the century, William Montague wrote in his travel report of 'some few inconsiderable toy-shops at one end above stairs'.[64]

The filling-up of the new neighbourhoods and the city centre's unrivalled position as the main shopping area gave special significance to the radial streets that linked the centre to the canal ring and peripheral neighbourhoods. They became crowded approach routes that were perfect, from a shopkeeper's perspective, for intercepting passers-by—something that we discussed in terms of linear accessibility in the first chapter. The appeal of these radials to retail businesses was reinforced by the city-wide distribution of markets, which fanned out over Amsterdam in the course of the seventeenth century. And this was also necessary because in the new and much larger city, it was impossible for the medieval centre to accommodate all of the markets. The new market locations were not chosen at random; Figure 3.9 clearly shows that they fit well with the radial streets that transected the city.

As we know from the banns deeds, the radial streets were popular among suppliers of consumer durables. To a certain extent, they could be considered linear bulges in the core retail system located on the Dam and the streets on both sides of the Amstel. The rents on the radials would have been lower than on the main shopping thoroughfares, and although we lack information about this, one could expect that the hat sellers, silk vendors, sellers of Nuremberg wares and other retailers who were located there offered a different range from that on the main shopping thoroughfares. This would have been even more true of shops established in working-class neighbourhoods, such as the Jordaan and the Lastage.

Suppliers of food and beverages were not located in large numbers on the main shopping thoroughfares. Commercial property was expensive on these streets, and the advantages of a prime location did not weigh heavily for bakers and tobacco sellers. After all, consumers from other parts of the city were unlikely to travel to the centre to purchase bread and tobacco. The providers of these goods would have relied on consumers in the immediate surroundings and would have attempted to achieve a monopolistic position in a geographically limited part of the market. Bakers and tobacco sellers were thus distributed over the urban area much more widely than retailers selling durable goods. Given the nature of their merchandise, we would also expect these sellers to have been the first to set up shop in new neighbourhoods. Although we are unable to

63 Van Domselaer, *Beschryvinge van Amsterdam*, Book III, pp. 225–226 and 254–255.

64 Breen, 'Topografische geschiedenis van den Dam', p. 150, and Mountague, *The Delights of Holland*, p. 162. In London, too, the popularity of retail booths in exchange buildings was declining sharply (Baer, 'Early Retailing').

test this assumption properly due to the relatively small-scale nature of the research in the registers of banns and the limits of this source, it is striking that in the Fourth Expansion area, the bakers began appearing from 1666, the tobacco sellers from 1674 and the hat sellers from 1682. Sellers of silk and Nuremberg wares did not appear until 1700.[65]

In view of all of this, it will have become clear that the retail landscape of Amsterdam in the seventeenth century was highly consistent with what we might expect from the structure of the urban grid and modern location theories. This suggests that the policies pursued by the city government and institutions such as guilds had little influence on the location behaviour of retailers—something that is confirmed when we consult Amsterdam's sizeable volumes of by-laws. At first glance, these give the impression that nothing escaped the regulatory zeal of the city government, but closer inspection reveals that the location of shops was of little interest. The extensive building regulations of 1565, for example, which remained in force until the nineteenth century, did not contain any articles that limited shopkeepers in their choice of location. Even when it came to bakers, whose trade brought a risk of fire, only the quality of the ovens was monitored and there were no requirements regarding location. The only exception to this liberal establishment policy was the sale of meat and fish (Figure 3.10). For reasons of public health (and the payment of taxes), the merchandise on sale was monitored and the wares were clustered in the meat and fish stalls that were rented out by the city government.[66] This aside, anyone who belonged to a shopkeeper's guild was free to set up shop wherever they saw fit.

The fact that location patterns in early modern Amsterdam can be construed so effectively using modern location theories raises the question of whether contemporaries themselves were aware of the importance of location when running a shop. This cannot simply be assumed, as in everyday practice many retailers would have adapted their choice of location to the existing pattern of shops in their sector and the amount of rent that they were willing and able to pay. The striking number of shops selling Nuremberg wares in Warmoesstraat would then rightly be seen as an indication that many customers shopped for Nuremberg wares in that street, and that in Halsteeg one could be assured of customers who were looking for shoes. Bakers, by contrast, were rarely to be found in close proximity to one another, and few would have been tempted to open a business next door to an existing bakery. Van Domselaer was also drawing upon his own observations when he wrote in 1665 that the radials to the heart of the city that had been built during the Third Expansion were crowded with 'passers-by' and that the houses along the radials were therefore offering 'all kinds of wares' for sale.[67]

Nevertheless, it is clear that people also had a more abstract understanding of the value of a good location. In *Le parfait négociant*, published in 1675, Jacques Savary showed that he understood the importance of location, and he even referred to the difference in location patterns for durable goods and more frequently purchased goods. Among the key things that an aspiring retailer should consider, in Savary's

65 In the earliest years of the Third Expansion, hardly any tobacco sellers are mentioned in the bann deeds. Their numbers only started to increase from the end of the 1620s. Considering the early history of tobacco consumption, this was to be be expected (H.K. Roessingh, *Inlandse tabak*, p. 88 ff).

66 Kistemaker, 'De Amsterdamse markten', pp. 25–42.

67 Van Domselaer, *Beschryvinge van Amsterdam*, Book III, p. 259.

Figure 3.10: The fish market with covered fish stalls seen from Damrak, 1693.

view, was location, 'for there are places that are much more efficient than others for certain types of wares'.[68] And he followed this up with examples of consumer durables and the main streets in Paris where these could be bought. Grocers, by contrast, as well as artisans and those selling *kramers*' wares and light woollen cloth 'live without distinction throughout the city'. But even then, certain locations were more suitable than others, the author added, and he continued by remarking that although his examples might relate to Paris, his recommendations were also applicable elsewhere.

Although the Dutch translation of Savary's *Le parfait négociant* remained in print until the end of the eighteenth century, and the number of copies in Dutch libraries suggests that the book was quite popular, few aspiring shopkeepers would have consulted his work when searching for a suitable retail location. Nevertheless, there are indications that many were aware of the importance of a good location and that people were able to interpret the structure of the urban grid in terms of accessibility and pedestrian flows. This was evident when, during the auction of lots in 1614, the city fathers decided to add an extra radial street (Huidenstraat) to the canal ring in the expansion plan. This met with some resistance because those who had already purchased lots

68 Jacques Savary, *De volmaakte koopman*, pp. 283–284.

in the somewhat more northerly Wolvenstraat were only too well aware of the implications of this decision for the value of their property and responded without delay.[69] In their notice of objection, they explained that they had purchased their lots on the assumption that Wolvenstraat would be the most southerly transverse street in the planned part of the canal ring. This was what had been shown on the issuance map displayed during the auction. Anticipating that Wolvenstraat would become an important traffic route to the city centre, they had been planning to rent out or run their premises as shops, thereby profiting from what was described above as linear accessibility. Due to the extra transverse street, they argued, traffic flows would be divided over the two streets and their property would yield less than expected. They were thus demanding compensation for future damages. This compensation was not granted, but the city government was sympathetic to their cause and allowed them to return their lots to the city without charge.

We should add that this was not the only time when residents protested against changes to the infrastructure. Even earlier, in 1594, the city fathers had wanted to move the bridge over Singel by the Jan Rodenpoortstoren to the northern side of the tower so that it would form a continuation of Molsteeg and Torensteeg. The bridge had previously formed a continuation of Oude Leliestraat on the other side of Singel, and although it would only have been moved a few dozen metres, the residents of Oude Leliestraat were vociferous in their protests. They had paid a lot of money for their land, due to 'the trade that they assumed would follow from the crossing'.[70] They demanded that the old situation be maintained by the city government—which, in turn, acknowledged the reasonable nature of their objections and, perhaps fearing damage claims, granted their wish. With their protests, all of these citizens of Amsterdam revealed that they had a good understanding of the influence of the street network on the magnitude of traffic flows and the commercial potential of their properties. It does not seem an exaggeration to suggest that this awareness would have been more widespread than among the traders of Oude Leliestraat and the buyers of lots in Wolvenstraat alone.[71]

69 Abrahamse, *Metropolis in the Making*, chapter 2 ('Damages due to planning').

70 '[D]e neringe die apparentelijck aldaer deur de passagie soude volgen' (Ibidem, p. 282).

71 The commercial potential of corner houses was also known in the seventeenth century. During the urban expansions, plots on the corner of radial streets in the canal ring yielded a higher price per square metre than plots elsewhere in these streets and along the canals themselves. In the Fourth Expansion, these plots were even put up for auction separately (Ibidem, pp. 62 and 182).

4. The retail landscape and the consumer in the seventeenth century

Abstract
Given the profound changes in the distribution system in the decades around 1600 and the highly varied character of the retailing industry, it is striking that the display of wares continued to be on and in front of the façade. Nevertheless, the street scene changed radically, and this was mainly due to the fact that houses used exclusively as residential homes increasingly acquired a more closed character. Shop interiors varied as widely as exteriors, but in the course of the seventeenth century at the upper end of the market the design and decoration of the shop interior definitely became more important as a means to attract (wealthy) customers. In poor neighbourhoods, shop interiors continued to be very basic.

Keywords: continuity in shop exteriors, increasing differentiation in shop interiors

When painting a picture of the retail landscape of Amsterdam in the age of the great city expansions, we should not limit ourselves to dispersal maps and street patterns. We also want to know what Amsterdam's streets and shops looked like in the seventeenth century. In this chapter, we shall therefore focus on paving, street lighting and the hustle and bustle of the street, and particularly on residential and commercial housing in Amsterdam, and the ways in which the exterior and interior were made suitable for retail sales. And, although the available source material is scarce and incomplete, we shall also attempt to find out what the daily interchanges between shopkeepers and consumers were like in practice.

The street

Let us begin by observing that the streets were crowded—very crowded. Although the built-up area of the city had expanded significantly in the seventeenth century, it had not become less busy, particularly in the old centre where the main shopping streets were located. The old centre was home to Amsterdam's central square, the important public buildings, the inner harbour where inland vessels from every corner of the Republic were moored, and there were also markets and shops; in short, this was where much of urban life took place. Precisely because of this clustering of functions, the centre would have been even more crowded than in the sixteenth century, when the population size and activity would have encroached less upon the available space. What is more, a growing number of wealthy citizens preferred to travel through the city by horse and carriage. This was comfortable in busy traffic, and it was also a way to show off one's economic success.

The city government responded to the traffic problems with a whole raft of measures. In the immediate surroundings of the Dam, alleyways and streets were widened whenever possible and affordable, to help the young metropolis cope with the growing traffic flows

Lesger, C., *Shopping Spaces and the Urban Landscape in Early Modern Amsterdam*, 1550–1850.
Taylor & Francis Group, 2020
DOI: 10.5117/9789463720625_CH04

that largely had to be absorbed by the small medieval centre.[1] Corner houses were chamfered to facilitate throughflow, and obstacles were removed along the busiest routes, including the *kassen* (booths) rented out by the city. The city government also used by-laws in its attempt to clamp down on the display of merchandise and the storage of building materials on public roads. At the same time, traffic measures were taken. The city announced one-way traffic in a number of access streets to the Dam, sometimes in combination with a prohibition on stopping, and it was determined that the traffic on Heiligeweg leaving the city would take precedence over incoming traffic. In order to limit cargo traffic in the city as much as possible, parking for carts and wagons was created at the major city gates (Haarlemmerpoort, Leidsepoort, Weesperpoort and Utrechtsepoort), where wagoners could park their carts and transfer their goods to smaller-scale forms of transport.[2]

In 1634, draconian measures were taken against the use of 'coaches, carriages, calèches and suchlike'. As they could only squeeze through the narrow streets and alleyways with difficulty, and the horses 'were prone to bolt', they posed a great risk to other road users. Moreover, the city fathers considered driving through the city an improper expression of laziness that encouraged imitation, including by those who could not afford a carriage and horses, leading to 'the ruin of their fortunes'.[3] This policy was not maintained for very long. Several decades later, the use of carriages was permitted so long as they were used exclusively for journeys to and from places outside the city and provided that the shortest route within the city was taken. From 1679, an exception was made for physicians; they were allowed to travel to patients in a one-horse carriage displaying the word *Medicijn* (doctor) on the back in yellow or golden letters. The carriage ban was eventually lifted altogether, and the introduction of a luxury tax on the possession of a carriage made a virtue of a necessity. Even before that time, though, the ban was ignored by many, and pleasure carriages contributed to the huge crowds, especially in the old centre of the city.

The city government had also long objected to the use of carriages because they caused significant damage to the road surface. In the first chapter, we noted that in the course of the sixteenth century the government assumed responsibility for the city's paving. With the great city expansions of the seventeenth century, this responsibility brought significant costs, but this was also an opportunity to provide the new districts with more or less uniform paving. In the existing city, too, the paving was renovated in a way that was consistent with what had become standard in the new districts.[4] This standard was one that took account of use of the road surface. When it came to carts, carriages, sledges and other vehicles, durability was a key factor. Not only did sledge runners and carriage wheels do damage but horses' horseshoes in particular were responsible for a constant assault on the paving because they

1 Abrahamse, *Metropolis in the Making*, chapter 5 ('Passage and hauling'), and Breen, 'Topografische geschiedenis van den Dam'.

2 Schmal, 'De overheid als verkeersregelaar', pp. 56–59, and Abrahamse, *Metropolis in the Making*, chapter 5 ('Traffic regulations').

3 De Roever, *Uit onze oude Amstelstad*, p. 226. See also Schmal, 'De overheid als verkeersregelaar'; Abrahamse, *Metropolis in the Making*, chapter 5 ('Comfort and status'), and Noordkerk, *Handvesten ofte privilegiën*, pp. 739–742.

4 Sandifort, 'Onze stadsweg', pp. 229–236; Abrahamse, *Metropolis in the Making*, chapter 5 ('Paving the streets'), and see also the website of Vereniging Vrienden van de Amsterdamse Binnenstad.

featured iron caps and clips in order to give the horses a grip on the road surface. In order to avoid slippages and falls, the surface could not be slippery. For this reason, in practice, stone cobblestones made of materials such as granite or basalt were used for the traffic lanes. This surface was nothing less than a disaster for pedestrians. The cobblestones were uncomfortable to walk on and the irregular surface filled up with street dirt and manure. A strip of pavement was thus added, paved with clinker bricks placed on their sides. This provided a smooth, comfortable surface that was also easy to keep clean. As the clinker bricks were much less hard and durable than the cobblestones, carts, sledges and horses were forbidden from riding on the bricks, upon a penalty of six guilders.[5] Clinker bricks were also laid along the quaysides, on the strip where the trees lined the canals.

The paving of the front step of a house—the strip in front of the façade containing stairs, shutters, cellar entrances, *pothuizen* and various other things—was paid for by the owner of the house. In a by-law of September 1634, house-owners were reminded to level and pave their front steps if they had not already done so. In 1672, it was decreed that all owners of houses and property had to pave their front steps with yellow clinker bricks.[6] It is very possible that the city had already been using these same bricks to pave footpaths and quaysides for many years and that the decree was intended to bring more uniformity to the cityscape. What is certain is that on coloured images from the eighteenth and nineteenth centuries, the yellow clinker bricks and the cobblestones on the road are clearly visible.[7] Even on a monotone print of a shabby canal in the Jordaan, published in the *Fire Engine Book* by Jan van der Heyden, we can clearly distinguish the different kinds of paving (Figure 4.1).[8]

The system of gutters and sewers that carried away rainwater and waste water was also subject to change. In the sixteenth century, these had formed part of the surface of the street and could only partially be covered with planks or stone slabs. By the beginning of the seventeenth century, this situation was considered undesirable. In 1605, the city government decided to 'embellish' the city, and determined that the half-open drains—also in view of the risk that they posed to road-users—should be replaced with brick gutters under the road surface.[9] The by-law referred to 'all drains that run through or over streets to the [canal] waters'. Indeed, in pictures of the canals, we do not see any gutters in the surface of the road. This was also true of one of the poorest canals in the city, both then and in later years: Goudsbloemgracht (now Willemstraat) in the north of the Jordaan. To the extent that there were sewers and gutters there, they would have lain under the paving, but apart from that, the rainwater and dirt most likely simply flowed over the road surface into the canal. If there were no canals in the neighbourhood, this was not so straightforward. In one of the streets depicted by Jan van der Heyden around 1680, we see that

5 Noordkerk, *Handvesten ofte privilegiën*, p. 732. About a century later, during his visit to Amsterdam in 1759, Bengt Ferrner reported that as soon as the road surface was damaged, even if only a little, repairs were immediately carried out by men who had been specially appointed for that purpose (Kernkamp, 'Bengt Ferrner's dagboek', p. 331).

6 Noordkerk, *Handvesten ofte privilegiën*, pp. 731–734.

7 See the figures 4.5, 4.6, 4.12, 4.13 and 4.14 below.

8 Van der Heyden, *Beschryving der nieuwlijks uitgevonden en geoctrojeerde slang-brand-spuiten*.

9 '[A]lle de Goten, die door of over de Straten na de Wateren loopen' (Noordkerk, *Handvesten ofte privilegiën*, p. 732).

Figure 4.1: Paving on Passeerdersgracht, second half of the seventeenth century.

there is still a gutter in the road surface, running parallel to the pavement and covered with planks (Figure 4.2). Likewise, a by-law of August 1642 referred insouciantly to 'the gutters running in front of the houses'.[10] But this does not detract from the fact that in large parts of the city, the streets did become more passable in the seventeenth century.

This latter development was also aided by the waste collection system. Already in the late fifteenth century, there were public refuse bins in Amsterdam that were emptied with some regularity by the city's refuse collectors. This system was maintained for many years, although it had its limits. The capacity of the system was insufficient, particularly in working-class neighbourhoods with high living densities, narrow streets and multiple tenements on alleyways and passageways.[11] To the government's consternation, refuse was dumped on the streets, bridges and quays, and it responded

10 '[D]e goten voor de huysen loopende' (Ibidem, p. 734).

11 See for the following Abrahamse, *Metropolis in the Making*, chapter 6 ('City cleansing').

Figure 4.2: A plank-covered drain in the road, second half of the seventeenth century.

by increasing capacity and strengthening monitoring.

From the 1660s, for example, wooden *kassen* or booths were placed in strategic locations in the city. They provided a base for cobblers to practise their craft, but as well as their shoemaking, these artisans had to prevent refuse being dumped on the street or in the canals. Moreover, after the final great city expansion, the cleaning service was reorganized and put under the supervision of overseers. From that time onwards, barges would sail the canals on working days and remove the refuse dumps from the quays. In the streets, barrows were used for the same purpose; 200 street sweepers worked in the city at that time. This was not sufficient to remove all of the industrial and private waste, but the major shopping thoroughfares and the main canals were kept tidy.[12] Problems tended to arise in working-class neighbourhoods and industrial areas on the periphery of the city as well as in the slums and alleyways of the old inner city.

What is more, public roads became more negotiable at dusk and at night, thanks to a radical transformation of the city's street lighting. During the sixteenth century, street lighting was a very scarce commodity, and passers-by had to make do with the small lights that innkeepers and publicans were obliged to display in the *voorhuis* and the lanterns that were hung on or by bridges to prevent pedestrians from stumbling into the water and drowning on moonless nights. Sometimes there were

12 However, the quality of the water in the canals remained problematic, and there are countless complaints about the nasty smell of the Amsterdam canals. See for example Van Strien, *De ontdekking van de Nederlanden*, p. 99. Problems with water circulation are discussed in great detail in Abrahamse, *Metropolis in the Making*, chapter 6.

also candles burning by statues of saints on façades or in alcoves, but this tradition ended when the city joined the Protestant camp. In 1595, it was decreed that the occupants of every twelfth house should display a lantern with a burning candle when it grew dark. There soon appeared to be little enthusiasm for this, and in 1597 the city government appointed lantern lighters. The costs of this semi-public lighting system were covered by the introduction of a tax, the *lantaarngeld*.[13]

These measures would have had little impact because many lantern windows were made not of glass but horn and yielded little light. The problems are clearly expressed in a plan to improve the city lighting, discussed in the Council in 1668: 'to prevent accidents befalling the many people who fall in the water and drown when it is dark; also, so that the *Ratelwacht* (night watch) can do their rounds without having to carry lanterns; third, so that the civic guard can do their rounds, and all other citizens and inhabitants can use the streets, without having to carry lanterns; moreover, to discover and to prevent break-ins, and also in case of fire always to have a light to hand'.[14] The great change occurred when the painter, inventor and entrepreneur Jan van der Heyden presented the city with a detailed plan for public lighting using the street lamps he had invented. His oil lamps, which featured windowpanes, mirrors and airholes; provided much more light; and worked better than the existing candle lanterns. The city agreed to much of his proposal, and not long after, Amsterdam was lit at night by around 2,000 lanterns, a number that would rise to as many as 2,600 in 1681.[15]

Careful planning and sufficient financial resources ensured that the lanterns were also actually kept burning after dark. The inventor did not come out of it badly, either. In his proposal, he had offered to manage the entire street lighting system. Although the burgomasters did not agree to this, they did make Van der Heyden 'overseer and director of the night-lanterns', and from 1670 until his death in 1712, he received an annual salary of no less than 2,000 guilders.[16] At the end of the seventeenth century, the British traveller William Montague wrote admiringly that 'between their houses are most pleasant rows of trees and lamps between them, and very thick, (one to two dwellings,) which in night give a delightful prospect, and burn late, to answer the ends of business, or conversation'.[17]

The revolutionary nature of this public street-lighting system should not be underestimated. In the past, the city had been somewhere that people preferred to avoid after dark. With the construction of an effective system of street lighting, this was no longer the case;

13 Zahn Jr., *De geschiedenis der verlichting*, p. 4.

14 '[O]m te verhoeden het verongelucken van veele menschen, die bij duysternis in 't water vallen eñ versmoren; ten anderen om de Ratelwacht sonder Licht in de hand te doen gaen; ten derden om de burgerwacht ende ronden, mitsgaders alle andere burgers en ingesetenen, sonder lantarens de straet te konnen doen gebruyken; wijders om huysbraken te ontdecken ende moetwille te weren, ende dan oock om bij brant allomme licht bij de hand te hebben' (Breen, 'Jan van der Heijden', pp. 42–44).

15 Abrahamse, *Metropolis in the Making*, chapter 5 ('Street lighting'). Jan Wagenaar mentions that in the 1760s the city had 2815 lanterns, which were on average 8 to 10 houses apart (Zahn Jr., *De geschiedenis der verlichting*, p. 16).

16 Breen, 'Jan van der Heijden', pp. 42–44.

17 Mountague, *The Delights of Holland*, p. 136. Mountague also pointed to how safe Amsterdam was at night (Ibidem, pp. 138–139). In the last quarter of the eighteenth century, Parisian Louis Desjobert still noticed that the streets of Amsterdam were well-lit at night (Desjobert, 'Voyage aux Pays Bas', p. 140). Van der Heyden's street lighting system was quickly adopted in a number of Dutch cities and also in Berlin (1682), Cologne (1682) and Leipzig (1701). See Multhauf, 'The Light of Lamp-Lanterns', p. 250.

public life in Amsterdam was released from the grip of the seasons, and people could also go out on winter evenings. The foundations were thereby laid for the nightlife that we are familiar with today as well as for shops that offered their services in the evening. As such, the city increasingly stood out from the countryside, where public life still came to a halt after darkness fell.[18]

Shopfronts

In early modern Amsterdam, particularly in the city centre, retail trade had a prominent presence and was highly varied. It ranged from shops to the workplaces of artisan sellers, the barrows, carts, baskets and boxes of street traders, and the stalls and barges on which goods were presented to customers at the daily, weekly and annual markets. The focus of this study is limited to shops, that is to say, fixed locations where consumers can buy goods that are not produced on-site. Even within this category, however, we encounter great variety. As a result, it is not easy to give an impression of the interiors and exteriors of shops in this period. Nevertheless, one aspect of the shop remained unchanged in the seventeenth century, and that was its open character.[19] Even if the inspection, comparison, negotiation and purchase of goods might take place inside the shop, the barrier of the façade and shop door was overcome, as it were, by the display of wares on and in front of the façade; and this continuity with the preceding period was highly contingent on the way in which Amsterdam's townhouses were built.

As noted above, by the end of the sixteenth century, houses made entirely out of timber had largely disappeared from Amsterdam's cityscape, but the façade of the average dwelling was reminiscent of the old construction. This was because the front façade often consisted of a tall timbered lower façade, topped with a thin stone façade. Unlike a heavy stone façade, many high windows could be placed in a timber façade, allowing more light into the *voorhuis* and adding to its suitability as a workshop or shop. Nevertheless, one should not make too much of the view that customers would have had into the interior of the shop *voorhuis*. Early in the morning and at dusk, it would have been difficult to make out anything inside the building, as artificial lighting was expensive. Indeed, in the many inventories of shop estates studied for this research, only now and then did I come across a lantern in a *voorhuis* or, very occasionally, a copper chandelier.[20] Even in daytime, however, the view into the shop interior would have been limited. The leaded windowpanes were small, the glass was much less transparent than modern glass, and the oft-present canopy dimmed the interior. In addition, the three-foot-wide (ca. 85 cm) front step that was present in most Amsterdam streets prevented pedestrians from walking right up to the façade and looking at the

18 The effect of good street lighting can be seen, among other things, from the sharp increase in the number of complaints about prostitution in the first years after 1670 (Prak, 'Stad van tegenstellingen', p. 288).

19 Wholesalers who occasionally sold *en détail* are not included here. Their businesses are often referred to in the sources as 'closed shops' (*gesloten winkels* or *toe-winkels*).

20 SAA, Desolate boedelkamer, inv. nr. 571, fol. 157 v-161 (20 January 1646) and inv. nr. 622, fol.208 v-211 (26 November 1699). Apparently, chandeliers were used earlier in shops than in *voorhuizen* with a residential function only. Compare Fock, '1600–1650', pp. 43–44, and idem, '1650–1700', p. 109. For the lack of light in Amsterdam houses, see Muizelaar and Phillips, *Picturing Men and Women*, pp. 56–61.

Figure 4.3: The brush maker.

contents of shops in passing.[21] This is because there were stairs, basement entrances, *pothuizen*, benches, fencing and countless other obstacles in and on the front step. As a result, retailers were forced to display at least some of their merchandise on the façade and in front of their shops, and that is exactly what they did.

In the upper part of the timber façade, the leaded windows were mounted directly in the frame, but in the lower part of the façade there was no glass, or the glass was mounted in wooden frames that could be opened or removed. This not only provided more light, it also created space to display wares in the windows, and this space could be enlarged further by folding down the wooden shutters to a horizontal position.[22] This situation is captured clearly in a print entitled 'The brushmaker' in *Het menselyk bedrijf* by Jan and Caspar Luiken (1694) (Figure 4.3).[23] The brush

21 In the canal ring, the width of the front step was set at a maximum of four Amsterdam feet (approximately 115 cm). See Binnenstad 235 (August 2009) as published on www.amsterdamsebinnenstad.nl (last accessed 9 August 2019).

22 This is one of the reasons that Simon Stevin shows himself to be a strong proponent of this type of horizontally hung shutters (Van den Heuvel, *'De Huysbou'*, p. 262).

23 Luiken, *Het menselyk bedryf.*

Figure 4.4: Display cases on the shutters of shop premises in Kalverstraat, ca. 1700.

maker is reaching through the open window, and brushes of various types and sizes lie on the lower shutters. A considerable quantity of wares could be displayed in the window in this way. At the windows of Franchoys van Berken's shop on Oudebrugsteeg, there was a bundle of wood chips, 10 boxes containing all kinds of nails, 600 horn lantern panes, 50 small canes, 100 marbles, 50 *stuytknickers* (marbles made of baked earth), some locks and 6 pounds of whetstones.[24]

What we do not see in the print by Luiken are the upper shutters and the canopy, from which much more merchandise would have hung. The canopy was a handy place to hang wares, but it also extended out over the front step and thereby protected the displayed wares, the shopkeeper and the customer from all kinds of weather.

Despite this, there were also disadvantages to displaying shop goods in the window and in front of the façade. Some goods suffered from exposure to the blowing dust and dirt of the street, and there was always the risk of wares being pocketed by thieves. In an early modern city such as Amsterdam, where a considerable part of the population had extremely limited financial means, many must have been tempted to supplement their income with occasional or more frequent acts of theft. Shopkeepers protected themselves from loss by displaying small objects in cases known as *kasjens*. There were several in the loft of a lace and fabric shop on Warmoesstraat, described as 'painted *kasjens* to be placed in the windows'. And in the *voorhuis,*

24 SAA, Desolate boedelkamer, inv. nr. 570, fol. 253-283v (6 July 1644).

Figure 4.5: Outdoor display case on a shop premises in Kalverstraat, ca. 1700.

it was reported, there was 'a glass and a wooden case in the window'.[25] These were self-standing cases with glass panes that could be placed in the windows or on the lower shutters or hung on the lower façade. As well as providing protection from street dirt and theft, they also allowed shopkeepers to display items attractively. It would not be going too far to compare them to the velvet-lined display cases that are still popular today for displaying jewellery and watches.

Display cases such as these can be seen in a late-seventeenth-century picture of the house on the corner of Kalverstraat-Wijde Kapelsteeg and the adjacent booths on Nieuwezijdskapel (Figure 4.4). On the lower shutters are sloping cases with glass lids, which allowed customers to view the goods on display without the latter becoming dirty or being stolen. A little further up Kalverstraat, on the corner with Heiligeweg, a shopkeeper is standing under a canopy (Figure 4.5). He is leaning against a large outdoor case, mounted on the lower façade. A cloth is draped over the case, possibly to shield its contents from sunlight and discolouration. Finally, we see a beautiful display case on the lower shutters of the house by the Oudezijdskapel (Figure 4.6). This is a sloping multi-angular case, with panes set in copper or lead. The female shopkeeper is standing behind the half-door that gives access to the shop, surveying the street.

25 SAA, Notarieel archief, inv. nr. 5628, fol. 991–992 (30 November 1706).

Figure 4.6: Outdoor display case on the lower shutters of a shop premises on Zeedijk, second half of the seventeenth century.

On Sundays, when the shops had to close, the windows and shutters were opened but not filled with wares. Evidently, not everyone observed Sunday as a day of rest with the same zeal, and this was monitored. We know this, for example, from the fact that Hendrick Jansz de Reyer, who sold jugs and glass on Nes, felt compelled in July 1616 to ask two neighbours to declare before the notary that he 'opened his shop windows facing the street on Sundays in order to create more light in the *voorhuis*, and placed the screens in the lower windows without placing any jugs, glasses or other goods in his window on Sunday or putting them for sale'.[26] This tells us that De Reyer did not have glass in his windows, and he was not the only one to do without glass in the lower façade.[27] The heavy *hor*, or screen, which we occasionally come across in estate inventories (see further below) and in pictures, was intended to prevent uninvited guests from forcing their way

26 '[D]es Sondaechs sijn winckelveynsteren aen de straet boven toe laet hangen ende onder open nederwaerts, om licht in sijn voorhuys te scheppen, settende in de onderste veynsteren horden, sonder dat d'selve oyt by hen, getuygen, weten op Sondach eenige kannen, glasen ofte ander goet uuyt sijn winckel voor de veynsteren geset ofte te coope voorgestelt heeft' (Van Dillen, *Bronnen bedrijfsleven en gildewezen*, II, nr. 300). See also the by-law in Noordkerk, *Handvesten ofte privilegiën*, pp. 117–118.

27 The absence of glass in the lower part of the façade can be clearly seen in the picture of a mid-seventeenth-century goldsmith's shop in Fock, '1650–1700', p. 116. For residential houses without a commercial function, the use of glass is of course obvious.

Figure 4.7: Shop premises with canopy in Kalverstraat opposite the Nieuwezijdskapel, ca. 1650.

into the *voorhuis* or stealing things through the open window.

The canopy, with its hanging shop wares (in this case stockings) and display in the windows and in front of the façade are clearly visible in a picture of a house on Kalverstraat opposite the Nieuwezijdskapel (Figure 4.7). The image also captures the open character of shops in this period.[28] All things considered, the external appearance of shops was still similar to that of the stalls that were set up in the city on market days. This is hardly surprising, because in the first half of the seventeenth century in particular, some shopkeepers ran a market stall as well as a shop.[29] In order to be somewhat shielded from the street nevertheless, some shopkeepers used curtains. Fokkens mentions them explicitly in relation to Warmoesstraat; the shops in this main shopping street had a cloth in the door that 'could be pushed aside like a curtain'.[30]

28 For the open character of picture galleries in this period, see Bok, '"Schilderien te coop"', pp. 12–13.

29 For example, Lourens Danielsen in St. Annenstraat 'in the gilded mirror'. In the *voorhuis* he did indeed run a shop in mirrors, but the estate also contains a stall with three canvases (SAA, Desolate boedelkamer, inv. nr. 572, fol. 61v-67 (13 June 1646)).

30 Fokkens, *Beschrijvinge der wijdt-vermaarde koop-stadt Amstelredam*, p. 92. Door curtains are also mentioned in SAA, Desolate boedelkamer, inv. nr. 571, fol. 200 v (1646); inv. nr. 572, fol. 23 (1646) and inv. nr. 622, fol. 124 (1699).

Despite the fact that almost all shops in the seventeenth century shared this open character, the differences between them were still uncommonly large. In addition to shopkeepers' individual preferences regarding the exterior and interior of their shops, three factors seem to have played a major role in explaining the range of manifestations: location, offering and previous history. To begin with location: on the Dam and the main shopping thoroughfares, property prices were high and the shops were substantial. The aforementioned Melchior Fokkens, a contemporary, wrote of 'commercial' streets and 'respectable shopkeepers'. According to him, rents on Damrak came to around 800 to 1,500 guilders per year, and in Warmoesstraat and Nieuwendijk, 1,000 to 1,600 guilders.[31] That was a lot of money. For the townhouses on Oude Turfmarkt (the other side of Rokin), built around 1650, proprietors charged rents of 1,200 to 1,400 guilders. Only the large double houses in the canal ring were more expensive than this.[32]

The approach streets to the centre were also ideally located for shops, but property was much cheaper there, and the shops lacked the impact of the large businesses on the Dam, Warmoesstraat, Nieuwendijk and the other main shopping streets. The differences are clear if we compare a picture (ca. 1690) of the house on the corner of the Dam and Kalverstraat with a drawing, also made by Jan van der Heyden, of an unknown shopping street from the same era (Figures 4.8 and 4.9).[33] The architecture of the house on the Dam is beautiful; the timbered lower façade features finely carved balusters, and there is a substantial, lavishly decorated edge around the canopy. The adjacent premises, only part of which can be seen, also make a distinguished impression. Let us then compare this with the situation in the less distinguished shopping street. The houses are smaller, the simple buildings are topped with rather unspectacular stepped gables, and the lower façade and shutters are functional but simple. In particular, the canopy suspended from the partially burned-out house has an unusually simple construction. The open character of the lower façades, the crowded front step and the gutter covered with wooden planks are depicted here in detail. All in all, this drawing offers a rare view of shopfronts in a typical street in Amsterdam.

Figure 4.8: Shop premises on Kalverstraat near the Dam, second half of the seventeenth century.

31 Fokkens, *Beschrijvinge der wijdt-vermaarde koop-stadt Amstelredam*, pp. 92–93.

32 Lesger, *Huur en conjunctuur*, appendices 2 and 3.

33 Both pictures were intended as advertising material for the fire engine designed by this versatile entrepreneur, artist and technician. The shopping street is identified by some as Gravenstraat (Muizelaar and Phillips, *Picturing Men and Women*, p. 27).

Figure 4.9: A shopping street in Amsterdam, second half of the seventeenth century.

Nevertheless, the Dam and the main shopping thoroughfares were not only home to spacious and beautifully built retail properties; the excellent accessibility of these locations and the large flows of passers-by resulted in very intensive land use, as shown by the presence of the *kassen*. *Kassen* were wooden or stone constructions that had the character of permanent market stalls. In general, they provided enough room for the vendor and their wares but hardly enough for customers. The latter therefore stayed outside to inspect the wares that were displayed in or in front of the booth. In the sixteenth century, there had been *kassen* on the Oude Brug, among other places, but they were removed due to increasing traffic

Figure 4.10: The old city hall with shop-booths, situation before 1652.

on the bridge. In the seventeenth century, they were mainly documented against the façades of public buildings. In a painting by Pieter Saenredam (1597–1665), we see *kassen* against the façade of the old city hall (Figure 4.10). Although this painting, which dates from 1657, was produced several years after the fire in the city hall (1652), the painter had already made a detailed study in 1641.[34] The folded shutters function as a counter, and the canopies above protect the goods on display from the weather, wind and bird droppings. The booth to the left undoubtedly specializes in the sale of books and maps, items that were traditionally sold in the surroundings of the Dam and Damrak.

34 The preliminary study in SAA, Beeldbank, nr. 010001000168. For the *kassen* against the façade of the old city hall, see Breen, 'Topografische geschiedenis van den Dam', p. 135.

There was no room for *kassen* against the new city hall built on the Dam in the 1650s, a building whose imposing size and rich decoration were intended to demonstrate the power and wealth of the city and its governors. *Kassen* would have broken the strict classical lines of the building and might have undermined its effect on the beholder. But that is not to say that *kassen* disappeared from the street altogether—on the contrary. A stone's throw away from the city hall, they were to be found against the façade of the Nieuwe Kerk on the Dam and at the foot of the never-completed church tower (Figure 4.11). There were also *kassen* against the façades of the Nieuwezijdskapel on Kalverstraat and the Oudezijdskapel on St Olofspoort (Figure 4.12). Financial considerations also lay behind the establishment of the abovementioned *kassen* on the first floor of the Exchange, across the water of Rokin. This allowed

Figure 4.11: The Nieuwe Kerk on the Dam with shop-booths against the facade and tower, 1693.

the government to exploit the three layers of the site simultaneously in the densely built, crowded city centre: above the wet infrastructure of the Amstel, a partly covered exchange square was built for commerce, and above this, a shopping arcade that initially had no fewer than 123 *kassen*.[35]

But the phenomenon did not end there. Throughout the city, shops were run from hundreds of *pothuizen* and basements, and this is also likely to have been the case for the main shopping streets. Topographical representations of the major shopping streets are scarce. Only when retail facilities were located on or in the immediate vicinity of public buildings were they preserved for posterity in prints, drawings and paintings. It is thus fortunate for us that the artist who drew the Oudezijdskapel or Olofskapel for Commelins' *Beschryvinge van Amsterdam* (1694) also included the adjoining premises (Figure 4.13). The drawing beautifully captures the intensive use of land in the immediate vicinity of Warmoesstraat and the harbour. We can make out three houses with large canopies. Judging from the wares that hang from the canopies of the two houses on the left, they are a hat shop and a second-hand shop. But sales were not limited to the *voorhuizen*; against the façades, we see a whole series of *pothuizen* that can be accessed from inside the

35 Walsh argues that these shopping arcades, which were also found in the exchange buildings of Antwerp, London and elsewhere, can be regarded as precursors of the nineteenth-century department stores (Walsh, 'The Newness of the Department Store', and Idem, 'Social Meaning and Social Space'). See also Baer, 'Early Retailing'.

Figure 4.12: Shop-booths against the facade of the Oudezijdskapel, mid-seventeenth century.

house (on the left, without a door) or directly from the street (others, with doors). *Pothuizen* with separate street entrances were usually rented out, as their location on the yellow paved footpath made them perfect for commercial activities. Cobblers often had workplaces there, but *pothuizen* could also house shops. With some effort, we can also make out numerous people in and in front of the *pothuizen*, which lie partly below street level.[36]

It will have become clear from the above that the exterior of shops varied with the commercial status of the streets on which the shops were located, but we have also seen that even on the same street, consumer goods were sold from very different spaces: *voorhuizen, kassen, pothuizen* and basement shops, which we have yet to discuss. Concerning the latter category, I was unable to find any seventeenth-century pictures showing wares on display, but one does regularly come across estate inventories of basement shops in the archives of notaries and officials working on the financial settlement of bankruptcies. Once again, a print from Jan van der Heyden's *Fire Engine Book* gives a good impression of what the entrance to a basement shop would have looked like (Figure 4.14). Here, we see a corner building on Bloedstraat after a fire in July 1684. The basement runs under the whole house (see the basement window in the side street) and the entrance to

36 A *pothuis* with a commercial function also on Dam Square is on a hand-coloured print from the end of the seventeenth century: SAA, Beeldbank 010097010890.

Figure 4.13: Shops and shop *pothuizen* on Zeedijk, second half of the seventeenth century.

the basement is located next to the front step, which provides access to the *voorhuis* (above street level). Like *pothuizen* with separate entrances (also shown), basements with separate entrances were also rented out, as their proximity to the street made them ideal as shops. This very detailed print shows the leaded glass mounted directly in the frame in the upper part of the timber façade and, under the canopy, the shutters that could be opened upwards and downwards. A wooden beam catches the lower shutters above the *pothuis,* whilst the shutters above the cellar entrance have wooden supports. The stairs and entrance in the side street tell us that the upper storeys were rented out separately. This was very common in a city such as Amsterdam, with its densely packed residential population.[37]

Not only did a shop's location within Amsterdam's retail landscape affect its external appearance, it was also shaped by what was for sale. It stands to reason that sellers of daily necessities would have felt less need than sellers of consumer durables to bring their trade to the attention of the consumer with the aid of signboards and suchlike. In particular,

37 The print also shows a gutter in the road surface that is at right angles to the side wall and covered with boards.

Figure 4.14: Lower facade of a premises on Bloedstraat, second half of the seventeenth century.

bakers, *komenijen* (sellers of bacon, dairy and dry goods), grocers and other food suppliers were dispersed over the city and drew many of their customers from the immediate vicinity. These customers knew the shopkeepers and would not have wanted to compare the offering in various shops every time they bought bread or groceries. But shopkeepers could try to lure customers away from the competition in order to increase their market share and turnover. As bakers were bound to use fixed bread prices (the *broodzetting*), they were reliant on means other than price to beat the competition. How they might do so is captured in a decree of 1649, in which the city government determined, at the request of the bakers' guild, 'that no bakers here in the city shall be permitted to give away bread, *duivekaters* [sweet festive white bread] or other gifts, whatever these might be, to their clients'.[38]

Nevertheless, the use of signs was so established that they were often present even when there appeared to be little need for

38 '[D]at geene backers hier ter stede aen yemand van hunne calanten of die broodt t'haren huyse halen, eenige deuvecaters oft andere giften, hoedanigh die zouden mogen wesen, zullen mogen vereeren' (Van Dillen, *Bronnen bedrijfsleven en gildewezen*, III, nr. 1649).

Figure 4.15: Shop premises with canopy and display sign (to the left in the foreground) on the Dam, second half of the seventeenth century.

them. Some trades always used the same signs, more or less; shops selling meat, dairy and dry goods, for example, could be recognized from a painted wooden pile of cheeses, topped with one or several pats of butter. The protruding canopy was the ideal place for signs such as these, as is clear from a print showing the city hall fire of 1652 (Figure 4.15). To give other examples, the sign that was commonly used for tobacco shops showed wooden rolls of tobacco that were fixed to the façade or canopy, grocers often announced their presence with little sacks of coffee, corn chandlers with a little windmill, and sugar and spice shops with a sugar chest.[39]

We would expect signboards to play a more important role for sellers of durable goods. After all, the nature of their trade meant that they preferred to set up shop in the centre, close to similar sellers. As noted above, this was indeed the case in Amsterdam. Warmoesstraat was the place to find silk, Nuremberg wares and *Franse winkels* selling fashion accessories. On

39 Van Lennep and Ter Gouw, *De uithangteekens*, p. 115 ff.

Nieuwendijk, one could buy a strikingly wide range of fabrics, and Halsteeg—so as not to limit ourselves to the main shopping streets—was home to many shoe shops. In all of these cases, the clustering of shops in the same sector gave customers a wide choice and allowed them to compare the price, quality and appearance of the goods. For the shopkeepers themselves, surrounded by competitors with a similar offering, it was essential to attract the attention of potential clients. They would no doubt have done so with beautiful displays of shop wares in the windows and in front of the façade, but signs also played an important role, as they were meant to inform the customer—even from afar—about what was on sale.

Whether they always succeeded in doing so is another matter. Fokkens writes of Warmoesstraat that there were 220 houses and 230 signs,[40] and if this had been the case, one could hardly have had a clear view down the street. In addition, many of the houses would have had canopies, *pothuizen*, outside staircases, shutters and other things that obscured the view. It is hardly surprising that there were so many signs in Warmoesstraat, of all places, for until the mid-seventeenth century it was by far the most important shopping street in the city. This makes it all the more regrettable that we lack images of the street during this period. Nor do the wonderful bird's-eye-view maps by Balthasar Florisz van Berckenrode help, as they do not show any of the things that would have been on the steps and the façades. A by-law of 1642 perhaps offers the best impression of the appearance of the crowded shopping streets. Every day, according to the by-law, the legislators observed that 'the signs, or the brackets or wood on which they hang, stick out so far that the view of the streets is impeded and deformed'. For this reason, no one was henceforth permitted to have a sign that protruded further than the canopy was deep, and in the absence of a canopy, the sign had to be placed against the façade.[41] There is no indication that this or similar by-laws had the desired effect in the short term, and nor should we expect this, as the shopkeepers were vying for customers' attention and would have therefore tried to beat the competition with larger, more striking signs that stuck out even further into the street.

Third, and finally, the exterior of shops also varied due to what one might call the previous history of the shop premises. There was almost no mass production of buildings in Amsterdam at this time, meaning that every building had its own character and history. This created specific opportunities, but it also imposed limits on running a shop. Moreover, the function of retail premises changed on a regular basis. Different shopkeepers and trades would follow one another, each leaving their own traces. *Voorhuizen* were also converted into shop spaces (and vice versa) whenever the owner or tenant pleased. There were limits to the extent to which exteriors could vary, of course, but these limits were not particularly narrow. On the Dam and main shopping thoroughfares, the high rents alone meant that there would have been great pressure to keep up with the

40 Fokkens, *Beschrijvinge der wijdt-vermaarde koop-stadt Amstelredam*, p. 92. The number of 220 houses is fairly accurate. Around the middle of the sixteenth century, there were 207 houses in Warmoesstraat, but given the population growth and increasing demand for housing, it is not unlikely that a few buildings were split after that time. The figure of 207 in Van der Leeuw-Kistemaker, *Wonen en werken in de Warmoesstraat*, p. 12.

41 '[D]e uythangborden ofte de ysers of houten, daer deselve aen hangen, soo verre uyt-steken, dat 't gesicht van de straten verhindert ende gedeformeert wort' (Van Lennep and Ter Gouw, *De uithangteekens*, p. 85).

demands of the age and ensure that one's shop was attuned to the desired clientele. Even on the Dam, however—the commercial, administrative and religious heart of the city—next to distinguished houses with imposing stone façades, we come across old-fashioned timber façades (Figure 4.15). In the seventeenth century, these evidently still met the demands placed on houses in a prime location.

All of the above may give the impression that in the course of the seventeenth century, the appearance of shops in Amsterdam changed little. Throughout the century and even earlier, shops were run in *voorhuizen*, *kassen*, *pothuizen* and basements. There was also continuity in the open character of retail trade, the presence of the canopied front step and the use of signs and other indications. Despite this, the street scene did change radically, and this was mainly to do with the fact that houses used exclusively as residential homes were increasingly distinguished from those that had a commercial or a mixed commercial-residential function.

In houses with a fully residential function, it was increasingly common to have a side room (*zijkamer*) in the *voorhuis* in the first half of the seventeenth century. The side room had long been a feature of larger houses, but this trend was now adopted by smaller middle-class households. The open space of the *voorhuis* shrank as a result and increasingly assumed the character of an entrance hall.[42] Over time, the side room was transformed into a full-fledged living room, complete with heating. By adding a connection to the room at the back of the house, a *kamer en suite* was created: a front and back room linked by adjoining doors. By now, all that remained of the original *voorhuis* was the entrance to a long corridor that ran to the back of the house. In large houses, there was a preference for a central corridor for reasons of symmetry, but here, too, the traditional *voorhuis* disappeared.

When the side room became a full-fledged living room, it was no longer considered desirable to have a timbered lower façade. In the seventeenth century, new homes were increasingly built with façades made entirely out of stone, and existing timbered façades were replaced with masonry. The façade acquired a more closed character as a result, and this was precisely the intention.[43] There were also further differences between residential homes and houses where a craft was practised or a shop was run. The canopy, which had drawn the front step area into the house, as it were, was increasingly omitted or removed. Traditional signs also seem to have been replaced with stone *bas-reliëfs* mounted on the façade.[44] And particularly in the case of the more distinguished houses, the front step was cleared. The latter no longer functioned as the zone where street life and private life ran into one another but as a strip that separated the public and private domains. Passers-by were no longer invited to enter this semi-public part of the house but were kept at a distance by the step. On Amsterdam's most distinguished canals, this change was aptly symbolized by the use of fencing and poles with chains to block access to the front step.

These changes did not occur, or occurred to a much lesser extent, in houses with a commercial function. There, by contrast, maintaining a direct relationship with the street was a condition for commercial success. For shopkeepers and artisan sellers, the step was not a barrier but functioned as an invitation to passers-by and

42 Meischke, *Het Nederlandse woonhuis*, pp. 99–100, 427–429.

43 Ibidem, pp. 99–100, 437.

44 Van Lennep and Ter Gouw, *De uithangteekens*, p. 69.

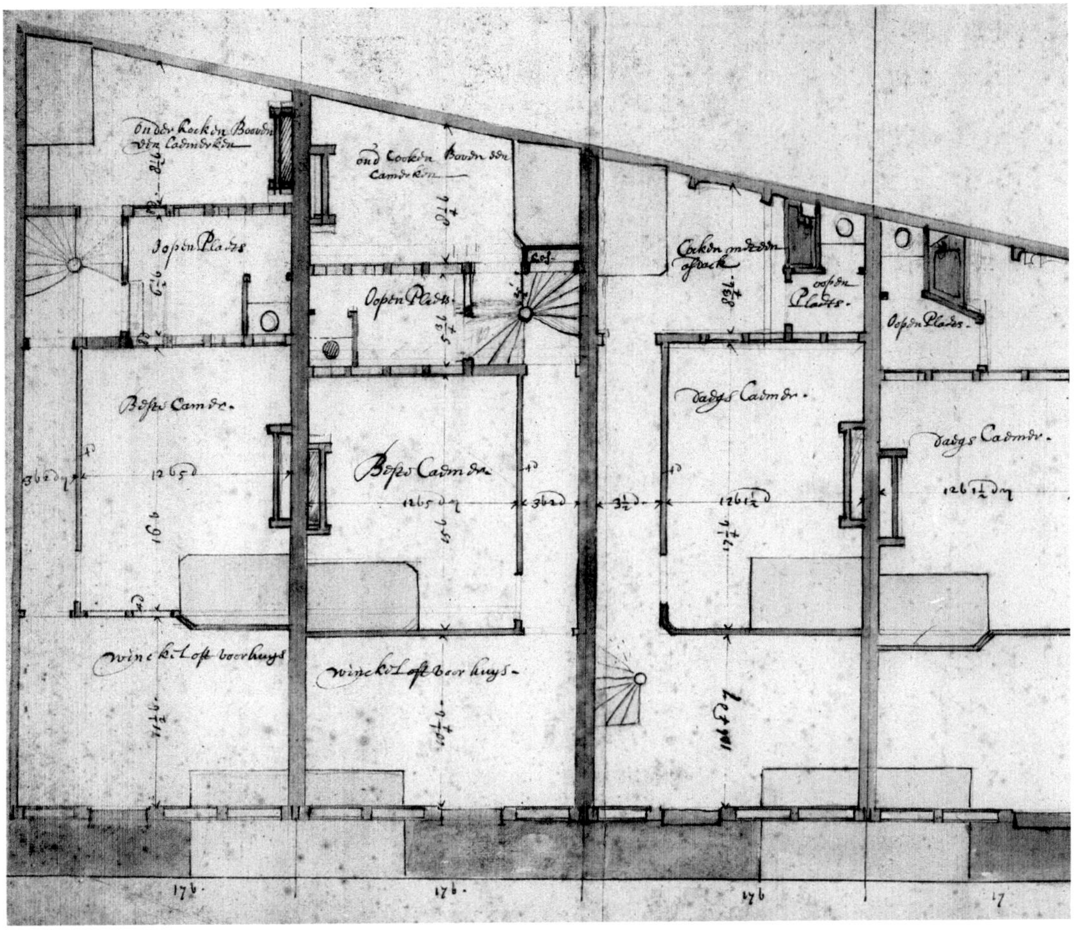

Figure 4.16: Design by Philip Vingboons for shop premises on St Luciensteeg, 1652.

an attempt to bring the merchandise for sale to the attention of potential buyers as strikingly as possible, in broad daylight. What is more, a canopy was almost indispensable, given that it protected the merchandise and customers from rain and bright sunlight. The *voorhuis* also maintained its key role as a shop space and workshop. For this reason, side rooms were rarely added, and the timbered lower façade, and the ample light that it let in, remained popular.

The traditional character of the shop in Amsterdam is nicely illustrated by a design produced in 1652 for the construction of a number of houses with commercial functions on St Luciënsteeg. The design was for a project, ultimately never realized, by the *Burgerweeshuis* (city orphanage) and the city government to widen the alleyway and replace the existing houses with new ones.[45] They commissioned the architect Philips Vingboons (1607–1678), a well-known architect who was popular with Amsterdam's elite at that time. He designed a row of eight simple rental houses, a number of which were suitable for use as shops. As it is usually only the drawings for more prestigious

45 Ottenheym, *Philip Vingboons*, pp. 84–86 and also Zantkuijl, *Bouwen in Amsterdam*, pp. 341–343.

Figure 4.17: Design by Philip Vingboons for shop premises on St Luciensteeg, 1652.

houses and public buildings that survive, Vingboons' design is of great significance. In his design, only the larger corner house with an entrance on Kalverstraat has a side room as a well as a *voorhuis*. The three adjacent houses on St Luciënsteeg are so small that they could not have been intended for commercial use, but for the next pair, Vingboons drew a 'shop or *voorhuis*' on the street side, spanning the full width of the house (Figure 4.16). Behind this, off the corridor to the *achterhuis*, lay the living room or parlour (*beste caemer*). From the appearance of the façade, we can see that the houses had the timbered lower façade that was so suited to commercial purposes, and on the front step we can see a *pothuis* and benches (Figure 4.17). Vingboons' design shows how an experienced and highly esteemed architect imagined residential-commercial houses at that time, and it is clear that this did not deviate from what had already been commonplace in Amsterdam for many years.

Shop interiors

With Vingboons' design, we have been able to step from the exterior into the interior. Architects' plans and façade drawings can tell us little about the interiors of shops, however. For this, we need to tap other sources. In addition to the few pictures that we have of shop interiors, I largely relied on estate inventories, *boedelinventarissen* in Dutch. This is a term that was already used several times above, but what exactly are estate inventories?

Estate inventories are lists of goods that were found in a particular house.[46] Lists such as these were drawn up when one or both parents died, leaving minor children. They served as documentation for the *weeskamer* (orphans' board), a municipal institution that represented

46 For estate inventories, see Wijsenbeek-Olthuis, *Achter de gevels van Delft*, chapter III, and Muizelaar and Phillips, *Picturing Men and Women*, appendix.

the interests of minor orphans as well as adult orphans who, due to a physical or mental disability, were considered incapable of acting for their own interests. The main purpose of management of the estate by the *weeskamer* was to prevent family members and guardians from enriching themselves illegally. In addition, estate inventories were also drawn up upon bankruptcy. In this case, they served as documentation for a different municipal institution, the *desolate boedelkamer* (insolvent estates board), which oversaw the interests of creditors.[47]

Estate inventories play an important role in this study because the clerks who drew up the lists often did so room by room, allowing us to discover what was in all of the rooms in a house, to the extent that this was movable property. Immovable property that formed part of the building was not included in the estate inventory but was sometimes mentioned in passing. This immediately reveals the limitation of this source: immovable parts of the shop interior, such as certain shelves and racks, were not listed in the descriptions. The inventories also leave us in the dark regarding what, precisely, these fixed elements would have looked like; were they decorated, and if so, how, and with what? The descriptions of shopkeepers' estates in the archive of the *desolate boedelkamer* also list the shop's stock, of course, but sometimes this information is missing, perhaps because the shop had ceased to exist long before it went bankrupt, or because a bankrupt or creditor had been able to remove the goods from the estate. The present study did consider estates such as these, but preference was given to estates where the presence of a stock inventory indicated that a business had recently been in operation.[48]

Drawing on pictures and estate inventories, what were the striking elements of shop interiors in the seventeenth century? In the first place, there was the counter (*toonbank*), also described in the sources as a *toombanck* or *tooghbanck*. In today's world of supermarkets, department stores and self-service stores, the old-fashioned counter has lost its original function, but in the seventeenth century it was still the place where shop wares were shown, something to which I shall return below. Like the shops discussed above, these counters came in a wide range of sizes and appearances. Some were small and extremely simple. Jan Vermeulen, who ran a shop in a basement on Vissteeg until his bankruptcy in 1646, had a 'suijckerkiste toonbanck': a counter, in other words, consisting or made out of an old sugar crate (*suikerkist*).[49] He was certainly not the only one to make do in such fashion, but even when the sources simply refer to a *toonbanck* or *toonbanckie*, it is striking that some were valued for meagre amounts. This implies that they were probably roughly built items, worth little more than the wood that constituted them. We can see a simple counter such as this on a seventeenth-century stone plaque (*gevelsteen*) showing the interior of a sugar shop (Figure 4.18). The *lompen* referred to in the caption are the cones of refined sugar, packed in blue paper, which were also known as *suikerbroden* or 'sugar loaves'.

At the other end of the spectrum were the counters that were clearly made at a furniture-maker's workshop. In an anonymous painting

47 More information on the *desolate boedelkamer* in Oldewelt, 'Twee eeuwen Amsterdamse faillissementen'.

48 In addition to estates in the archives of the *desolate boedelkamer*, use has been made of estates in the notarial archives. These have been selected from Van Dillen, *Bronnen bedrijfsleven en gildewezen*, II; Van Dillen, *Bronnen bedrijfsleven en gildewezen*, III, and from the index to the notarial archives for the years 1701–1710 (SAA, archief Hart (30452), Collectie S, inv. nrs. 737–739).

49 SAA, Desolate boedelkamer, inv. nr. 572, fol. 67v-68 (13 June 1646).

Figure 4.18: Plaque with interior of a sugar shop, seventeenth century.

of a pharmacist's shop from the mid-seventeenth century, we see the pharmacist, his wife and a shop assistant (Figure 4.19). The pharmacist himself is standing in front of the counter, which is made of an expensive type of wood, has beautiful panels and is decorated with ebony inlay.[50] Sometimes we also come across walnut-wood counters in the estates, but most items were made of pine. More impact was then achieved by painting the whole thing; indeed, the bankruptcy estate of Jacob van Mollem lists a 'large painted pinewood counter'.[51]

The estate descriptions never include the dimensions of the counters, so we have to go by what we can see in the pictures. In these, many of the counters are around 1.5 to 2.5 metres long, which is consistent with the fact that there were often two counters in a shop.[52] But we also come across much larger counters. Looking at Salomon de Bray's drawing of a book and art dealer's shop, made around 1628, it is clear that the counter ran around the walls with books and art (Figure 4.20), providing ample room for a number of clients to peruse the merchandise. The counter also seems to have been used as a space for displaying books and prints to the public.[53]

50 I would like to thank the Swedish *Apotekarsocieteten* for allowing me to reproduce the painting in this book.

51 SAA, Desolate boedelkamer, inv. nr. 572, fol. 212v-215v (14 November 1646).

52 For example SAA, Desolate boedelkamer, inv. nr. 571, fol. 80v-83v (18 July 1645); fol. 128v-133v (29 November 1645); fol. 194v-204 (16 March 1646); inv. nr. 572, fol. 61v-67 (12–13 June 1646), and inv. nr. 621, fol. 51v-54v (9 May 1695).

53 The picture to be discussed below of the fabric shop 'De blauwen Haen' run by Anthoni van Helsdingen shows a similar counter.

Figure 4.19: Interior of a pharmacy around the mid-seventeenth century.

Figure 4.20: Interior of a bookshop, ca. 1628.

Figure 4.21: Interior of a bookshop, ca. 1661.

A long counter like this one must have stood in the shop run by Daniël le Caillet, a candle-maker and chandler on Kalverstraat. In 1628, when the heads of the chandlers' guild and their assistants wanted to take a bunch of candles weighing around two pounds without paying, Le Caillet made every attempt to climb over his '*tooghbanck*'. He was knocked back repeatedly by the guild heads, and when several of them walked out of the door with the candles whilst others blocked his exit, he sprang out of the window 'to get his candles back'. His efforts were to no avail, so he sought a few witnesses to give an account of the event before a notary.[54] Although we do not know how the story ended, it is clear that the counter must have run at least the full length of the wall, and that Le Caillet could not simply step around it.

The counter was not always a separate piece of furniture that could be listed in the estate inventory by a clerk. The printer's mark of the bookseller and publisher Johannes van Den Bergh shows the interior of a bookshop in Amsterdam around the mid-seventeenth century, and here we can see that the counter was integrated, as it were, into the wall cabinet on the right (Figure 4.21).[55] The section with the counter is closed off, but it probably provided enough space for stock, or what the clerks described in the sources as *rommelingh* (junk) and did not take the trouble to specify further. The fact that counters were indeed used for storage is shown by the bankrupt estate of Jan van Lennep, a silk merchant on Warmoesstraat.[56] Under the counter were three drawer units, each containing five drawers full of silk stockings, ribbons, sewing silk and other items. It was shop goods such as these that the estate inventory was all about; the fact that they were kept in drawers under the counter was only noted in passing. When Christina Mijnders, the widow of Harmanus Grim, left minor children upon her death, a very extensive inventory was made of the shop on Warmoesstraat, 'daar de Oijevaar en de kant-winkel uithangt [under the sign of the stork and the lace-shop]'. The shop was found to contain, among other things, a 'large counter with chests', two walnut-wood counters with drawers, and yet

Figure 4.22: Shop with table and cloth, second half of the seventeenth century.

54 Van Dillen, *Bronnen bedrijfsleven en gildewezen*, II, nr. 1144. In this shop, too, the windows either seem to have been open or there were no windows at all in the lower part of the façade.

55 Van Zanten, *Spiegel der gedenckweerdighste wonderen*.

56 SAA, Desolate boedelkamer, inv. nr. 624, fol. 218v-219v (November 1701).

Figure 4.23: The tinsmith, end of the seventeenth century.

another 'large counter with sixteen drawers'.[57] A great deal could be stowed away under such counters; one even contained no fewer than 9,222 yards (more than 6,300 metres) of lace. In addition to the two counters, widow Grim's

57 SAA, Notarieel Archief, inv. nr. 5628, fol. 977–1011 (30 November 1706). Information about this house, the current number 193, is also included in Kam, *Waar was dat huis in de Warmoesstraat*, pp. 420–421.

Figure 4.24: Plaque with the interior of a stockings shop in Amsterdam, seventeenth century.

voorhuis also featured a table with a top made of Swedish stone. We also come across tables in shops in other inventories, too. On the title page of *De Amsterdammer apotheek* from 1683, we see a table draped with a cloth (Figure 4.22).[58] Counters were not usually covered with cloths, but an exception was the counter of the fabric shop run by Deonijs de Glabays on Oudezijds Voorburgwal, 'daer de Seepton boven de deur staet [under the sign of the soap barrel]'. Not only did a green curtain hang in the windows, there was also a green cloth on the counter.[59]

Aside from the counter, another particularly striking element of the shop interior that we encounter in pictures is that of the shelves and cabinets where the shop goods were stored. It is hardly surprising that these were rarely listed in estate inventories from the 1640s. The few depictions that we have from the first half of the century show that shop fixtures were still extremely simple in this period. Standing against the walls were shelves made of boards, upon which stood the packages, boxes, bottles and other containers that were used for storing the shop wares. As these shelves formed part of the immovable property, they were not included in the estate or registered. The simple shelves are clearly visible in the interiors of the bookshops, pharmacy and sugar shop shown above. The beautiful plaque of the 'Groninger kousse winkel [Groningen stockings shop]' and the tinsmith's shop from *Het menselyk bedrijf* by Jan and Caspar Luiken also show the simple shelves that evidently sufficed for many years (Figures 4.23 and 4.24).

By the end of the century, we come across an increasing number of references to *houten winkeltjes*, or 'little wooden shops'. I puzzled over this until it was suggested I consult the *Proeve van taal- en dichtkunde* by Huydecoper and Van Lelyveld, published in 1791. The entry on *winkel* (shop) contains the following: '*Houses* where something is offered for sale, more specifically

58 *Pharmacopaea Amstelredamensis*, and SAA, Desolate boedelkamer, inv. nr. 570, fol. 80-84v (February 1644).
59 SAA, Desolate boedelkamer, inv. nr. 572, fol. 104-111v (July 1646).

the *Voorhuis* or *Vertrek*, where the wares are kept; most specifically, the storage provided by boards, etc., against the wall, on which lie goods for sale.' [italics in original][60] It is this 'storage provided by boards, etc., against the wall' that is implied by the term *houten winkeltjes* in the estate inventories, and the fact that they were recorded and valued at all means that they were counted as movable property. In other words, they were separate pieces of furniture and no longer the built-in shelves from the first half of the century. It is no simple matter to identify when this change occurred. In by far the majority of cases, the *winkeltje* is referred to in one and the same breath as the counter ('*een houte winckel & toonbanck*' or '*toonbanck met 't winkeltie*') and also valued with the counter. This suggests that the shop furniture was increasingly being seen as a whole. This change was evidently quite general, because in the inventories I studied, the value of the combination varied from three to forty guilders. When the counter and the *houten winkel* were valued separately, the latter was worth significantly more. In Jan de Waert's *voorhuis* on Leidsestraat, for example, the two counters were valued together at six guilders, and the '*houte winckel*' at sixteen guilders; and one shop on Kalverstraat contained a counter valued at three guilders and a '*houten winkel*' at 25 guilders.[61] From this, it is also clear that these were proper pieces of furniture and not simply some loose planks.[62]

I believe that I can make out a simple variant of what is described in the sources as a *houten winkel* on the trade card of the Amsterdam fabric shop Jacob & George Roeters from around 1697 (Figure 4.25). Cards such as these did not usually give a realistic impression of the shop interior because they were meant to show different aspects of the business. For example, the weaving mill that we see in the background was certainly not in the same building as the shop.[63] The depiction of the separate elements in the interior is much more realistic, however, and this is probably also true of the simple wooden cabinets standing against the walls. On a trade card produced by Jan Luiken for the widow Christiaan Beuningen & sons on Herengracht, dating from the last decade of the seventeenth century, we see a more stylish cabinet (Figure 4.26). The top is covered with a plank that is wider than the side panels, and the lower section has been closed off with panel doors. The latter were useful when exposure to daylight and dust threatened the quality and value of the merchandise.

Open shelves were often protected, too. On the print of 'De Blauwen Haen [the blue cock]', we see curtains on the left-hand side of the wall cabinet (Figure 4.27).[64] As well as protection, these curtains may also have formed part of a sales ritual, whereby the theatrical opening of the curtains and display of the merchandise was intended to spark the consumer's desire. The protection of merchandise is also clearly evident on a plaque that was found in the cistern of a building on Rozenstraat in the 1930s

60 '*Huizen* daar iets te koop is, bepaalder 't *Voorhuis* of 't *Vertrek*, waarin de waaren zich bevinden; allerbepaaldst de opslag van planken enz. tegen den wand opgericht, in welken de koopgoederen liggen' (Huydecoper, *Proeve van taal- en dichtkunde*, p. 220). I am indebted to Mrs. A. Gosliga for drawing my attention to this publication.
61 SAA, Desolate boedelkamer, inv. nr. 622, fol. 82v-90 (15 October 1698) and fol. 90v-92 (28 October 1698).
62 This is also evident from SAA, Notarieel archief, inv. nr. 5559 (29 March 1705).
63 For a critical assessment of these trade cards, see Colenbrander, 'Zolang de weefkunst bloeit', p. 161.
64 Curtains are also mentioned in the lace and fabric shop of the widow Harmanus Grim in Warmoesstraat (SAA, Notarieel archief, inv. nr. 5628, fol. 993–994 [30 November 1706]).

Figure 4.25: Trade card of the firm Jacob and George Roeters, end of the seventeenth century.

(Figure 4.28). The beautiful seventeenth-century stone plaque shows the interior of a ribbon shop, complete with a counter and a wall cabinet that can be closed with a shutter that is rolled up to the ceiling. Behind the counter and in front of the cabinet of wares, the shopkeeper, yardstick in hand, is ready to measure out the desired quantity.[65] Shopkeepers also protected precious textiles by storing them on the shelves packed in dark wrapping paper and by only getting them out during the process of showing, inspecting, negotiating and selling.[66]

65 Boers, 'Amsterdamse gevelstenen'.

66 See the picture of a shop interior by Matthys Naiveu to be discussed below. Dark wrapping paper is regularly found in shop inventories.

Packaging is the third element that was prominent in seventeenth-century shop interiors. As a rule, the merchandise did not lie within hand's reach but was fetched, shown and preferably also sold from the container by the shopkeeper or personnel. Lying on the shelves, in the cabinets and in the drawers were often dozens of boxes, packages, crates, casks, bottles, sacks and barrels—the list goes on. Larger shops, particularly those selling groceries or dry goods, sometimes kept an incredible variety of containers. Take, for example, the insolvent estate of the grocer on the corner of Oude Nieuwstraat, 'daer de Stadt Lubeck uythangt [under the sign of the Town of Lubeck]'. On 20 January 1646, in the *voorhuis* where the shop was run, the clerk found the following packaging materials: 24

Figure 4.26: Trade card of the firm Van Beuningen, end of the seventeenth century.

square boxes, 28 round boxes, 10 tin canisters, 80 white pots, 36 white casks, 7 'normal' casks, 11 vats, 2 barrels, 2 tubs, 2 sacks, 1 bag, 1 drawer, 20 wooden storage bins, 1 pine crate, 4 pewter jugs, 1 oil basin, bundles of torches, liquorice and wormwood, and finally, 41 bunches of poppy-heads. But this was not all, because in the parlour he found another 31 boxes, 24 casks, 16 pots and 9 bottles, and in the basement 15 tubs, 26 bottles, 4 barrels, 3 casks, 1 sack and 1 iron pot containing sulphur.[67] A painting

67 SAA, Desolate boedelkamer, inv. nr. 571, fol. 157v-164 (20 January 1646). For comparable shop inventories, see ibidem fol. 139v-144 (20–21 December 1645), and inv. nr. 622, fol. 103-108v (22 December 1698).

Figure 4.27: Trade card of Anthonie van Helsdingen, seventeenth century.

by Willem van Mieris gives a good impression of the interior of a grocer's shop (Figure 4.29). Although the stone archway bears no relation to reality, the shop would have done, with its shelves, boxes, canisters, sieves, casks, baskets, barrels and bags. In the background, we see the stepladder used by the shopkeeper to reach the merchandise at the top. On a plaque dating from 1660, we see a tin box (with a soldered joint), like the one listed in the estate inventory of the grocery on Oude Nieuwstraat (Figure 4.30).

Shops that sold durable goods such as fabric, lace and ribbons had a narrower range of containers, but here, too, we come across many boxes and packages. The boxes are clearly visible on the shelves and in the foreground of the trade card of the shop of the widow Christiaan

Figure 4.28: Plaque showing interior of Amsterdam ribbon shop, seventeenth century.

Beuningen & sons (Figure 4.26). Boxes also formed part of the insolvent estate of Eduwijn Sandtvoordt, a former *pluimecier* (feather seller) on Vijgendam, who had left without notice before the inventory of his possessions was drawn up in December 1645. As a *pluimecier*, Sandtvoordt prepared plant-based plumes and probably also bird feathers, which were used to decorate hats and other headgear. The *voorhuis* contained simple wooden shelves that were not listed in the inventory and no fewer than 48 large boxes, each containing from several dozen to more than 100 feathers or 200–300 feather points. Elsewhere in the house, there were yet more boxes and crates of feathers. And the shop on Nieuwezijds Voorburgwal known as 'd'Stadt Venloo [under the sign of the Town of Venloo]', run by Anna Rumswinkel, a shopkeeper selling lace, fabric and fashion accessories, was found to contain 52 wooden shop-boxes in March 1646.[68] In a certain class of shop, these boxes would also have looked attractive; one regularly comes across painted boxes or cupboards in the inventories.[69] At Eduwijn Sandtvoordt's shop, the 'rough pine crate' containing feathers was not kept in the *voorhuis* but in the back room. From what are often very detailed descriptions of shop goods in the estate lists, it can be inferred that the numerous boxes, drawers, barrels, compartments, packages, crates and other storage containers were also used to create order in the shop. Related articles were often kept together, and

68 SAA, Desolate boedelkamer, inv. nr. 571, fol. 128v-133v (29 November 1645) for the Sandtvoordt shop and ibidem fol. 194v-204 (16 March 1646) for the shop run by Anna Rumswinkel.

69 This was for example the case in a shop on Geldersekade (SAA, Desolate boedelkamer, inv. nr. 622, fol. 73v-75 [26 August 1698]).

Figure 4.29: Interior of a grocer's store, 1717.

this allowed the shopkeeper and staff to show customers different models and qualities of a product without too much searching.

In most shops, the estate was not limited to the shop's wares, the counter, the cabinets and the containers and packaging. The other things that a shop contained might best be discussed with reference to a painting by Matthys Naiveu (1647–1726), a painter from Leiden who spent much of his working life in Amsterdam. The painting is a detailed rendering of a gold brocade shop (in Amsterdam?) from the upper

Figure 4.30: Plaque with a tin box, 1660.

Figure 4.31: Interior of a gold brocade shop, 1709.

end of the market (Figure 4.31). The lower edge is signed and dated 1709.[70] Many of the objects in the shop also feature in seventeenth-century estate descriptions, which justifies the use of this picture in this chapter.[71] Note how the interior of the shop echoes the expensive gold brocade that was sold there and the taste of the affluent clientele. A great deal of attention has been paid to the interior. The wall units are decorated with pilasters, for example, and the moulding and the capitals are golden. The purple-brown tone of the wall units is repeated in the doorframes and window frames, and green panels in the cabinet doors provide an accent of colour. The use of colour in the shop thereby reflected the colours that were popular in people's homes at that time.[72] On the cabinet, we see two bronze vases and a bronze bust. In 1698, the porcelain shop run by Hendrick te Water in Kalverstraat also featured two bronze vases standing on a cabinet, and this shop also targeted a wealthy clientele.[73] In Naiveu's painting, skeins of silk lie in the wall units, and the costly fabrics in the cabinet are wrapped in dark wrapping paper.

In front of the wall units we can see an oak counter, and on the left, fixed to the window frame, there is an iron bracket with scales for weighing merchandise. On the windowsill, we see an accompanying copper weighing pan. Scales in kind and measures, and the weighing pans and weights that went with them, were present in almost every shop estate. In shops selling fabric and fashion accessories, there was often one or several pairs of scales with copper weighing pans, and at most several dozen pounds of copper or iron weights. But at one shop on Nieuwendijk, in addition to four iron scales with copper weighing pans, the shopkeeper or wholesaler trading in colonial wares also had a 'large iron beam with two wooden weighing pans' and no fewer than 1,200 pounds of iron weights.[74] To the right of the counter in the painting, we see a chair upholstered in leather, something that we often encounter in inventories; they tend to be described as 'Spanish leather chairs'. In the fabric shop of Juriaen Robbertse on Leidsestraat in 1695, for example, there were also two cheap rush-bottomed chairs and three leather chair-cushions.[75] Rush-bottomed chairs and *driestallen*—three-legged chairs—were regularly recorded by clerks, and chair cushions were not an exception either. Finally, our attention is caught by the birdcage in Naiveu's painting. Such cages cropped up in shop inventories throughout the seventeenth century. They were present in small, simple shops selling foodstuffs and in large, distinguished emporia selling durable goods on the main shopping thoroughfares. One baker had a cage with three canaries hanging in his shop, another a cage with two turtle doves, and in Christina Mijnders' luxurious lace shop on Warmoesstraat, a 'tin parrot cage' was hung.[76] In those days, the cheeping and cooing of canaries and turtle doves or a talking parrot were a means of enticing customers. People's attention would also have been caught by a parrot's colourful and exotic appearance.[77]

70 A picture and description of the painting is also in Pijzel-Dommisse, '1700–1750', p. 207.

71 This is not to say, of course, that the painting is an accurate reproduction of a shop interior that existed at the time.

72 Pijzel-Dommisse, '1700–1750', pp. 194–195.

73 SAA, Desolate boedelkamer, inv. nr. 622, fol. 82v-90 (15 October 1698).

74 SAA, Desolate boedelkamer, inv. nr. 570, fol. 1-10v (7 November 1643).

75 SAA, Desolate boedelkamer, inv. nr. 621, fol. 57v-62 (29 June 1695).

76 SAA, Desolate boedelkamer, inv. nr. 572, fol. 199v-202 (8 November 1646); ibidem, inv. nr. 621, fol. 43–44 (20 April 1695), and SAA, Notarieel archief, inv. nr. 5628, fol. 997 (30 November 1706).

77 Birdcages were also found in shops in Antwerp and Middelburg and therefore appear to have been

One item that was not depicted by Naiveu but that was regularly listed in shop inventories is *soldertjes* or *sitsoldertjes*. Those were the wooden platforms that were meant to protect the shopkeeper somewhat from rising cold in the unheated *voorhuis* in winter. The fact that they are sometimes mentioned in the same breath as the counter suggests that they lay behind the counter, where the shopkeeper would have spent much of his day. Nor can we see mirrors in the visible part of Naiveu's shop interior. Naturally, these would have hung in shops where the client wanted to see the effect of a garment, headpiece or accessory prior to purchase. Thus, there was one hanging at the *pluimecier* on Vijgendam, and one at Juriaen Robbertse's fabric shop on Leidsestraat, but we do not find them in grocery or dry-goods stores. At the end of the seventeenth century, it was much more common to have a mirror in the shop, and they also hung in porcelain shops and even at a few tobacconists. The opposite seems to have been the case with paintings. These did not always hang in shops, by any means, but we encounter them more often in the 1640s than in the 1690s.[78]

The shop painted by Naiveu had evidently spread beyond the traditional *voorhuis*. On the right, there is an upstairs room reached by a little flight of steps, and along the wall we see simple wooden shelves stacked with fabrics. This upstairs room probably served as a storage area from which fabrics were brought out to show to customers, but we cannot know for sure. When Christina Mijnders, the widow of Harmanus Grim, died in November 1706, an estate inventory was drawn up.[79] As the shop had already been in operation for many years, the inventory gives a good impression of a large lace and fabric shop on Warmoesstraat at the end of the seventeenth century. The shop was indeed large, as it covered three separate rooms: the *voorhuis*, the hall or shop room, and the upstairs room or large front parlour.[80] Each of these rooms contained cabinets, large quantities of merchandise and a counter. The hall almost exclusively contained lace, and lace and (linen) fabrics were also kept in the *voorhuis* and upstairs parlour. According to the description of the estate, the hall had shelves on both sides, '*met der zelven schuyven*': probably shutters or doors to protect the contents. There were paintings on the walls, and there was a desk and chairs.

The upstairs parlour or large parlour contained a considerable quantity of linen and a large counter with sixteen drawers in which lace was stored. Nevertheless, this room seems to have had a more private atmosphere than the others. There was a small tea table, for instance, and the clerk noted the presence of porcelain. In addition to paintings, a large mirror with a black frame hung on the wall, and the room contained four armchairs, an uncovered chair and two couches with mattresses. Merchandise was probably stored in an oak cabinet as well as the counter, and a round birdcage made of braided copper hung from the ceiling.

a usual shop accessory during this period (Van Damme, *Verleiden en verkopen*, p. 144 and table 3.1, and De Graaf and Polderman, *D' Guld Waerrelt*, pp. 252 and 259).

78 Blondé and Van Damme ('The Shop, the Home, and the Retail Revolution', p. 344 ff.) interpret the disappearance of paintings from shops in Antwerp as an indication that commercial space and living space were separated more strictly than before, all the more so because no other objects seem to have replaced them in Antwerp. In Amsterdam, on the other hand, the number of mirrors seems to have increased.

79 SAA, Notarieel archief, inv. nr. 5628, fol. 977–1011 (30 November 1706).

80 The latter may be comparable to the upstairs room in the Naiveu painting.

In addition to the counter, there was also a walnut tabletop on trestles. This room was where the widow kept the shop's cash in an iron chest and ebony cabinet, out of the direct reach of the *voorhuis*. Unlike the hall or the *voorhuis*, the room also had a fireplace and could be heated in winter. It is quite possible that distinguished customers were invited here to inspect the goods and make their selection in peace.[81]

The commotion of the shop would have been manifest in the *voorhuis,* the entrance to the shop. This was also where the relationship with the street was most direct, and there was a display case made of glass and wood in the window. There were wooden cabinets (*houten winkels*) with accompanying drawers on both sides of the *voorhuis*. There were also two handsome walnut-wood counters and the above-mentioned table with a top made of Swedish stone. A ladder provided access to the upper sections of the wall cabinets. There were no paintings, but there was a mirror with a black frame and an ebony birdcage. There were also chairs—three in total, with cushions—but unlike in the large parlour, they were not armchairs.

It is clear that this was a large and professionally equipped shop. Given the nature of the merchandise and the intended clientele, the rooms were furnished and had chairs, but there was otherwise a clear separation between the shop space and the private rooms elsewhere in the house on Warmoesstraat. This separation between the shop and private rooms was not yet universal in the seventeenth century. In the 1640s, we sometimes come across an alcove bed and bed linen in a shop *voorhuis*. Take the house belonging to Franchoys van Bercken, for example, a seller of Nuremberg wares on Oudebrugsteeg. This house was literally packed to the rafters with merchandise, and it must have been particularly difficult to get through the *voorhuis*. It is telling that the estate inventory was drawn up on 6 July 1644 'and on the following days'. Nevertheless, in addition to all the goods, the *voorhuis* also contained a bed (i.e., a mattress), two cushions, a bolster, three blankets and two sheets, and an alcove bed was evidently present and in use.[82] We still come across such cases at the end of the century. When Hendrick te Water went bankrupt in 1698, for example, he was running a shop selling tea and porcelain in Kalverstraat, and like the lace shop on Warmoesstraat, his shop contained several rooms. It remains unclear whether the living room was used exclusively for storage. In addition to 165 pounds of tea, it contained a large quantity of porcelain. There was no counter, however. There was likewise a large quantity of porcelain divided over five cupboards in the *voorhuis*, and there was also a counter, four scales with weighing pans, a small mirror, two chairs with cushions and also a mattress, bolster, cushions, blankets and sheets. Here, too, there was evidently an alcove bed in the shop, and to judge from the bedding, it was still in use.[83] Quite clearly, the stricter separation between reception rooms and private rooms that one increasingly finds in affluent households in the second half of the seventeenth century, and that we also saw in the lace shop on Warmoesstraat, did not apply in Te Water's case.[84]

Given our focus on large shops on important shopping streets, we should not forget that the majority of shops in Amsterdam would have

81 For these special retail spaces in Belgian cities, see Van Damme, *Verleiden en verkopen*, p. 144 ff.

82 SAA, Desolate boedelkamer, inv. nr. 570, fol. 253-283v (6 July 1644), and for beds/mattresses Fock, '1600–1650', p. 40.

83 SAA, Desolate boedelkamer, inv. nr. 622, fol. 82v-90 (15 October 1698).

84 Fock, '1650–1700', pp. 86–87 for residential houses.

had much plainer interiors. One example is the simple cheese shop run by Barent Harmanse and Geesje Wouters on Marken in the Jewish Quarter. The *voorhuis* contained no more than a counter and wooden shelves, 22 Edam cheeses, ten Leiden cumin cheeses, two green cheeses and two wooden scales with twelve pounds in weights.[85] Even a relatively pricey beverage such as tea could sometimes be sold from extremely simple shops such as these. In the *voorhuis* of Lambertus Brouwer on Nes, on the corner with Halsteeg, the clerk found few items: six empty tin tea caddies, a counter and wooden shelves, a small set of scales with half a pound of weights, a wooden drawer for storing the weights, an 'iron' (perhaps an iron balance?) and some 'junk' (*rommeling*). A wooden tea caddy functioned as a shop sign in the window.[86]

When asking how shop interiors changed in the course of the seventeenth century, it is important to recognize that at the lower end of the market, in marginal shops such as those described above, there were very few changes at all. It is also obvious that shops selling daily necessities would not have changed significantly. For suppliers of durable and luxury goods, the situation was more complicated. Around 1700, tea was also sold in poorer shops, but those that focused on selling chic goods to a wealthy and status-conscious clientele could not afford to ignore trends in home furnishings, and interiors had to keep up with the fashions of the time.

Indeed, such adjustments do appear to have been made. As far as we can ascertain, shops selling durable and luxury items in the first half of the seventeenth century were also furnished exceptionally plainly, with simple wooden racks and shelves for storing merchandise. In the book trade, little seems to have changed, but suppliers of fashionable items such as fabric and fashion accessories did start to decorate their shops more ostentatiously. Simple shelves were replaced by wall-mounted cabinets, and the painting by Naiveu shows us that the colour, design and decoration of the shop interior were considered very important. The golden accents on the wall cabinet in the gold brocade shop would have reflected the elite's taste for gilded carving and striking ornamentation in residential interiors in the second half of the seventeenth century. In shops, just as in people's homes, mirrors also played a more significant role in the interior than in the past, whilst paintings became less popular.[87] In the lace shop on Warmoesstraat, we can discern steps in the direction of a more large-scale, professional retail operation. No fewer than three rooms in the house had been made suitable for shop sales, and these rooms no longer contained beds. Just like the residential homes belonging to Amsterdam's bourgeoisie, a distinction was made between reception rooms and private rooms, but this did not rule out a personal approach.[88] On the contrary, the presence of multiple retail spaces made it possible

85 The couple lived in the only other room in the house and there, too, the interior was extremely austere, not to say shabby (SAA, Desolate boedelkamer, inv. nr. 622, fol. 55v-56 (20 January 1698)).
86 SAA, Notarieel archief, inv. nr. 6973, fol. 70–72. More estates of marginal shops in SAA, Notarieel archief, inv. nr. 5559, fol. 937 and fol. 1847–1848; inv. nr. 5973, fol. 151–154; inv. nr. 6973, fol. 1059–1060, and inv. nr. 6974, fol. 347–349.
87 In Amsterdam, the changes to the shop interior were therefore more radical than Blondé and Van Damme established for Antwerp (Blondé and Van Damme, 'The Shop, the Home, and the Retail Revolution') but not as radical as in Paris and London in the eighteenth century (Coquery, 'The Language of Success', and Walsh, 'Shop Design'). For paintings and mirrors in Dutch residential houses, see Fock, '1650–1700', pp. 98–99.
88 Fock, '1650–1700', pp. 84–88.

to invite some clients to examine, discuss and negotiate the price of wares beyond the hustle and bustle of the *voorhuis*.

Buying and selling

The process of displaying, examining, inspecting and negotiating is the final theme that we shall address in this chapter. As we have already seen, shop goods were usually packaged and stored in boxes and cupboards, and this implies that every customer required personal assistance. In the case of food and other daily necessities, serving the client would not have taken much time, but when durable goods were being purchased, there was more going on. The shopkeeper would have needed to talk to the customer to ascertain their wishes and financial possibilities, so that they could then fetch suitable articles and display them on the counter. From interrogations of people accused of shop theft, we know that this is what happened in practice.[89] During this period, the standard scenario of shop theft was for the thief to enter a shop and get the shopkeeper to display all kinds of wares on the counter, under the pretext of wanting to buy something. For the thief, it was then a question of slipping things under their clothing unnoticed, breaking off the purchase and leaving the shop. Naturally, the whole thing went even more smoothly if the shopkeeper was distracted. For this reason, thieves often operated in small gangs that entered a shop together, or their accomplices would join them in the shop after a few minutes and also act as though they wanted to buy something. In this case, there were soon so many goods on the counter and the shopkeeper was so preoccupied that one of the thieves would be able to slip the wares under their clothing and leave the shop.[90]

How shopkeepers and clients interacted varied enormously, of course. Exchanges in the street and at markets will often have been none too delicate, but incidents also took place at the booths above the Exchange. In 1615, when a customer there wanted to exchange a badly fitting pair of trousers, the shopkeeper refused, despite an earlier promise. When a bystander took the customer's side, Jan Barentsz sprang out of his booth in a rage and stabbed the bystander in the head with a pair of scissors. Violence of this kind was a frequent occurrence. This can be inferred, at least, from the fact that the ordinance on the booths above the Exchange included the prospect of punishment for those who abused, slandered or injured others. If a shopkeeper drew or took hold of a knife in the event of a dispute, he had to pay an additional fine of 20 stivers.[91] Thus, manners in Amsterdam's retail community were not always perfect, something that should perhaps come as no surprise. When, as was the case in seventeenth-century Amsterdam, shops had an open character, there were displays by the windows, the streets were crowded and there was lots of competition between shopkeepers, tension would have built up quickly.

In particular, poaching another's clients would have led to much disagreement and abuse. It is no coincidence that the shopkeepers in the booths above the Exchange were explicitly forbidden to call to, follow or entice customers away from another shopkeeper's

89 I am indebted to Dr. J. Mispelaere of Uppsala Universitet in Sweden for references to shoplifting in the Amsterdam judicial archive.

90 SAA, Rechterlijk archief, Confessieboek 318, fol. 46 (21 January 1668) and the same file for more allegations of shoplifting. See also Van Dillen, *Bronnen bedrijfsleven en gildewezen*, II, nr. 1194.

91 Ibidem, nr. 205 for the stabbing. The ordinance in Noordkerk, *Handvesten ofte privilegiën*, p. 1059, and Dapper, *Historische beschryving der stadt Amsterdam*, p. 452.

counter.[92] Such practices were evidently not uncommon among shopkeepers, and there were clearly also attempts to poach others' clients in the streets. This would have made it impossible to shop in peace, and affluent clients in particular would have wanted to avoid such scenes. Moreover, the fact that the range of fashionable products was growing and changing did not make things any easier for customers. When it came to changing fashions, it was very important to have expert advice, and the shopkeeper was best-informed about recent trends and preferences.[93] Seen from this perspective, it is hardly surprising that some shopkeepers selling chic products such as textiles and fashion accessories embellished their shop interiors and created opportunities to receive customers beyond the commotion of the street and the open *voorhuis*. The trade cards shown above and the painting by Naiveu exude an atmosphere of polite interchange. Regardless of how realistic these images were, this is the image that people wanted to project. The shopkeeper, dressed in a housecoat, displays the wares, praises their quality and offers advice. Nothing in these scenes resembles the retail trade that took place in the street.

Something that did not change—and this remained strikingly consistent throughout the seventeenth century and beyond—was the presence of the lady of the house in the shop. From the estate inventories drawn up upon bankruptcy and death, we know that many shops were run by widows. As women tended to live longer than men in the early modern period, this is hardly surprising. The question is whether they were already active in the shop prior to their husband's death. Research by Van den Heuvel into the situation in a number of Dutch towns in the eighteenth century makes it clear that this was indeed the case. Although we lack accurate data, the scarce data that we do have seem to indicate that this was likewise the case for Amsterdam in the seventeenth century. On the eve of the seventeenth century, for example, Cornelis Plancius referred to the notably large number of women in Amsterdam 'who not unsuccessfully ply their trade in open shops'.[94] And at the end of the century, William Montague wrote of the situation in Amsterdam: ''t is very observable here, more women are found in the shops and business in general than men; they have the conduct of the purse and commerce, and manage it rarely well, they are careful and diligent, capable of affairs, (besides domestick), having an education suitable, and a genius wholly adapted to it'.[95] The independence of Dutch women is a topos in early modern travel accounts, but in the case of Montague, as Van den Heuvel rightly argues, we have a description of the situation specifically in Amsterdam, and it does seem to have been based on his own observations.

There are also other indications. When, in 1596, the furniture makers established a common showroom and salesroom at the cabinet makers' premises on Kalverstraat, sales were put in the hands of two women who were appointed and sworn in by the city. Moreover, a furniture maker's wife was allowed to sell her husband's products.[96] This suggests that retail

92 Noordkerk, *Handvesten ofte privilegiën*, p. 1059, and Dapper, *Historische beschryving der stadt Amsterdam*, p. 453.

93 For Antwerp, see Van Damme, *Verleiden en verkopen*, in particular chapter 4.

94 '[D]ie niet ongeluckelijck met open winckelen [...] haren handel drijven' (Plancius, 'Beschrivinge der loflijcke ende wijtvermaerde coopstede Aemstelredamme', p. 9).

95 Mountague, *The Delights of Holland*, p. 183, and see also Van den Heuvel, *Women and Entrepreneurship*, pp. 41–42.

96 Van Dillen, *Bronnen bedrijfsleven en gildewezen*, I, nr. 889.

sales by women were far from uncommon in Amsterdam. This is also suggested by the fact that in 1605, Anthoinette Cornelis and her sister Petronella Cornelis decided to open a shop selling fabrics and bone lace on the corner of Halsteeg. They pooled together 150 Flemish pounds (900 guilders), and yet another sum of 200 Flemish pounds was invested by Anna van der Heijden and her brother, Heyndrick Bormans. In the contract, we read that the three parties would share the profits and losses in proportion to their investments, but it also reveals that Anthoinette and her sister would operate the shop 'on their own [...] both in the buying and selling'.[97] And in 1634, two more sisters, Janneken and Sara Willems, went to the notary to terminate their eight-year collaboration in a jointly run shop selling fabric and lace. Janneke took over the shop and the stock for 1,400 guilders, and a modern-sounding competition clause stipulated that her sister was forbidden from engaging in the sale of similar products in Amsterdam or the surroundings for the coming one and a half years.[98]

Even when a man was involved in the business, however, women were also present. This is shown by a statement by a silk winder, for example, who bought black silk from a male shop assistant in a shop on Warmoesstraat. In 1629, she reported to the notary that the lady of the house and her mother-in-law had also been present.[99] It is also shown by the images presented above: in almost every image, a woman is (also) standing behind the counter. It is the case for the bookshop drawn by Salomon de Bray around 1628, for the picture of the pharmacy from the mid-seventeenth century, for the plaque with the Groningen stockings shop, the trade card of 'De Blauwen Haen' from the second half of the seventeenth century, and the painting by Naiveu from 1709. All things considered, it seems that William Montague was not exaggerating when he claimed that women played a major role in Amsterdam's shops.

97 '[A]lleen [...] soo in 't incoopen als vercoopen' (Ibidem, nr. 1060).

98 Van Dillen, *Bronnen bedrijfsleven en gildewezen*, III, nr. 100.

99 Van Dillen, *Bronnen bedrijfsleven en gildewezen*, II, nr. 1221.

5. The location of shops in Amsterdam in the mid-eighteenth century

Abstract

The availability of a detailed tax record for 1742 made it possible to establish, with more certainty than before, the location patterns of Amsterdam's early modern retail industry. This chapter also shows that we can usefully draw on location principles formulated in twentieth-century liberal economies when analyzing and explaining early modern location patterns. The reason is that in early modern Amsterdam too, the use of property was subject to the rules of the 'free market'. This does not rule out the influence of the local context. After all, the actual distribution of shops and the range of goods they sold were strongly determined by the urban and socio-spatial structure of the city as it had developed over the preceding centuries.

Keywords: location patterns, modern location theory, accessibility, daily necessities, consumer durables

During the eighteenth century and the first half of the nineteenth century, the period on which we shall focus in the coming chapters, the population of Amsterdam initially grew to between 230,000 and 240,000 inhabitants in 1730. After this, however, population growth stagnated, and in the decades around 1800, there was even a sharp decline in the population. The recovery was slow, and around the middle of the nineteenth century Amsterdam still had no more than 220,000 inhabitants. Throughout this period, the population could thus easily be accommodated in the city as it had developed during the major seventeenth-century expansions. The urban grid—and with it the accessibility of the streets, canals and squares—also remained unchanged. This stable spatial framework forms the background to our study of shops in the period between 1700 and 1850.

In this chapter, we shall focus on the location behaviour of retailers. For the period prior to the seventeenth century, there is only fragmentary source material available for this type of research, but for the year 1742, we have a source that covers a considerable part of Amsterdam's retail landscape. We first examine this source in more detail, after which we map out the distribution of shops. In doing so, it is possible to make a distinction between shops selling daily necessities and those selling durable goods. We then compare the location patterns in Amsterdam with the three forms of accessibility introduced in the first chapter: general, linear and special accessibility. Finally, we reflect on the influence of general location principles and local context on the location behaviour of Amsterdam's retailers and on the spatial patterns that emerged from this.[1]

1 Part of this chapter was also published in Lesger, 'Patterns of Retail Location'.

Lesger, C., *Shopping Spaces and the Urban Landscape in Early Modern Amsterdam, 1550–1850.*
Taylor & Francis Group, 2020
DOI: 10.5117/9789463720625_CH05

Sources and location patterns: A first exploration

The source on which a substantial part of this chapter is based is the *Personele Quotatie* that was collected in the year 1742. Imposed on the whole of Holland, this tax was meant to provide the provincial government with means to meet the financial obligations arising from the principal and interest on a 3-million-guilder loan. The loan had been contracted in relation to the War of the Austrian Succession that broke out in December 1740 and the pressing need to maintain the Republic's defences.[2]

The value of the source for this research lies mainly in the fact that of the 3,757 people with a shop listed in the *Personele Quotisatie* registers of Amsterdam, just ten were described using the general term 'shopkeeper' (*winkelier*). In all other cases, the nature of the shop was also mentioned, and this allows us to make a distinction between providers of daily necessities and shopkeepers who sold durable goods that were purchased less frequently. When drawing up the lists, use was made of the so-called *verpondingregisters*—registers used to administer a provincial tax on real property—and as a result, we also know the fiscal numbers of the houses for this tax. Although house-numbering did not exist in Amsterdam before the French period, we are able to 'translate' this administrative fiscal number into a more or less exact location in a street. The procedure is cumbersome and extremely time-consuming, but I know of no other source from the early modern period that allows one to do this.

There are also some specific problems associated with the source, the most important undoubtedly being its lack of completeness. People with an annual income of less than 600 guilders were exempt from the tax and thus were unfortunately not registered. Elsewhere, I have calculated that around three-quarters of Amsterdam's population thereby remain out of the picture.[3] But that is not to say that three-quarters of Amsterdam's shopkeepers escape our observation as a result. After all, the sizeable lower stratum of society consisted largely of wage-dependents, not shopkeepers. By simultaneously making use of information from the archives of the shopkeepers' guild and the *desolate boedelkamer,* the city board for the financial settlement of bankruptcies, I have nevertheless attempted to give an impression of the part of Amsterdam's retail system that was not included in the register of the *Personele Quotisatie.*

In the theoretical literature, it is argued that shops selling daily necessities show a high degree of dispersion. The source material available for the seventeenth century does not allow us to show effectively whether this high level of dispersion also existed at that time, and even the *Personele Quotisatie* does not offer a complete picture. After all, especially in the poorer neighbourhoods, only some shopkeepers were assessed for this tax. Fortunately, a comparison of the number of bread bakers registered in the *Personele Quotisatie* (451) with a list of members of the bakers' guild in 1688 (412 people) and the number of bakeries in 1800 (391) reveals that almost all bakers were included in the group of Amsterdam's citizens with sufficient income to be eligible for the *Personele Quotisatie* of 1742.[4] In the following, the spatial distribution of bakeries is thus assumed to be

2 The levy is discussed in detail in Oldewelt, *Kohier van de Personeele Quotisatie,* and in Van Nierop, 'Het kohier van de personele quotisatie'.

3 Lesger, 'Stagnatie en stabiliteit', p. 259, table 13.

4 Oldewelt, *Kohier van de Personeele Quotisatie,* Volume 1, p. 12, and Diederiks, *Een stad in verval,* p. 312. According to Wagenaar (*Amsterdam, in zyne opkomst,* Part IV, p. 465), the bakers' guild had over 400 members at the start of the eighteenth century. There are no indications that the number of bread bakers per 1,000 inhabitants in 1742 was much higher or lower than in the other years.

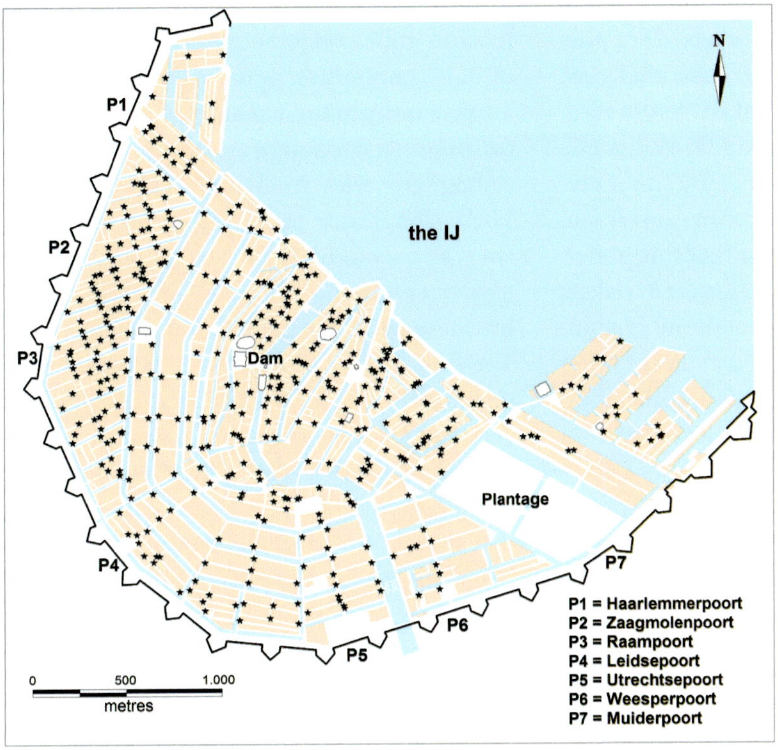

Figure 5.1: Location of bakeries, 1742.

indicative of the distribution of shops selling daily necessities in general.[5]

Where did Amsterdam's bakers practise their profession? One initial indication that their businesses did show a considerable degree of dispersion is the fact that there were bakeries in 226 of the roughly 880 streets in Amsterdam. But we cannot leave it at this, of course. The distribution of almost all of the bakeries across the city has therefore been mapped out in Figure 5.1.[6] In order to interpret the situation correctly, it is important to understand that in the period until around the mid-nineteenth century, when the first bread factories appeared, bread production and bread sales were inextricably linked. The baker and his assistants baked bread at night and began selling early in the morning. The map leaves us in no doubt that bakers' shops showed a high degree of dispersion, meaning that the distance to the consumer was minimized. Evidently, the early modern consumer did not wish to travel large distances to buy a daily necessity such as bread, and the level of demand also made it possible for these shops to be dispersed across the city.[7]

One striking phenomenon is the marked preference of bakers for a location on or nearby a street corner. On the map, we can easily make out this preference in the canal ring, where the

5 A detailed account of Amsterdam bakers and journeymen bakers in the seventeenth century can be found in Kuijpers, *Migrantenstad*, pp. 226–244.

6 Of 438 of the 451 bakeries, I was able to determine the location with sufficient certainty.

7 There was a similar degree of dispersion in New York in 1840 (Pred, *The Spatial Dynamics*, p. 206).

bakers were almost exclusively located on the corners of canals and side streets. This phenomenon was not limited to the canal ring, though. Of the total of 438 bakers whose locations I was able to discover, no fewer than 64 per cent were located on or nearby street corners.[8] From a report on bakeries in Amsterdam published in 1903, it is evident that this preference for corner buildings on the part of bakers persisted into the second half of the nineteenth century. The report also notes that these corner buildings had often been used as bakeries since they were first built.[9] This high degree of continuity in the location of Amsterdam's bakers is, of course, related to the presence of a fixed brick oven (and possibly a specially adapted chimney) in the bakery building, which made it relatively expensive to establish a bakery in a property that had previously been used for a different purpose. The striking preference for corner buildings is not surprising and is consistent with what one would expect on theoretical grounds: corner buildings, especially those that intersect with radials or tangentials, are sought-after locations for retailers because they generate more customers than shops elsewhere in the street, and because they offer the possibility of having display windows on two sides.[10]

In order to shore up the claim that, just as in later times, eighteenth-century suppliers of daily necessities were located in immediate proximity to their customers, I also looked for information about the location of shops selling groceries known as *komenijswaren*. These shops not only sold fat-based wares such as bacon, ham, butter and candles but also beer, groats, beans, pearl barley, flour, brushes, wrapping paper and much more.[11] The *komenij* was thus typically a shop where one purchased daily necessities, making it very suitable for testing the picture sketched above for bakeries against location behaviour in a different sector.

One hundred and eighty-six such grocers (*komenijshouders*) are listed in the *Personele Quotisatie*, but they are just the tip of the proverbial iceberg. This can be inferred from the records of the shopkeepers' guild, to which these grocers were required to belong. By the end of the year 1751, the guild heads must have lost patience with the large numbers of citizens of Amsterdam who were opening shops without joining the guild and paying the admission fee, as they asked the burgomasters' permission to tackle evasion of the rules, which they were granted on 25 January 1752. In the decree issued on the case, it was stated that those who had not yet paid the admission fee of four guilders should do so within six weeks, on penalty of a fine of two guilders in addition to the amount they already owed.[12] The governors of the guild could be satisfied with the outcome of their

8 The distinction between corner houses and adjacent buildings could not always be made.

9 Serrurier et al., *Het bakkersbedrijf te Amsterdam*, p. 3. See also Knotter, *Economische transformatie*, p. 195, and Een-Amsterdammer, *Physiologie van Amsterdam*, p. 27.

10 The question why it was mainly bakers who managed to seize the more attractive (and expensive) corner houses cannot be easily answered. Their relative prosperity among providers of daily necessities may have played a role in this. They were also among the first to settle into new neighbourhoods, and that gave them the chance to seize the best locations (namely those on street corners). For the (family) continuity of baker shops in Brussels, see Burm and De Munck, 'Het broodje gebakken?'.

11 Van Lennep and Ter Gouw, *De uithangteekens*, pp. 116–117.

12 For more information on this guild, see SAA, Archief gilden, inv. nr. 560, 'Ordonnanties van het kleinkramersgilde', pp. 46–48, and Wagenaar, *Amsterdam, in zyne opkomst*, Part IV.

Table 5.1 Location of *komenijshouders* (grocers) among the new members of the shopkeepers' guild in 1752 and distribution of the total population across Amsterdam's neighbourhoods in 1795

	komenij 1752 (a)	population 1795 (b)	ratio (a/b x 100)
City centre, *Oude zijde* (east)	7.4%	8.3%	89
City centre, *Nieuwe zijde* (west)	4.8%	10.0%	48
canal ring, northwest	4.4%	6.9%	64
canal ring, south	2.1%	4.8%	43
canal ring, southeast	2.3%	3.6%	64
Noordse Bos and surroundings	6.2%	8.1%	77
Plantage	0.5%	0.5%	92
Waterlooplein and surroundings	4.8%	8.8%	55
Rembrandtplein and surroundings	3.7%	2.8%	132
Lastage	7.4%	6.2%	119
Jordaan	27.9%	24.8%	113
Western Islands	7.6%	6.1%	125
Eastern Islands	13.6%	6.9%	197
unclassifiable	6.2%		
outside of Amsterdam	0.7%	2.2%	
place of residence unknown	0.2%		
total	100.0%	100.0%	100
N =	433	217024	

Sources: SAA, archief gilden, inv.nr. 564 and Farret, Verster and Van Swinden, *Rapport over de telling van het volk van Amsterdam*.
* The numbers in the table have been rounded off and therefore do not always add up to 100.

offensive, for between 10 February and 16 March 1752, they received the four-guilder overdue admission fee from hundreds of people as well as the 18 stivers that every new member had to deposit for the guild regulations. In 1752, a total of 619 people registered, and it was reported that 433 of these new members ran a *komenij*. Let us thus see where these shops were located.

In Table 5.1, the city has been divided into thirteen districts, and I have shown where the new guild members ran their businesses. For the purposes of comparison, I have also included the distribution of the total population in 1795 and the ratio between the two series. From the table, it is clear that the 'legalized' *komenijen* were spread throughout the city.[13] This confirms the expectation expressed above regarding the location of groceries and of suppliers of daily necessities in general. The table also reveals that these small, marginal businesses were underrepresented in the city centre and affluent neighbourhoods such as the canal ring. By contrast, they were

13 The records of the shopkeepers' guild usually only mention the names of the streets where the *komenijen* were located. A map with the district layout used here in Lesger, 'Migranten in Amsterdam', p. 45.

Table 5.2 Spatial distribution of shops in daily necessities and durable goods, 1742

sector	street	proportion of shops in sector	N =
Daily necessities			
tobacconist	Damrak	4.2%	236
bread-baker	Prinsengracht	3.1%	451
Durable goods			
silk shop	Nieuwendijk	44.4%	27
bed shop	Nieuwendijk	33.3%	33
linen shop	Nieuwendijk	28.2%	78
Franse winkel	Kalverstraat	22.4%	49
Nuremburg shop	Warmoesstraat	18.5%	27
cloth shop	Nieuwendijk	17.5%	63
book shop	Rokin	17.4%	121
chintz shop	Nieuwendijk	14.8%	81
cotton shop	Nieuwendijk	10.1%	79

Source: Calculated on the basis of Oldewelt, *Kohier van de Personeele Quotisatie*.

overrepresented in poorer parts of the city such as Rembrandtplein and its surroundings, the Lastage, the Jordaan, and the Western and Eastern Islands.[14] In the *Personele Quotisatie*, we lack a sufficiently comprehensive picture of the facilities available in these neighbourhoods, but it is clear that the population not only had bakers but also had access to a large number of grocers when buying daily necessities. We should add that these small shops were not established in the many passageways to be found throughout the city; even marginal shops were dependent on customers and showed a preference for more accessible locations in their neighbourhoods.

In order to investigate whether shops selling durable goods were less widely dispersed than those selling daily necessities, in Table 5.2 information has been collated on location patterns in a series of sectors. For every sector, the street has been named on which this sector was represented in the largest numbers. In the case of daily necessities, we would expect none of the streets to be home to a large proportion of all shops in the given sector. In the case of durable goods, it is obvious that this would be the case. That is because a cluster of shops in the same sector is attractive to consumers who want to compare the price, quality and appearance of these kinds of occasionally purchased goods. The shopkeeper, in turn, profits from the fact that this same concentration increases the attractiveness of the shopping area and thereby allows for a higher potential turnover than an isolated location.

These assumptions are confirmed by the data in the table. Looking at the information on the distribution of tobacconists and bread bakers, we see that Damrak, where the largest numbers of tobacconists were to be found, was nevertheless home to just 4.2 per cent of all tobacconists registered in the *Personele Quotisatie*, and Prinsengracht was home to only 3.1 per cent of all bakeries. In the durable goods sector, these percentages were much higher. More than 44 per cent of all registered silk shops and more than 33 per cent of all bed shops were to be found on Nieuwendijk. As we can see from the table, this street was by far the most important shopping street for fabric in Amsterdam; no fewer than 80 of the 207 shops on Nieuwendijk listed in the *Personele Quotisatie* were shops that sold fabric.[15] Nieuwendijk is thereby a textbook example of a shopping street. As well as fabric shops, however, there were also striking concentrations of *Franse winkels* ('French shops' that sold fashion accessories), Nuremberg shops

14 The fact that the books of the shopkeepers' guild record a relatively small number of registrations in the Jewish Quarter obviously reflects the prohibition on Jews becoming a member of the guild.

15 In total, there were 265 buildings in Nieuwendijk.

(luxury utensils and decorative articles) and bookshops.

So far, we have found the empirical evidence to be consistent with the theory. In the previous chapters, it was cautiously suggested that when it comes to daily necessities and durable goods, the location behaviour of shopkeepers in the past was driven by the same logic that prevails in modern cities, and this statement was supported and confirmed by the analysis above. The next question is whether the three forms of accessibility identified by Davies and Bennison also shaped the retail landscape of eighteenth-century Amsterdam.

The retail system in the city centre: The main shopping streets

Although we took a detailed look at the work of Davies and Bennison in the first chapter, it will do no harm to reiterate here the distinction they made between general, linear and special accessibility. General accessibility concerns the accessibility of locations to consumers from the immediate neighbourhood in the case of daily necessities, and to consumers from a much wider area in the case of providers of less frequently purchased items. By linear accessibility, we mean locations that allow a shopkeeper to intercept passers-by; in practice, these are locations on important access roads and through-routes. Special accessibility refers to locations that derive their attractiveness from the nature of the immediate surroundings: an affluent neighbourhood, say, or the presence of crowded markets, or the proximity of important public buildings.

In order to get a general impression of the spatial distribution of Amsterdam's retail facilities, the most important shopping streets have been mapped out in Figure 5.2. These are streets with shop densities of 30 per cent or more in the *Personele Quotisatie*.[16] For the time being, let us limit the analysis to the heart of the city. Here we would expect to find locations that are associated in the literature with a high degree of general accessibility: 'the need to be central to a surrounding consumer body'.[17] And this was also the case in Amsterdam in 1742: measured by the number of shops in the *Personele Quotisatie*, the highest densities were to be found in the old centre of the city.

As is true of all cities that develop organically, the retail heart of Amsterdam consisted of a series of streets with a pattern that revealed much of the situation in previous phases of the city's development. As we have already observed, the oldest commercial activities took place on or around the Dam on the Amstel. As the city's population and the economy grew, the space on the Dam was no longer sufficient, and the old river dikes—the access roads to the Dam—developed into shopping streets. The same was true of Damrak and Rokin, streets that had been built on the western bank of the river. Along with the Dam, these six north-south axes formed the retail heart of the city. From west to east, they were Nieuwendijk, and by extension Kalverstraat; the Damrak-Rokin axis, located directly on the water; and to the east of the Amstel, the Warmoesstraat-Nes axis.[18]

The main shopping thoroughfares had traditionally profited from excellent accessibility, both to the city's inhabitants and to people from outside the city. The latter group

16 I have calculated shop densities by relating for every street with at least five shops the number of shops to the number of buildings according to the registers of the *verponding* (a general property tax levied in 1733).

17 Davies and Bennison, 'Retailing in the City Centre', p. 271.

18 For the end of the eighteenth century, the above is corroborated almost literally by the fictitious dialogue in Martinet, *Het vaderland*, p. 34.

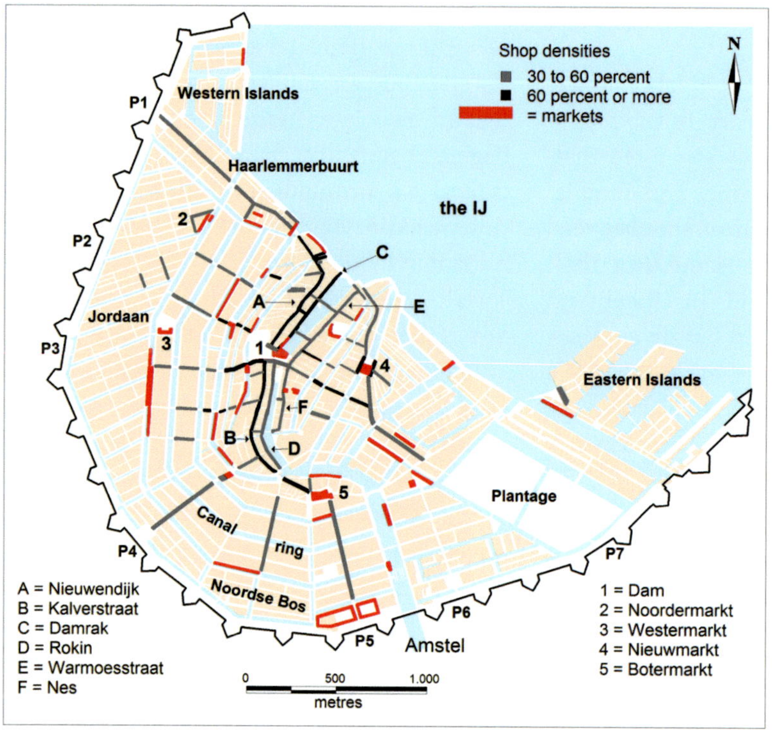

Figure 5.2: Shopping streets (black) and markets (red) in Amsterdam, 1742.

reached the centre via the many country roads that were connected to streets on both sides of the Amstel or via Amsterdam's inner harbour, the Damrak. The inner harbour was extremely busy; it was from the Damrak and the harbour front that many of the 800 weekly sailings to 180 different destinations took place.[19]

In view of its central location, the old city centre of Amsterdam was also where we would expect to find a relatively large number of shops selling durable goods; and that was indeed the case, as we can see from Table 5.3. In the table, I have divided all of the shops into suppliers of daily necessities and suppliers of durable goods.

Along the main thoroughfares, less than 30 per cent of the shops registered in the *Personele Quotisatie* sold food, beverages and tobacco; in the rest of the city, this number was almost 56 per cent. In practice, the contrast will have been even greater because it is evident that the marginal shops that were not included in the *Personele Quotisatie* would have been located mainly outside the main axes, and it was precisely this group that included many providers of daily necessities. Conversely, the main axes were dominated by shops selling durable goods, which featured much less often in the rest of the city in the registers of the *Personele Quotisatie*.

19 Kistemaker, 'Functiekaarten', p. 108, and see also Lesger, 'Intraregional trade'. Elsewhere I have argued that there was a hierarchy of service centres (central places) in early modern Holland, with Amsterdam and The Hague occupying the top positions (Lesger, 'Regions, urban systems and historical central place analysis').

Table 5.3 Division of shops registered in the *Personele Quotisatie* by type of goods, 1742

	main shopping streets	elsewhere in the city
Daily necessities	29.4%	55.7%
Durable goods		
fabrics	22.8%	8.8%
clothing accessories	13.9%	9.1%
other	33.8%	26.4%
total	100.0%	100.0%
N =	674	3073

Source: Calculated on the basis of Oldewelt, *Kohier van de Personeele Quotisatie*.
* The 10 shops without further specification are not included. The main shopping streets are the Dam, Nieuwendijk, Kalverstraat, Damrak, Rokin, Warmoesstraat and Nes.
** The numbers in the table have been rounded off and therefore do not always add up to 100.

This contrast between the main axes and the rest of the city does not alter the fact that each of the six main shopping streets on both sides of the Amstel and the Dam had its own character. This is also evident from Table 5.4, where we can make out considerable differences in the relationships between the various categories of goods. The shops on the Dam, Nieuwendijk, Warmoesstraat and Kalverstraat, for example, largely sold fabric and clothing accessories, whilst a relatively large amount of food, beverages and tobacco was sold on Damrak and Nes.

Exactly what products did these shops sell? Although it would make little sense to review every street and every shop, several findings deserve emphasis. With 206 shops registered in the *Personele Quotisatie* and a shop density of 78 per cent, in quantitative terms, Nieuwendijk was by far the most important shopping street and an excellent place to buy fabric. In certain sections of the street, fabric shops were established almost door-to-door. And it did not end there; the street was also home to 22 businesses where one could buy related items: eight hat shops, five ribbon shops, four shops selling stockings, two *Franse winkels*, two sagathy (worsted) shops and one lace shop. The other main shopping streets also sold specific types of goods. In the case of Warmoesstraat, this was mainly Nuremberg wares, in addition to

Table 5.4 Division of shops located on the main shopping streets by type of goods, 1742

	daily necessities	fabrics	clothing accessories	other	total	shop density (%)	N =
Dam	28.0%	12.0%	36.0%	24.0%	100.0%	56	25
Nieuwendijk	24.8%	38.8%	9.7%	26.7%	100.0%	78	206
Kalverstraat	28.0%	15.4%	18.9%	37.8%	100.0%	61	143
Damrak	39.7%	5.2%	3.4%	51.7%	100.0%	69	58
Rokin	30.6%	2.8%	9.7%	56.9%	100.0%	42	72
Warmoesstraat	26.6%	30.3%	17.4%	25.7%	100.0%	58	109
Nes	42.6%	18.0%	16.4%	23.0%	100.0%	53	61

Sources: Calculated on the basis of Oldewelt, *Kohier van de Personeele Quotisatie* and SAA, *Legger van de verponding*, 1733.
* The numbers in the table have been rounded off and therefore do not always add up to 100.

fabric and fashion accessories.[20] The Dam and Kalverstraat sold a striking number of fashion accessories as well as books. On nearby Rokin, we find a similar clustering of 22 book and map shops. Taking a short walk from the Dam via Kalverstraat to the Munt and back along Rokin, the book-loving consumer would have encountered no fewer than 44 book and map shops, and an additional four bookshops could be perused in the adjacent side streets. Not only the residents of Amsterdam but also visitors from the wider region would have benefited from this enormous offering. On the whole, Kalverstraat offered a relatively large range of luxury goods, and a glance at the map clearly shows why. Via Heiligeweg and Vijzelstraat, Kalverstraat enjoyed an almost direct link with the southerly and most affluent part of the canal ring. Nieuwendijk, by contrast, could be accessed easily from the slightly less wealthy northern part of the canal ring and from working-class neighbourhoods such as the Jordaan and Haarlemmerbuurt.

In view of the above, it will again have become clear that the empirical evidence is consistent with the theory. In terms of general accessibility, we expected Amsterdam's medieval heart to be the most attractive location for shops, and that indeed turned out to be the case. The six most important shopping streets in eighteenth-century Amsterdam ran along the three main axes on both sides of the Amstel. More so than elsewhere in the city, the goods for sale along the main axes were dominated by consumer durables, and this, too, is consistent with the claims made by modern location theories. After all, these were typically goods for which customers wanted to get a feel for what was for sale, and this was only possible when a large number of similar shops were clustered in a relatively small area.

In addition—and this deserves some emphasis—a variety of shops for purchasing food, beverages and tobacco were also located along the central shopping axes. Their clients would have included the inhabitants of the city centre as well as passers-by, and they were many in number. In 1795, in the first proper census, the area encircled by Singel, Kloveniersburgwal and Geldersekade was found to have almost 40,000 inhabitants, more than 18 per cent of Amsterdam's population.[21]

Shops outside the city centre

In order to evaluate the retail trade beyond the core retail area, let us take another look at the distribution of shopping streets in Figure 5.2. Two things in particular strike us: first, that beyond the core retail area, the streets with high shop densities in the *Personele Quotisatie* were almost exclusively radials that provided access to the heart of the city; and second, that the city gates and daily/weekly markets played an important structuring role in Amsterdam's retail landscape. It was here that linear and special accessibility came together, as it were, because the radials linked these structural elements with the old centre of the city on the Amstel and the Dam.

Amsterdam's most important city gates were at P1 (Haarlemmerpoort), P4 (Leidsepoort) and P5 (Utrechtsepoort), which linked the city to the busy roads to Haarlem, Leiden and Utrecht, respectively—the largest cities in

20 Van Nierop, 'De handeldrijvende middenstand', pp. 209–210. Shops in Nuremberg wares were already located in Warmoesstraat in the seventeenth century.

21 Farret, Verster and Van Swinden, *Rapport over de telling van het volk van Amsterdam.*

Amsterdam's surroundings (see also figure 5.1). At P1 and P4, there was also parking for wagons: open spaces where people could park vehicles that they did not need, wish or were not permitted to bring into the narrow city streets.[22] In view of the importance of these exit roads, it will come as no surprise that the shop density on the radial roads was relatively high and that these shopkeepers were wealthy enough to merit inclusion in the registers of the *Personele Quotisatie*. The gates at P2 (Zaagmolenpoort) and P3 (Raampoort) were much less important due to the poor connections between the streets of the Jordaan and the canal ring and city centre—a legacy of the days when the canal ring and the Jordaan were built.[23] There are indications that a shopping street ran through the Jordaan in the direction of P3, but the population of the Jordaan was by no means affluent, and the number of listings of shopkeepers in the *Personele Quotisatie* is too small for Nieuwe Leliestraat to show up on the map. A similar situation existed for the route to Weesperpoort (P6, also with wagon parking). Moreover, compared to the Jordaan, the surroundings of Weesperstraat were not very densely populated, and demand for retail goods there remained limited.[24] The access road to the Muiderpoort (P7) ran through the Plantage; this part of the city had remained free of buildings since the overly ambitious city expansion of 1656–1662 and was eventually converted into pleasure gardens. Residential homes were not permitted there, just a small residence for the gardener and his family.[25]

22 Schmal, 'De overheid als verkeersregelaar'.

23 See chapter 3 above.

24 In 1795, only 3.6 per cent of the urban population lived in this area (calculated on the basis of Farret, Verster and Van Swinden, *Rapport over de telling van het volk van Amsterdam*).

25 Wagenaar, 'De Plantage'.

What kinds of goods were for sale on these radials? Table 5.5 shows that the division of shops by type of goods is consistent with the retail facilities along the main axes, but the offering of daily necessities was larger there, and durable goods were thus offered less frequently. Concerning the radials, when we distinguish between the streets in the medieval centre of the city and those beyond, we also see that the share of the daily necessities sector was larger in peripheral parts of the city, and the percentage of durable goods was correspondingly lower. There is a high degree of consistency between these findings and what one would expect based on the work by Davies and others. In view of their intercepting function, shops on radials indeed have a well-developed offering with a relatively high number of durable goods. In studies on modern cities, radials are therefore viewed as 'linear bulges' in the central retail area. It is also evident that the offering of durable goods became scarcer the further one travelled away from the centre. After all, the centre was the most accessible location for the largest number of consumers, and as such it was the most suitable location for shops selling durable goods. Where the radials branched off from the main shopping axes, there was thus much more benefit to be gained from the proximity of the buying public than in the peripheral parts of the radials, and the shop offering adapted itself accordingly. The same logic of linear accessibility explains the relatively high shop density along streets that gave access to the city's major daily and weekly markets, as these were also locations with excellent potential for intercepting passers-by.

The general overview from Table 5.5 conceils substantial differences between the radial streets themselves and even between the radials in the city centre. Some streets mainly sold durable goods, whilst elsewhere the picture was strongly determined by shops selling

Table 5.5 Division of shops registered in the *Personele Quotisatie* by type of goods, 1742

	main shopping streets	radials in the city centre	other radials
Daily necessities	29.4%	40.5%	50.6%
Durable goods			
fabrics	22.8%	11.9%	10.0%
clothing accessories	13.9%	16.8%	9.7%
other	33.8%	30.8%	29.7%
total	100.0%	100.0%	100.0%
N =	674	464	630

Sources: Calculated on the basis of Oldewelt, *Kohier van de Personeele Quotisatie* and SAA, *Legger van de verponding*, 1733.

* The city centre is the area of Amsterdam encircled by the waters of the Singel, Kloveniersburgwal and Geldersekade canals and the open harbour front to the north.

** Only the radial streets with shop densities of at least 30 percent in the *Kohier van de Personeele Quotisatie* are included.

*** The numbers in the table have been rounded off and therefore do not always add up to 100.

daily necessities: bakers, confectioners, grocers, corn chandlers, *komenijen*, tea shops and shops selling tobacco and snuff. Nevertheless, the radials showed much higher shop densities than the side streets and backstreets. After all, when tapping flows of passers-by, it made a significant difference whether a shopkeeper was located on a connecting axis or on a street with little through-traffic. Thus, as is also the case today, in the mid-eighteenth century there was a direct relationship between the location of a shop relative to flows of passers-by and the possibility of earning an income in this location.

The markets were an expression of what Davies and others call special accessibility: 'the need to occupy areas exhibiting prestige, historical affiliations or some particular environmental attribute'. But what of other examples of special accessibility? Here a particularly relevant question is whether shopping areas developed outside the city centre, with retail systems tailored to the level of prosperity of the residents. We have already established that this did not happen in the canal ring in the seventeenth century. Over the course of time, however, the canal ring increasingly became an elite domain, and side streets such as Herenstraat, Hartenstraat, Wolvenstraat and Huidenstraat—which were strategically located between Herengracht and Keizersgracht—could have accommodated a variety of luxury shops that competed with the retail system in the city centre.

From Table 5.6, we can see that this did not happen. Even in the immediate proximity of an elite clientele, the shop offering did not consist exclusively of high-value durable consumer items, and in Wolvenstraat, as much as 60 per cent of the offering fell into the 'daily necessities' category. Despite this, it is clear that the neighbours were wealthy. Cornelis Grave, a pastry cook on Herenstraat, had an annual income of 3,000 guilders; along with a colleague on Nieuwendijk, this made him one of the highest-earning pastry cooks in the city. And with an income of 4,000 guilders, J. Ketelhoet, the manager of a chintz shop on Hartenstraat, enjoyed the highest income in his sector. On the whole, we can also gauge the influence of the surroundings from the relatively luxurious nature of the wares for sale, especially in Herenstraat and Hartenstraat. In those streets, for example, we find a striking number of patisseries among those selling food, although the amounts earned were not large. In Herenstraat and Hartenstraat, the average income of the registered shopkeepers amounted to 800 guilders per year, and in Wolvenstraat and Huidenstraat, 600 guilders per year. On Damrak, Nieuwendijk, Kalverstraat and Warmoesstraat, the figure was 1,500 guilders, and on Rokin, 1,000 guilders. All in all, we

Table 5.6 Retail offering on transverse streets between Herengracht and Keizersgracht, 1742

	Herenstraat	Hartenstraat	Wolvenstraat	Huidenstraat
Daily necessities	31.8%	40.9%	58.3%	54.5%
Durable goods				
fabrics	13.6%	13.6%	8.3%	18.2%
clothing accessories	18.2%	22.7%	8.3%	9.1%
other	36.4%	22.7%	25.0%	18.2%
total	100.0%	100.0%	100.0%	100.0%
N =	22	22	12	11
shop density (%)	59	56	38	31

Source: Calculated on the basis of Oldewelt, *Kohier van de Personeele Quotisatie*.
* The numbers in the table have been rounded off and therefore do not always add up to 100.

are justified in concluding that whilst the retail offering in the streets connecting Herengracht and Keizersgracht reflected the prosperity of the neighbourhood's inhabitants, these streets did not develop into a shopping area that could compete with the centre.

The explanation for this is the same as that formulated for the seventeenth century: unlike cities such as Brussels and Paris, where there was a concentration of affluent consumers around the court, the elongated form of the canal ring prevented the development of a compact luxury quarter. The emergence of a secondary shopping district tailored to the tastes and spending power of the elite was therefore nipped in the bud.[26] The city centre was easy to access from the canal ring, however, and as a result, it remained the preferred place for purchasing durable goods. It was also home to shops that maintained direct relations with suppliers in Paris, Lyon, Brussels and other places, far and wide, for purchasing stock.[27]

When it comes to neighbourhoods with lower incomes, it is more difficult to research the existence of shopping areas outside the heart of the city because the registers for the *Personele Quotisatie* did not include people with an income of less than 600 guilders. Despite this, clusters of shops, particularly around Noordermarkt and Nieuwmarkt (see Figure 5.2), indicate that shopping areas may have emerged. In order to investigate this, I looked for supplementary sources that could provide information about the locations of shops owned by less wealthy shopkeepers, and I found such a source in the above-mentioned archive of the *desolate boedelkamer* in Amsterdam.[28] Although the archive is extensive, in the records that have survived from around 1742, the type of shop is, unfortunately enough, hardly ever specified. Aside from the most obvious cases, it is impossible to make out from the paper records exactly what kind of shop one is dealing with. After the *boedelkamer* was reorganized in 1777, this kind of information was included in most of the dossiers. To supplement the register of the *Personele Quotisatie*, I therefore used the address data of bed shops, *Franse winkels* and fancy goods shops from the archive of the *desolate boedelkamer* for the period between 1777 and 1795.

Figure 5.3 shows the location of all of the bed shops that were included in the register of the *Personele Quotisatie* as well as the location of the eight bed shopkeepers who went

26 For the situation in Brussels, see Bruneel and Delporte, 'Approche socio-professionelle', in particular figure 4, and Bruneel, 'La localisation du commerce', p. 179.

27 See for example the lists of creditors in SAA, Desolate boedelkamer, inv. nrs 3480 and 3949.

28 An introduction to the archive and an overview of the number of bankruptcies per year can be found in Oldewelt, 'Twee eeuwen Amsterdamse faillissementen'.

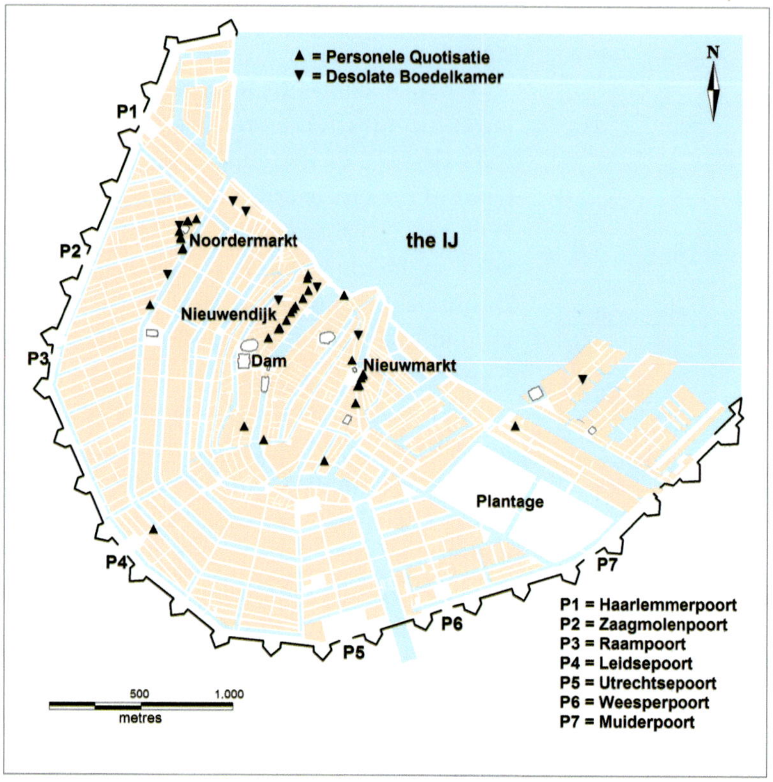

Figure 5.3: Location of bed shops in the register of the *Personele Quotisatie* (1742) and the archive of the *desolate boedelkamer* (1777–1795).

bankrupt and were thus listed in the archives of the *desolate boedelkamer* between 1777 and 1795.[29] It should be noted that the address details from the register of the *Personele Quotisatie* are more accurate than those in the *boedelkamer* files, where one frequently comes across overly general descriptions such as 'on Haarlemmerdijk near Buiten Brouwerstraat'. Nevertheless, the picture is clear. Bed shops—where pillows, blankets and bed linen were sold in addition to mattresses—were clustered in three places: at Noordermarkt, Nieuwendijk and Nieuwmarkt. There were evidently very few bed shops beyond the immediate surroundings of these clusters. This is consistent with the durable nature of bedding and beds, articles that the client would have wanted to compare carefully in terms of price and quality before making a purchase. It is thus no wonder that Nieuwendijk was home to the largest number of bed shops. After all, it lay in the heart of the city and could be accessed easily by the largest number of residents, and also by visitors from outside Amsterdam.

The clusters at Noordermarkt and Nieuwmarkt lay on the edge of densely populated neighbourhoods such as the Jordaan in the west and the Lastage and Jewish Quarter in the east of the city. It would seem reasonable to assume that the shops there had a more neighbourhood-oriented character than those on Nieuwendijk and stocked a range that reflected the limited purchasing power of the clientele

29 SAA, Desolate boedelkamer, inv. nrs. 3092, 3348, 3555, 3786, 5157, 5442, 5458 and 5593.

in these parts of the city. Unfortunately, we lack precise data about what was for sale in the bed shops, but the considerable differences in the incomes of the bed shopkeepers suggest that Noordermarkt and Nieuwmarkt served a different segment of Amsterdam's population from Nieuwendijk. On the latter street, the average annual income of the eleven bed shopkeepers in 1742 was 1,964 guilders, whereas the six shopkeepers on Noordermarkt had to make do with an average of 800 guilders per year, and those on Nieuwmarkt, 760 guilders.

The fact that the peripheral and poorer parts of the city were supplied with beds and related items from Noordermarkt and Nieuwmarkt in particular will have been no accident. Weekly markets were also held on both squares, which drew many people and made them attractive locations for shops. Moreover, the wares sold by the market traders increased the level of choice for consumers and thereby the attractiveness of these shopping areas. This was certainly true of Noordermarkt, where bed linen was explicitly mentioned in the by-laws that regulated what was sold at the weekly market.[30] At Nieuwmarkt, the shopkeepers not only benefited from the passing clientele on the weekly market day but also from its favourable location on the through-route from the eastern city district to the harbour front and the IJ. Thus, it seems beyond doubt that at the markets in peripheral parts of the city, there was a retail system centred on the financial capacity and preferences of the residents in the immediate surroundings. The shops and stalls at these markets will also have played a key role in providing the neighbourhood's population with daily necessities and durable goods.

Nevertheless, it is important to emphasize that for less affluent consumers, the offering was not limited to these markets. It has already been established that bread bakers were dispersed throughout the city, and the same was true of *komenijen*. But durable goods could also be purchased outside the city centre and the large market squares, as shown by Figure 5.4. This shows the geographical distribution of *Franse winkels* and fancy goods shops in the register of the *Personele Quotisatie* and the archive of the *desolate boedelkamer*. It concerns a total of 105 address listings of businesses where people could purchase fashion items and clothing accessories. Here, too, we see a clustering of shops in the centre of the city, but whereas the bed shops were mostly located on Nieuwendijk, suppliers of French fashion articles and fancy goods were mostly located on Dam Square and along Kalverstraat. A number of radials in the canal ring and the radial running from the Dam in a south-easterly direction through Halsteeg (now Damstraat), Oude Doelenstraat and Hoogstraat were also well-provided with these kinds of shops. By contrast, at Noordermarkt, there was not a single shop in this sector, and at Nieuwmarkt, only one. On the map, there are evidently concentrations on Prinsengracht between Tuinstraat and Egelantiersgracht, and in the surroundings of Haarlemmerstraat. The estate inventories that were drawn up upon bankruptcy give the impression that these were relatively marginal, small shops, which also explains why no French accessories shops or fancy goods shops are to be found at this location in the register of the *Personele Quotisatie*.[31]

Although the limitations of the source material prevent us from drawing any firm conclusions, certain things are nevertheless clear. The

30 Wagenaar, *Amsterdam, in zyne opkomst*, Part IV, Book 1 under the heading 'Noorder-markt'.

31 SAA, Desolate boedelkamer, inv. nrs. 3420, 3438, 5510 and 5583.

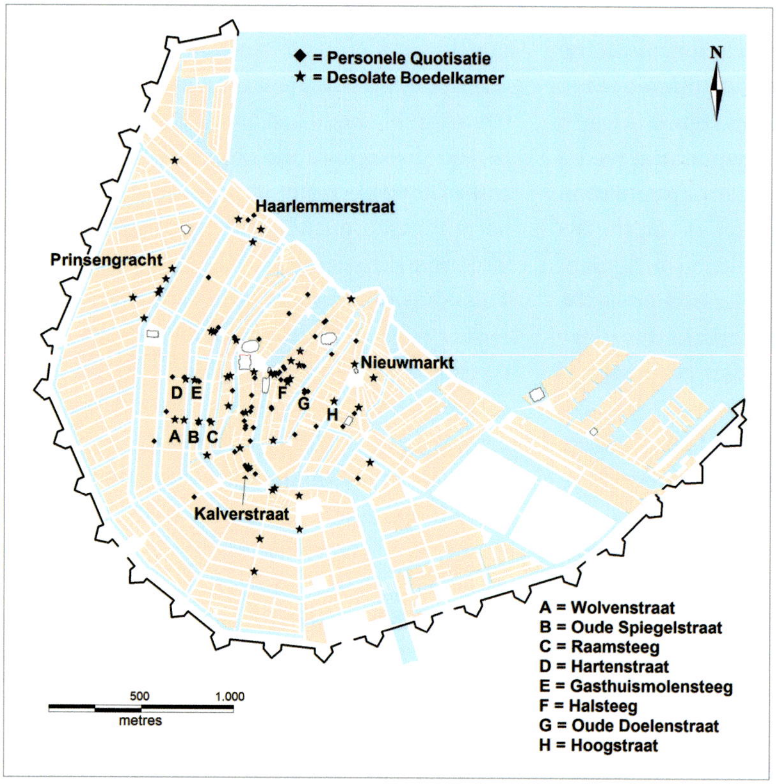

Figure 5.4: Location of *Franse winkels* and fancy goods shops in the register of the *Personele Quotisatie* (1742) and the archive of the *desolate boedelkamer* (1777–1795).

distribution pattern of bed shops, *Franse winkels* and fancy goods shops confirms the importance of the central shopping axes and the radials for the supply of consumer durables in Amsterdam. But at the same time, we now know that these kinds of goods were also sold elsewhere in the city and that this offering, in keeping with the character of shopping goods, was usually concentrated in clusters of shops in the same sector. These clusters did not develop into what we would today call 'secondary retail centres', however; Noordermarkt and Nieuwmarkt did not function as large and varied shopping facilities for peripheral neighbourhoods. Rather, it seems to have been a case of sector clustering at street level. If they wished to buy beds, pillows, bed linen and related items, the residents of the Jordaan went to Noordermarkt; and if they wished to purchase fashion items, people went to Prinsengracht.[32] It does not seem to be an exaggeration to suggest that a similar pattern would have existed for other parts of the consumer durables sector. It goes without saying, of course, that the specific offering in these shops would have been of a different quality and price than that in the shops on the Dam and main shopping thoroughfares.

Forms of accessibility and the urban grid in Amsterdam

The availability of a source such as the *Personele Quotisatie* of 1742 makes it possible to establish, with more certainty than the

32 I thus assume that the bankruptcies are indicative of concentrations of these types of shops on Prinsengracht. Of the four files, two date from 1781 and two from 1795.

seventeenth-century source material allows, that we can usefully draw on location principles formulated in the twentieth century when analyzing and explaining the location patterns of shops in early modern Amsterdam. Thus, the different location preferences of providers of daily necessities and durable goods and the three forms of accessibility also determined, to a considerable extent, where shops were established in the urban landscape. In this sense, that landscape could be described as 'modern'. The principle of general accessibility—that is to say, accessible to the population living in a particular area—was reflected in the high-quality character of the goods sold by shops in the centre of Amsterdam and the distribution of shops selling daily necessities over different parts of the city. The essence of the principle of linear accessibility, in turn, concerns the interception of passers-by. As one would expect, the best locations for 'intercepting' shops are major through-roads and access routes to the centre, a logic that could also be applied to Amsterdam. A series of radials linked the main shopping axes and created connections between the city centre, several key markets and the city gates. These radials, which can be viewed as linear bulges in the central shopping area, were the site of relatively high-quality shops. But the fact that the further one travelled from the city centre, the scarcer the offering along the radials became is also easy to explain with reference to general location principles. And with demand for retail facilities in neighbourhoods outside the centre, we come to the third form of accessibility: special accessibility. This was difficult to study in view of the available source material. From the situation in the connecting streets between Herengracht and Keizersgracht as well as the distribution of several sectors over the city, however, it is clear that whilst the offering varied with the prosperity of the neighbourhood in question, there were no sizeable secondary shopping centres. Here, too, we can analyze the situation in the eighteenth century with the aid of an instrument that draws heavily on location practices in the twentieth century.

In Davies' complex model (see Figure 1 in Chapter 1), the three forms of accessibility overlap with one another, as it were. A pattern thereby emerges in which the concentric structure of general accessibility, the elongated structures of linear accessibility and the clusters of shops created by special accessibility intersect with one another. For the present research, the complex model largely derives its value from the fact that it reminds us that the distinction between the three forms of accessibility, used above, is an analytical and explanatory tool. On the whole, shop locations possess a combination of general, linear and special accessibility, with one form of accessibility dominating in one situation and another form in another. Nevertheless, it is important to underline that this kind of diagrammatic representation also has its limits. For example, we often get the impression that the retail heart of a city consists of a continuous, unbroken area. Davies himself noted that this is not the case, an observation that is also confirmed by the situation in Amsterdam.[33] The central retail system in Amsterdam consisted of the Dam and half a dozen streets that also functioned as linear approach routes but that became the main shopping area over time. They gave the city centre its retail character, but the city centre contained more than these streets alone. In many of the side streets, backstreets, slums and alleyways located in the immediate surroundings of the main shopping streets, there were no shops or hardly any, meaning that the picture was much more varied than diagrammatic representations would suggest.

33 Davies, 'Structural Models', p. 78.

The striking consistency between what one would expect, based on modern location theories, and the actual distribution of shops in early modern Amsterdam raises the question of the influence of institutional and historical context on the location pattern of Amsterdam's shops. In relation to the seventeenth century, we already observed that with the exception of fishmongers and butchers, who had to sell their perishable wares in the city's meat and fish markets, the city government and the guilds did not interfere in shopkeepers' location behaviour—and this was still the case in the eighteenth century. Contrary to what one might expect, in view of the corporate organization of Amsterdam's economy in the early modern period, the use of property was subject to the rules of the 'free market'. This explains why the general principles that were formulated on the basis of the situation in modern cities with liberal economic policies also have explanatory power in early modern Amsterdam.[34]

This does not mean, of course, that local context played an insignificant role—on the contrary. After all, the actual distribution of shops and the range of goods they sold were strongly determined by the urban and socio-spatial structure of the city as it had developed over the preceding centuries. It was argued above that the urban grid had a great influence on the accessibility of locations and an almost compelling impact on the location pattern of shops. This is confirmed by comparing the accessibility of streets, as found by using Space Syntax Analysis (Figure 8 in Chapter 3), with the shop densities calculated on the basis of the *Personele Quotisatie* (Figure 5.2 above). The main shopping streets in the mid-eighteenth century continued to be streets with a high degree of accessibility as generated by the urban grid. The city government's decisions in relation to the location of markets and the range of goods that could be sold there also had an effect on the pattern of shops in the city. Not coincidentally, many radials were connected to important markets in the city. Moreover, the city government had an indirect influence on the quality of the goods that were for sale in different parts of the city. After all, when the city was enlarged in the seventeenth century, there was a conscious attempt to achieve a certain degree of segregation between social groups. The goods on sale in the canal ring were thus of a different quality and price from those in working-class areas such as the Jordaan and the Western and Eastern Islands.

34 That is also the conclusion of Brown in his research into location patterns in Belfast in the years 1910–1980 (Brown, 'The Complex Model', p. 16).

6. Stagnation and modernization in Amsterdam's retail sector, 1700–1850

Abstract:
The fact that the spatial distribution of shops remained unaltered does not imply that the period from 1700 to 1850 passed without changes. On the contrary, the street scene and the character of shops changed fundamentally. In line with the general trend in residential housing, shops on the main streets retreated, as it were, behind their façade. From the second half of the eighteenth century, the first examples of purposely designed shop facades began turning up, and along the main shopping streets canopies and signboards were taken down and front steps were cleared of obstacles such as stairs and fences. Nevertheless, even these fashionable shopping streets of Amsterdam could not stand comparison with those in metropolises like Paris and London.

Keywords: street scene, shop interiors, indoor sales, shop exteriors

The shop distribution pattern that I was able to reconstruct on the basis of the *Personele Quotisatie* of 1742 remained unchanged until after the mid-nineteenth century. Indeed, this is what one would expect, as there were in essence no changes to the structure of Amsterdam's urban grid during this period, nor was there a change in the spatial distribution of income groups. But this need not mean that there were no changes at all. In England, for example, the eighteenth century was a time of fundamental change. In this chapter, we shall first focus on the situation on the other side of the North Sea before turning to examine whether similar developments also took place in Amsterdam.

Shops in Britain in the eighteenth century

In order to find out how the retail shop developed in Britain in the eighteenth century, we need briefly to examine the somewhat older literature on British retail trade in the nineteenth and twentieth centuries. Many of these works have made much of the changes that took place in this period, and not unjustifiably. The most striking expression of these changes in retail trade was, of course, the rise and rapid expansion of large-scale retail businesses. Here it is important to note that scholars studying the modern shop tended to be dismissive of the situation before the mid-nineteenth century, labelling it as 'traditional' and 'underdeveloped'. On the very first page of his influential study *Retail trading in Britain,* James B. Jefferys argues: '[t]he wholesale and retail trades in Britain in the middle of the nineteenth century were examples of those trades that still bore the marks of the old system rather than of the new'.[1] Nor was he alone in believing that before around 1800, shops—that is to say, fixed points of sale of

1 Jefferys, *Retail Trading in Britain*, p. 1.

Lesger, C., *Shopping Spaces and the Urban Landscape in Early Modern Amsterdam, 1550–1850.*
Taylor & Francis Group, 2020
DOI: 10.5117/9789463720625_CH06

goods that were not produced on the premises—were of little or no significance.[2]

The 1980s saw the rise of a countermovement in England, where the history of retail trade has traditionally attracted more interest than on the Continent. In a series of publications, it became clear that shops in eighteenth-century England were much more common than had been suggested and that they were concentrated in typical shopping streets. Nor were all shops dark, unattractive and strictly functional. In fact, according to various authors, a 'culture of shopping' developed in this period. This was no longer exclusively about the strictly commercial exchange of money and goods in soberly furnished shopping spaces; rather, such transactions formed part of the leisure activities of the wealthy and were embedded in a whole repertoire of courteous interchange between the shopkeeper and the client. In this context, the term used in the literature is 'polite consumption'.[3] Naturally, this meant adapting shops and shopping streets to the needs of the affluent buying public. British research thus emphasizes that in the course of the eighteenth century, shops in the upper segment of the market were decorated increasingly lavishly and given a look that was in keeping with the status of their intended clientele. In order to facilitate comfortable 'shopping', the urban landscape also needed to be addressed, 'in order to make a fashionable social space for enlightened cultural activity, an infrastructure of pleasure'.[4]

When we review the literature on British retail trade in the eighteenth century, we can identify four elements characterizing the modernization process. First, there was a striking rise in the number of shops. Second, more so than in the past, these shops formed clusters in the centre of the city. Third, the city centre—and more specifically the major shopping streets in the centre—was adapted to the requirements of shopping as a leisure activity for the affluent upper classes. The term for this that is commonly used in the literature is 'urban improvement'. And finally, there was a whole series of changes that can be summarized under the heading of 'retail practices', including marketing techniques and forms of interchange between the shopkeeper and the consumer.[5] Below, we will try to establish the extent to which these changes also took place in Amsterdam. The degree of detail to which we are accustomed in the British studies will never be achieved, as there are almost no preliminary studies available for the Netherlands and Amsterdam, meaning that the picture is necessarily sketchy. At the same time, it is striking that British historians have tended to show great interest in shops selling durable goods in the upper segment of the market to an affluent clientele. As the aim of the present study is broader here, greater emphasis will be put on diversity within Amsterdam's retail landscape.

2 Ibidem. For an extensive treatment of the older literature, see the introduction to Mui and Mui, *Shops and Shopkeeping*, p. 5, and Cox, *The Complete Tradesman*, pp. 11–14.

3 For the presence of significant numbers of shops in England, see Mui and Mui, *Shops and Shopkeeping*. For shop exteriors, shop interiors and daily routine in the retail trade, see especially Walsh, 'Shop Design'; Stobart, 'Shopping Streets as Social Space'; Cox, *The Complete Tradesman*; Cox and Walsh, '"Their Shops are Dens"'; Stobart and Hann, 'Retailing Revolution in the Eighteenth Century?'; and Stobart, Hann and Morgan, *Spaces of Consumption*.

4 Clark, *European Cities and Towns*, p. 195, and see also Alexander, *Retailing in England*, p. 6 ff, and Stobart, Hann and Morgan, *Spaces of Consumption*.

5 Compare Stobart and Hann, 'Retailing Revolution in the Eighteenth Century?', p. 171, and Jefferys, *Retail Trading in Britain*.

The number and location of shops in Amsterdam

In the light of the chapters above, it is indisputable that there were shops in Amsterdam long before the eighteenth century. It is less straightforward, however, to establish whether the number of shops grew in the eighteenth century and the first half of the nineteenth century, and whether the relative importance of the shop grew compared to other forms of retail trade. Due to the poor state of Amsterdam's guild archives, it is impossible to reconstruct the development of the number of guild members. Moreover, we have already observed that registration for the shopkeepers' guild, which included a large proportion of the shopkeepers, was anything but comprehensive. In 1752, many hundreds of citizens of Amsterdam were running groceries or grain chandleries without ever having joined a guild.

Although we lack hard data, it is unlikely that Amsterdam's retail sector became full-fledged as late as between 1700 and 1850. This had already happened in the preceding period, from the late sixteenth century onwards, when Amsterdam's population exploded and its distribution system started to become differentiated and specialized. This was the era in which the number of job titles in retail trade multiplied (see Chapter 2) and the shop flourished as never before. From the end of the seventeenth century, the population of Amsterdam grew only slowly, to a maximum of ca. 240,000 around 1730, and it would fluctuate around this level until the final quarter of the century. After this, it started to fall, and despite a recovery in the second quarter of the nineteenth century, in 1850, the number of people living in Amsterdam was still considerably lower than it had been around 1730.[6]

6 Van Leeuwen and Oeppen, 'Reconstructing the Demographic Regime of Amsterdam', table 9.

In such a period of demographic stagnation, decline and slow recovery, a substantial expansion could only take place in the retail sector if new products were introduced that were sold exclusively in shops and if shop sales superseded other forms of retail trade. This latter development does not seem to have occurred. Admittedly, the Dam lost some of its seventeenth-century market-square character, but on the whole, the number of daily and weekly markets remained constant.[7] In the first half of the nineteenth century, a number of very specific markets—such as those for medicinal herbs or for ladders and well hooks—were no longer listed in the market regulations, but again, there were few significant changes.[8] And the situation could hardly be otherwise because given the lack of refrigeration and modern transport, the town's population was and continued to be dependent for food and beverages on the supply from market gardeners, dairy farmers and poultry farmers in the immediate vicinity. They would sail to Amsterdam's markets with their wares early in the morning (Figure 6.1). Once there, they sold directly to the consumer but also to street traders, who in turn sold the goods in the city. This system was very common, especially for the trade in vegetables and fruit, and remained so until far into the nineteenth century.[9] Only then did shops take on a large and growing part of food provision. All in all, it is unlikely that the size of Amsterdam's shop sector increased markedly in the years between 1700 and 1850 by superseding market trading and street trading.

When it comes to the introduction of new products, the main contenders were coffee, tea and tobacco. By European standards, the Dutch

7 Kistemaker, 'De Amsterdamse markten', p. 86, and the maps on page 84.
8 Wagenaar, 'De Amsterdamse markten', p. 104.
9 Kistemaker, 'De Amsterdamse markten', p. 92, and Wagenaar, 'De Amsterdamse markten', pp. 101–104.

Figure 6.1: The vegetable market on Prinsengracht, first half of the eighteenth century.

encountered coffee at an early stage. This happened in Mocha in 1616, when Pieter van den Broecke came across what he described as a 'a type of black bean [...], used to make black water, drunk hot'.[10] The first quantities of 'cauwa [coffee] de Mocha' turn up in the sales records of the Amsterdam Chamber of the VOC in the 1660s, but it would be several decades before coffee became a common beverage. In 1686, it was noted by Stephanus Blankaert, a physician in Amsterdam, that 'even twenty years ago, only some foreigners who had travelled in Turkey and elsewhere were familiar with it. But now the drink has become so common that the coffee houses are full to bursting with people.'[11] Plenty of coffee was consumed in private homes, too. According to François Valentijn, by the 1720s the drink had become so common that 'the maids and the seamstresses must take their coffee in the morning, or the thread will not go through the eye of the needle'.[12] That coffee became a popular drink only at the end of the seventeenth century is confirmed by the small number of coffee sellers among Amsterdam's bridegrooms in the years between 1691

10 '[E]en spetie van swarte boontjes [...], daer swart water van maken en warm indrincken' (Glamann, *Dutch-Asiatic Trade*, p. 183). For the introduction of coffee in the Netherlands, see Reinders and Wijsenbeek, *Koffie in Nederland.*

11 '[S]elfs over twintig jaar was deselve maar by sommige buitenlanders bekendt, die in Turkyen en elders gesworven hadden. Maar nu is die drank soo gemeen geworden, dat men de Coffi-huisen tot Amsterdam soo vol van menschen siet dat se gepropt zijn' (Reinders, De Wit and Nijboer, '"Een specie van swarte boontjes"', p. 11).

12 '[D]e meijden en naeisters nu smorgens hare coffi moeten hebben, of de draed wil door het oog van de naald niet' (Glamann, *Dutch-Asiatic Trade*, p. 185).

and 1700.[13] After this, the situation changed rapidly: in the registers of the *Personele Quotisatie* of 1742, which included only citizens of Amsterdam with an income of 600 guilders or more, we come across 70 coffee shopkeepers and seven shopkeepers selling coffee and tea.[14]

Tea, like coffee, was initially seen as a medicine, and not everyone was enthusiastic about the taste. In his history of the East Indies, the above-mentioned François Valentijn wrote that he had tried tea for the first time in 1681 and that, in his opinion, it tasted 'no better than hay-water'.[15] Tea was still extremely expensive at that time; around 80 guilders per pound, according to Valentijn. From the end of the seventeenth century, and particularly in the 1720s, when the Chinese port city of Canton was opened up to European merchants, the price of tea fell. Imports grew spectacularly, and tea, like coffee, became a beverage consumed by large swathes of the population. In the banns deeds dating from the last decade of the seventeenth century, only one tea seller is listed, but the rapid growth of consumption in the first half of the eighteenth century is reflected in the 108 tea shopkeepers among those liable for tax in the *Personele Quotisatie*.

Tobacco, a crop from America, was introduced to Europe via Spain. Smoking, sniffing and chewing tobacco quickly became extremely popular among Europeans. Around 1530, the first commercial tobacco plantation was established in the islands of the Caribbean.[16] Tobacco exports from Virginia give an impression of the enormous European demand for this stimulant. In 1616, just 500 kilos of tobacco were exported from this production area; by 1620, this had already risen to 20,000 kilos; by 1629, more than 700,000 kilos; and by 1750, no fewer than 25 million kilos.[17] Amsterdam was a major centre for trading and processing imported tobacco, and, as was also the case for Chinese porcelain and Indian cotton fabrics, demand in the Netherlands was so great that people spotted opportunities for import substitution. Around 1710, tobacco was being grown in the sandy soil of Utrecht and Gelderland on an enormous scale, producing around seven to nine million kilos a year.[18] Compared to coffee and tea, tobacco entered the consumption package relatively early on. This is also shown by the fact that nineteen tobacco sellers were already listed in banns deeds in Amsterdam in the years between 1641 and 1650, a number that would rise to 62 in the last decade of the century. In 1742, the *Personele Quotisatie* registered no fewer than 233 tobacconists and three tobacco sellers. If sales of coffee, tea and tobacco are taken together, there were more than 400 shops in 1742. That is certainly an underestimation of the actual number, because shopkeepers with meagre incomes were not included in the registers of the *Personele Quotisatie*.

Only in the French period—in 1810 to be precise—do we get an impression of the total number of shopkeepers selling tea, coffee, tobacco and chocolate. In the *patentbelasting* of that year—a tax levied on businesses and industries in accordance with size, location and profitability—919 large and small retailers who sold these stimulants were registered.[19] In comparison to the low number in the early

13 In the years 1586–1595 and 1641–1650, no coffee sellers are mentioned in the registers of intended marriages.

14 Oldewelt, *Kohier van de Personeele Quotisatie*, Volume II. The figures in Oldewelt, Volume I, appendix deviate slightly from my direct counts in the register (Volume II).

15 '[N]iet beter dan hooy-water smaakte' (Glamann, *Dutch-Asiatic Trade*, p. 212).

16 Roessingh, *Inlandse tabak*, p. 44.

17 Ibidem, p. 47, and Steensgaard, 'Commodities, Bullion and Services', p. 12.

18 Roessingh, *Inlandse tabak*, p. 340.

19 The original registration has not been preserved, but total figures can be found in SAA, Archief Burgemeesters, inv. nr. 718. See also Diederiks, *Een stad in verval*, pp. 375–376.

eighteenth century, when consumption, particularly of tea and coffee, was still rather insignificant, the number of shopkeepers in this sector had therefore increased strongly. Because the figures from the French period do not give the impression that the number of shopkeepers in other sectors fell strikingly, the net result will have been an increase in the total number of shopkeepers. Despite this, we should again emphasize that the real growth in Amsterdam's retail system took place in the late sixteenth and early seventeenth centuries, and not in the eighteenth century.[20]

Likewise, when we consider the second element of the modernization process, the increasing concentration of shops in the city centre, the period between 1700 and 1850 does not appear to have been one of great change. As we saw above, a well-developed and differentiated retail system emerged in Amsterdam as early as the end of the sixteenth century, with clusters of shops selling durable goods mainly in the city centre and widespread distribution of shops selling daily necessities. The relatively modern location patterns that only developed in many British cities in the course of the eighteenth century thus had a much longer history in Amsterdam.

Urban improvement in Amsterdam

The third component of the modernization process in Britain was that of making public space suitable for social and cultural pursuits, particularly those of the well-off. Viewed in the broadest sense, this urban improvement entailed much more than the creation of an infrastructure that could make shopping a pleasurable pastime. In *Spaces of Consumption,* the authors focus on the total range of leisure activities on offer, from horseracing and shopping to theatre visits and reading library books.[21] Here, we limit our focus to those aspects that are directly relevant to the functioning of shops: paving, waste removal, lighting, traffic regulation and the appearance of the shop premises. In many British towns, these aspects were only addressed in the course of the eighteenth century and sometimes not until the beginning of the nineteenth century. Until that time, the financial resources tended to be lacking, as was a government with sufficient authority to implement the measures. The results were hardly spectacular, particularly in the eighteenth century. Only 45 streetlights were installed in Liverpool in 1718, for example, and there were only a few such lights in Birmingham in the 1790s.[22]

In Amsterdam, by contrast, the city government had capitalized upon the urban expansions of the seventeenth century to bring the organization and maintenance of public space under the city's oversight. This was not only the case for the new city districts but also for the public space in the old city centre, and it was there in particular that the main shopping thoroughfares were located. As we saw above, paving was made uniform throughout the city, with a traffic lane of stone cobbles and footpaths of yellow clinker bricks laid on their sides. Drains were built under the pavements to carry away waste water and rain water, and there was also a waste removal system that functioned well by early modern standards. The negotiability and safety of the city at dusk and during the night were greatly improved

20 In the eighteenth century, the number of retailers was also increasing in Antwerp and Maastricht: see Van Aert, 'Leven of overleven?', pp. 153–154, 284–297, and Steegen, *Kleinhandel en stedelijke ontwikkeling*, chapter 3.

21 Stobart, Hann and Morgan, *Spaces of Consumption*, in particular the tables 2.1 and 2.4.

22 Ibidem, pp. 88–89.

by the street lighting designed by Jan van der Heyden in the second half of the seventeenth century, and traffic flows were regulated with orders and prohibitions. During the Fourth Expansion, the city government went even further by constructing a well-planned system of traffic streets. Moreover, markets that caused significant disturbance and pollution were moved to the periphery of the city, which added to the suitability of the centre for use by wealthy citizens.

Taken altogether, it is justifiable to discuss seventeenth-century Amsterdam in terms of 'urban improvement', a phenomenon that would not play a role in British towns until a much later stage. This integral approach to the city centre was exceptional in European terms. Of the great European metropolises, Amsterdam was undoubtedly the city where planning and management had the greatest impact on the urban landscape. This had to do with the fact that several capable administrators had learned from the problems experienced during the Third Expansion, the fact that key positions in the official apparatus were filled by engineers and designers such as Daniël Stalpaert, and the structure of the real estate market.[23] Plans were also made in England and France in the seventeenth century, and the Great Fire of London in 1666 even provided an excellent opportunity for the urban landscape to be reorganized. That it did not come to this, despite the designs produced by Christopher Wren and others, can largely be attributed to the vested interests of the landowning classes.[24] There were landowners in Amsterdam too, of course, but they consisted almost exclusively of small private landowners who were unable to take a stand against the city government when confronted with plans for expropriation—a condition for integral urban planning. In England, in particular, but also elsewhere, expropriation was much less straightforward, as much land was owned by aristocratic families and influential institutions such as religious houses, churches and universities, which proved more tenacious. The building projects that were realized in England were thus of a self-contained nature and hindered the integral management of the urban space. By contrast, there was no extensive aristocratic land ownership in Amsterdam; most of the property of the religious houses and churches had been expropriated at the time of the *Alteratie*; and social care institutions did not own extensive and continuous property in the city. In short, the underlying conditions for the planning and management of urban space were much more favourable in Amsterdam than elsewhere.

Now that it is clear that many of the matters classified as 'urban improvement' in Britain in the eighteenth century had already been realized in Amsterdam during the preceding century, there remains the question of whether this also applied to the appearance of the shopping streets. After all, in British cities, urban improvement also concerned the architecture of houses and the ways in which these were combined in rows of façades. Uniformity and having a distinguished appearance were prized very highly.[25] For commercial reasons—the creation of a pleasant shopping environment—shopkeepers in particular made great efforts. They often took the initiative to reconstruct a façade, either completely or partially. One example is that of the celebrated renovation of Colmore Row in Birmingham in 1830. West wrote in his *History, topography and directory of Warwickshire* that 'the style of architecture, and the light and airy mode of fronting

23 Abrahamse, *Metropolis in the Making*, chapter 7.
24 Stobart, Hann and Morgan, *Spaces of Consumption*, p. 59.
25 Ibidem, chapter 4.

the houses, together with the elegance of the shops, has rendered this quarter of the town very attractive'.[26]

Were renovations such as these also undertaken in shopping areas in Amsterdam? Before we answer this question, it is important to note that the appearance of many British cities was practically medieval before the urban improvement. In provincial towns such as Warwick, Worcester and Chester, houses on the main shopping streets were built with timbered frames, a construction technique that had disappeared almost completely from Amsterdam by the beginning of the eighteenth century. In this respect, too, British urban improvement was partially a matter of catching up.[27] This is also shown by the fact that the classical style of architecture that was popular in British towns had been used on a large scale in Amsterdam since the mid-seventeenth century, albeit mainly for public buildings and the homes of the wealthy elite in the canal ring. For this reason, there was presumably less need for an extensive reconstruction of shopping streets in Amsterdam than on the other side of the Channel.

That is not to say, though, that there were no changes to the appearance of shops and shopping streets in Amsterdam between 1700 and 1850. Admittedly, the traditional design of the small bourgeois house remained unchanged, and the *voorhuis* was still the place best suited to a shop or workspace, but the façade—and with it the appearance of the street—did change. In new buildings or renovations, for example, the timbered lower façade was often replaced with a stone façade, not only in residential homes but also frequently in shop premises.[28] The façades of Amsterdam's houses also changed in response to changing fashions. These were expressed most powerfully in newly built homes, but even in the case of existing houses, the façade could be removed without too much difficulty and replaced with one that better reflected the architectural fashions of the time and the tastes of the owner.[29] As a result of these adjustments, from the end of the seventeenth century, the Dutch renaissance style and Dutch classicism were less dominant in the streets, and the expressive Baroque and Rococo (Louis XV style) movements began to influence the proportions and decoration of façades. From the final quarter of the eighteenth century, architecture became less lavish, and particularly in the final years of the Republic and during the French period, there was a revival of interest in classical architecture. The influence of classicism remained considerable until the mid-nineteenth century.[30]

How radical the changes to existing façades could be is illustrated by a building on Kalverstraat that was occupied for many years by publishers and booksellers, known as 'Bibliopolum'. We have a picture of this part of Kalverstraat from the year 1768 because the booksellers Jacob Yntema and

26 Quoted in ibidem, p. 97. It is striking that the appearance of Amsterdam's streets and shops hardly received any attention in city descriptions and travel guides from the eighteenth and first half of the nineteenth centuries. See, for example, Kernkamp, 'Bengt Ferrner's dagboek'; *Le guide, ou nouvelle description d'Amsterdam* (1722, 1772); *Le guide d'Amsterdam* (1793), and Maaskamp, *Nouveau tableau statistique* (1845). But compare Van Damme, *Verleiden en verkopen*, p. 171 for the Southern Low Countries.

27 See, for example, the picture from around 1817 (!) of Eastgate Street in Chester as depicted in Stobart, '"A Settled Little Society of Trading People"?', p. 209.

28 Meischke, *Het Nederlandse woonhuis*, p. 437.

29 As the joisting in Amsterdam houses usually rested in the side walls, front and rear façades had no constructive function and could easily be removed and replaced.

30 Zantkuijl, *Bouwen in Amsterdam*, pp. 482–524 and 558–559. See also Koldeweij, '1750–1800', pp. 264–265, and Eliëns, '1800–1850', p. 343.

Figure 6.2: Bibliopolum on Kalverstraat, 1768.

Jacob Tieboel threw a pamphlet out of a first-floor window, directed at the city architect Jan Smit (Figure 6.2). Then there is a painting from 1779 that shows a crowd gathering in front of what was then not only a bookshop but also a lottery office (Figure 6.3).[31] The framing is almost identical to that of the engraving of 1768, and we can clearly see how much the appearance of a façade could change. The lower façades in particular are almost unrecognizable and have a completely different appearance—one that was modern for that time.[32] It is important to remember that not all of Amsterdam's houses would have been subject to every stylistic change; the changes were often less radical than in this part of Kalverstraat. As a result, an extremely varied street scene developed over time, one that reflected the efforts that people made, by making small and large adjustments, to adapt their living environment to what they saw at the time as an appropriate backdrop to their daily lives and commercial activities.

Linked to changing stylistic fashions and of great relevance to research into retail trade are the radical changes made to window frames and windowpanes. Amsterdam's residential buildings had traditionally had heavy wooden cross-windows. In the picture of Bibliopolum from 1768 we can see

31 More information on this building and its occupants can be found on www.bibliopolis.nl (last accessed 9 August 2019).

32 This modernity does not alter the fact that the basement under the building was used by a herring seller. This is indicated by the herring crown protruding from the cellar (Ter Brugge, "'Een eigen Hollandsch feest'").

Figure 6.3: Bibliopolum on Kalverstraat, 1779.

examples of these on the first floor: the top half is closed with leaded glass that is mounted directly in the frame, whilst the bottom half has a hinged window and shutters on the outside of the frame. Due to the heavily built frame, the small leaded windows and the opacity of the glass, little light would have penetrated through to the rooms behind. In the second half of the seventeenth century, fashions inspired by English and French examples led to more demand from trend-setting and affluent citizens for daylight in residential rooms. This wish was granted by replacing the leaded glass with larger panes of clear glass that were fixed in wooden glazing bars. By the end of the seventeenth century, the heavy mullion and transom were also removed from the cross-window when possible and desirable, creating enough space to put a grid window over the entire width of the window opening.[33] Finally, the amount of light in the room beyond was further improved by enlarging the window opening. For the buildings next to Bibliopolum, this had been done before 1768. At Bibliopolum itself, the window openings on the first floor were enlarged considerably between 1768 and 1779.

These same larger windowpanes set in wooden glazing bars were also used in shops and offered a much better view of the shop interior. It is no coincidence that the modern grid windows with clear glass that were still lacking from the first floor of Bibliopolum in 1768 *had* been placed in the lower façade, behind which the shop was located. And the trend towards using more and more glass did not end there.

33 Zantkuijl, *Bouwen in Amsterdam*, p. 210. For the wish for more daylight in residential houses, see also Pijzel-Dommisse, '1700–1750', pp. 187 and 194.

Figure 6.4: Shop premises on Kalverstraat, second half of the eighteenth century.

In the eighteenth century, the glazing bars were placed further and further apart, a trend that would continue into the nineteenth century.[34] All of this had significant implications for shops. In the sixteenth and seventeenth centuries, shops usually had an open character: with their displays in the window and in front of the façade, they were still highly reminiscent of market stalls. These types of shops still existed in the eighteenth and nineteenth centuries—there should be no doubt about it—but we can detect a change. More than previously, selling became an activity that took place behind rather than in front of the lower façade. And now this was also possible because the larger panes and improved light maintained the link with passers-by in the street—albeit in a new way—that was so essential for sales.

34 Zantkuijl, *Bouwen in Amsterdam*, p. 216.

This development did not occur in isolation but was related to the changes that had already taken place in the homes of the bourgeoisie. In the latter, the separation of public and private space had begun in the seventeenth century, and the front step now functioned more as a barrier than as the smooth transitional space between home and the outside world that it had once been (see Chapter 4). It is therefore clear that this more closed form of shopkeeping would have been introduced on the major shopping thoroughfares first and only later spread to working-class neighbourhoods such as the Jordaan and the Jewish Quarter and was presumably less common there. The changes that occurred on the main streets are clearly illustrated by a shop premises neighbouring the Nieuwezijdskapel, meaning that it was depicted a number of times (Figure 6.4). Figure .4 in Chapter 4 shows the situation around 1700. With

Figure 6.5: Shop premises on the corner of Heiligeweg and Kalverstraat, last quarter of the seventeenth century.

two display cases on the shutters on the façade and wares hanging from the canopy, the appearance of this shop could be described as 'traditional'. By the second half of the eighteenth century, much had changed. Not only did the first floor of the façade now feature modern window frames, but the canopy and the shutters in front of the windows in the lower façade had disappeared and with this the possibility of displaying merchandise in front of the façade. What remained were small barrels in the window as a kind of outdoor advertising, informing the consumer in this busy shopping street what kinds of wares could be purchased there.

The disappearance of canopies was one of the most striking changes in the eighteenth-century retail landscape and contributed to the fading of the association between the shop and the market stall. Now that actual sales and the display of merchandise increasingly took place behind—and not in front of—the façade, the canopy lost its function of protecting clients and shop goods from all kinds of weather. In fact, when it came to selling and presenting goods in a shop, the canopy even blocked the free entry of natural light and had to be removed. Blinds were sometimes used to protect the consumer and the merchandise from the sun.[35] These changes are captured in Figures 6.5 and 6.6, which show the cabinet makers' building on Kalverstraat, viewed from Heiligeweg. In the final quarter of the seventeenth century (Figure 6.5), all of the buildings depicted had large canopies on and under which merchandise was displayed. Moreover, the cabinet makers' building, a showroom and salesroom for products made by Amsterdam's furniture makers, still had a traditional timbered lower

35 SAA, Desolate boedelkamer, inv. nr. 6241.

Figure 6.6: Shop premises on the corner of Heiligeweg and Kalverstraat, 1774.

façade with leaded glass windows and cross windows on the upper floors.

By 1774 (Figure 6.6), the lower façade and first-floor window frames of the cabinet makers' building had been modernized and, even more importantly, all of the canopies had disappeared. Instead, display boards had been added to the cabinet makers' building and the façade on the right; these were much lighter in construction and let more daylight into the shop. The same effect was achieved by placing grid windows in the lower façade. One is also struck by the prominent presence of signboards on the façade. Passers-by could be in no doubt that stockings were for sale in the building on the right and that ironmongery could be bought in the building on the left. With the disappearance of displays in front of the façade and canopies, how to highlight the merchandise and lure consumers into the shop remained a matter of concern for retailers. The owner of the house on the left in the background has resorted to a tried and trusted method: using the window sill as an outdoor showcase for pottery and porcelain (Figure 6.7). Likewise, the female vegetable seller in the

Figure 6.7: Display of shop wares on windowsill, 1774.

basement on the right is still displaying her wares in the street to draw attention to her trade. In the second half of the eighteenth century, it was the large display boards, signs, door displays and the lack of 'real' shop windows that caused visitors from England and France to observe that the shops of Amsterdam looked old-fashioned in comparison with those in London and Paris.[36]

Something that is also clear from depictions of eighteenth-century Amsterdam is that although canopies and displays in front of the façade had become less common, the traditional front step—with its *pothuizen*, basement entrances, benches, fencing and many other things—remained. The strip of pavement directly adjacent to the façade was still regarded as belonging to the house and could be used as the owner saw fit, and this did not change until after the mid-nineteenth century. Nevertheless, in an important shopping street such as Kalverstraat, shopkeepers did remove obstacles in front of the façade of their own accord. This is hardly surprising, because when the display of merchandise was moved to the interior, potential clients needed to be able to get right up to the shop window—and this was more difficult if it was cluttered with *pothuizen*, cellar entrances and fencing. Real pavements did not yet exist in 1850. In *Physiologie van de Kalverstraat*, published in 1844, a fictitious dialogue between a citizen of Amsterdam and a stranger features the following remark: 'By the way, do you see that endless flat step,

36 Desjobert ('Voyage aux Pays Bas', 338) wrote: 'Les enseignes des boutiques sont très grandes, comme jadis à Paris'. Smith noted that the busy streets of Amsterdam gave a good impression of 'what Cheapside and Ludgate-street were in the last century' (Smith, *A Sketch of a Tour on the Continent*, p. 22). I wish to thank Mr C.D. van Strien for his help in finding these references.

Figure 6.8: Kalverstraat in the second half of the eighteenth century.

which looks a little like the pavements in Paris and London? It was hoped that the whole of Kalverstraat would have steps like that […].'[37] Indeed, in London and Paris, the private steps with fencing and outbuildings were removed and replaced with contiguous raised pavements, something that undoubtedly proved more comfortable for pedestrians than the situation in Amsterdam.[38]

But on the whole, the street scene in the main shopping streets and major approach streets did become more peaceful. This is clear from Figure 6.8, which shows the situation in

37 'Apropos, ziet gij daar die eindelooze platte stoep, dat lijkt wel wat naar de Parijsche en Londensche trottoirs. Het was te hoopen, dat de geheele Kalverstraat zulke stoepen had […]' (Een-Humorist, *Physiologie van de Kalverstraat*, p. 25).

38 Pavements were laid in London in the second half of the eighteenth century and in Paris towards the end of the century (Van Strien-Chardonneau, *'Le voyage de Hollande'*, p. 162). In 1794, Radcliffe noticed the lack of 'raised pavement' in Amsterdam (Radcliffe, *A Journey through Holland*, p. 73).

Kalverstraat in the second half of the eighteenth century. The pedestrian could usually get right up to the façade of the shops, recognizable from the signboards hanging far into the street, as there were no *pothuizen* or other constructions.[39] Only when the buildings still had an exclusively residential function did the front step have a (stone) staircase that gave access to the *voorhuis,* which lay above street level. The canopies, which had once dominated the street scene, had almost completely disappeared.

In the light of all of the above, it will come as no surprise that the appearance of the lower façade changed. When the sale and display of merchandise moved inside the shop, the function of the shopfront became more important. It needed to provide the privacy that the consumer valued when inspecting, choosing and buying, but at the same time it had to give customers a sufficient impression of the interior and tempt them inside. Enlarging the glass window, removing the canopy and clearing away the *pothuizen* and other constructions were attempts to achieve this, but they were not the only ones. Presumably in imitation of what had already been done in canal houses, some shopkeepers replaced the wooden doors with glass ones. In Figure 6.9, we see a shop with just such a glass door.[40]

In the end, all of these adaptations led to the development of a style of façade that was specifically adapted to retail trade. In practice, such façades did not exist until the second half of the eighteenth century. They were almost always a variant on the lower façade of the traditional private home, adapted to a greater or lesser extent. Judging from architectural drawings and images, the 'emancipation' of the shopfront was achieved by maximizing the quantity of glass and accentuating the main entrance of the building. The latter was often done by placing the entrance centrally in the façade, adding architectural and decorative accents, and by installing a double door (glass or otherwise). A fine example of this new type of shopfront is the lower façade of Bibliopolum in Kalverstraat (Figure 6.3), which was renovated between 1768 and 1779. Architectural drawings from around 1800 show a similar picture and demonstrate how far the shopfront had come from the design that Philips Vingboons had produced for the shops on St Luciënsteeg around the middle of the seventeenth century (Figure 4.17). These had not yet been distinguishable from middle-class homes in any way. From figures 6.10 and 6.11, we can see at a glance that the specialized shopfront had made its entrance into Amsterdam's retail landscape by the second half of the eighteenth century.

That some still had to adjust to the new situation is shown by a novel by Willem Kist, published in 1800. When the protagonist, who comes from the provinces, goes into raptures when he sees the shops in Kalverstraat, his companion quips that 'the shops here were perfect for luring people, just as one would put out a net to catch birds', and it was precisely for this reason that 'the most and the most beautiful [things are displayed] in the windows'.[41] Even though Amsterdam's shopfronts had been modernized, Amsterdam's shops could not necessarily stand comparison with those in a metropolis such as London. In 1794, Ann Radcliff wrote: 'The shops [...] in the interior [of the city] have a mean appearance to those who

39 Estate inventories from the years 1743–1746 confirm that signboards and signs were still very common.

40 For glass doors, see Zantkuijl, *Bouwen in Amsterdam*, pp. 289–290.

41 '[D]at de winkels hier juist geschikt waren om de menschen te verlokken, even als men netten spant om vogels te vangen' [...] 'het meeste en fraaiste [...] uitgespreid voor de glazen' (Kist, *Het leven, gevoelens en zonderlinge reize*, p. 200).

Figure 6.9: Glass door in a shop on Oudekerksplein, second half of the eighteenth century.

try them by the standard of London conveniences and elegance.'[42] And similar voices could be heard at the beginning of the nineteenth century. After a visit to Amsterdam in 1806, August Niemeijer wrote: 'There are countless shops, and full of goods, but mostly located in narrow streets. They also don't leave as much of an impression as English shops.'[43]

As noted above, contact with passers-by in the street remained a constant source of concern for shopkeepers. In the major shopping thoroughfares, extensive displays in front of the façade were a thing of the past, and during the French Period the signboards that had hung out far into the street disappeared. Now customers' attention had to be caught by a fine shopfront and clear view of the shop interior.[44] Outdoor display cases also fulfilled this function, however. Already in use in the seventeenth century, these were still being used in the eighteenth and the early nineteenth

42 Radcliffe, *A Journey through Holland*, p. 75. See also Smith, *A Sketch of a Tour on the Continent*, p. 22, which describes the situation in the second half of the 1780s.

43 'Die Kaufläden sind zahllos, und reich ausgestattet; aber sie liegen grösztentheils in engen Straszen. Auch machen sie bey weitem nicht den Eindruck wie die englischen' (Niemeyer, *Beobachtungen auf einer Reise*, pp. 102–103). See also Huber, *Bemerkungen über Holland*, p. 137.

44 For the disappearance of sign boards and shop signs, see Witsen Geysbeek, *Het tegenwoordig Amsterdam*, pp. 42–43, and see also Garrioch, 'House Names, Shop Signs and Social Organization'.

Figure 6.10: Design of the lower facade of a shop, ca. 1800.

centuries—something that visitors from metropolises such as London and Paris considered old-fashioned at the end of the eighteenth century.[45] In 1787, H.P. Schouten produced a beautifully painted example of one on the façade of a house on the corner of Kalverstraat and Munt (Figure 6.12), and in 1819, Gerrit Lamberts captured an outdoor display case filled with silverware on the right-hand side of the Beurspoort (Figure 6.13).

On the left-hand side of the Beurspoort, on the lower façade, we see not a self-standing display case but an extended shop window that can only be accessed from inside the shop. Indeed, this was a new weapon in the battle for the attention of passers-by and the shopping public. Possibly influenced by British and French examples, self-standing display cases were integrated into the façade, as it were, and were also made bigger.[46] An early example of a large extended display window such as this can be seen in a depiction of Kalverstraat by Christiaan Andriessen in 1807. In a street that is shrouded in darkness, one's

45 Radcliffe, *A Journey through Holland*, p. 34.

46 See the extended display windows on the Strand in London around 1790 as depicted in Cox, *The Complete Tradesman*, p. 69.

Figure 6.11: Design of the lower facade of Matthis Schoonveld's bookshop on Rokin, 1802.

eye was immediately caught by the illuminated display.[47]

Around 1825, this type of extended display window was quite common in busy shopping streets such as Kalverstraat. This is clear from a print of Kalverstraat published by Frans Buffa, which, not coincidentally, also features his own print shop (Figure 6.14, in the foreground on the right).[48] The print shop had flat display windows with a grid frame, as was common, but on both the left and right-hand sides of the street we see a number of extended display windows that present their contents emphatically to passers-by. With glass on three sides and good light, they were perfect for displaying merchandise. In the same period, Buffa had a similar print made of the southerly end of Kalverstraat near the Munttoren, and in this we can likewise clearly make out the extended display windows. But as well as similarities, there are also differences. The changes to the street scene were most far-reaching at the northerly end of the street, near the Dam. Display boards, which had still been ubiquitous in the eighteenth century, were nowhere to be seen around 1825. And although the front step area still existed and fencing can be seen every now and

47 Hoogenboom, Gerlagh and Stroop, *De wereld van Christiaan Andriessen*, figure 43, and SAA, Beeldbank 010094000042.

48 More information on the Buffa print shop can be found in Heijbroek, 'Van eenvoudige prentenkoopman'.

Figure 6.12: Outdoor display case on the facade of the corner house on Kalverstraat-Munt, 1787.

then, we see no trace of *pothuizen*, displays or benches. The situation near the Munt was different. There, signs such as barrels or rows of stockings had been placed on the façades, *pothuizen* were present in considerable numbers, and the traditional benches were still present (Figure 6.15, in the foreground on the left). These differences can be explained by the fact that, more than at the southern end of Kalverstraat, the northern part of the street directly adjacent to the Dam was in the heart of the central retail area. It was there that accessibility was greatest, the commercial potential of locations was best, and the urge for innovation was most strongly felt.[49]

49 For the accessibility of the northern part of Kalverstraat, see chapter 3. The author of *Physiologie van de Kalverstraat* also makes a distinction between the different parts of Kalverstraat and reports for the southernmost part that it 'has nothing special except for the two shops of Puttenaar and the *Heerenmagazijn*' (Een-Humorist, *Physiologie van de Kalverstraat*, p. 21).

Figure 6.13: Outdoor display case on Beurspoort, 1819.

We are fortunate that Buffa & Sons was still based in the same premises on Kalverstraat in the mid-nineteenth century and considered it commercially worthwhile to publish yet another print of the street. The view presented by the artist, Cornelis Springer, was almost identical to that captured by his predecessor a few decades earlier. The front step still existed, but the rest of the street scene had changed radically (Figure 6.16). This is clearly evident in the first place from the gables of the houses. Many of the stepped gables, neck gables and Dutch gables had been replaced with straight cornice gables. These were more in line with contemporary tastes and also cheaper when the stone façades had to be replaced or repaired. But it is also clear that the extended display windows had been removed and the panes in the grid windows were larger than before. Like many of the gables, the lower façades were also finished with a ledge, which was used for inscriptions—and Buffa & Sons was no exception (on the right in the foreground).

There is no simple explanation for the relatively rapid disappearance of the extended display windows from Kalverstraat. Increasing crowding in the street and the removal of obstacles that hindered traffic flows have been suggested as explanations but appear unlikely in this case.[50] After all, the front step continued to exist, as did the fencing at right angles to the façade. Thus, it was not simply a question of allowing for an unimpeded flow of traffic. An alternative explanation could be that this was related to the introduction of gas lighting and its use in shop

50 Rouwhorst, 'Oog voor detail: uitstal- of winkelkasten'.

Figure 6.14: Kalverstraat near the Dam, 1825.

windows. The extended display windows benefitted maximally from the amount of available natural light, but the introduction of gas lighting offered unprecedented opportunities for shopkeepers. The bright light was perfect for lighting items displayed in a window, but the fittings had to be mounted close to the windowpane. This was because the light had to shine from the front onto the merchandise and not from behind, which would have placed the goods in the shadow. The glass side walls of extended display cases were ill-suited to the mounting of gas fittings, and hanging lamps from above would have obstructed the view. Moreover, until the 1860s, gas lights gave off a large amount of heat, and this could not be conveyed away easily in extended display windows.[51] The usual method of displaying items, which I shall address in more detail below, also led to problems. Extended window display cases were normally divided into separate levels or storeys, which did not work well with gas lighting: the light could not cover all of the levels simultaneously, and the conveyance of heat from the lamp was seriously impeded. All of these problems disappeared when goods were displayed slightly further back in the shop, the extended display window was replaced with a flat windowpane, and the gas light was mounted between the window and the display. It would not be far-fetched to say that

51 Dil and Homburg, 'Gas', p. 125.

Figure 6.15: Kalverstraat near the Muntplein, 1825.

when making these changes, Dutch shopkeepers were probably inspired by their English colleagues. Gas lighting had been introduced earlier in England, meaning that shopkeepers there had already found solutions to the problems raised by the new lighting source.

When it came to shops in prominent locations in the retail landscape, the radical changes that took place during the eighteenth century and the first half of the nineteenth century are clearly illustrated by Figures 6.17 to 6.19, which show houses on the corner of the Dam and Kalverstraat. As shown in the drawing, this was the location of a fire in the first half of the eighteenth century (Figure 6.17). The appearance of the corner building is clearly still traditional. The building has a timbered lower façade and a substantial canopy at the front and side onto which the firemen have climbed, using ladders, to fight the fire. The other houses on the Dam likewise have the usual timbered lower façades and canopies. We also have several images from the second half of the eighteenth century, which show that few changes had been made to the corner house by then, but after this, an almost complete metamorphosis took place.[52] The result can be seen in a somewhat inept drawing that depicts the situation before 1838

52 For the situation in the second half of the eighteenth century, see SAA, Beeldbank 010097002533, 010097010846, 010094001161 and 010001000769.

Figure 6.16: Kalverstraat near the Dam, 1850.

Figure 6.17: The corner house on Dam-Kalverstraat, first half of the eighteenth century.

(Figure 6.18). We are interested in the building on the right, on the corner of the Dam and Kalverstraat (which has been drawn as far too narrow). The timbered lower façade and canopies have disappeared and been replaced by large extended display windows, with substantial windowpanes in wooden frames.[53]

An advertising print or letterhead from around 1850 reveals that this was a branch of the draper's shop belonging to A. Heyman (Figure 6.19). His shop had three large semi-circular shop windows facing onto the Dam and one onto Kalverstraat. Unlike previous examples, these shop windows ran all the way down to street level and no longer had the character of display cases hung on the façade. The shop windows of the firm Brandon & Partners, located somewhat further up Kalverstraat, though not semi-circular, had the same construction down to street level and likewise maximized the amount of potential display space (Figure 6.20). The large display windows made a great impression on contemporaries. The anonymous author of *Physiologie van de Kalverstraat* wrote: 'To our right, to our left, in front of us, behind us, large, extremely large glass windows and Brandon everywhere.'[54] The appearance of these renovated shopfronts no longer differed significantly from those on important shopping streets in London.[55] Amsterdam's shops, which had been described as 'old-fashioned' by visitors from London and Paris at the end of the eighteenth century, were starting to catch up.[56]

Dating from the same period is a beautiful drawing of the Dam in the evening, showing the brightly illuminated display windows winding like white ribbons around the Dam and through the neighbouring streets (Figure 6.21). Having begun in the eighteenth century, the trend towards presenting wares in, rather than in front of, the façade had come to full fruition in the retail heart of the city. It was now the shop windows and shop interiors, not the displays on the front step, that caught the attention of shoppers. Although the association with the market stall had almost completely disappeared, the way in which the wares were displayed was nonetheless still traditional. Just as market stalls were hung from top to bottom with wares, display windows were also packed with items. This is clearly evident from a detail in the print by Buffa dating from 1825, discussed above (Figure 6.22), which shows how extended display windows were divided into 'storeys' at the height of the bars, each with their own display. This technique was still common in the middle of the century. This is illustrated by Figure 6.23, for example, which shows a fragment of a price list produced by the firm Focke & Meltzer, a shop selling glassware and porcelain.[57]

The depictions of the shops belonging to A. Heyman and Brandon & Partners clearly show that in the first half of the nineteenth century, the first steps were taken towards scaling-up—something that had been virtually impossible in the past, due to guild regulations and the guild culture. Nevertheless, Heyman and Brandon were not pioneers in this respect. This

53 The semicircular windows look like the *bow windows* found in UK cities. See for example the picture from around 1800 in Cox, *The Complete Tradesman*, opposite the title page.

54 'Aan onze regterzijde, aan onze linkerzijde, vóór ons, achter ons, overal groote, zeer groote glasruiten en Brandon' (Een-Humorist, *Physiologie van de Kalverstraat*, p. 143).

55 Armstrong, *Victorian Glassworlds*, figures 29–32. However, there were no shops the size of E. Moses & Son (ibidem, figure 28) in Amsterdam.

56 Not everyone would agree. See for example the critical notes on Kalverstraat in Nolet de Brauwere van Steeland, *Een reisje in het noorde*, p. 17.

57 See also the advertising bill of the F.J. Winter shop in SAA, Beeldbank 010094006952.

Figure 6.18: The corner house on Dam-Kalverstraat, before 1838.

Figure 6.19: The corner house on Dam-Kalverstraat, around 1850.

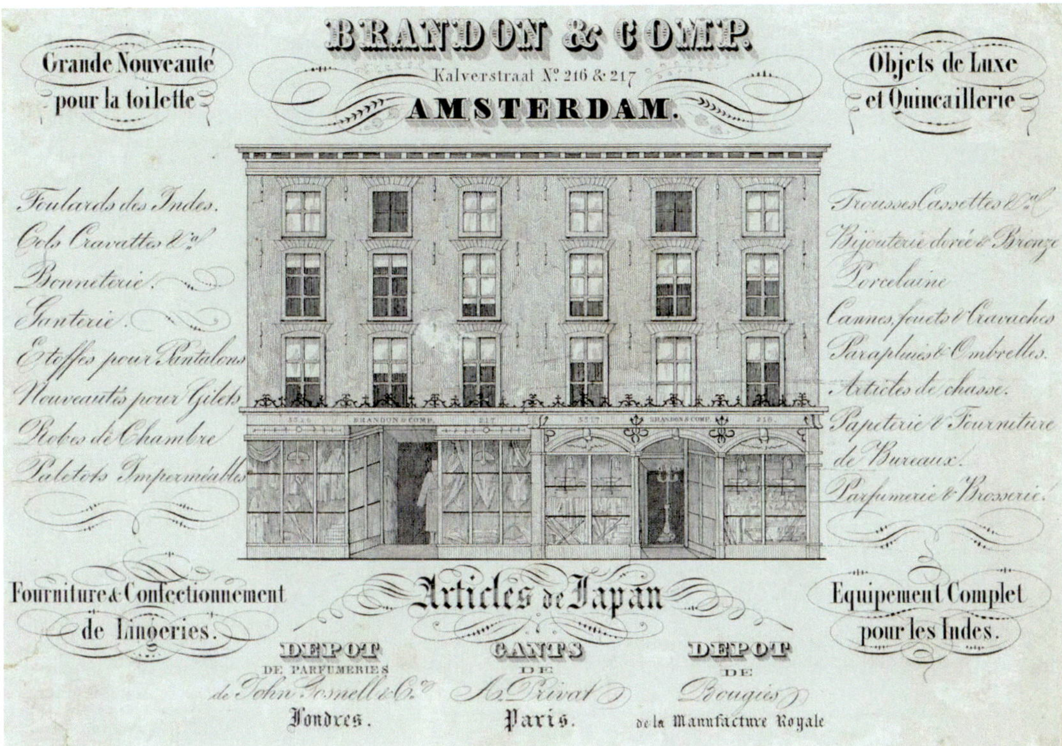

Figure 6.20: Display window of the firm Brandon & Partners on Kalverstraat, around 1850.

Figure 6.21: The Dam and surroundings by evening, 1852.

Figure 6.22: Display window in Kalverstraat near the Dam, 1825.

Figure 6.23: Display window of Focke & Meltzer in Kalverstraat near the Dam, ca. 1850.

honour is usually reserved for Michael Anton Sinkel, a migrant from Germany and founder of the celebrated 'Winkel van Sinkel [Sinkel's shop]' on Nieuwendijk. In the first decade of the nineteenth century, Sinkel established a draper's business in Amsterdam, and in 1821—himself a widower—he married Agnes Moormann-Ten Brink, the widow of a rich merchant from Westphalia.[58] It was probably her capital that allowed him to expand the business. In the same year, he bought the neighbouring premises, had both houses demolished, and built a brand-new shop on the double lot, designed by the architect J. van Straaten (Figure 6.24).

The lower façade had a striking design for a shop premises: it featured five openings with semi-circular arches, three of which served as shop windows and two as entrances. The whole thing was strongly reminiscent of the lower façade of the Franse Schouwburg (French theatre) on the Amstel, now known as De Kleine Komedie, which was designed by Abraham van de Hart in 1786.[59] Perhaps there was a search for a suitable design for a type of shop that was completely new in Amsterdam at the time. Whatever the case, on 22 April 1822, Sinkel announced in a circular that he, 'in his new building on Nieuwendijk, which opens today, will continue his celebrated business selling all kinds of wool, cotton and silk drapery, with a new full range befitting the size of the premises'.[60]

In the same period, Paris saw the emergence of the first large-scale retail businesses selling a mixed range of goods, the so-called bazaars.[61] But it is not in this tradition that we should place Sinkel's shop; his enterprise was limited to the sale of drapery and thereby followed in the tradition of Westphalian tradesmen, who had plied their trade in the Netherlands long before 1800.[62] These 'Tödden' or hawkers travelled throughout the Netherlands selling (linen) fabrics and stockings that were made on farms in their home region. They extended their product range over time, adding merchandise that had been manufactured elsewhere. In addition to pedlary, Westphalians also engaged in more large-scale trade. At the beginning of the nineteenth century, Sinkel belonged to a trading company run by two internationally operating merchants. His international contacts would have been useful when stocking his shop, and he made frequent visits to annual fairs in Germany to buy stock. This allowed him to cut out the middleman, and his commercial success in the Netherlands was clearly in part attributable to the fact that he was able to undercut the competition.

It is evident from Figure 6.24 that Sinkel's business, which was modern for that time, still made use of traditional practices, too, such as displaying merchandise on trestle tables to catch the attention and whet the appetite of the public. Modern shops were also operating in a retail landscape that still resembled that of past centuries in many respects. See, for example, the boned carcass hanging by the door of the butcher's shop to the right of Sinkel's shop. And

58 For the famous Sinkel shop, see Miellet, *Honderd jaar grootwinkelbedrijf*, pp. 38–41, and Schrover, *Een kolonie van Duitsers*, chapter 10.

59 Zantkuijl, *Bouwen in Amsterdam*, pp. 587 and 550. Similar arches can be found in Van Straaten, *De vignola der ambachtslieden*, figure xviii.

60 '[I]n zijn nieuwe gebouw aan den Nieuwendijk, hetwelk heden zal geopend worden, zijne alom bekende affaire in alle soorten wollen, catoenen en zijden manufacturen zal voortzetten en tot dien einde met een nieuw compleet assortiment, evenredig aan de grootte van zijn lokaal is voorzien' (Miellet, *Honderd jaar grootwinkelbedrijf*, p. 38). A slightly different version of the text on this circular can be found in Fuchs and Simons, *In de winkel van Sinkel*.

61 Gillet, 'Innovation and tradition', and the literature cited there.

62 Miellet, *Honderd jaar grootwinkelbedrijf*, and ibidem, 'Immigratie van katholieke Westfalers'.

Figure 6.24: Sinkel's shop on Nieuwendijk, ca. 1830.

this should come as no surprise; unlike with the sale of durable goods such as fabrics and luxury items, there was no great urge to innovate in the daily necessities sector. These shops were distributed much more widely across the city and enjoyed a quasi-monopolistic position in a market area of limited size, meaning that they had less to fear from the chill winds of competition. Thus, Leendertsz's pharmacy on Leidsestraat, pictured here around 1850, with its front step and cellar entrance in front of the façade and traditional *gaper* sign, still had many of the characteristics of the traditional shop-house in Amsterdam. To judge from the display on the front step to the right, there was a cellar under the adjoining bread shop from which vegetables were sold. Likewise, the appearance of the tobacco shop known as 'De Keulsche Waag [Cologne weighing-house]' on Schippersgracht, with its four wooden rolls of tobacco on the lower façade, was still strikingly traditional (Figures 6.25 and 6.26).

This could also be said of a shop on the corner of Nieuwendijk and Singel that served as a preliminary study for a now-lost panorama by Cornelis de Kruijf from 1817. Not only do we see the now-uncommon canopy hanging on the façade, but the front step still functioned as a shop window and crowd-puller, and perhaps as a storage space, too (Figure 6.27).[63]

63 I am indebted to Ester Wouthuysen for drawing my attention to this picture. See for this panorama her 'Panorama uit 1817 teruggevonden'.

Figure 6.25: Leendertsz's pharmacy on Leidsestraat, ca. 1850.

A very varied retail landscape thereby emerged in which traditional shops continued to exist alongside experimentation with novelties such as extended display windows. In time, the latter also fell out of fashion but continued to exist in the shelter of side-streets—sometimes until the present day.[64]

Retail trade practices in Amsterdam

Finally, we turn to the fourth component of the modernization process: changes that can be summarized under the heading 'retail trade practices'. As these largely took place within the shop, it is time to focus our attention on the shop interior and what happened behind and in front of the counter. We have already established that in the seventeenth century, counters, cabinets and packaging were the main elements of the shop interior, and this was still the case between 1700 and 1850. It was also emphasized that there were many different kinds of shop interiors, and that this was related to the type of goods on sale and the intended clientele. For providers of daily necessities and wares such as ironmongery, it was not essential to push the boat out and purchase a beautifully decorated interior. The same was generally true of shopkeepers selling luxury items and durable goods in shops located beyond the main shopping thoroughfares and busy approach routes. Often there were no chairs in these shops, and the decoration was sober. A very different impression was created by the centrally located

64 Extended display windows can still be admired in Oude Spiegelstraat and Gasthuismolensteeg.

Figure 6.26: Tobacco shop 'De Keulsche Waag' on Schippersgracht, ca. 1850.

shops in the upper segment of the market. We have already looked in detail at the shop selling fabrics and lace that was run by Christina Mijnders, the widow of Harmanus Grim, on Warmoesstraat in the years around 1700. This had counters in three different rooms, making it possible to receive wealthy customers in the seclusion of the heated upstairs parlour. It is clear from the estate inventories and from the painting of the interior of the gold brocade shop (probably in Amsterdam) by Matthys Naiveu that in the upper segment of the market, a great deal of attention was also paid to decorating and furnishing shops; and this does not yet seem to have been the case in the early seventeenth century. The increasing attention that some of Amsterdam's shopkeepers now paid to the appearance of their shops was indeed a new phenomenon.

Between 1700 and 1850, there was a high degree of continuity with the preceding period, especially in the daily necessities sector. This is something we know from, among other things, the study of inventories of shop estates dating from the mid-eighteenth and early nineteenth centuries.[65] These were still shops run in the traditional *voorhuis* or in basements, and aside from a counter, cabinet and numerous casks, boxes, cans, barrels, grain bins and other storage materials, they were furnished in sober style. Take, for example, the tobacconist's run by Samuel David Calf and his wife on Korte Houtstraat in Amsterdam's Jewish Quarter. In 1743, this shop contained a counter, a cupboard

65 I have selected inventories of shop estates from the archives of the *desolate boedelkamer* for the years 1743–1746 and 1800–1810.

Figure 6.27: Shop in a preliminary study for a panorama by Cornelis de Kruijf, 1817.

with shelves, a small pair of iron scales with copper weighing dishes and weights, eight casks with remnants of (curly-cut) tobacco, two Cologne jars of snuff, baskets of pipes, a few pots, bottles and boxes, an empty wooden chest, a copper sconce (a low dish-shaped candlestick), a small table and '*wat rommelingh*' ('some junk')[66]—all in all, a shop interior that differed little from those that had been common in the past.

The baker's shop captured by J.A. Langendijk in 1806 was also furnished simply (Figure 6.28). A small painting hangs above the entrance to the bakery and there are curtains in the windows, but the decoration is otherwise limited to oval moulding on the front of the counter and the shelving on the back wall. We would not expect to see luxurious and costly decorations in a bread shop, of course, but the appearance of bookshops also continued to be strictly functional for many years. It was only later that more attention was paid to the interior. In 1763, for example, the bookshop run by Hermanus de Wit on the corner of Molsteeg and Nieuwezijds Voorburgwal did admittedly have a chair for clients, but we can see from the wall on the right that the books were still kept in simple wooden units (Figure 6.29).[67] Only the cabinet behind the counter was decorated and more like a proper piece of furniture. We should also note that

66 SAA, Desolate boedelkamer, inv. nr. 663, fol. 48–49. Comparable inventories in inv. nr. 663, fol. 29–31, 34–38, 161–162 and 234–237; inv. nr. 664, fol. 34–39, and in the file with inv. nr. 7054 in the same archive.

67 *Naam-register van veele capitaale-net-geconditioneerde* [...] *boeken*, Volume 2, frontispiece.

Figure 6.28: Bakery, 1806.

the ceiling still consisted of the rough joists and floorboards of the floor above—something that was very uncommon in the homes of wealthier citizens in this period. As early as the seventeenth century, wooden ceilings in residential buildings were painted decoratively or covered with stucco and hidden from view.[68]

We can also see an unfinished ceiling in a very detailed painting, dating from 1820, of the bookshop run by Pieter Meijer Warnars on Vijgendam. Well after 1800, the interior of this distinguished bookshop could still be described as rather sober (Figure 6.30). A round mat lies on the simple wooden floor, and high shelves with bound books run along the walls. The lower part of the shelving unit has been closed off with panel doors. The latter may have been used to store the loose quires, which were bound into books using the bookbinders' tools on the floor. The decoration is not limited to the embellished counter and the wooden casing of the *comptoirtje* (small office space) on the right of the entrance; there is also a series of paintings of triumphal chariots around the ceiling, a decorative element lacking in older depictions of bookshops. This, too, confirms that the decoration of shops in the upper segment of the market became more common over time.

What applied to bookshops also seems to have applied to shops selling fabrics: decorative elements were not entirely lacking but were anything but lavish. 'Very sober' would be an apt description of the interior of the fabric shop in Adriaan Spinniker's *Vervolg der leerzame zinnebeelden* (Figure 6.31). This print by Vincent van der Vinne, which dates from the end of the seventeenth century, shows the kind of interior with which we are already familiar: piles of fabric on wall-mounted shelves and a cabinet containing

68 Koldeweij, '1750–1800', p. 268.

Figure 6.29: Officina Wittiana, 1763.

rolls of fabric (velvet?) that have been placed upright to prevent the fabric from being crushed and spoiled.[69] The situation in the second quarter of the nineteenth century was not very different, as shown by an advertising print from the 1830s of the fabric shop run by D.H. Dahleman.[70] The print presents the company as much larger than it could have been in the relatively small building on Herenstraat, but again, we see the simple shelves containing rolls of cloth and other fabrics (Figure 6.32). To the left of the entrance, there is a small office, and above the open doors, we see a clock. Like Meijer Warnars' bookshop,

69 Spinniker, *Vervolg der leerzaame zinnebeelden*.

70 The print from the collection of the Koninklijk Oudheidkundig Genootschap is not dated, but advertisements in *Algemeen Handelsblad* make it clear that the business on Herenstraat was in operation in 1838. The shopkeeper, Detloff Hendrik Dahleman, died in 1849 according to an advertisement in the same newspaper (https://www.delpher.nl/nl/kranten; last accessed 9 August 2019).

Figure 6.30: Pieter Meijer Warnars' bookshop on Vijgendam, 1820.

Dahleman's shop had a simple wooden floor. Even in Sinkel's newly built premises on Nieuwendijk, the decoration was what one would call sober. Here, too, the rolls of fabric were piled up on simple shelves behind the counters, with staff behind the counter to show the fabrics to customers upon request (see Figure 6.38 below).

The fancy goods shop ran by François Haram Rilliet and his wife Nanette Françoise Rilliet was furnished in a more lavish fashion. At the time of their bankruptcy in 1791, the wall was hung with fourteen pictures in gilded frames with glass, and there were also two mirrors with painted frames. Even if they were hanging for sale, such items would have given the shop interior an ambiance that was often lacking elsewhere. This was also the case for the clock and the three French barometers; it was explicitly noted in the inventory that the latter were 'beautifully gilded'. For the benefit of clients, there were four *taboret* stools, three traditional chairs with rush seats, and two fabric-covered couches. Exceptionally, there was also a stove with a pipe, which meant that, in contrast to most shops, this shop was heated in inclement and chilly weather.[71]

Nevertheless, it will have become clear that the lavish decorations that are reported in British research were not very common in Amsterdam, and even shops selling durable goods such as books and fabrics were also furnished relatively simply. Despite this, changes were

71 SAA, Desolate boedelkamer, inv. nr. 4879.

Figure 6.31: Fabric shop, late seventeenth century.

made to shop interiors in Amsterdam similar to those documented for British shops in the upper segment of the market. These included the increasing use of glass in display cases and the growing importance of artificial light in the shop interior—two things that are closely related to the earlier-mentioned practice of displaying wares in the shop space itself instead of in front of the façade.

The fact that glass was used more widely can be gleaned from shop estate inventories. Counters, cabinets and boxes featuring glass are rarely mentioned in estates dating from before 1700. By contrast, we come across many examples from the 1740s and the beginning of the nineteenth century, and we even encounter glass in shops in the lower segment of the market. The small coffee and grocery shop run by Meijer Hendriks in the Jewish Quarter featured a counter with a 'little glass window', for example, and the bankruptcy records for the tobacconist's run by the above-mentioned Samuel David Calf and his wife include a counter with two glass panes.[72] In Kalverstraat, the shop selling writing pens run by Gerrit Lem and his wife Jacoba Hardenberg had a counter with a sliding window, and we also come across frequent references to counters with glass windows in other estates from the 1740s.[73]

By the beginning of the nineteenth century, counters with glass windows were seldom recorded in estate inventories anymore, whilst

72 SAA, Desolate boedelkamer, inv. nr. 663, fol. 161 and 48.

73 SAA, Desolate boedelkamer, inv. nr. 663, fol. 234–237, 90–94, 335; inv. nr. 664, fol. 175–183.

Figure 6.32: The fabric shop run by D.H. Dahleman, ca. 1835–1840.

self-standing display cases that were placed on the counter gained in popularity. In the records from that time, we come across references to 'counter-top cases' and 'glass display cases'.[74] In *Afbeeldingen van de kleeding, zeden en gewoonten in de Bataafsche Republiek* (*Images of the clothing, manners and customs of the Batavian Republic*), published in 1803, we see a corner counter with two such display cases (Figure 6.33).[75] The case on the left, which is made of glass and has a bar down the centre, has an open lid, and the seller is showing the woman a piece of golden or gilded jewellery. Such display cases are still used today at flea markets and antiques markets to display watches and jewellery. The cases are usually lined with dark fabric to set off the objects on display, and the situation in the past would have been no different. Display cases on the counter were by no means novel, as an eighteenth-century print of a fashion boutique by Hendrik Numan shows a glass display case on the counter displaying 'decorations', against which lower-class children are warned in the accompanying moralistic text (Figure 6.34).[76] We have already seen that in

74 '[T]oonbankkasten' and 'glazen legkasten' (SAA, Desolate boedelkamer, inv. nrs. 7255 and 7261).

75 Maaskamp, *Afbeeldingen van de kleeding, zeden en gewoonten.*

76 Noman, *Verzameling van Nederlandsche tafereelen*, Volume 4. The edition used here was published in 1829, but the prints by Hendrik Numan (1736–1788) date from the eighteenth century. For this type of prints, see www.hetoudekinderboek.nl (last accessed 9 August 2019).

Figure 6.33: Glass display cases, around 1800.

Figure 6.34: Fashion boutique, third quarter of the eighteenth century.

the past, these types of display cases were hung by the door and on the lower façades of shops. In 1746, Leendert Swanenburg and his wife Aaltie Steenberg also had a glass display case in front of the façade of their fashion boutique shop on Barndesteeg, no doubt to show off the 'decorated flowers' and 'gilt' that could be purchased there.[77]

It did not end with counters with glass panes and glass display cases; in inventories, we also come across glass cabinets, which were evidently available in various shapes and sizes. Some were quite large, with a closed bottom section and drawers.[78] It is a cabinet such as this that we can probably see in a print of a lace maker's shop, also by Hendrik Numan (Figure 6.35), showing a solidly built cabinet with a glass door. On the shelves, we see the boxes and packages that undoubtedly contained the lace made by the lace maker. There are more boxes on top of the cabinet, on the counter and on the floor. There is a cupboard (perhaps for storage?) without glass hanging on the wall, and such cupboards are also mentioned in the inventories.

There was a sturdy cabinet in the *Franse winkel* run by Johan Gottlieb Wentzel on Prinsengracht, near the intersection with Molenpad. The estate inventory, dating from 1800, mentions a 'large cabinet with 2 glass sliding windows'. The contents were quite something: it was full of (paper) cartons and boxes containing items that ranged from 'girls' bonnets' to needles. It also contained pieces of cloth, packets of yarn, towels, chamois ladies' gloves and much more.[79] In the course of the eighteenth century, these types of cabinets with glass doors seem to have replaced the *kevie*, a cabinet with a latticed or gauze door. As well as these large pieces of furniture, there must have been smaller cabinets, too. The sources often refer to 'little cabinets' (*kastjes*), and some shops contained so many cabinets and display cases that these must have been closer in size to boxes than cupboards. This would also make sense in view of the scant contents of the small cabinets and display cases.[80]

The extent to which glass could be used in the interior of shops in the upper segment of the market is illustrated by a picture of the looting of Thiensma's silverware shop on Nieuwendijk on the night of 2 June 1787.[81] The political unrest of that era can hardly have been pleasant for the Orangist Thiensma, but it did mean that his shop interior was captured for posterity (Figure 6.36). In the foreground, we see the shop's sales area with its long counter, over which one of the looters is climbing. There is jewellery on the floor, and two looters are holding a glass display case. In the middle of the room, there is a heavily decorated partition wall with a passage through to the room behind. On both sides of this passageway are display cases with glass doors, all of which have been smashed in order to grab the contents. Despite the darkness of the night, it is nevertheless clear that much attention had been paid to the interior of this silversmith's shop and that glass had played an important role in its decoration.

The latter could also be said of the interior of a patisserie from around 1780. Located on the corner of Herengracht and Utrechtsestraat, the shop served affluent customers from the southern canal ring. These days, the interior—which

77 SAA, Desolate boedelkamer, inv. nr. 665, fol. 255–259.

78 SAA, Desolate boedelkamer, inv. nr. 663, fol. 7–27.

79 SAA, Desolate boedelkamer, inv. nr. 6241.

80 See, for example, the scant contents of the seven glass shop cabinets in the French shop of Maximiliaan de Lorme and wife at Rokin in 1802 (SAA, Desolate boedelkamer, inv. nr. 6432) and the thirteen shop cabinets and two display cabinets in the French shop of Hendrik Hilbus and wife on Prinsengracht in 1803 (ibidem, inv. nr. 6514).

81 Carasso-Kok, *Amsterdam Historisch*, pp. 98–99.

Figure 6.35: Lacemaker's shop with shop cabinet, third quarter of the eighteenth century.

consists of cabinets and a counter—is in storage, having been moved numerous times and having fallen into a deplorable state, but a photograph that predates its disassembly gives a good impression of this ornate shop interior in neoclassical Louis XVI style. The strong use of symmetry, the imitation marble columns with their gilded capitals, the garlands and urns on the moulding, and the clock surrounded by horns of plenty form a harmonious and carefully considered whole (Figure 6.37). Mirrors have been incorporated into the open display case under the clock, and part of the wall unit (not visible in the photo) is closed off with glass doors. Even the glass pots on the shelves probably featured in the original interior.[82]

The increasing use of glass, both for windows on the outer façade and for shop furniture, was linked to the fact that the distinction between public and private space was gradually becoming sharper. The need to retreat into the private domain was originally perceptible among the wealthy upper classes; as early as the seventeenth century, the front façade of their homes acquired a more closed character,

82 A description of this shop interior can be found in Vullers and Deenik, 'Het banketbakkersinterieur'.

Figure 6.36: Looting of the silversmith's shop owned by G.A. Thiensma on Nieuwendijk, 1787.

and the front step functioned more as a barrier than as a fluid and semi-public transition to the interior. Shopkeepers lagged behind in this development because for them, by contrast, it was very important to maintain a fluid movement from street to shop. Large displays in front of the façade thus remained a striking characteristic of shops for many years. Nevertheless, shopkeepers were not isolated from the broad social tendency towards privatization, and between 1700 and 1850, the canopies and displays in front of the lower façade disappeared, particularly on major shopping thoroughfares. The connection with the street was then maintained by adding more glass to the lower façade, a development that was also linked to the growing need for daylight in Amsterdam's homes and the introduction of the grid window.

With the disappearance of displays in front of the façade, there was also an increasing need to display the merchandise visibly in the shop, a need that was met by having glass display cabinets and counters with glass windows. The use of glass in the façade and the shop interior was supported by technological developments in glass manufacturing. As early as the sixteenth century, 'sheet glass' was developed in addition to traditional 'crown glass'. Whilst crown glass was made by using centrifugal force to stretch

Figure 6.37: Interior of patisserie, ca. 1780.

a red-hot globe of glass into a more or less flat disc, in the case of sheet glass, the glassblower blew a large globe of glass, which was stretched into a hollow cylinder of around a metre long and then cut open and stretched flat.[83] Both products were used in the Netherlands until the beginning of the nineteenth century, but it was the cylinder method that was best suited to large-scale use. France was at the forefront of this development and even produced fully industrially manufactured glass at the beginning of the nineteenth century. By the middle of the century, the Belgian town of Charleroi had become the most important manufacturing centre for sheet glass. The scaling-up of glass production in the eighteenth century and first half of the nineteenth century undoubtedly led to a drop in the price. Falling prices would also explain why we can observe a trend towards the use of more glass in the interior, even in marginal shops.[84]

When the display of merchandise was moved from the front step and the façade to the shop interior, lighting the interior became more important than before. It should thus come as no surprise that we encounter more

83 Zantkuijl, *Bouwen in Amsterdam*, p. 198, and the pictures in Douglas and Frank, *A History of Glassmaking*, chapter 6. For the production and use of glass and other building materials see also Van Leeuwen, 'Woning- en utiliteitsbouw'.

84 According to the description by Gerrit Lamberts, around 1830 large shops such as those of Bahlman on Nieuwendijk even had a '*spiegelglazen wand*' (mirror-glass wall) (SAA, Collectie Handschriften, inv. nr. 77).

lighting elements in shop estates from the 1740s than in seventeenth-century records. In most cases, these were sconces—low dish-shaped candlesticks that were suitable for burning candles.[85] At dusk and in the evening hours, they helped to light the shop, but the amount of light they provided was minimal, and beyond the direct reach of the candlelight it must have been pitch dark; all the more so because the most important source of artificial light—the hearth fire—was lacking in shops.

Important technological breakthroughs were achieved in the second half of the eighteenth century, giving a major boost to the amount of light provided by the traditional oil lamp. These innovations continued in the tradition of the work of individuals such as Jan van der Heyden, who had already made improvements to the oil lamp in the seventeenth century. But they also reflected the spirit of the age because the combustion process had been studied scientifically and this knowledge was used to improve lighting. The new oil lamp was named after François-Pierre Ami Argand (1750–1803), who was born in Switzerland but worked in France and England. The Argand lamp had three fundamental advantages over the traditional oil lamp. First, thanks to the use of a circular wick, air could also be drawn in from inside of the wick, making the combustion process more efficient and the light much brighter. Second, the glass around the flame worked like a chimney, ensuring that the combustion gases were removed efficiently and preventing smoking and irregular burning when the flame was high. And finally, Argand introduced a mechanism to turn the wick up or down, whereby the brightness could be controlled.[86] His invention had a major impact: here was a lamp that provided lots of light, produced very little smoke, and had a wick that did not need to be snuffed. It was said of the lamp that 'its very white light, very bright and almost blinding, exceeds that of all lamps known until now'.[87] For the first time in history, people had access to a form of artificial light that almost allowed them to forget it was dark outside.

Around the middle of the 1780s, the Argand lamp was manufactured in both France and England. Despite its high purchase price and substantial fuel consumption, the lamp was soon being used in public spaces. The Nederduitsche Schouwburg theatre in Amsterdam seems to have been in the vanguard, purchasing 'English lamps', as they were commonly known, in 1788. Their use was not limited to theatres and societies, however; shopkeepers also understood the benefits of good lighting. We do not know when the first shop was equipped with this new source of light, but in 1791, François Haram Rilliet and his wife Nanette Françoise Rilliet had an English lamp in the 'parlour' they presumably used as an annex to their fancy goods shop.[88] Later, the above-mentioned Johan Gottlieb Wentzel on Prinsengracht even had two such lights in his *Franse winkel*, and the bankrupt estate of a *Franse winkel* on Kloveniersburgwal mentions an 'English shop-lamp'. By then, the use of the Argand lamp in shops was evidently no longer exceptional.[89] At the bookshop run by Meijer Warnars on Vijgendam, a height-adjustable Argand lamp hung in the front room of the shop by the counter (Figure 6.30 above).[90]

85 SAA, Desolate boedelkamer, inv. nr. 663, fol. 29–31, 34–38, 48–50, 161–162; inv. nr. 664, fol. 293–334.

86 Berkers, 'Een nieuw licht', p. 98, and Schrøder, *The Argand burner*.

87 '[H]aar zeer witte licht, zeer helder en bijna verblindend, overtreft dat van alle tot nu bekende lampen' (Berkers, 'Een nieuw licht', p. 100).

88 SAA, Desolate boedelkamer, inv. nr. 4879.

89 This applies in particular to Kalverstraat (Kouwenaar, *Tussen Dam en Muntplein*, pp. 82–83). Argand lamps ('patentlampen') also in SAA, Desolate boedelkamer, inv. nrs. 6241, 6379, 6749 and 6774.

90 Berkers, 'Een nieuw licht', p. 90.

Figure 6.38: Interior of Sinkel's shop on Nieuwendijk, ca. 1830.

The picture of the interior of Sinkel's shop on Nieuwendijk is less detailed, but we know that it was lit with a whole series of Argand lamps. Indeed, the use of bright artificial light was particularly important for large fabric stores such as Sinkel's, where daylight could not penetrate to the back of the shop (Figure 6.38). Nevertheless, the use of such lamps was far from universal at the beginning of the nineteenth century. In November 1808, Barend Joseph Banken and his wife Geertruij Kelderman had two *spiegellusters* (double wall-sconces with candles) in their grocery.[91] At that time, many shops still had no form of artificial light at all; if it got too dark, a sconce would simply be fetched from elsewhere in the building.

The introduction and spread of the Argand lamp did not bring an end to technological innovations in the area of artificial light. In the first half of the nineteenth century, gas lighting gained ground. The use of gas for lighting

91 SAA, Desolate boedelkamer, inv. nr. 7054, and Koldeweij, '1750–1800', p. 283.

purposes was driven by inventors from the Netherlands, France and England. It was in England, with its ample availability of capital, its developed machine industry and its high lamp-oil prices, that coal gas was first used on a large scale. Around 1825, gas lighting was available in large cities, and several decades later, the same was true of many small towns and even villages.[92]

In the Netherlands, the first demonstration of gas lighting was held in 1816 in Amsterdam's home for the elderly, known as the Oude Mannen- en Vrouwenhuis. Even when compared to the Argand lamp, gas lighting proved to be of superior brightness. Following one of the demonstrations, it was remarked of gas lighting that 'normal street and lamp lights appear to be just flames and not lights by comparison'.[93] The early history of gas lighting was one of searching for the most suitable and profitable manufacturing and distribution techniques. For several decades, it remained unclear whether coal gas or oil gas from vegetable oils would win the day; and in addition to distribution via a pipe network, gas was successfully packed in large gas canisters by the company Droinet and delivered to people's homes. There continued to be a market for Droinet, particularly in the years when the gas pipe network remained small. Only around the middle of the century did it become clear that coal gas and distribution via a pipe network had a future, and at this point, large towns also opted for this system for lighting public spaces.

Coal gas lighting only became suitable for lighting private homes in the second half of the century. Until that time, the connection fees and cost of the lighting fixtures remained too high for many. Moreover, gas lighting gave off a large amount of heat, a problem that would only be solved in the 1860s. Finally, until purification techniques were developed in the 1840s, coal gas often gave off an unpleasant smell caused by the combustion of impurities in the coal. This objection would have weighed less heavily in larger spaces, and we can therefore assume that shops on the main shopping streets were among the earliest adopters of coal gas. Until the 1840s, when the use of coal gas grew rapidly, they would also have been the main consumers of Droinet's bottled gas.[94] The fact that shopkeepers indeed used coal is shown by an account of a stroll through Amsterdam written in verse by the artist Gerrit Lamberts in the early 1830s, in which he referred to *lichtend kolengaz* ('shining coal gas'). He wrote:

> As the silver moon glimmers in the sky's firmament, Gaslight, you spread your silent radiance and glow, When the dusk of evening falls, you open your taps, And light winds its way into our shops.[95]

The fact that his enthusiasm was not shared by all is clear from a tirade by the author of *Physiologie van de Kalverstraat* directed against the 'universally-celebrated and infamous fancy-good shops of Kalverstraat [...] with your French-style display windows [...] your blinding gas lighting,

92 Berkers, 'Een nieuw licht'. For the following, see Dil and Homburg, 'Gas', and Stolp, 'F. J. Hallo als fabrikant van vloeibaar gas'.

93 '[D]e gewone straat- en lamplichten schijnen daarbij slechts vlammen en geene lichten te zijn' (Dil and Homburg, 'Gas', p. 107).

94 The advantages of oil-gas over coal gas in Mac Lean, *Geschiedenis der gasverlichting*, p. 28.

95 'Gelijk de zilvere maan gloort aan des hemels trans, Verspreidt ge O Gazlicht ook uw stillen schijn en glans; Als d'avond scheemring daalt dan opent ge Uwe kranen, En 't licht komt zich een weg in onze winkels banen.' (SAA, Collectie Handschriften, inv. nr. 77, 'wandeling van Koningsplein naar Heiligeweg'). For these walks and the drawings by Gerrit Lamberts, see Van de Waal and De Vries, *Amsterdam omstreeks 1800*.

and, God help us, your portable gas, which sets off the whole garish medley so superbly'.[96]

The lighting innovations that took place from the end of the eighteenth century resulted in brightly lit shop rooms and display windows on the main shopping thoroughfares and wherever shopkeepers could afford the relatively high lighting costs. The centuries-long dependence on daylight thereby came to an end, and there was no longer a need to display merchandise in front of the façade in broad daylight. Shops on the main streets now retreated behind the façade for good, but artificial lighting and the much-enlarged glass panes of the windows and display windows maintained the essential connection with passers-by and the shopping public in the street. With the development of well-functioning and affordable artificial lighting, an important condition for scaling up retail businesses was also met. Goods could now be displayed and presented to clients beyond the direct reach of daylight. And with this observation, let us now turn back to the changes in the shop interior between 1700 and 1850 and the retail practices that accompanied them.

Great significance is ascribed to the development of the shop interior in British research. In a widely cited article, Walsh argues that shop design in the eighteenth century was important because it contributed to the attractiveness of the wares that were presented in carefully designed shops; because the interior gave a message to potential consumers about the status of the shop, the reputation of the shopkeeper and the intended clientele; and because a beautiful shop interior added to the charm of shopping as a leisure activity.[97] Did these aspects also play a role in Amsterdam?

It can hardly be disputed that a carefully designed and decorated interior would have contributed to the impact of the wares for sale. Particularly for sellers of luxury articles and durable goods in the city centre, it would have been important to have an attractive shop interior. After all, they faced intensive competition from shops selling similar goods, and they could also expect consumers to familiarize themselves with the ranges in several shops before making a purchase; for, as we noted above, there were clusters of shops in the same sector in the town centre. The growing use of glass display cases and the increasing focus on decoration that we saw in Meijer Warnars' bookshop, the silversmith's shop on Nieuwendijk and the patisserie on Utrechtsestraat—all shops on major shopping streets that were aimed at an affluent clientele—are indications that in Amsterdam, too, at least some shopkeepers were fully aware that the shop interior could make a contribution to turnover and customer loyalty.[98]

Just as the interior of a luxury department store such as Bloomingdale's or Harrods, or the interior of a budget clothing store such as Target or Primark, give messages to today's consumer, this was also the case in the early

96 '[O]veral beroemde en beruchte galanteriewinkels van de Kalverstraat [...] met uwe uitgetimmerde, naar Fransch model gemaakte winkelkasten, [...] met uw oogverblindend gazlicht, en, God betere het, met uw portatif gaz, dat de kakelbonte mengeling nog eens zoo schoon doet uitkomen' (Een-Humorist, *Physiologie van de Kalverstraat*, p. 107). Somewhat later, the new lighting and presentation techniques were adopted by shops on the other main shopping streets (Van der Vijver, *Geschiedkundige beschrijving der stad Amsterdam*, Volume 4, pp. 329–330).

97 Walsh, 'Shop Design', pp. 167–168.

98 That is apparently less the case in Antwerp. Blonde and Van Damme remark that 'throughout the early modern period shops [in Antwerp] were rarely subjected to decorative improvement schemes' (Blondé and Van Damme, 'The Shop, the Home, and the Retail Revolution', p. 350).

modern period. Unlike today, however, in the early modern period the shop interior was almost all the consumer could rely on to form an impression of the quality and price of the offering, and this was related to the fact that branded goods and quality standards hardly existed.[99] Although lead quality seals were used for cloth and barrels of herring were branded, these signs were mainly used in wholesale trade, especially for import and export. By the time products reached the retail circuit, all of these marks and seals had long disappeared. Moreover, the early modern retailer had a much wider range of tasks than his modern colleagues, and only rarely did a wholesaler's products cross the counter in an unmodified form or composition. The shopkeeper would mix various qualities of coffee, tea or dry goods to reach the desired composition, and he would roast and pack the coffee. The shopkeeper also played a key role in the non-food sector, where he would combine separate components into saleable products. This can also be seen in the picture, shown above, of the fashion boutique (Figure 6.34). On the counter lie the materials that will be made into 'decorations' by the shopkeeper and her female assistant. The image is supported by the accompanying verse, which reads:

I make, out of shining paper,
Out of feather, cloth and wire;
Decorations to adorn the parties
Of the upper and middle classes.[100]

Precisely because the shopkeeper played a major role in determining the composition and quality of the product, it was very difficult for consumers to establish beforehand whether it met their requirements. In other words, there was an information asymmetry at play, and more so than in an age of branded goods and consumer forums, the consumer would have had to reply on the shopkeeper's reputation and the appearance of the shop. Reputation was also important because fixed prices were not commonly used, and the client had to negotiate the price.

It is in this context that we should see the trade cards of manufacturers and shopkeepers.[101] These usually featured the name and address of the supplier and gave a rough indication of the goods that were for sale. When it comes to tobacco shops, we often see an image of some rolls and casks of tobacco, and text to the effect that these and other types of tobacco could be purchased from the tobacconist with such and such a name and address (Figures 6.39 and 6.40).

Nor did the trade cards used by shopkeepers selling durable goods give anything more than a rough indication of the articles that they sold, and there is never a specific list of qualities and prices (Figures 6.41–6.43). The trade cards are therefore not comparable to modern leaflets or pamphlets that advertise certain articles at low prices, to encourage people to visit the shop. When it came to most products, it was not possible to use this form of canvassing before the nineteenth century, as there were hardly any standard branded goods and it was therefore difficult to advertise fixed prices.[102] Trade cards were used in a very different

99 See also Van Damme, *Verleiden en verkopen*, chapter 4 on this matter.

100 'Ik maak uit blinkende papieren, Uit veeren doek en ijzerdraad; Versiersels die de feesten sieren, Van hooge en middelbare staat.' (Noman, *Verzameling van Nederlandsche tafereelen*, Volume 4).

101 Trade cards can be found in the collections of the Koninklijk Oudheidkundig Genootschap, in the Beeldbank of the SAA, and in the collection 'Atlas W.J.R. Dreesmann', also in SAA.

102 On the trade cards, information about prices is limited to remarks such as 'to a civil price' and 'everything to a reasonable price'.

Figure 6.39: Trade card of a tobacconist, 1775–1825.

way. The shopkeeper would hand them out to customers who visited the business, and they served as a reminder and a business card. The shopkeeper would also ask customers to recommend their shop to others, whereupon the trade card could be passed on. The often-extensive address details, which in many cases mention the house name, are evidence of their usefulness. The trade card used by J.P. van Bergen in Warmoesstraat even asked explicitly for 'everyone's respective favour and recommendation.'[103]

103 '[E]en ieders respective gunst en recommandatie' (SAA, collectie Atlas Dreesmann).

Trade cards thus formed part of a retail system where personal relationships between buyers and sellers played a key role. Establishing a personal relationship and trust was important to the seller because it bound clients to his business and because he was dependent on word-of-mouth recommendations to expand his client base. For the consumer, it was important to have a personal relationship based on trust when negotiating prices, not least because quality standards were lacking for most goods and one was therefore reliant on the shopkeeper's word. Moreover, with the growing importance of fashion and more rapidly changing trends than in the seventeenth

Figure 6.40: Trade card of a tobacconist, 1775–1825.

century, the shopkeeper became a fount of information. He would keep the consumer informed of developments in the world of consumption and give advice on clothing, home furnishings, and all the other things that communicate to the world who you are or who you aspire to be. Nor is it surprising, given the importance of personal relationships, that prior to the nineteenth century, shopkeepers selling luxury items and other shopping goods made very little use of adverts in an impersonal medium such as the newspaper.[104] Nevertheless, the possibility of placing ads certainly existed; from the late seventeenth century, *De Amsterdamsche Courant* contained a growing number of adverts. These were mainly used by brokers or to find missing persons and lost or stolen items. The only retailers to advertise there with any frequency were booksellers,

104 Similar conclusions in Lyna and Van Damme, 'A Strategy of Seduction?'.

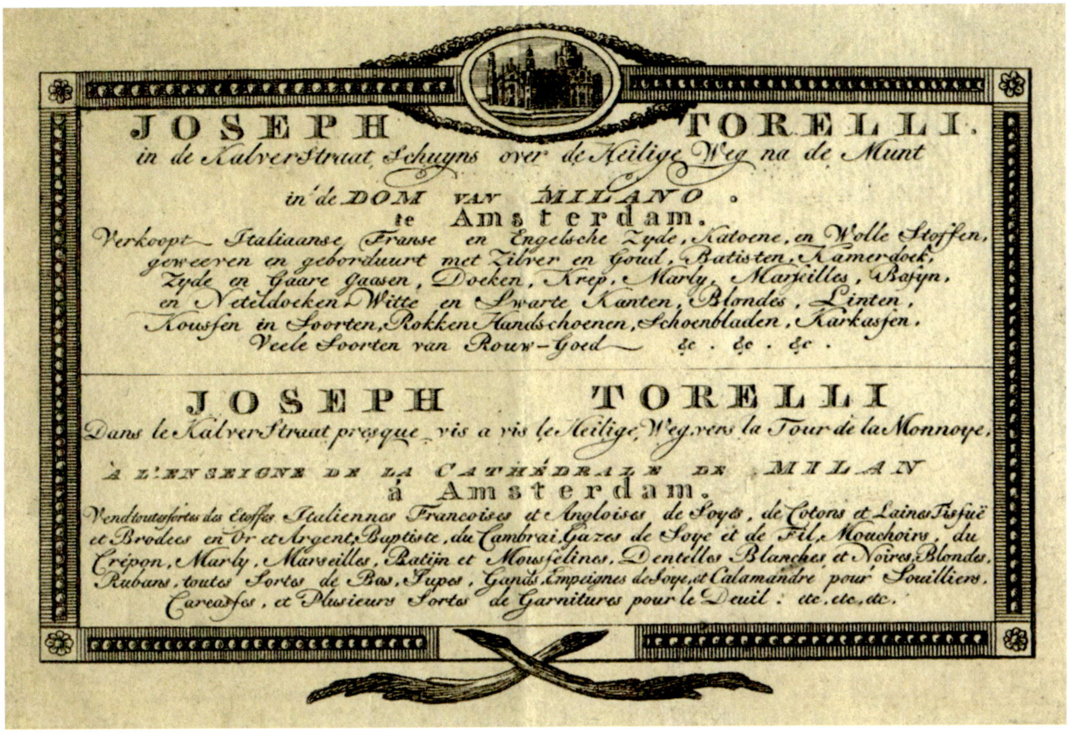
JOSEPH TORELLI.
in de Kalverstraat, Schuyns over de Heilige Weg na de Munt
in de DOM VAN MILANO.
te Amsterdam.
Verkoopt Italiaanse, Franse en Engelsche Zyde, Katoene, en Wolle Stoffen, geweeven en geborduurt met Zilver en Goud, Batisten, Kamerdoek, Zyde en Gaare Gaasen, Doeken, Krep, Marly, Marseilles, Basyn, en Neteldoeken, Witte en Swarte Kanten, Blondes, Linten, Kousfen in Soorten, Rokken, Handschoenen, Schoenbladen, Karkasfen, Veele Soorten van Rouw-Goed &c. &c. &c.

JOSEPH TORELLI
Dans le Kalverstraat presque vis a vis le Heilige Weg, vers la Tour de la Monnoye,
À L'ENSEIGNE DE LA CATHÉDRALE DE MILAN
á Amsterdam.
Vend toutes sortes des Etoffes Italiennes Francoises et Angloises de Soyes, de Cotons et Laines Tissuë et Brodees en Or et Argent, Baptiste, du Cambrai, Gazes de Soye et de Fil, Mouchoirs, du Crépon, Marly, Marseilles, Batijn et Mousselines, Dentelles Blanches et Noires, Blondes, Rubans, toutes Sortes de Bas, Jupes, Gands, Empeignes de Soye, et Calamandre pour Souilliers, Carcasses, et Plusieurs Sortes de Garnitures pour le Deuil: etc. etc. etc.

Figure 6.41: Trade card of Joseph Torelli, late eighteenth century.

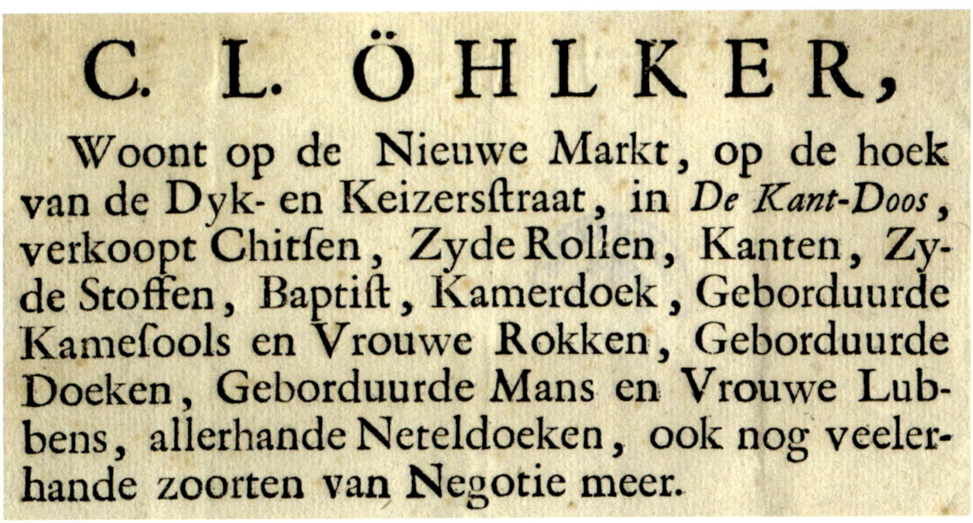
C. L. ÖHLKER,
Woont op de Nieuwe Markt, op de hoek van de Dyk- en Keizersſtraat, in *De Kant-Doos*, verkoopt Chitſen, Zyde Rollen, Kanten, Zyde Stoffen, Baptiſt, Kamerdoek, Geborduurde Kameſools en Vrouwe Rokken, Geborduurde Doeken, Geborduurde Mans en Vrouwe Lubbens, allerhande Neteldoeken, ook nog veelerhande zoorten van Negotie meer.

Figure 6.42: Trade card of C.L. Öhlker, ca. 1760.

Figure 6.43: Design of a trade card for J.C. Hagendoorn, first quarter of the nineteenth century.

which is hardly surprising, given that they also produced and distributed the *Courant*.[105]

This implies that shopkeepers who sold shopping goods could market their shops almost exclusively by distinguishing themselves based on the shop's design, the quality and quantity of the offering, and their professional knowledge, reliability and customer service. Once a personal relationship had been established with a customer, word-of-mouth advertising ensured the expansion of the customer base. Trade cards could play a role in this, but it remains unclear how general the use of trade cards was. As the cards were typically printed materials that were not carefully preserved, we only have a few dozen examples from early modern Amsterdam. The fact that trade cards have also survived from shopkeepers and craftsmen in the Jordaan, the Haarlemmer Houttuinen and Bethanienstraat suggests that their use was not confined to the higher segment of the market.[106]

According to Walsh, a shop's interior is not only important because it reinforces the attractiveness of the wares and communicates a message to potential customers about the shop's status and the reputation of the shopkeeper, but also because an attractive interior adds to the charm of shopping as a leisure activity. In British research, much attention has been paid to the social and cultural function of shopping, and the question arises as to whether shop interiors in Amsterdam had the potential to transform shopping into a pleasant

105 For Amsterdam newspapers and advertisements, see Sautijn Kluit, 'De Amsterdamsche Courant'; Stolp, *De eerste couranten in Holland*; Van Eeghen, 'De Amsterdamsche Courant'; Schipper-van Lottum, *Advertenties en berichten*, and Van der Krogt, *Advertenties voor kaarten, atlassen, globes e.d.*.

106 See for example SAA, Beeldbank 10094006774 and 010094006730, and see also the trade cards in the collection 'Atlas Dreesmann'.

pastime.[107] Broadly speaking, it is not possible to answer this question. The interiors, shown above, of the gold brocade shop in the painting by Naiveu (1709), the patisserie from around 1780 and the silversmith's shop from 1787 were designed with care and undoubtedly made shopping a visually attractive experience. But as hardly any shop interiors have survived the years intact and images of them are scarce, representativeness remains a problem. Was the gold brocade shop the subject of a painting because its decoration was so remarkably beautiful? And why, of all the shops that were looted, was it Thiensma's silversmith's shop on Nieuwendijk that was captured in a painting? As for the interior of the patisserie in Louis XVI style, we can be sure that it evaded demolition and modernization precisely because of its lovely appearance!

Unfortunately, estate inventories from Amsterdam do not provide enough information about the appearance and decoration of shop furnishings, but when the inventories do contain valuations, these do not indicate that the shop cabinets and counters were expensive. In most cases, shop furniture was only worth a few guilders. Likewise, in the chapters above it was already noted that shop decoration was relatively sober. Sometimes there were a few chairs, perhaps a table, and there might have been paintings on the wall or a mirror here and there, but on the whole, the impression that we have is one of functionality rather than lavish decoration. What is more, shop interiors must have been cold and clammy for much of the year, as there was no chimney in the traditional *voorhuis*.

We noted above that shopkeepers in the upper segment of the market probably received important clients in rooms above or behind the shop. The decoration there would have been less sober, there would have been a fire in the hearth, and the customers' wishes and possible choices could be addressed in a more personal atmosphere. The fact that the distinction between the shop space and private rooms was not absolute is likewise shown by reports from travellers who visited Amsterdam. Zacharias Conrad von Uffenbach, for example, made a journey through Holland around 1710 and also visited Amsterdam. He visited a whole series of art dealers there as well as shops selling porcelain and instruments and the cabinet makers' building on Kalverstraat. In the art shops (paintings, prints) in particular, it was evidently common for the wares to be spread over a number of rooms. Von Uffenbach bought prints and maps from an art shop on the Dam, for example. He was clearly taken around the whole house because, as he wrote in his travel journal, in a small room he was shown '[...] sechs unvergleichlich schöne Stucke, von Lairesse, gemahlt'.[108] Such tours proved the rule rather than the exception during Von Uffenbach's trip, and many of the rooms that he was shown evidently had the character of showrooms. We can well imagine that discussions about potential purchases would not have taken place in the shop itself, but in the more private atmosphere of one of the other rooms. The shop in the *voorhuis* would then have served mainly for smaller purchases that did not require detailed negotiations. This assumption is supported by a remark that Margaret Steuart Calderwood made in her travel journal in 1756. She visited a large porcelain shop in Amsterdam, selling wares that she believed to be worth at least 40,000 British pounds. In doing so, she observed that the upper floor contained 'all the fine', and the floor below 'all the common'. The

107 Shopping as a pleasant pastime is extensively dealt with in Stobart, Hann and Morgan, *Spaces of Consumption*.

108 Von Uffenbach, *Merkwürdige Reisen*, Volume 3, p. 541.

latter included plates, dishes and bowls ('very good for making salads').[109]

The presence of a number of rooms made it possible for a shopkeeper to adapt their selling strategies and approach to the customer. Particularly when it came to expensive items such as art and porcelain, important clients would have been given preferential treatment in the privacy of back and upstairs rooms, whilst others would have gotten no further than the shop room in the *voorhuis*. This was consistent with the situation in Paris and in British towns in the eighteenth century, where various social groups visited the same shops but received different treatment and were served in separate parts of the shop.[110]

It is no straightforward matter to establish how common such practices were. Perhaps we should err on the side of caution and say that there are indications that some shops in Amsterdam had multiple rooms, giving the shopkeeper the option of adapting their sales strategy to the size of the transaction and the social status of the client. Naturally, this phenomenon was limited to shops of a certain size in the upper segment of the market for durable goods. In other words, there was indeed the potential for shopping to develop into a pleasant pastime, as it had done in British towns, but did this actually happen? To date, there is virtually no material available to answer this question in relation to the eighteenth century. To the extent that foreign travellers mentioned their purchases, mostly art and books, they seem to have shopped in a relatively targeted fashion. Perhaps they only mentioned the shops in their journals that they considered worth mentioning, however, and these travellers may not have been the type to fritter away much time on shopping. After all, this was also something that they could do in their own country. In addition, the lack of pavements and large shop windows meant that the infrastructure was less suitable for shopping than in cities such as London and Paris. This is supported by the comments about the old-fashioned nature of Amsterdam's shops.

A different perspective was taken by less indulged individuals, such as Isabella van Ittersum of the country estate of Het Relaer, southeast of Zwolle. Around 1800, on paying a visit to Amsterdam, she reported that Kalverstraat was full of 'belles boutiques, qui surpassaient tout ce qu'on voit dans d'autres villes'. Isabella clearly considered shopping a pleasant pastime and something on which to judge the attractiveness of a town. She noted, for example, that the situation in Zutphen, a town in the Province of Gelderland, was much improved in recent years, thanks to the establishment of 'luxe et belles boutiques, qui avaient fort augmentée'.[111]

The pavements that had been noted by foreign visitors as missing continued to be absent until the mid-nineteenth century, but in the early nineteenth century, the slowly changing exteriors and interiors of Amsterdam's shops entered a phase in which 'real' shop windows were introduced in order to give passers-by an impression of the goods for sale. The oldest example of which I am aware is the abovementioned picture by Christiaan Andriessen of an extended display window in Kalverstraat in 1807.[112] The development that subsequently took place was supported by technological progress in the manufacture of glass and artificial lighting. This resulted in a situation on the main

109 Calderwood, *Letters and Journals*, p. 113.
110 Cox, *The Complete Tradesman*, pp. 99–101; Coquery, 'The Language of Success', p. 87, and Van Damme, *Verleiden en verkopen*, pp. 143–144.
111 Both quotations from Streng, *Vrijheid, gelijkheid, broederschap en gezelligheid*, p. 43.
112 Hoogenboom, Gerlagh and Stroop, *De wereld van Christiaan Andriessen*, figure 43, and SAA, Beeldbank 010094000042.

shopping streets that bore much resemblance to what we call 'shopping' today. This becomes clear when we take another look at Figure 6.16. At the northern end of Kalverstraat, where we would expect the changes to have been most rapid and most radical, we see small groups of people sauntering past the shop windows. They are chatting, and some have paused to admire the contents of a shop window. With their ever-larger glass panes, the latter caught the attention of the public and tempted them to enter. The atmosphere that dominates this image from the middle of the century is one that is highly consistent with the notion of shopping as a pleasant pastime. And that is also precisely what the anonymous author ('a humorist') of the *Physiologie van de Kalverstraat* (published in 1844) tells us:

> For [the ladies], Kalverstraat is truly a form of amusement; [...] and believe me, it is one they enjoy; with a few fivers tucked into a finely embroidered handkerchief, off they go, arm in arm. They stand before the windows of one shop, they take a look in another, they enter a third, they inquire about the price in the fourth, they negotiate in the fifth, and in the sixth they buy a small trifle, on condition that if it does not keep its colour or contains too much starch, they might bring it back.[113]

But it was not only ladies who saw shopping in Kalverstraat as a pleasurable activity. According to the author, 'male flaneurs' would not know how to while away the time 'if they could not stand in front of the colossal glass windowpanes [of your fancy goods shops] and take everything in, all the curiosities in your display windows'.[114] Even the exceptionally courteous treatment of customers that is considered in the British research to be typical of the culture of shopping was evidently encountered in Kalverstraat. The humorist scoffed at the fancy good shops: 'with your courteous and trained shop attendants, who "enchant" people, as it is called, so that they might spend more'.[115] The impression that shopping and parading came to full fruition only after 1800 is supported by the 'humorist's' exceptionally negative attitude to shopping, to (foreign) shopkeepers and to French influence on the Dutch language and culture, which suggests that he was battling with a relatively new phenomenon.

From the writings of contemporaries, we know that Kalverstraat was undoubtedly the most elegant of Amsterdam's shopping streets, although it was by no means an exclusive place to wander. The authors of a fictitious account of a visit to Amsterdam describe Kalverstraat

113 '[D]e Kalverstraat is voor haar [dametjes] eene regte uitspanning; [...] en geloof mij, zij jouisseren; met een paar vijfjes in de punt van de fijn geborduurde zakdoek, gaan zij arm aan arm op weg. Voor den eenen winkel staan zij voor de glazen, voor den anderen winkel kijken zij eens, in een' derden gaan zij eens in, in een' vierden vragen zij naar den prijs, in den vijfden overleggen zij eens, en in den zesden koopen zij een *bagatelletje*, onder beding dat, als het geen kleur houdt, of er te veel stijfsel in is, zij het mogen terugbrengen' (Een-Humorist, *Physiologie van de Kalverstraat*, p. 83). It is striking that the author gives an excellent description of what we now call *winkelen* (shopping) but does not use the word itself. In its modern sense, the term only came into vogue later.

114 '[A]ls zij niet voor uwe [galanteriewinkels] kolossale glasruiten stonden, en alles eens konden opnemen, wat van rariteiten zich in uwe kasten bevindt' (Een-Humorist, *Physiologie van de Kalverstraat*, pp. 107–108).

115 '[M]et uwe beleefde en gedresseerde winkelbedienden, die de menschen zoogenoemd *enchanteeren* om nog meer *depenses* te maken' (Ibidem, p. 107). For the depiction of shop staff in England, see for example Cox, *The Complete Tradesman*, figure 3.5, and Walsh, 'Shop Design', figure 7 ('The Haberdasher Dandy').

and Nieuwendijk as the most crowded streets in the city.[116] Elsewhere in the account, we learn that the crowds there were extremely diverse: 'such an overwhelmingly large number of people of both genders, of every class, as genteel and bourgeois as you could imagine, and as low as possible, with the thousands of nuances this brings'.[117] Despite the social mix described here, the fact remains that on Monday mornings, a remarkable number of farmers from North Holland would walk down the street and on Saturdays many Jewish citizens of Amsterdam. There was also a certain degree of differentiation through the day. Certain times of the day were dominated by the traders and staff of the nearby Exchange, others by the ladies and maids who came to make purchases. During exchange hours and in the evenings after 10 pm, when the shops were closed, Kalverstraat was the domain of prostitutes.[118] Prostitution was by no means a new phenomenon in the street in the mid-nineteenth century; in 1642, mention was already made of a *Kalverstraets hoer* ('Kalverstraat whore').[119]

It seems unlikely that Kalverstraat was the place for Amsterdam's elite to see and be seen, a function that is often fulfilled by elegant shopping streets. They would have been deterred by the pressing crowds, the presence of the middle and lower classes and the street's longstanding association with prostitution. Moreover, Amsterdam's *beau monde* had Keizersgracht as a backdrop for the public display of wealth, taste and good manners. Particularly on Sunday afternoons between 2 pm and 4.30 pm, the stretch of Keizersgracht between the Amstel and Oude Leliestraat functioned as a stage for what was known as the *Pantoffelparade* ('parade of slippers'): a promenade under the trees by the edge of the canal. It was there that one would find the elite, 'dressed as splendidly as their finances or the credit they had with their seamstress or tailor would allow'.[120]

For those who could not afford to mingle with the promenading *beau monde* on Keizersgracht, Kalverstraat was the place to be; but at the same time, of course, this 'avenue of all kinds of fancy-goods and other shops' was also a street where one could stroll pleasantly past the shop windows and marvel at the things on display.[121] This phenomenon was not entirely absent elsewhere in the main shopping streets, but it was precisely thanks to the striking presence of shops selling luxury articles such as fancy goods, crystal and art prints that Kalverstraat was *the* shopping street in Amsterdam and received more attention than all the other streets put together in the writings of contemporaries. It was there that trends in shop design and fashion took shape before they percolated down to other segments of the retail system and the buying public.

In this chapter, we compared the developments in Amsterdam to what is known about modern trends in British retail trade in the eighteenth century and the first half of the nineteenth century. The now commonly held

116 Boom and Lesturgeon, *Een Drentsch gemeente-assessor*, Volume 1, p. 197.

117 '[Z]oo ontelbaar vele menschen van beider geslacht, van elken stand, zoo hoog deftig-burgerlijk, en zoo laag met de duizenderlei nuances van dien' (Ibidem, p. 228).

118 Een-Humorist, *Physiologie van de Kalverstraat*, chapters 3 and 5. Prostitution in Kalverstraat also receives ample attention in Een-Amsterdammer, *Physiologie van Amsterdam*, chapter 3.

119 Van de Pol, *Het Amsterdams hoerdom*, p. 79.

120 '[Z]oo prachtig uitgedoscht, als hunne finantiën of het crediet, dat zij bij de modemaakster of den kleêrmaker hebben, zulks toelaat' (Een-Amsterdammer, *Physiologie van Amsterdam*, pp. 27–28). See also Een-Humorist, *Physiologie van de Kalverstraat*, p. 36.

121 The characterization of Kalverstraat in Een-Humorist, *Physiologie van de Kalverstraat*, p. 19.

view is that shops were already extensive before the mid-nineteenth century and underwent considerable changes, a picture that was also found to be true for Amsterdam. At the same time, though, it is clear that there were significant differences between the situation in Britain and the situation in Amsterdam. In British research, historians tend to identify the eighteenth century as the time when the number of shops rose sharply, modern location patterns took shape, urban improvement schemes were used to adapt town centres to the demands of the age, and new practices arose in the presentation and sale of goods—especially durable goods to wealthy customers. The latter is an important addition because it did indeed concern changes that took place largely in the upper segment of the market.

In Amsterdam, too, we mainly looked at the changes that took place in the upper segment of the market for luxury items and other durable goods, but we found key differences with the situation across the North Sea, mostly having to do with chronology. Much more so than in Great Britain, it was the late sixteenth century and particularly the seventeenth century that saw the modernization of the retail industry in Amsterdam. This was the period in which the number of shops grew sharply and differentiation emerged between different retail sectors. It was also the period that saw the emergence of modern location patterns, which did not change substantially between 1700 and 1850. Moreover, paving, lighting, waste removal and traffic regulation had become the responsibility of the city authorities during the urban expansions, and in this context, it is not an exaggeration to speak of 'urban improvement' on a scale that remained uncommon in many British towns in the eighteenth century and even at the beginning of the nineteenth century. The radical changes that British towns underwent in this period should thus be seen more as a matter of making up for lost ground than as breaking away from the pack.

The fact that as early as the seventeenth century, the retail industry in Amsterdam could already be called modern in many respects does not imply that the period between 1700 and 1850 passed without changes. On the contrary, the street scene and the character of the shop changed fundamentally. In line with the general trend in residential housing, shops on the main streets retreated, as it were, behind the façade. The substantial canopies and extensive displays in front of the façade disappeared, and the street scene became calmer. This was also possible because the area of glass in façades was simultaneously enlarged and the development of artificial light underwent spectacular technological changes from the final quarter of the eighteenth century onwards. As a result, people could enjoy a much better view of the shop interior and the wares that were displayed there on counters and in cabinets, which, in turn, also had glass panes and doors. In the second half of the eighteenth century, the changes to the shop exterior led to the first purposely designed shop façades and retail spaces. On major streets such as Kalverstraat, shops increasingly broke loose from the traditional *voorhuis* where they had always been run and where many shops were still run in large parts of the city until long after 1800.

Nevertheless, it is clear that by the second half of the eighteenth century, neither Amsterdam's shops nor the appearance of the city's shopping streets could stand comparison with metropolises such as Paris and London any longer. Precisely because the latter cities embarked at a relatively late stage on the type of urban improvement that Amsterdam had already undergone in the seventeenth century, it was possible to incorporate the newest insights and technologies. Whilst Amsterdam continued for many years to use the street lighting that had been introduced by Jan van der Heyden in the years around 1670, in London a new generation of oil lamps was installed, followed by gas lighting at the beginning of the nineteenth century.[122] The signboards hanging far into the street and the front steps with their fencing, *pothuizen*, cellar entrances and other things likewise made an old-fashioned impression on visitors from London and Paris. They also remarked upon the absence of the large display windows that were already common elsewhere in the late eighteenth century. The shops in Kalverstraat did make a great impression on visitors with more provincial backgrounds. Nevertheless, only in the first half of the nineteenth century did 'real' display windows, large-scale shopping facilities and the modern phenomenon of shopping as an enjoyable pastime become established in Amsterdam, a development to which the examples of London and Paris and the entrepreneurship of migrants and other newcomers to Amsterdam's retail trade made no small contribution.

122 Witsen Geysbeek, *Het tegenwoordig Amsterdam*, pp. 40–41.

Conclusion: Continuity and change in Amsterdam's retail landscape

In the introduction, we observed how the nineteenth century has assumed a dominant position in much research on the history of retail trade. This century is seen as a watershed between an age dominated by markets and small, primitive shops and a new age characterized by scaling-up, rationalization and the emergence of modern retail businesses. The large department stores and fashion boutiques that arose in Western cities after the mid-nineteenth century were icons of this new age. For a long time, it was possible to maintain this image of under-developed shops in the years before large department stores and clothing shops made their mark on the urban landscape because the source material for the early modern period is relatively scarce and not particularly accessible. But another factor was also at play, as I argued above. On the whole, the towns that were studied were still small at the beginning of the nineteenth century, meaning that their shopping systems were underdeveloped. This only changed when these towns grew in the course of the nineteenth century and new industrial towns penetrated the highest echelons of the urban hierarchy. The link between industrialization, modernization and the emergence of the modern retail system was then easily drawn. Amsterdam was chosen for the present study because this city was already relatively large in the early modern period, meaning that the existence of a differentiated retail system was not ruled out in advance. Moreover, by taking the long view, we gained an overview of continuities and discontinuities that would otherwise have remained hidden, and I should like to highlight some of them here.

One of the most striking findings of this research is the spatial continuity of the retail system in the city. The area that formed the heart of Amsterdam's retail landscape in the second half of the sixteenth century was still the city's shopping heart in the mid-nineteenth century, and even today, the real estate prices per square metre on Kalverstraat and Nieuwendijk are among the highest in the city (and the Netherlands). This is a key observation because it is consistent with the significance that this study has ascribed to the urban grid and how it determines the accessibility of locations in a city. The urban grid shaped shopkeepers' location preferences and thereby determined the distribution of shops across the urban landscape to a major degree. The urban grid itself was the result of the phases of urban expansion that were discussed in this study. It was this urban grid at the heart of the city, one that was anchored in the pre-urban landscape and hardly changed over the centuries, that lay at the basis of Amsterdam's retail landscape. The core of the area was formed by the Dam on the Amstel, the city's oldest market square, and the dike roads on both sides of the river, which were connected on the Dam. Although it has not been possible to document this to date, it is obvious that the situation that existed in the sixteenth century was the product of an older development whereby the role of retail trade

Lesger, C., *Shopping Spaces and the Urban Landscape in Early Modern Amsterdam, 1550–1850*.
Taylor & Francis Group, 2020
DOI: 10.5117/9789463720625_CONCLUSION

in Amsterdam expanded as the city grew, from the central market square on the Dam to the main approach streets that ran along the river dikes.

As shown by the use of Space Syntax Analysis, the position of the city centre as the area with the greatest level of accessibility was not affected when the large city expansions began in the seventeenth century and the appearance of Amsterdam changed completely. There were, however, shifts in the relative accessibility of the various main shopping axes. Due to the western and southwestern orientation of the expansions, Warmoesstraat, for example, on the eastern side of the Amstel, lost its position as a main shopping street, whilst the significance of Kalverstraat grew for the same reason. But aside from such shifts, the Dam and the old river dikes (and Damrak and Rokin, constructed on the filled-in channels of the Amstel) remain the city's main shopping area to this very day. The fact that the medieval urban grid pattern at the heart of the city has withstood the centuries fundamentally unchanged is not without significance, but it is not the only important factor. When shops were established on the main axes thanks to their high level of accessibility in the urban grid, this strengthened the pull of these axes on retail businesses, and this, too, ensured continuity.

It should be noted, though, that continuity in retail location patterns was not limited to the main shopping axes. As the city grew in the seventeenth century, radials spread out from the city centre to the peripheral parts of the city and the city gates. In many cases, these radials were also anchored in the pre-urban landscape of low-lying ground and the dike roads to other towns in Holland and the countryside. Due to their role as approach streets to the centre, they were attractive locations for shops, and many of these radials likewise retain their retail function to this day.

This study used the complex model, introduced at the beginning, to delve more deeply into the retail patterns described above. In the complex model, Davies makes a distinction between three forms of accessibility: general accessibility, linear accessibility and special accessibility. The first, general accessibility, concerns locations that enjoy a central location relative to the intended clientele. In the case of infrequently purchased durable and luxury goods, this clientele had to be drawn from a large area, making a location in the city centre attractive; and in the case of frequently purchased daily necessities, it was sufficient to have a market area of much more limited size. General accessibility can be represented diagrammatically as a series of concentric zones around the city centre. The expectation that durable goods would have a prominent presence in the offering in the city centre and would be much less prominent in the urban periphery was confirmed time and again in this study of shops in Amsterdam. Throughout the period under study, we saw that the concentration of shops selling durable items fell as the distance to the centre increased. It was suppliers of daily necessities who first set up shops in newly built neighbourhoods. They moved with the residents, supplying them with food and other wares that were purchased frequently and for which people did not wish to travel long distances. When the extent of demand in the new neighbourhoods allowed, they were followed by shops selling more durable goods.

In the case of linear accessibility, Davies' model focuses on the location of shops on key access roads and through-routes. The above-mentioned radial streets are one example of this, but elsewhere in the city, too, linear shopping patterns were common. In the long period until the mid-nineteenth century, these radials were a characteristic feature of Amsterdam's shopping landscape, and they supplied both residents in the surrounding neighbourhoods and passers-by with consumer goods. At the same time, we established that whilst the supply of durable items on the radials was greater than in the surrounding neighbourhoods, it became scarcer as the distance to the centre increased. This makes it clear that the patterns of general and linear accessibility overlapped with one another—something that is argued by Davies and was confirmed here.

The final element of the complex model is special accessibility, the term used to describe locations that derive their appeal from the specific characteristics of their surroundings, such as the proximity of an affluent clientele or the presence of public buildings or a popular market. This form of accessibility also existed in Amsterdam's retail landscape in the early modern era. When the city was expanded from the end of the sixteenth century, greater spatial divisions were created between the various income groups, and Amsterdam's new neighbourhoods acquired a specific socio-economic composition. Retail areas with specific characteristics also arose as part of this process. The transverse streets in the canal ring in the early modern period, for example, had a very different character from the transverse streets of the Jordaan or the retail system in the Jewish Quarter.

The complex model puts flesh on the bare bones of location patterns derived from the urban grid and accessibility because it clearly shows which types of shops we might expect to find where. When we consider the empirical case of Amsterdam presented in this study, it becomes clear that this model, based on modern location theories, can also be applied to a situation in the distant past. This observation is not without significance because all too often it has been suggested that 'modern' location patterns such as these resulted from changes associated with the Industrial Revolution and the modernization of economic life in the nineteenth century. As we have seen, this is not the case. The present research on shops in Amsterdam has shown that 'modern' location patterns existed long before the dawn of modern manufacturing and distribution technologies and that they were linked, in particular, to the lack of regulations governing location and to the scale of the city. In this latter respect, Amsterdam was unique among virtually all other early modern cities. Long before 1800, Amsterdam had already become a truly large city, with a distribution apparatus befitting its size and complexity.

Although there was a high degree of continuity in the location of Amsterdam's shops, this is not to say that the retail landscape that was observed and experienced by the public did not change over the centuries. Particularly at times of rising purchasing power, growing population size and city expansion, the retail landscape underwent radical changes. This happened in the seventeenth century, for example, when Amsterdam shed its medieval character and assumed a very different appearance. The city government seized upon the expansions undertaken at that time to bring the design and maintenance of public space in the old city and the new neighbourhoods under its control. Paving, waste removal, lighting and traffic regulation played a particularly important role in the functioning of retail businesses. The measures that were taken in relation to these can be summarized under the term 'urban improvement', and they supported the retail function of Amsterdam's city centre. The city was thereby far ahead of many British towns, for example, where comparable measures were mainly taken in the eighteenth century, and sometimes only in the nineteenth century.

Compared to the interventions in public space, the changes to the appearance of shops in the seventeenth century could be described as modest. This appearance was anchored, as it were, in the building characteristics of Amsterdam's townhouses. Although there were hardly any fully timbered houses left in the city around 1600, the front façade was still characterized by a tall wooden lower façade in front of the *voorhuis*. As it allowed for a relatively large amount of natural light, this latter room was ideal for running a business. A large canopy was often hung from the wooden lower façade, as were signboards, which functioned as identifiers and outdoor advertising. Displays in front of, in and on the façade were the norm at this time, a role to which the front step—a transitional area between the private and public domains—was perfectly suited; all the more so because the overhanging canopy protected the customers and wares from the fickle Dutch weather. Precisely because shops were run largely in front of the façade, relatively little attention was paid to the interior. Rough wooden shelves, simple counters and the occasional stool or chair were the standard kit in most shops. The wares themselves were packed in an indescribable variety of cases, crates, boxes, packages, barrels, casks, vats, pots, bottles, baskets, sacks and bales and were usually only fetched and displayed at the customer's behest.

Only from the end of the seventeenth century and especially in the eighteenth century did the appearance of shops change on the major shopping streets. In essence, the changes entailed replacing the timbered lower façade with a stone façade and introducing greater transparency via the installation of larger panes of clear glass and the removal of the canopy. This made it easier to display goods in the shop than it had been in the past. This process turned out to be well-documented, particularly on Kalverstraat, and it reflected the increasing preference of Amsterdam's bourgeoisie for privacy and distance from the busy life of the street. In the second half of the eighteenth century, we also saw the development of shop façades that were specifically oriented towards retail, a phenomenon that did not occur prior to this time. Moreover, some shopkeepers took it upon themselves to remove *pothuizen*, cellar entrances, stairways and other obstacles from the front step. After all, as wares were no longer displayed on the front step, it was essential for the public to be able to step right up to the façade and the shop windows.

Now that the shop space itself had become important, more attention was paid to the interior. On the better shopping streets, wooden shelves and simple counters made way for more presentable pieces of shop furniture, and the interaction between customers and shopkeepers likewise assumed a more refined and ritualized character. The trend towards closed shops was supported by the introduction at the end of the eighteenth century of the Argand oil lamp that produced sufficient light on dark days and at dusk to light the shop interior and the wares. Beyond the main shopping streets and in shops selling daily necessities, the old, extensive displays in front of the façade and simple interiors still remained common. Nevertheless, at the end of the eighteenth century, even 'modernized' shops and shopping streets were described as 'old-fashioned' by visitors familiar with the situation in London and Paris. They pointed to, among other things, the traditional front steps, the lack of pavements, the large display boards, the absence of modern display windows and the lack of refinement and elegance. Only in the first half of the nineteenth century did the shop in Amsterdam, influenced by examples abroad, slowly make up lost ground.

Popular shopping streets such as Kalverstraat and Nieuwendijk now featured real display windows, the display boards and the remaining canopies disappeared, the shop—exemplified by firms such as Sinkel's—underwent a process of scaling-up, and gas lighting was introduced. And not coincidentally, it was precisely at this time that promenading and shopping as a pleasurable pastime reached their full potential.

Appendix: Sources for the location of shops in Amsterdam and selection of sectors

A range of sources was used to reconstruct the location patterns of shops in Amsterdam, but two sources in particular stand out: the *Capitale Impositie* and the *Personele Quotisatie*. The oldest of the two is the register of the *Capitale Impositie* of 1585, published by Van Dillen.[1] The main limitation of this source is its incompleteness: only 3,000 of the 7,000 to 8,000 households in Amsterdam contributed to the tax, and Van Dillen was only able to establish the professions of 1,400 households. On the other hand, it does give us a rough impression of where the people in the register lived in the city, and thereby an impression of the location of what were undoubtedly relatively affluent retailers in Amsterdam. As the proceeds of the tax were used for the relief of Antwerp, Catholics are likely to have minimized their contributions, but as we do not consider the amount of tax contributed here, this disadvantage does not weigh very heavily.[2] The data of 338 people were retrieved from the source, spread over 25 professional groups:

Shops selling daily necessities:

Apple seller, bacon buyer, baker, beer seller, beer trader, brandy seller, butcher, cake baker, dairy buyer, flour buyer, grocer, grocer/pharmacist, herring buyer, pie baker, vegetable seller, waffle baker, wine buyer (147 people in total).

Shops selling durable and luxury goods:

Book seller, cloth buyer, jug seller, *kramer* (non-itinerant seller), pharmacist, second-hand dealer, silk-cloth buyer, *wantsnijder* (selling fabric by the yard) (191 people in total).

In Chapter 1, it was argued that it is justifiable to include specialized traders such as herring buyers and dairy buyers in retail trade in this period on the basis that they were seldom exclusively wholesalers but also sold *en detail*.

For the mid-eighteenth century, the *Personele Quotisatie* of 1742—published by Oldewelt and discussed in detail in Chapter 5—was available.[3] The *Personele Quotisatie* was also a tax, one that was intended to provide Holland with the funds to pay the interest and principal on a loan that had been taken out to strengthen the defences. The War of the Austrian Succession, which broke out in 1740, was the immediate reason for reinforcing the military strength of the Republic. Like the *Capitale Impositie*, this tax only provides information about the affluent part of Amsterdam's population. It has been estimated that three-quarters of the population did not meet the tax threshold of 600 guilders of income a year, and they

1 Van Dillen, *Amsterdam in 1585*.
2 For the objections of Catholics to contributing to this tax, see Dudok van Heel, 'Waar waren de Amsterdamse katholieken'.
3 Oldewelt, *Kohier van de Personeele Quotisatie*.

Lesger, C., *Shopping Spaces and the Urban Landscape in Early Modern Amsterdam, 1550–1850*.
Taylor & Francis Group, 2020
DOI: 10.5117/9789463720625_APP

were—unfortunately for us—not registered in the source. For shopkeepers with sufficient income, though, the *Personele Quotisatie* is a wonderful source, for it not only reports the taxpayer's profession and gives an indication of their address, it also states their income, the (estimated) rental value of their home and an estimate of their capital wealth. Moreover, numbers of servants, country estates, carriages or vessels and horses were noted as indicators of prosperity. No other source from the early modern era contains so much information about such a large group of citizens in Amsterdam. The fact that the specializations of shopkeepers were registered in great detail makes this source even more valuable to this research. Of the 3,757 retailers we encounter in the source, only ten are described exclusively as 'shopkeepers'; for the rest, the nature of the shop is recorded. Specifically, it concerns 118 different retail activities and shop types:[4]

Shops selling daily necessities:
bacon butcher, baker, butcher, cake baker, cheese shop, coffee shop, coffee and tea shop, dry goods shop, egg shop, French baker, fresh water seller, fruit shop, grocery, ham shop, jam shop, *komenij* (bacon, dairy and dry goods), oyster shop, pastry cook, pie baker, rusk baker, snuff shop, tea shop, tobacconist's, vegetable shop, victuals shop, waffle baker (1,910 people in total).

Shops selling durable and luxury goods:
basket shop, bed shop, bombazine shop, (whale) bone shop, bonnet shop, book printer's, bookshop, broom shop, brush shop, button shop, can shop, candle shop, cane shop, card shop, chemist's, children's shop, chintz shop, cloth shop, clothes shop, comb shop, copper shop, cord shop, corset shop, cotton shop, curiosity shop, decorations shop, Delft shop, dolls shop, English fabric shop, fabric shop, fan shop, fancy goods shop, feathers shop, flag shop, flax shop, *Franse winkel*, fur shop, glass shop, gloves shop, hat shop, ironmongery, jeweller's, knife shop, lace shop, leather shop, linen shop, linen and stockings shop, matting shop, mirror shop, moquette shop, netting (gauze) shop, Nuremberg wares shop, paint shop, paper shop, parchment shop, pen shop, pen and varnish shop, pharmacist, pipe shop, porcelain shop, pot shop, pottery shop, powder shop, ribbon shop, rope shop, sagathy shop, salt and soap shop, scales shop, second-hand shop, seed shop, shackles shop, shoe shop, silk shop, silk stockings shop, silversmith's, silversmith's tools shop, spurs shop, stockings shop, stone shop, straw hat shop, tin shop, (sailors') trousers shop, trunk shop, varnish shop, wallpaper shop, watchmaker, watch shop, wig shop, wood shop, yarn shop, yarn and ribbon shop (1,837 people in total).

Nature of the shop not specified: 10 people.

4 Persons who have been included in the register with several professional titles (for example goldsmith and wallpaper shop) have been included in this research under their retail activity.

List of consulted sources and literature

Primary sources

Stadsarchief Amsterdam (SAA):

- Aalmoezeniersweeshuis (archief 343)
- Archief Burgemeesters (archief 5028)
- Archief gilden (archief 366)
- Archief Hart (archief 30452)
- Beeldbank
- Collectie handschriften (archief 5059)
- Collectie Hart (archief 883)
- Desolate boedelkamer (archief 5072)
- Notarissen (archief 5075)
- Poorterboeken and indices
- Rechterlijk archief (archief 5061)

Bibliography

Abrahamse, Jaap Evert, *De grote uitleg van Amsterdam. Stadsontwikkeling in de zeventiende eeuw* (Bussum 2010).

Abrahamse, Jaap Evert, *Metropolis in the Making. A Planning History of Amsterdam in the Dutch Golden Age* (Turnhout, forthcoming).

Aert, Laura van, 'Buurtwinkels en winkelstraten. De evolutie van het Antwerpse winkelbedrijf in de nieuwe tijd', *Stadsgeschiedenis* 4 (2009): 21–44.

Aert, Laura van, *Leven of overleven? Winkelhouden in crisistijd: de Antwerpse meerseniers, ca.1648 - ca.1748* (PhD thesis, University of Antwerp 2007).

Alexander, David, *Retailing in England During the Industrial Revolution* (London 1970).

Armstrong, Isobel, *Victorian Glassworlds. Glass Culture and the Imagination 1830–1880* (Oxford 2008).

Baer, William C., 'Early Retailing. London's Shopping Exchanges, 1550–1700', *Business History* 49 (2007): 29–51.

Bairoch, P., J. Batou and P. Chèvre, *La population des villes Européennes. Banque de données et analyse sommaire des résultats, 800–1850* (Geneva 1988).

Bakker, Boudewijn, 'De stadsuitleg van 1610 en het ideaal van de "volcomen stad"', *Jaarboek Amstelodamum* 87 (1995): 71–96.

Bakker, Boudewijn, 'De zichtbare stad 1578–1813', in: Willem Frijhoff and Maarten Prak (eds.) *Geschiedenis van Amsterdam. Centrum van de wereld 1578–1650*, II-1 (Amsterdam 2004), pp. 17–101.

Barlaeus, Caspar and Joost van den Vondel, *Blyde inkomst van Maria de Medicis / Medicea Hospes* (Amsterdam 1639) Digitale bibliotheek voor de Nederlandse letteren (https://www.dbnl.org/tekst/vond001dewe03_01/vond001dewe03_01_0137.php; last accessed 9 August 2019).

Bavel, Bas J.P. van, *Manors and Markets. Economy and Society in the Low Countries, 500–1600.* (Oxford 2010).

Benson, John and Laura Ugolini (eds.), *Cultures of Selling. Perspectives on Consumption and Society since 1700, The History of Retailing and Consumption* (Aldershot 2006).

Benson, John and Laura Ugolini (eds.), *A Nation of Shopkeepers. Five Centuries of British Retailing* (London and New York 2003).

Berkers, E., 'Een nieuw licht', in: Harry Lintsen and Martijn Bakker (eds.) *Geschiedenis van de techniek in Nederland. De wording van een moderne samenleving 1800–1890, III, Textiel*; Gas, licht en elektriciteit; Bouw (The Hague and Zutphen 1993), pp. 91–105.

Berry, Brian J.L, *Commercial Structure and Commercial Blight. Retail Patterns and Processes in the City of Chicago.* University of Chicago, Department of Geography, Research Paper 85. (Chicago, IL 1963).

Berry, Helen, 'Polite Consumption: Shopping in Eighteenth-Century England', *Transactions of the Royal Historical Society* 12 (2002): 375–394.

Blondé, Bruno, *Een economie met verschillende snelheden. Ongelijkheden in de opbouw en de ontwikkeling van het Brabantse stedelijke netwerk (ca. 1750 - ca. 1790)* (Brussels 1999).

Blondé, Bruno and Ilja van Damme, 'Een crisis als uitdaging? Kleinhandelsrevoluties en verbruiksveranderingen te Antwerpen (ca. 1648 - ca. 1748)', *Tijdschrift voor Sociale en Economische Geschiedenis* 4 (2007): 61–88.

Blondé, Bruno and Ilja van Damme, 'The Shop, the Home, and the Retail Revolution. Antwerp, Seventeenth-Eighteenth Centuries', *Città e Storia* 2 (2007): 335–350.

Blondé, Bruno and Hilde Greefs, 'Werk aan de winkel. De Antwerpse meerseniers: aspecten van de kleinhandel en het verbruik in de 17de en 18de eeuw', *Bijdragen tot de Geschiedenis* 84 (2001): 207–229.

Blondé, Bruno et al., 'Retail Circuits and Practices in Medieval and Early Modern Europe: An Introduction', in: Marc Boone (ed.) *Buyers and Sellers. Retail Circuits and Practices in Medieval and Early Modern Europe*, Studies in European Urban History, 9 (Turnhout 2006), pp. 7–29.

Blondé, Bruno et al. (eds.), *Retailers and Consumer Changes in Early Modern Europe. England, France, Italy and the Low Countries*, Collection Perspectives Historiques, 14 (Tours 2005).

Boeken, A., *Amsterdamse stoepen* (Amsterdam 1950).

Boers, Onno W., *De gevelstenen van Amsterdam* (Hilversum 2007).

Boers, Onno W., 'Amsterdamse gevelstenen. Twee zeventiende-eeuwse winkelinterieurs', *Binnenstad. Uitgave van de Vereniging Vrienden van de Amsterdamse Binnenstad* 234 (June 2009) and also available on the website of the *Vereniging Vrienden van de Amsterdamse Binnenstad.*

Bok, Marten Jan, '"Schilderien te coop". Nieuwe marketingtechnieken op de Nederlandse kunstmarkt van de Gouden Eeuw', in: Martine Gosselink et al. (eds.) *Thuis in de Gouden Eeuw. Kleine meesterwerken uit de SØR Rusche collectie* (Zwolle 2008), pp. 9–29.

Boom, Harm and Alexander Lodewijk Lesturgeon, *Een Drentsch gemeente-assessor met zijne twee neven op reis naar Amsterdam, in 't voorjaar van 1843*, deel 1 (Groningen 1845).

Bourdieu, Pierre, *Distinction: A Social Critique of the Judgement of Taste* (Cambridge, MA 1984).

Bredero, Gerbrand Adriaensz., *Kluchten* (ed. Jo Daan) (Culemborg 1971).

Breen, Joh.C., 'Jan van der Heijden', *Jaarboek Amstelodamum* 11 (1913): 29–63.

Breen, Joh.C., *Rechtsbronnen der stad Amsterdam*, Oud Vaderlandsche Rechtsbronnen (The Hague 1902).

Breen, Joh.C., 'Topografische geschiedenis van den Dam te Amsterdam', *Jaarboek Amstelodamum* 7 (1909): 99–196.

Breen, Joh.C., 'De verordeningen op het bouwen te Amsterdam vóór de negentiende eeuw', *Jaarboek Amstelodamum* 6 (1908): 107–148.

Briels, J., *De Zuidnederlandse immigratie 1572–1630* (Haarlem 1978).

Brouwer Ancher, A.J.M. and J.C. Breen, 'De doleantie van een deel der burgerij van Amsterdam tegen den Magistraat dier stad in 1564 en 1565', *Bijdragen en Mededeelingen van het Historisch Genootschap* 24 (1903): 59–200.

Brouwer, T., *Stoepen, stoeppalen, stoephekken*, Heemschut serie (Zutphen 1985).

Brown, Stephen, 'The Complex Model of City Centre Retailing: An Historical Application', *Transactions of the Institute of British Geographers, new series* 12 (1987): 4–18.

Brugge, Jeroen ter, '"Een eigen Hollandsch feest". Gebruiken rondom de Nieuwe Haring', *Holland* 38 (2006): 187–234.

Brugmans, H., *Geschiedenis van Amsterdam*, Deel 6. Opgaand getij 1848/1925 (Utrecht and Antwerp 1973).

Bruneel, Claude, 'La localisation du commerce et de l'artisanat à Bruxelles au milieu du XVIIIe siècle', in: P. Guignet (ed.) *Le peuple des villes dans l'Europe du Nord-Ouest (fin du Moyen Âge-1945)*, p. 1 (Rijsel 2000), pp. 167–191.

Bruneel, Claude and Luc Delporte, 'Approche socio-professionelle de la population bruxelloise en 1783', *Revue du Nord* 79 (1997): 463–494.

Bucklin, Louis P., *Competition and Evolution in the Distributive Trades* (Englewood Cliffs, NJ 1972).
Burger jr., C.P., 'Amsterdam in het einde der zestiende eeuw. Studie bij de uitgaaf van den grooten plattegrond van 1597', *Jaarboek Amstelodamum* 16 (1918): 1–101.
Burm, Ellen and Bert de Munck, 'Het broodje gebakken? Huwelijksstrategieën en partnerkeuze van bakkers(kinderen) te Brussel in de overgang van het Ancien Régime naar de negentiende eeuw', *Stadsgeschiedenis* 5 (2010): 148–168.
Buursink, J., *Stad en ruimte. Inleiding in de stadsgeografie* (Assen 1980).
Calderwood, Margaret Steuart, *Letters and Journals of Mrs. Calderwood of Polton, from England, Holland and the Low Countries in 1756*, Alexander Fergusson (ed.) (Edinburgh 1884).
Carasso-Kok, Marijke, *Amsterdam Historisch. Een stadsgeschiedenis aan de hand van de collectie van het Amsterdams Historisch Museum* (Bussum 1975).
Carasso-Kok, Marijke (ed.) *Geschiedenis van Amsterdam. Een stad uit het niets. Tot 1578*, I (Amsterdam 2004).
Carter, Harold, *The Study of Urban Geography* (London 1972).
Clark, Peter, *European Cities and Towns 400–2000* (Oxford 2009).
Colenbrander, Sjoukje, 'Zolang de weefkunst bloeit. Zijdeweverijen in Amsterdam en Haarlem, 1585–1750', (PhD thesis, University of Amsterdam 2010).
Colijn, Yvonne, 'Amsterdamse graanhandel, "sincere" katholieken en keizer Karel V: over de politieke context van Cornelis Anthoniszoons "Gezicht in vogelvlucht op Amsterdam"', *Jaarboek Amstelodamum* 100 (2008): 178–209.
Commelin, Caspar, *Beschryvinge van Amsterdam, etc.* (Amsterdam 1693).
Conzen, Michael R.G., 'Zur Morphologie der englischen Stadt im Industriezeitalter', in: Helmut Jäger (ed.) *Probleme des Städtewesens im Industriellen Zeitalter* (Cologne/Vienna 1978), pp. 1–48.
Coquery, Natacha, 'The Language of Success. Marketing and Distributing Semi-Luxury Goods in Eighteenth-Century Paris', *Journal of design history* 17 (2004): 71–89.
Coquery, Natacha, *Tenir boutique á Paris au XVIIIe siècle. Luxe et demi-luxe* (Paris 2011).
Cox, Nancy, *The Complete Tradesman. A Study of Retailing, 1550–1820*. The History of Retailing and Consumption (Aldershot 2000).
Cox, Nancy and Claire Walsh, '"Their Shops Are Dens, the Buyer Is Their Prey": Shop Design and Sale Techniques', in: Nancy Cox (ed.) *The Complete Tradesman. A Study of Retailing, 1550–1820* (Aldershot 2000), pp. 76–115.
Damme, Ilja van, 'Pendelen tussen revoluties en tradities. Recent historisch onderzoek naar de kleinhandel in de late middeleeuwen en de nieuwe tijd (ca.1450-ca.1850)', *Stadsgeschiedenis* 2 (2007) 1, pp. 54–65.
Damme, Ilja van, *Verleiden en verkopen. Antwerpse kleinhandelaars en hun klanten in tijden van crisis (ca. 1648-ca. 1748)* (Amsterdam 2007).
Damme, Ilja van, 'Zotte verwaandheid. Over Franse verleiding en Zuid-Nederlands onbehagen, 1650–1750', in: Raf de Bont and Tom Verschaffel (eds.), *Het verderf van Parijs* (Leuven 2004), pp. 187–203.
Dapper, Olfert, *Historische beschryving der stadt Amsterdam, waerin de voornaemste geschiedenissen ... vertoont worden* (Amsterdam 1663).
Davies, R.L., 'Structural Models of Retail Distribution. Analogies with Settlement and Urban Land-Use Theories', *Transactions of the Institute of British Geographers* 57 (1972): 59–82.
Davies, R.L. and D.J. Bennison, 'Retailing in the City Centre: The Characters of Shopping Streets', *Tijdschrift voor Economische en Sociale Geografie* 69 (1978): 270–285.
Desjobert, Louis, 'Voyage aux Pays Bas en 1778', *De Navorscher* 59 (1910): 337 ff.
Desjobert, Louis, 'Voyage aux Pays Bas en 1778', *De Navorscher* 60 (1911).
Dibbits, Hester and Harm Nijboer, 'Retailers and the Marketing of Coffee and Tea in the Dutch Republic, 1650–1800' (forthcoming).
Diederiks, Herman, *Een stad in verval. Amsterdam omstreeks 1800: demografisch, economisch, ruimtelijk*, Amsterdamse Historische Reeks, 4 (Amsterdam 1982).
Dil, G. and E. Homburg, 'Gas', in: Harry Lintsen and Martijn Bakker (eds.) *Geschiedenis van de techniek in Nederland. De wording van een moderne samenleving 1800–1890, III, Textiel*; Gas, licht en elektriciteit; Bouw (The Hague and Zutphen 1993), pp. 107–133.
Dillen, J.G. van, *Amsterdam in 1585. Het kohier der capitale impositie van 1585* (Amsterdam 1941).

Dillen, J.G. van, 'Bloeitijd der Amsterdamse Wisselbank 1687–1781', in: J.G. van Dillen (ed.) *Mensen en achtergronden. Studies uitgegeven ter gelegenheid van de tachtigste jaardag van de schrijver* (Groningen 1964), pp. 385–415.

Dillen, J.G. van, 'Een eeuw economische en sociale ontwikkeling (1848–1948)', in: A.E. d'Ailly (ed.) *Zeven eeuwen Amsterdam*, V (Amsterdam 1950), pp. 157–207.

Dillen, J.G. van, *Van rijkdom en regenten. Handboek tot de economische en sociale geschiedenis van Nederland tijdens de Republiek* (The Hague 1970).

Dillen, J.G. van (ed.) *Bronnen tot de geschiedenis van het bedrijfsleven en het gildewezen van Amsterdam*, Rijks Geschiedkundige Publicatiën, 69 (Grote Serie), I, 1512–1611 (The Hague 1929).

Dillen, J.G. van (ed.) *Bronnen tot de geschiedenis van het bedrijfsleven en het gildewezen van Amsterdam*, Rijks Geschiedkundige Publicatiën, 78 (Grote Serie), II, 1612–1632 (The Hague 1933).

Dillen, J.G. van (ed.) *Bronnen tot de geschiedenis van het bedrijfsleven en het gildewezen van Amsterdam*, Rijks Geschiedkundige Publicatiën, 144 (Grote Serie), III, 1633–1672 (The Hague 1974).

Domselaer, Tobias van, *Beschryvinge van Amsterdam, haar eerste oorspronk ... tot dezen tegenwoordige jare 1665, is voorgevallen* (Amsterdam 1665).

Douglas, R.W. and Susan Frank, *A History of Glassmaking* (Henley-on-Thames, Oxfordshire 1972).

Dudok van Heel, S.A.C., 'Regent Families and Urban Development in Amsterdam', in: Peter van Kessel and Elisja Schulte (eds.) *Rome - Amsterdam. Two Growing Cities in Seventeenth-Century Europe* (Amsterdam 1997), pp. 124–145.

Dudok van Heel, S.A.C., 'Waar waren de Amsterdamse katholieken in de zomer van 1585. Enkele aantekeningen bij de uitgave van het kohier van 1585', *Jaarboek Amstelodamum* 77 (1985): 13–53.

Dyer, C., 'The Consumer and the Market in the Later Middle Ages', *Economic History Review* 42 (1989): 305–327.

Eeghen, I.H. van, 'De Amsterdamsche Courant in de achttiende eeuw', *Jaarboek Amstelodamum* 44 (1950): 31–58.

Eeghen, I.H. van, 'Uitdraagster 't zij man of vrouw', *Maandblad Amstelodamum* 56 (1969): 102–110.

Een-Amsterdammer, *Physiologie van Amsterdam door een' Amsterdammer* (Amsterdam 1844).

Een-Humorist, *Physiologie van de Kalverstraat door een Humorist* (Amsterdam 1844).

Elias, Johan E., *Het geslacht Elias. De geschiedenis van een Amsterdamsche regentenfamilie* (The Hague 1937).

Elias, Johan E., *De vroedschap van Amsterdam 1578–1795*, two volumes (Haarlem 1903–1905).

Eliëns, Titus M., '1800–1850', in: C. Willemijn Fock (ed.) *Het Nederlandse interieur in beeld 1600–1900* (Zwolle 2001), pp. 342–403.

Engel, Henk and Esther Gramsbergen, 'Het eerste beursgebouw en de vorming van het centrum van Amsterdam', *OverHolland. Architectonische studies voor de Hollandse stad* 3 (2006): 57–87.

Farret, J.P., A.G. Verster and J.H. van Swinden, *Rapport over de telling van het volk van Amsterdam. Overgegeven aan de representanten van hetzelve Volk op den 20sten October 1795* (Amsterdam 1795).

Fock, C. Willemijn, '1600–1650', in: C. Willemijn Fock (ed.) *Het Nederlandse interieur in beeld 1600–1900* (Zwolle 2001), pp. 16–79.

Fock, C. Willemijn, '1650–1700', in: C. Willemijn Fock (ed.) *Het Nederlandse interieur in beeld 1600–1900* (Zwolle 2001), pp. 81–179.

Fokkens, Melchior, *Beschrijvinge der wijdt-vermaarde koop-stadt Amstelredam, van haar eerste beginselen, oude voorrechten ... en, haar tegenwoordigen standt* (Amsterdam 1662).

Fokkens, Melchior, *Beschrijvingh der wijdt-vermaarde koop-stadt Amstelredam, van haar eerste beginselen, zedert den jare 1203 ... tot den iare 1664 toe* (Amsterdam 1664).

Frederiks, J.G. and P.J. Frederiks, *Kohier van den tweehonderdsten penning voor Amsterdam en onderhoorige plaatsen over 1631* (Amsterdam 1890).

Frijhoff, Willem and Maarten Prak (eds.) *Geschiedenis van Amsterdam. Centrum van de wereld 1578–1650*, II-1 (Amsterdam 2004).

Fuchs, J.M., *Beurt- en wagenveren* (The Hague 1946).

Fuchs, J.M. and W.J. Simons, *In de winkel van Sinkel. Kopen en verkopen in Nederland* (Amsterdam ca. 1963).

Furnée, Jan Hein, '"Om te winkelen, zoo als het in de residentie heet". Consumptiecultuur en stedelijke ruimte in Den Haag 1850–1890', *Jaarboek voor Vrouwengeschiedenis* 22 (2002): 28–55.

Furnée, Jan Hein, 'Winkeletalages als moderne massamedia. Visuele cultuur en sociale verhoudingen in Den Haag, 1850–1890', *Negentiende Eeuw* 27 (2003): 74–106.
Furnée, Jan Hein, '"Our Living Museum of Nouveautés": Visual and Social Pleasures in the Hague's Shopping Streets, 1650–1900', in: Jan Hein Furnée and Clé Lesger (eds.), *The Landscape of Consumption. Shopping Streets and Cultures in Western Europe, 1600–1900* (Houndmills 2014), pp. 208–231.
Furnée, Jan Hein and Clé Lesger (eds.), *The Landscape of Consumption. Shopping Streets and Cultures in Western Europe, 1600–1900* (Houndmills 2014).
Garrioch, David, 'House Names, Shop Signs and Social Organization in Western European Cities, 1500–1900', *Urban History* 21 (1994): 20–48.
Gelderblom, Oscar, *Zuid-Nederlandse kooplieden en de opkomst van de Amsterdamse stapelmarkt (1578–1630)* (Hilversum 2000).
Gillet, Marie, 'Innovation and Tradition in the Shopping Landscape of Paris and a Provincial City, 1800–1900', in: Jan Hein Furnée and Clé Lesger (eds.), *The Landscape of Consumption. Shopping Streets and Cultures in Western Europe, 1600–1900* (Houndmills 2014), pp. 184–207.
Gawronski, Jerzy, 'Ontstaan uit een storm. De vroegste geschiedenis van Amsterdam archeologisch en landschappelijk belicht', *Jaarboek Amstelodamum* 109 (2017): 54–91.
Glamann, Kristof, *Dutch-Asiatic Trade 1620–1740* (Copenhagen/The Hague 1981 [1958]).
Glennie, Paul, 'Consumption, Consumerism and Urban Form: Historical Perspectives', *Urban Studies* 35 (1998): 927–951.
Goinga, Johanna van, *Alom te bekomen: veranderingen in de boekdistributie in de Republiek 1720–1800* (Amsterdam 1999).
Gouw, J. ter, *Geschiedenis van Amsterdam*, 8 volumes (Amsterdam 1879–1893).
Graaf, Ed de and Tiny Polderman (eds.) *D' Guld Waerrelt. De wondere huisnaamwereld van Middelburg* (Vlissingen 2005).
Le guide d'Amsterdam, avec la description de tout ce qu'il y a de plus intéressant (Amsterdam 1793).
Le guide ou nouvelle description d'Amsterdam, enseignant aux voyageurs, et aux négoçians, sa splendeur, son commerce, et la description de ses édifices, ruës, etc.: la connoissance des poids, des mésures, etc. (Amsterdam 1722).
Le guide, ou nouvelle description d'Amsterdam; enseignant aux voyageurs, et aux negocians, son origine, ses aggrandissemens & son état actuel …; avec une description de sa belle maison de ville, et de tout ce qu'elle renferme de curieux (Amsterdam 1772).
Haccoû, J.F., *De groothandel. Functies, dynamiek en perspectieven* (Leiden 1969).
Haitsma Mulier, E.O.G., 'The Image of Amsterdam in Seventeenth-Century Descriptions', in: Peter van Kessel and Elisja Schulte (eds.) *Rome - Amsterdam. Two Growing Cities in Seventeenth-Century Europe* (Amsterdam 1997), pp. 13–23.
Haitsma Mulier, E.O.G., 'De zeventiende-eeuwse stadsbeschrijvingen van Amsterdam', *Maandblad Amstelodamum* 85 (1998): 107–115.
Hameleers, Marc, *Kaarten van Amsterdam 1538–1865* (Bussum and Amsterdam 2013).
Harms, Roeland, 'Handel in letteren. De ambulante handel in actueel drukwerk in zeventiende-eeuws Amsterdam', *De zeventiende eeuw* 23 (2007): 216–229.
Hart, Simon, 'Geschrift en getal. Onderzoek naar de samenstelling van de bevolking van Amsterdam in de 17e en 18e eeuw, op grond van gegevens over migratie, huwelijk, beroep en alfabetisme', in: Simon Hart (ed.) *Geschrift en getal. Een keuze uit de demografisch-, economisch- en sociaal-historische studiën op grond van Amsterdamse en Zaanse archivalia, 1600–1800* (Dordrecht 1976), pp. 115–181.
Heijbroek, J.F., 'Van eenvoudige prentenkoopman tot gerenommeerde kunsthandelaar: Frans Buffa & Zonen in Amsterdam (ca. 1785–1951)', *De Boekenwereld* 23 (2006–2007): 50–64.
Heinemeijer, W.F. and M.F. Wagenaar (eds.) *Amsterdam in kaarten. Verandering van de stad in vier eeuwen cartografie* (Ede and Antwerp 1987).
Hesselmans, A.N., 'Elektriciteit', in: Harry Lintsen and Martijn Bakker (eds.) *Geschiedenis van de techniek in Nederland. De wording van een moderne samenleving 1800–1890*, III, Textiel; Gas, licht en elektriciteit; Bouw (The Hague and Zutphen 1993), pp. 134–161.

Heuvel, Charles van den, *'De Huysbou'. A Reconstruction of an Unfinished Treatise on Architecture, Town Planning and Civil Engineering by Simon Stevin,* History of Science and Scholarship in the Netherlands, 7 (Amsterdam 2005).

Heuvel, Danielle van den, *Women and Entrepreneurship. Female Traders in the Northern Netherlands c. 1580–1815* (Amsterdam 2007).

Heuvel, Danielle van den and Sheilagh Ogilvie, 'Retail Development in the Consumer Revolution: The Netherlands, c. 1670 - c. 1815', *Explorations in Economic History* 50 (2013): 69–87.

Heyden, Jan van der, *Beschryving der nieuwlijks uitgevonden en geoctrojeerde slang-brand-spuiten, en haare wijze van brand-blussen tegenwoordig binnen Amsterdam in gebruik zijnde; Nevens beschryving der brand-ordres van de stad Amsterdam* (Amsterdam 1690).

Hillier, Bill, 'Cities as Movement Economies', *Urban Design International* 1 (1996): 41–60.

Hillier, Bill et al., 'Natural Movement: Or, Configuration and Attraction in Urban Pedestrian Movement', *Environment and Planning B, Planning and Design* 20 (1993): 29–66.

Hillier, Bill and Julienne Hanson, *The Social Logic of Space* (Cambridge 1984).

Hondelink, H.Ph., 'Vroom en Dreesmann, de oprichters en hun onderneming 1887–1912', *Jaarboek voor de geschiedenis van bedrijf en techniek* 9 (1992), pp. 159–184.

Hondelink, H.Ph. (ed.) *Historische Bedrijfsarchieven. Detailhandel. Een geschiedenis en bronnenoverzicht.*, Historische Bedrijfsarchieven, 14 (Amsterdam 1993).

Hoogenboom, Annemieke, Bert Gerlagh and Jan Stroop, *De wereld van Christiaan Andriessen. Amsterdamse dagboek-tekeningen 1805–1808* (Bussum and Amsterdam 2008).

Horlings, Edwin, *The Economic Development of the Dutch Service Sector 1800–1850. Trade and Transport in a Premodern Economy* (Amsterdam 1995).

Hortensius, Lambertus, *Het boeck van den oproer der weder-dooperen. Eerst int Lat. beschr. ende gedr. tot Basel ende nu in Ned. overgheset: mitsgaders een voor-reden van den selven autheur* (Enkhuizen 1614).

Huber, Therese, *Bemerkungen über Holland aus dem Reisejournal einer deutschen Frau* (Leipzig 1811).

Huydecoper, B., *Proeve van taal- en dichtkunde, behelzende uitvoerige bladwyzers op dezelve proeve naar de uitgave van wylen F. van Lelyveld* (Leiden 1791).

Jacobsen Jensen, J.N., 'Moryson's reis door en zijn karakteristiek van de Nederlanden; 1592–1595', *Bijdragen en Mededeelingen van het Historisch Genootschap* 39 (1918): 214–305.

Jansen, L., 'De derde vergroting van Amsterdam', *Jaarboek Amstelodamum* 52 (1960): 42–89.

Jansen, L., 'De stadsuitbreiding van 1663', *Ons Amsterdam* 15 (1963): 374–380.

Jansen, P.C., 'Armoede in Amsterdam aan het eind van de achttiende eeuw', *Tijdschrift voor Geschiedenis* 88 (1975): 613–625.

Jayasena, Ranjith, 'Amsterdam 1200–1300, stadswording aan de monding van de Amstel', *Jaarboek Amstelodamum* 109 (2017): 113–149.

Jefferys, J.B., *Retail Trading in Britain 1850–1950. A Study of Trends in Retailing with Special Reference to the Development of Co-Operative, Multiple Shop and Department Store Methods of Trading* (Cambridge 1954).

Jones, Fred Mitchell, *Middlemen in the Domestic Trade of the United States 1800–1860* (Urbana 1937).

Jones, Ken and Jim Simmons, *The Retail Environment* (London and New York 1990).

Kam, J.G., *Waar was dat huis in de Warmoesstraat* (Amsterdam 1968).

Kaptein, Herman, *Nijverheid op windkracht. Energietransities in Nederland 1500–1900* (Hilversum 2017).

Kaptein, Herman, 'Poort van Holland. De economische ontwikkeling 1200–1578', in: Marijke Carasso-Kok (ed.) *Geschiedenis van Amsterdam. Een stad uit het niets (tot 1578)*, I (Amsterdam 2004), pp. 109–173.

Keene, Derek, 'Sites of Desire: Shops, Selds and Wardrobes in London and Other English Cities, 1100–1550', in: Bruno Blondé et al. (eds.) *Buyers and Sellers. Retail Circuits and Practices in Medieval and Early Modern Europe*, Studies in European Urban History, 9 (Turnhout 2006), pp. 125–153.

Kerf, Raoul de, *De juiste prijs in de laatmiddeleeuwse stad. Een onderzoek naar middeleeuwse economische ethiek op de ambachtelijke markt en in moralistische literatuur,* Studies Stadsgeschiedenis (Amsterdam 2010).

Kernkamp, G.W., 'Bengt Ferrner's dagboek van zijne reis door Nederland in 1759', *Bijdragen en Mededeelingen van het Historisch Genootschap* 31 (1910): 314–509.

Ketner, F., 'Amsterdam en de binnenvaart door Holland in de 15e eeuw', *Bijdragen voor vaderlandsche geschiedenis en oudheidkunde* 8e reeks, IV and V (1943): 169–200, 33–59.

Ketner, F., *Handel en scheepvaart van Amsterdam in de vijftiende eeuw* (Leiden 1946).

Kist, Willem, *Het leven, gevoelens en zonderlinge reize van den landjonker Govert Hendrik Godefroi van Blankenheim tot den Stronk* (Haarlem 1800).

Kistemaker, Renée, 'De Amsterdamse markten van omstreeks 1300 tot 1815', in: Renée Kistemaker, Michiel Wagenaar and Jos van Assendelft, *Amsterdam marktstad* (Amsterdam 1984), pp. 15–95.

Kistemaker, Renée, 'Functiekaarten en de analyse van de economische en sociale structuur van Amsterdam in de zeventiende en achttiende eeuw', in: Michiel Jonker, Leo Noordegraaf and Michiel Wagenaar (eds.) *Van stadskern tot stadsgewest. Stedebouwkundige geschiedenis van Amsterdam* (Amsterdam 1984), pp. 101–112.

Kivell, P.T. and G. Shaw, 'The Study of Retail Location', in: John A. Dawson (ed.) *Retail Geography* (London 1980), pp. 95–155.

Klein, P.W., *De Trippen in de 17e eeuw. Een studie over het ondernemersgedrag op de Hollandse stapelmarkt* (Assen 1965).

Klep, P.M.M., 'Urban Decline in Brabant: The Traditionalization of Investments and Labour (1374/1806)', in: H. van der Wee (ed.), *The Rise and Decline of Urban Industries in Italy and in the Low Countries* (Leuven 1988), pp. 261–286.

Knotter, Ad, *Economische transformatie en stedelijke arbeidsmarkt. Amsterdam in de tweede helft van de negentiende eeuw* (Zwolle 1991).

Knotter, Ad and Hans Muskee, 'Conjunctuur en levensstandaard in Amsterdam 1815–1855. Een onderzoek op basis van plaatselijke accijnzen', *Tijdschrift voor Sociale Geschiedenis* 12 (1986): 153–181.

Kok, A.A., *Amsterdamsche woonhuizen* (Amsterdam 1943).

Koldeweij, Eloy F., '1750–1800', in: C. Willemijn Fock (ed.) *Het Nederlandse interieur in beeld 1600–1900* (Zwolle 2001), pp. 260–341.

Kooy, T.P. van der, *Hollands stapelmarkt en haar verval* (Amsterdam 1931).

Kouwenaar, D., *Tussen Dam en Muntplein. De levensgeschiedenis van de Kalverstraat* (The Hague 1950).

Krogt, P.C.J. van der, *Advertenties voor kaarten, atlassen, globes e.d. in Amsterdamse kranten 1621–1811* (Utrecht 1985).

Kuijpers, Erika, *Migrantenstad. Immigratie en sociale verhoudingen in 17e-eeuws Amsterdam* (Hilversum 2005).

Laan, P.H.J. van der (ed.) *Oorkondenboek van Amsterdam tot 1400*, Publikaties van de Gemeentelijke Archiefdienst van Amsterdam, 11 (Amsterdam 1975).

Laan, P.H.J. van der and R. Bessem (eds.), *Resoluties van de vroedschap van Amsterdam 1551–1565* (Hilversum 2008).

Leeuwen, Marco H.D. van, *Bijstand in Amsterdam, ca.1800–1850. Armenzorg als beheersings- en overlevingsstrategie* (Zwolle-Amsterdam 1992).

Leeuwen, Marco H.D. van and James E. Oeppen, 'Reconstructing the Demographic Regime of Amsterdam 1681–1920', *Economic and Social History in the Netherlands* 5 (1993): 61–102.

Leeuwen, Paul van, *Amsterdamse uithangborden en gevelstenen* (Amsterdam 1974).

Leeuwen, W.R.F. van, 'Woning- en utiliteitsbouw', in: Harry Lintsen and Martijn Bakker (eds.) *Geschiedenis van de techniek in Nederland. De wording van een moderne samenleving 1800–1890*, III, Textiel; Gas, licht en elektriciteit; Bouw (The Hague and Zutphen 1993), pp. 196–231.

Leeuw-Kistemaker, R.E. van der, *Wonen en werken in de Warmoesstraat van de 14de tot het midden van de 16de eeuw*, Werkschriften Historisch Seminarium van de Universiteit van Amsterdam, 7 (Amsterdam 1974).

Leguay, Jean-Pierre, *La rue au moyen age* (Rennes 1984).

Lennep, J. van and J. ter Gouw, *De uithangteekens, in verband met geschiedenis en volksleven beschouwd*, deel 1 (Amsterdam 1868).

Lesger, Clé, *Huur en conjunctuur. De woningmarkt in Amsterdam, 1550–1850*, Amsterdamse Historische Reeks, 10 (Amsterdam 1986).

Lesger, Clé, 'Hiërarchie en spreiding van regionale verzorgingscentra. Het centrale plaatsensysteem in Holland benoorden het IJ omstreeks 1800', *Tijdschrift voor Sociale Geschiedenis* 16 (1990): 128–153.

Lesger, Clé, *Hoorn als stedelijk knooppunt. Stedensystemen tijdens de late middeleeuwen en vroegmoderne tijd*, Hollandse Studiën, 26 (Hilversum 1990).

Lesger, Clé, 'Intraregional Trade and the Port System in Holland, 1400–1700', in: Karel Davids and Leo Noordegraaf (eds.) *The Dutch Economy in the Golden Age (Volume 4: Economic and Social History in the Netherlands)* (Amsterdam 1993), pp. 185–217.

Lesger, Clé, 'Migranten in Amsterdam in de achttiende eeuw. Residentiële spreiding en positie in de samenleving', *Jaarboek Amstelodamum* 89 (1997): 43–68.

Lesger, Clé, 'Regions, Urban Systems and Historical Central Place Analysis: Holland 1550–1800', in: Peter Ainsworth and Tom Scott (eds.) *Regions and Landscapes. Reality and Imagination in Late Medieval and Early Modern Europe* (Oxford 2000), 205–232.

Lesger, Clé, *The Rise of the Amsterdam Market and Information Exchange; Merchants, Commercial Expansion and Change in the Spatial Economy of the Low Countries, c. 1550–1630* (Aldershot 2006).

Lesger, Clé, 'De locatie van het Amsterdamse winkelbedrijf in de achttiende eeuw', *Tijdschrift voor Sociale en Economische Geschiedenis* 4 (2007): 4, 35–70.

Lesger, Clé, 'De wereld als horizon. De economie tussen 1578 en 1650', in: Willem Frijhoff and Maarten Prak (eds.) *Geschiedenis van Amsterdam. Centrum van de wereld 1578–1650*, II-1 (Amsterdam 2004), pp. 102–187, 473–476.

Lesger, Clé, 'Stagnatie en stabiliteit. De economie tussen 1730 en 1795', in: Willem Frijhoff and Maarten Prak (eds.) *Geschiedenis van Amsterdam. Zelfbewuste stadstaat 1650–1813*, II-2 (Amsterdam 2005), pp. 219–265, 506–508.

Lesger, Clé, 'Patterns of Retail Location and Urban Form in Amsterdam in the Eighteenth Century', *Urban History* 38 (2011): 24–47.

Lesger, Clé, *Het winkellandschap van Amsterdam. Stedelijke structuur en winkelbedrijf in de vroegmoderne en moderne tijd, 1550–2000* (Hilversum 2013).

Lesger, Clé and Jan Hein Furnée, 'Shopping Streets and Cultures from a Long-Term and Transnational Perspective: An Introduction', in: Jan Hein Furnée and Clé Lesger (eds.), *The Landscape of Consumption. Shopping Streets and Cultures in Western Europe, 1600–1900* (Houndmills 2014), pp. 1–15.

Lesger, Clé, Marco H.D. van Leeuwen and Bart Vissers, 'Residentiële segregatie in vroeg-moderne steden. Amsterdam in de eerste helft van de negentiende eeuw', *Tijdschrift voor Sociale en Economische Geschiedenis* 10 (2013): 102–132.

Lloyd, Peter E. and Peter Dicken, *Location in Space. A Theoretical Approach to Economic Geography* (London 1977).

Lomax, Susan, 'The View from the Shop: Window Display, the Shopper and the Formulation of Theory', in: John Benson and Laura Ugolini (eds.), *Cultures of Selling. Perspectives on Consumption and Society since 1700*, The History of Retailing and Consumption (Aldershot 2006), pp. 265–291.

Looijen, Taco K., *Ieder is hier vervuld van zijn voordeel ...; Amsterdam in de ogen van buitenlanders* (Amsterdam 1981).

Luiken, Jan and Caspar Luiken, *Het menselyk bedryf vertoond in 100 verbeeldingen van ambachten, konsten, hanteeringen en bedryven met versen* (Amsterdam 1694).

Lyna, Dries and Ilja van Damme, 'A Strategy of Seduction? The Role of Commercial Advertisements in the Eighteenth-Century Retailing Business of Antwerp', *Business History* 51 (2009): 100–121.

Maaskamp, E., *Afbeeldingen van de kleeding, zeden en gewoonten in de Bataafsche Republiek, met den aanvang der negentiende eeuw* (Amsterdam 1803).

Maaskamp, E., *Nouveau tableau statistique, historique, d'Amsterdam; ou Conducteur général de l'étranger dans cette ville* (Amsterdam [1845]).

Mac Lean, J., *Geschiedenis der gasverlichting in Nederland 1809–1850* (Zutphen 1977).

Mahieu, Paul, *De distributie. Groothandel en kleinhandel* (Antwerp 1948).

Malsen, H. van, *Geschiedenis van het makelaarsgild te Amsterdam, 1578–1933* (Amsterdam [1933]).

Marin, Pieter, *Nederduitsch en Fransch woordenboek, waarin de aart der beide taalen, naar de beste schrijvers naauwkeurig in acht genomen is* (Amsterdam 1793 [6th edition]).

Martinet, J.F., *Het vaderland, met geheel nieuw geteekende en gekleurde kaarten ... en zeer gewigtige vaderlandsche afbeeldingen* (Amsterdam 1791).

McKendrick, Neil, 'The Consumer Revolution of Eighteenth-Century England', in: Neil McKendrick, John Brewer and J.H. Plumb (eds.), *The Birth of a Consumer Society. The Commercialization of Eighteenth-Century England* (Bloomington 1982), pp. 9–33.

Meilink, P.A., 'Gegevens aangaande bedrijfskapitalen in den Hollandschen en Zeeuwschen handel in 1543', *Economisch-Historisch Jaarboek* 8 (1922): 254–277.

Meischke, R., *Het Nederlandse woonhuis van 1300–1800. Vijftig jaar Vereniging 'Hendrick de Keyser'* (Haarlem 1969).
Meischke, R. et al., *Huizen in Nederland: Amsterdam. Architectuurhistorische verkenningen aan de hand van het bezit van de Vereniging Hendrick de Keyser* (Zwolle and Amsterdam 1995).
Melker, B.R. de (ed.) *Oorkondenboek van Amsterdam tot 1400: supplement*, Apparaat voor de geschiedenis van Holland, 12 (Haarlem and Hilversum 1995).
Melle, Marius van, 'Waar vindt men uw's gelijk, verheuglijk Amsterdam? De 17de-eeuwers Fokkens, Van Domselaer en Commelin', *Ons Amsterdam* 49 (1997): 272–276.
Miellet, Roger, *Honderd jaar grootwinkelbedrijf in Nederland* (Zwolle 1993).
Miellet, Roger, 'Immigratie van katholieke Westfalers en de modernisering van de Nederlandse detailhandel', *Tijdschrift voor Geschiedenis* 100 (1987): 374–393.
Miellet, Roger, *Winkelen in weelde. Warenhuizen in West-Europa 1860–2000* (2001).
Mountague, William, *The Delights of Holland: Or, a Three Months Travel About That and the Other Provinces Etc.* (London 1696).
Mui, Hoh-Cheung and Lorna H. Mui, *Shops and Shopkeeping in Eighteenth-Century England* (London 1989).
Muiswinkel, F.L. van, *Handel, markt en beurs. Organisatie en techniek van de handel in theorie en praktijk* (Amsterdam 1957).
Muiswinkel, F.L. van and J.C. Berk (eds.) *Het kruideniersbedrijf. Een studie over het kruideniersbedrijf in Nederland* (Amsterdam 1951).
Muizelaar, Klaske and Derek Phillips, *Picturing Men and Women in the Dutch Golden Age. Paintings and People in Historical Perspective* (New Haven and London 2003).
Multhauf, Lettie S., 'The Light of Lamp-Lanterns. Street Lighting in 17th-Century Amsterdam', *Technology and Culture* 26 (1985): 236–252.
Mumford, L., *The City in History. Its Origins, Its Transformations, and Its Prospects* (London 1961).
Naam-register van veele capitaale-net-geconditioneerde Nederduitsche, en eenige Latynsche en Fransche boeken ... uit de boekwinkel van Herm. de Wit (Amsterdam 1768).
Nelson, Richard L., *The Selection of Retail Locations* (New York 1958).
Niemeyer, August Hermann, *Beobachtungen auf Reisen in und ausser Deutschland. Nebst Erinnerungen an denkwürdige Lebenserfahrungen und Zeitgenossen in den letzten fünfzig Jahren*, I-II Reise nach England (Halle 1820).
Niemeyer, August Hermann, *Beobachtungen auf einer Reise durch einen Theil von Westphalen und Holland. Nebst Erinnerungen an denkwürdige Lebenserfahrungen und Zeitgenossen in den letzten fünfzig Jahren* (Halle 1824).
Nierop, L. van, 'De bruidegoms van Amsterdam van 1578 tot 1601. Hun wording en getal', *Tijdschrift voor Geschiedenis* 48 (1933): 337–359.
Nierop, L. van, 'De handeldrijvende middenstand te Amsterdam in 1742', *Jaarboek Amstelodamum* 45 (1953): 193–230.
Nierop, L. van, 'Het kohier van de personele quotisatie te Amsterdam over het jaar 1742 en de Amsterdamse vrouw', *Jaarboek Amstelodamum* 43 (1949): 80–101.
Nierop, L. van, 'Naamregister van alle de voornaamste winkeliers der stad Amstelredam (1767)', *Jaarboek Amstelodamum* 29 (1932): 159–216.
Nieuwenhuijzen, Kees (ed.) *De vroegste foto's van Amsterdam* (Amsterdam 1974).
Nijs, Thimo de, *Op zoek naar de verdwenen middenstand. Handleiding voor onderzoek naar de detailhandel* (Hilversum 2007).
Nolet de Brauwere van Steeland, J.C.H., *Een reisje in het noorde* (Leuven and Rotterdam 1843).
Noman, Johannes, *Verzameling van Nederlandsche tafereelen van kunsten, ambachten en bedrijven, voor kinderen: met derzelver afbeeldingen, welke voorzien zijn van de noodige beschrijvingen van elke kunst, elk ambacht of bedrijf, en waarbij tevens toepasselijke versjes gevoegd zijn*, deel 4 (Zaltbommel 1829).
Noordegraaf, Leo and Gerrit Valk, *De gave Gods. De pest in Holland vanaf de late middeleeuwen* (Amsterdam 1996).
Noordkerk, H. (ed.) *Handvesten ofte privilegiën ende octroyen; mitsgaders willekeuren, costumen, ordonnantiën en handelingen der stad Amsterdam etc.* (Amsterdam 1748).
Nusteling, H., *Welvaart en werkgelegenheid in Amsterdam 1540–1860. Een relaas over demografie, economie en sociale politiek van een wereldstad* (Amsterdam 1985).

Oldewelt, W.F.H., 'Bescherming van merk en handelsnaam', in: W.F.H. Oldewelt (ed.) *Amsterdamsche archiefvondsten* (Amsterdam 1942), pp. 119–123.

Oldewelt, W.F.H., 'Twee eeuwen Amsterdamse faillissementen en het verloop van de conjunctuur (1636–1838)', *Tijdschrift voor Geschiedenis* 75 (1962): 421–435.

Oldewelt, W.F.H., (ed.) *Kohier van de Personeele Quotisatie te Amsterdam over het jaar 1742* (Amsterdam 1945).

Ottenheym, Koen, *Philip Vingboons (1607–1678) Architect* (Zutphen 1989).

Panhuysen, Bibi, *Maatwerk. Kleermakers, naaisters, oudkleerkopers en de gilden (1500–1800)* (Amsterdam 2000).

De Parijsche winkelhuizen. Keur der voornaamste bestaande winkelpuijen te Parijs ten dienste van architecten, timmerlieden, metselaars en verdere bouwkundigen, door eene vereeniging van architecten (Amsterdam 1850).

Pharmacopaea Amstelredamensis, of d'Amsterdammer apotheek, in welke allerlei medicamenten, zijnde tot Amsterdam in 't gebruik, konstiglijk bereid worden, als ook des selfs krachten en manier van ingeven (Amsterdam 1683).

Pijzel-Dommisse, Jet, '1700–1750', in: C. Willemijn Fock (ed.) *Het Nederlandse interieur in beeld 1600–1900* (Zwolle 2001), pp. 181–259.

Plancius, Cornelius, 'Beschrivinge der loflijcke ende wijtvermaerde coopstede Aemstelredamme, 1597', in: P. Scheltema (ed.) *Aemstel's Oudheid of gedenkwaardigheden van Amsterdam*, 2 (Amsterdam 1856), pp. 1–12.

Pol, Lotte van de, *Het Amsterdams hoerdom. Prostitutie in de zeventiende en achttiende eeuw* (Amsterdam 1996).

Polak, N.J., 'De taak van den tusschenhandel. Rede uitgesproken ter gelegenheid der elfde herdenking van de stichting der Nederlandsche handels-hoogeschool op 7 november 1924' in: N.J. Polak, W.J. van de Woestijne and S.C. Homan (eds.) *De functie van de groothandel. Beschouwingen van prof.dr. N.J. Polak, prof.dr. W.J. van de Woestijne en mr. S.C. Homan* (Rotterdam 1966), pp. 7–34.

Pontanus, Johannes Isacius, *Rerum et urbis Amstelodamensium historia* (Amsterdam 1611).

Posthumus, N.W., *De geschiedenis van de Leidsche lakenindustrie. II. De nieuwe tijd (zestiende tot achttiende eeuw) De lakenindustrie en verwante industrieën* (The Hague 1939).

Posthumus, N.W., *De Oosterse handel te Amsterdam; het oudst bewaarde koopmansboek van een Amsterdamse vennootschap betreffende de handel op de Oostzee, 1485–1490* (Leiden 1953).

Prak, Maarten, 'Stad van tegenstellingen 1730–1795', in: Willem Frijhoff and Maarten Prak (eds.) *Geschiedenis van Amsterdam. Zelfbewuste stadstaat 1650–1813*, II-2 (Amsterdam 2005), pp. 267–307.

Pred, Allan R., *The Spatial Dynamics of U.S. Urban-Industrial Growth, 1800–1914. Interpretive and Theoretical Essays* (Cambridge, MA 1966).

Radcliffe, Ann, *A Journey through Holland Made in the Summer of 1794*, A.G.H. Bachrach (ed.) (Leiden 1998 [1795]).

Ravesteyn Jr, W. van, *Onderzoekingen over de economische en sociale ontwikkeling van Amsterdam gedurende de 16de en het eerste kwart der 17de eeuw* (Amsterdam 1906).

Read, Stephen, *Function of urban PATTERN of urban function* (Delft 1996).

Regteren Altena, I.Q. van, 'Doove Barend, die schilder, en de wederdoopers', *Jaarboek Amstelodamum* 22 (1925): 111–123.

Reinders, Pim and Thera Wijsenbeek (eds.) *Koffie in Nederland. Vier eeuwen cultuurgeschiedenis* (Zutphen and Delft 1994).

Reinders, Pim, Annette de Wit and Harm Nijboer, '"Een specie van swarte boontjes". Voorspel van de koffie in Nederland', in: Pim Reinders and Thera Wijsenbeek (eds.) *Koffie in Nederland. Vier eeuwen cultuurgeschiedenis* (Zutphen and Delft 1994), pp. 11–24.

Ridder, B. de, *Verdwenen straatnamen* (Amsterdam 1958).

Roessingh, H.K., *Inlandse tabak. Expansie en contractie van een handelsgewas in de 17e en 18e eeuw in Nederland*, A.A.G. Bijdragen, 20 (Wageningen 1976).

Roever, N. de (ed.) *Uit onze oude Amstelstad. Schetsen en tafereelen betreffende de geschiedenis der veste, het leven en de zeden harer vroegere bewoners* (Amsterdam 1902 [2d edition]).

Rooseboom, Gerard, *Recueil van verscheijde Keuren en Costumen, midtsgaders Maniere van Procederen binnen de stadt Amsterdam* (Amsterdam 1656).

Rouwhorst, Theo, 'Oog voor detail: erkers', *Binnenstad. Uitgave van de Vereniging Vrienden van de Amsterdamse Binnenstad* 223/224 (2007).

Rouwhorst, Theo, 'Oog voor detail: pothuizen', *Binnenstad. Uitgave van de Vereniging Vrienden van de Amsterdamse Binnenstad* 234 (2009).

Rouwhorst, Theo, 'Oog voor detail: stoepen', *Binnenstad. Uitgave van de Vereniging Vrienden van de Amsterdamse Binnenstad* 235 (2009).
Rouwhorst, Theo, 'Oog voor detail: uitstal- of winkelkasten', *Binnenstad. Uitgave van de Vereniging Vrienden van de Amsterdamse Binnenstad* 222 (2007).
Roy van Zuydewijn, H.J.F de, *Amsterdamse bouwkunst 1815–1940* (Amsterdam ca. 1969).
Sandifort, P.A., 'Onze stadsweg. Grepen uit de historie van de Amsterdamse bestrating', *Ons Amsterdam* 30 (1978): 229–236.
Sautijn Kluit, W.P., 'De Amsterdamsche Courant', *Bijdragen voor Vaderlandsche Geschiedenis en Oudheidkunde* 5 (1868): 209–292.
Savary, Jacques, *Le parfait négociant, ou instruction générale pour ce qui regarde le commerce des marchandises de France & des pays étrangers* (Geneva 1752).
Savary, Jacques, *De volmaakte koopman, zynde een naaukeurige onderrechting van alles wat den Inlandschen en Uitlandschen koophandel betreft* [*enzovoort*] *in 't Nederduitsch gebracht door G. van Broekhuizen* (Amsterdam 1683).
Schipper-van Lottum, M.G.A., *Advertenties en berichten in de Amsterdamse Courant uitgetrokken op kleding, stoffen, sieraden en accessoires tussen de jaren 1672–1765* (Amsterdam and Groningen 1993–2004).
Schmal, H., 'De overheid als verkeersregelaar. Ongelukken en opstoppingen', in: W.F. Heinemeijer and M.F. Wagenaar (eds.) *Amsterdam in kaarten. Verandering van de stad in vier eeuwen cartografie* (Ede and Antwerp 1987), pp. 56–59.
Schötz, Susanne, *Handelsfrauen in Leipzig. Zur Geschichte von Arbeit und Geschlecht in der Neuzeit* (Cologne 2004).
Schrøder, Michael, *The Argand Burner: Its Origin and Development in France and England, 1780–1800. An Epoch in the History of Science, Illustrated by the Life and Work of the Physicist Ami Argand (1750–1803)* (Odense 1969).
Schrover, Marlou, *Een kolonie van Duitsers. Groepsvorming onder Duitse immigranten in Utrecht in de negentiende eeuw* (Amsterdam 2002).
Serrurier, L., et al., *Het bakkersbedrijf te Amsterdam* (*Rapport uitgebracht door de commissie, benoemd door de gemeentelijke commissie voor het onderzoek van arbeidstoestanden en de kamer van arbeid voor de voedings- en genotmiddelen te Amsterdam*) (Amsterdam 1903).
Simmons, James, *The Changing Pattern of Retail Location,* Department of Geography, Research Paper 92 (Chicago, IL 1964).
Six van Chandelier, J., ''s Amsterdammers Winter', in: J. Six van Chandelier, *Gedichten* (ed. A.E. Jacobs) (Assen and Maastricht 1991), pp. 101–125.
Smith, J.E., *A Sketch of a Tour on the Continent in the Years 1786 and 1787*, Part 1 (London 1793).
Speet, Ben, 'Een kleine nederzetting in het veen', in: Marijke Carasso-Kok (ed.) *Geschiedenis van Amsterdam. Een stad uit het niets (tot 1578)*, I (Amsterdam 2004), pp. 21–61.
Speet, Ben, 'Verstening, verdichting en vergroting', in: Marijke Carasso-Kok (ed.) *Geschiedenis van Amsterdam. Een stad uit het niets (tot 1578)*, I (Amsterdam 2004), pp. 75–107.
Spinniker, Adriaan, *Vervolg der leerzaame zinnebeelden, spiegel der boetvaardigheid en genade en eenige Stichtelyke gezangen* (Haarlem 1758).
Stabel, Peter, 'From the Market to the Shop. Retail and Urban Space in Late Medieval Bruges', in: Bruno Blondé et al. (eds.) *Buyers and Sellers. Retail Circuits and Practices in Medieval and Early Modern Europe*, Studies in European Urban History, 9 (Turnhout 2006), pp. 79–108.
Steegen, Erwin, *Kleinhandel en stedelijke ontwikkeling. Het kramersambacht te Maastricht in de vroegmoderne tijd*, Maaslandse Monografieën, 69 (Hilversum 2006).
Steensgaard, Niels, 'Commodities, Bullion and Services in Intercontinental Transactions before 1750', in: H. Pohl (ed.) *The European Discovery of the World and Its Economic Effects on the Preindustrial Society: 1500–1800*, VSWG Beihefte, 89 (Stuttgart 1990), pp. 9–23.
Stobart, Jon, '"A Settled Little Society of Trading People"? The Eighteenth-Century Retail Community of an English County Town', in: Bruno Blondé et al. (eds.) *Retailers and Consumer Changes in Early Modern Europe. England, France, Italy and the Low Countries*, Collection Perspectives Historiques, 14 (Tours 2005), pp. 189–212.
Stobart, Jon, 'Shopping Streets as Social Space. Leisure, Consumerism and Improvement in an Eighteenth-Century County Town', *Urban History* 25 (1998): 3–21.

Stobart, Jon, *Spend, Spend, Spend! A History of Shopping* (Stroud 2008).

Stobart, Jon, 'The Shopping Streets of Provincial England, 1650–1840', in: Jan Hein Furnée and Clé Lesger (eds.), *The Landscape of Consumption. Shopping Streets and Cultures in Western Europe, 1600–1900* (Houndmills 2014), pp. 16–36.

Stobart, Jon and Andrew Hann, 'Retailing Revolution in the Eighteenth Century? Evidence from North-West England', *Business History* 46 (2004): 2, 171–194.

Stobart, Jon, Andrew Hann and Victoria Morgan, *Spaces of Consumption. Leisure and Shopping in the English Town, c. 1680–1830* (London 2007).

Stolp, Annie, *De eerste couranten in Holland. Bijdrage tot de geschiedenis der geschreven nieuwstijdingen* (Haarlem [1938]).

Stolp, Annie, 'F. J. Hallo als fabrikant van vloeibaar gas', *Jaarboek Amstelodamum* 72 (1980): 120–137.

Straaten, Johannes van, *De vignola der ambachtslieden, of gemakkelijke wijze om de vijf bouworders te teekenen ... der gebouwen* (Amsterdam 1824).

Streng, J.C., *Vrijheid, gelijkheid, broederschap en gezelligheid. Het Zwolse Sint Nicolaasgilde tijdens het ancien régime* (Hilversum 2001).

Strien, Kees van, *De ontdekking van de Nederlanden. Britse en Franse reizigers in Holland en Vlaanderen, 1750–1795* (Utrecht 2001).

Strien-Chardonneau, Madeleine M.G. van, *'Le voyage de Hollande'. Recits de voyageurs Français dans les Provinces-Unies 1748–1795* (Groningen 1992).

Taverne, Ed, *In 't land van belofte: in de nieue stadt. Ideaal en werkelijkheid van de stadsuitleg in de Republiek 1580–1680* (Maarssen 1978).

Taverne, Ed, 'Een "tolerante" stedenbouw. De esthetiek van de Raadhuisstraat in Amsterdam (1895–1899)', *OverHolland. Architectonische studies voor de Hollandse stad* 4 (2007): 84–98.

Tussenbroek, Gabri van, *De toren van de Gouden Eeuw: een Hollandse strijd tussen gulden en God* (Amsterdam 2017).

Tussenbroek, Gabri van, 'Voor de grote uitleg. Stedelijke transformatie en huisbouw in Amsterdam, 1452–1578', *Stadsgeschiedenis* 10 (2015): 1–23.

Uffenbach, Zacharias Conrad von, *Merkwürdige Reisen durch Niedersachsen, Holland und Engelland,* deel 3 (Ulm 1754).

Uytven, R. van, 'Oudheid en Middeleeuwen', in: J.A. van Stuijvenberg (ed.), *De economische geschiedenis van Nederland* (Groningen 1977), pp. 1–48.

Vance Jr., James E., *The Merchant's World: The Geography of Wholesaling,* Foundations of Economic Geography Series (Englewood Cliffs, NJ 1970).

Veblen, Thorstein, *The Theory of the Leisure Class. An Economic Study of Institutions* (New York 1899).

Veluwenkamp, Jan Willem, *Ondernemersgedrag op de Hollandse stapelmarkt in de tijd van de Republiek. De Amsterdamse handelsfirma Jan Isaac de Neufville & Comp., 1730–1764* (Meppel 1981).

Verhoeff, J.M., *De oude Nederlandse maten en gewichten* (Amsterdam 1982).

Vernoegde, Petrus de, *De tien delicatessen des huwelyks. Of de wederlegging van de Tien vermakelykheden des huwelyks door Petrus de Vernoegde Getroude* (Amsterdam 1678).

Vijver, C. van der, *Geschiedkundige beschrijving der stad Amsterdam, sedert hare wording tot op den tegenwoordigen tijd; of Beknopt overzigt van den oorsprong, de uitbreiding, lotgevallen, bijzonderheden, geestelijke en wereldlijke inrigtingen en gebruiken dier stad / op eene, voor alle standen, bevattelijke en onderhoudende wijze beschreven, onder medewerking van eenige geschied- en letterkundigen,* 4 (Amsterdam 1848).

Vijver, C. van der, *Wandelingen in en om Amsterdam* (Amsterdam 1829).

Vries, Jan de, *Barges and Capitalism. Passenger Transportation in the Dutch Economy, 1632–1839* (Utrecht 1981 [original version 1978]).

Vries, Jan de, *European Urbanization 1500–1800* (Cambridge, MA 1984).

Vries, Jan de, 'The Industrial Revolution and the Industrious Revolution', *The Journal of Economic History* 54 (1994): 2, 249–270.

Vries, Jan de, *The Industrious Revolution. Consumer Behavior and the Household Economy, 1650 to the Present* (Cambridge 2008).

Vries, Jan de and Ad van der Woude, *The First Modern Economy. Success, Failure, and Perseverance of the Dutch Economy, 1500–1815* (Cambridge 1997).

Vriese, J., 'Pothuizen', *Ons Amsterdam* 9 (1957): 205–209.

Vriese, J., 'Stoepen', *Ons Amsterdam* 9 (1957): 346–350.

Vullers, Francisca and Roosmarij Deenik, *Het banketbakkersinterieur uit de collectie van het Amsterdams Historisch Museum: gered van de schroothoop ...*, interne publicatie Amsterdams Historisch Museum (Amsterdam 2009).

Waal, A.M. van de and Han de Vries, *Amsterdam omstreeks 1800. 100 tekeningen uit omstreeks 1800 en 100 foto's van nu* (Amsterdam 1965).

Waal, J.C., 'Oude winkelluyfels te Amsterdam', *De Winkelier, Officieel orgaan van de Algemeene Winkeliersvereeniging te Amsterdam* 23 (1923): 337–344.

Wagenaar, Jan, *Amsterdam, in zyne opkomst, aanwas, geschiedenissen, voorregten, koophandel, gebouwen, kerkenstaat, schoolen, schutterye, gilden en regeeringe* (Amsterdam 1760–1767).

Wagenaar, Michiel, 'De Amsterdamse markten van omstreeks 1815 tot 1945', in: Renée Kistemaker, Michiel Wagenaar and Jos van Assendelft (eds.) *Amsterdam marktstad* (Amsterdam 1984), pp. 96–138.

Wagenaar, M.F., 'De Plantage. Wonen in een lustoord', in: W.F. Heinemeijer and M.F. Wagenaar (eds.) *Amsterdam in kaarten. Verandering van de stad in vier eeuwen cartografie* (Ede and Antwerp 1987), pp. 132–135.

Walsh, Claire, 'The Newness of the Department Store. A View from the Eighteenth Century', in: Geoffrey Crossick and Serge Jaumain (eds.) *Cathedrals of Consumption. The European Department Store, 1850–1939*, The History of Retailing and Consumption (Aldershot 1999), pp. 46–71.

Walsh, Claire, 'Shop Design and the Display of Goods in Eighteenth-Century London' *Journal of Design History* 8 (1995): 157–176.

Walsh, Claire, 'Social Meaning and Social Space in the Shopping Galeries of Early Modern London', in: John Benson and Laura Ugolini (eds.) *A Nation of Shopkeepers. Five Centuries of British Retailing* (London and New York 2003), pp. 52–79.

Walsh, Claire, 'Stalls, Bulks, Shops and Long-Term Change in Seventeenth- and Eighteenth-Century England', in: Jan Hein Furnée and Clé Lesger (eds.), *The Landscape of Consumption. Shopping Streets and Cultures in Western Europe, 1600–1900* (Houndmills 2014), pp. 37–56.

Wee, H. van der, *The Growth of the Antwerp Market and the European Economy (14th-16th Centuries)* (The Hague 1963).

Westerfield, Ray Bert, *Middlemen in English Business Particularly between 1660 and 1760* (New Haven 1915).

Westermann, J.C., 'Beschouwingen over de opkomst en den bloei des handels in de Gouden Eeuw', in: A.E. d' Ailly (ed.) *Zeven eeuwen Amsterdam*, II (Amsterdam 1947), pp. 65–120.

Wijngaarden, Hilde van, 'Barber Jacobs en andere uitdraagsters. Werkende vrouwen in Amsterdam in de zestiende en zeventiende eeuw', *Tijdschrift voor Vrouwenstudies* 16 (1995): 334–347.

Wijsenbeek-Olthuis, Thera, *Achter de gevels van Delft. Bezit en bestaan van rijk en arm in een periode van achteruitgang (1700–1800)* (Hilversum 1987).

Wijsenbeek-Olthuis, Thera, 'Joodse winkels in de zeventiende en achttiende eeuw', in: *275 jaar Haagse Snoge. Nieuw elan in eeuwenoud gebouw* (The Hague 2002), pp. 79–104.

Wild, M.T. and G. Shaw, 'Locational Behaviour of Urban Retailing During the Nineteenth Century: The Example of Kingston Upon Hull', *Transactions of the Institute of British Geographers* 61 (1974): 101–118.

Wild, M.T. and G. Shaw, 'Trends in Urban Retailing: The British Experience During the Nineteenth Century', *Tijdschrift voor Economische en Sociale Geografie* 70 (1979): 35–44.

Willan, T.S., *The Inland Trade. Studies in English Internal Trade in the Sixteenth and Seventeenth Centuries* (Manchester 1976).

Winschooten, Wigardus à, *Seeman: behelsende een grondige uitlegging van de Nederlandse Konst, en spreekwoorden, voor soo veel die uit de Seevaart syn ontleend, en by de beste schryvers deeser eeuw gevonden werden* (Leiden 1681).

Witsen Geysbeek, P.G., *Het tegenwoordig Amsterdam* (Amsterdam 1809).

Woude, A.M. van der, 'Demografische ontwikkeling van de Noordelijke Nederlanden 1500–1800', in: *Algemene Geschiedenis der Nederlanden*, 5 (Haarlem 1980): 102–168.

Wouthuysen, Ester, 'Panorama uit 1817 teruggevonden', *Ons Amsterdam* 56 (2004): 28–33.

Zahn Jr., G.P., *De geschiedenis der verlichting van Amsterdam* (Amsterdam 1911).
Zande, J. van der, 'Amsterdamse stadsgeschiedschrijving vóór Wagenaar', *Holland* 17 (1985): 218–230.
Zanden, Jan Luiten van, *De industrialisatie in Amsterdam, 1825–1914* (Bergen 1987).
Zanden, Jan Luiten van and Arthur van Riel, *Nederland 1780–1914. Staat, instituties en economische ontwikkeling* (Amsterdam 2000).
Zandvliet, Kees, *De 250 rijksten van de Gouden Eeuw. Kapitaal, macht, familie en levensstijl* (Amsterdam 2006).
Zanten, Laurens van, *Spiegel der gedenckweerdighste wonderen en geschiedenissen onses tijds. Meestendeel voor-gevallen in Europa, en voornaemlijk in de Nederlanden, zedert het jaer 1600. tot den jare 1660. ...* (Amsterdam 1661).
Zantkuijl, H.J., *Bouwen in Amsterdam. Het woonhuis in de stad* (*een boek in afleveringen*) (Amsterdam 1975–1992).

List of tables

Image credits

Abbreviations

BC/UvA: Bijzondere Collecties, Universiteit van Amsterdam
KOG: Koninklijk Oudheidkundig Genootschap
RMA: Rijksmuseum Amsterdam
RPK: Rijksprentenkabinet Amsterdam
SAA: Stadsarchief Amsterdam
SAA/Bb: Stadsarchief Amsterdam, Beeldbank

Figure 1.1: after Davies, 'Structural Models of Retail Distribution', 75.
Figure 1.3: map by Cornelis Anthonisz, 1544, BC/UvA.
Figure 1.4: map by Cornelis Anthonisz, 1544, BC/UvA.
Figure 1.9: map by Cornelis Anthonisz, 1544, BC/UvA.
Figure 1.10: 'het spijzigen der hongerigen' by the Master of Alkmaar (ca. 1504); RMA, SK-A-2815-1.
Figure 1.11: drawing by (Anthonie?) Beerstraten; RMA, RP-T-1899-A-4201.
Figure 1.12: Dapper, *Historische beschryving der stadt Amsterdam*; SAA/Bb 010094003092.
Figure 1.13: Hortensius, *Het boeck van den oproer der weder-dooperen*; BC/UvA, 2 C 18.
Figure 1.14: Pontanus, *Rerum et urbis Amstelodamensium historia*; SAA/Bb 010097010845.
Figure 1.15: Hortensius, *Het boeck van den oproer der weder-dooperen*; BC/UvA, 2 C 18.
Figure 2.2: map by Balthasar Florisz, 1647; SAA.
Figure 3.2: map by Pieter Bast, 1597; SAA.
Figure 3.3: map by Balthasar Florisz, 1647; SAA.
Figure 3.4: map by Balthasar Florisz, 1647;SAA.
Figure 3.5: map published by Theodor Dankerts, ca.1700; SAA/Bb KOKA0010200000.
Figure 3.10: SAA/Bb 010094003391.
Figure 4.1: Jan van der Heyden, *Beschryving der slang-brand-spuiten*; SAA/Bb 010097004482.
Figure 4.2: Jan van der Heyden; SAA/Bb 010097010325.
Figure 4.3: Jan Luiken, *Het menselyk bedryf*; BC/UvA, OG 80-36.
Figure 4.4: SAA/Bb 010094000037.
Figure 4.5: SAA/Bb 010097002859.
Figure 4.6: Commelin, *Beschryvinge van Amsterdam*; SAA/Bb 010097011209.

Figure 4.7: SAA/Bb 010097011091.
Figure 4.8: Jan van der Heyden; SAA/Bb 010001000909.
Figure 4.9: Jan van der Heyden; SAA/Bb 010097010325.
Figure 4.10: painting by Pieter Jansz. Saenredam; RMA, SK-C-1409.
Figure 4.11: SAA/Bb 010097010890.
Figure 4.12: Dapper, *Historische beschryving der stadt Amsterdam*; SAA/Bb 010097003097.
Figure 4.13: Commelin, *Beschryvinge van Amsterdam*; SAA/Bb 010097011209.
Figure 4.14: Jan van der Heyden, *Beschryving der slang-brand-spuiten*; SAA/Bb 010001000644.
Figure 4.15: Jan van der Heyden, *Beschryving der slang-brand-spuiten*; SAA/Bb 010001000646.
Figure 4.16: SAA/Bb 010056916906.
Figure 4.17: SAA/Bb 010097016229.
Figure 4.18: Vereniging Vrienden van Amsterdamse Gevelstenen, photograph by P. van der Vlist.
Figure 4.19: painting attributed to Emanuel de Witte, Apotekarsocieteten, Stockholm.
Figure 4.20: RMA, RP-T-1884-A-291.
Figure 4.21: Van Zanten, *Spiegel der gedenckweerdighste wonderen*; BC/UvA, OK 63–281.
Figure 4.22: *Pharmacopaea Amstelredamensis*; BC/UvA, OK 62–355.
Figure 4.23: Jan Luiken, *Het menselyk bedryf*; BC/UvA, OG 80-36.
Figure 4.24: Vereniging Vrienden van Amsterdamse Gevelstenen, photograph by P. van der Vlist.
Figure 4.25: RMA, RP-P-1896-A-19368-1142.
Figure 4.26: SAA, library, collectie adreskaarten.
Figure 4.27: SAA, library, collectie adreskaarten.
Figure 4.28: Vereniging Vrienden van Amsterdamse Gevelstenen, photograph by P. van der Vlist.
Figure 4.29: Koninklijk Kabinet van Schilderijen Mauritshuis Den Haag, 109.
Figure 4.30: Vereniging Vrienden van Amsterdamse Gevelstenen, photograph by P. van der Vlist.
Figure 4.31: Museum De Lakenhal, Leiden.
Figure 6.1: print by J. Schenk; SAA/Bb 010094008206.
Figure 6.2: BC/UvA, Pr. K 819.
Figure 6.3: painting by Isaak Ouwater; RMA, SK-A-4026.
Figure 6.4: drawing by H.P. Schouten; SAA/Bb 010097010959.
Figure 6.5: SAA/Bb 010097002859.
Figure 6.6: drawing by H.P. Schouten; SAA/Bb 010001000548.
Figure 6.7: drawing by H.P. Schouten; SAA/Bb 010001000548.
Figure 6.8: drawing by H.P. Schouten; SAA/Bb 010097010959.

Figure 6.9: drawing by Reinier Vinkeles; SAA/Bb 010055000179.
Figure 6.10: SAA.
Figure 6.11: SAA/Bb 010056917858.
Figure 6.12: drawing by H.P. Schouten; SAA/Bb 010001000582.
Figure 6.13: drawing by Gerrit Lamberts; SAA/Bb 010097001186.
Figure 6.14: print published by Buffa & Zonen; SAA/Bb 010097002837.
Figure 6.15: print published by Buffa & Zonen; SAA/Bb 010097002824.
Figure 6.16: print published by Buffa & Zonen; SAA/Bb 010001000402.
Figure 6.17: drawing by A. Rademaker; SAA/Bb 010001000174.
Figure 6.18: drawing by G.F. Bergveld; SAA/Bb 010097001141.
Figure 6.19: letterhead of the firm of A. Heyman; SAA/Bb 010194000276.
Figure 6.20: SAA/Bb 010094006743.
Figure 6.21: drawing by Reinier Craeyvanger; SAA/Bb 010001000924.
Figure 6.22: print published by Buffa & Zonen; SAA/Bb 010097002837.
Figure 6.23: SAA/Bb 010094006771.
Figure 6.24: SAA/Bb 010097012533.
Figure 6.25: painting attributed to Jan Cornelis van Rossum; Amsterdam Museum, SA 38469.
Figure 6.26: SAA/Bb 010094006970.
Figure 6.27: panorama by Cornelis de Kruijf, KOG, Atlas Amsterdam, 3–10.
Figure 6.28: water colour by J.A. Langendijk; KOG, sectie Beroep en Bedrijf, ZG-1-13-B-16.
Figure 6.29: *Naam-register van boeken*, frontispiece by Reinier Vinkeles; BC/UvA, O 60–4869.
Figure 6.30: painting by Johannes Jelgerhuis; RMA, SK-A-662.
Figure 6.31: Spinniker, *Vervolg der leerzame zinnebeelden*; BC/UvA, OM 63–1835.
Figure 6.32: KOG, sectie Beroep en Bedrijf, ZG-1-11-H-32.
Figure 6.33: Maaskamp, *Afbeeldingen van de kleeding*; BC/UvA, KG 94-19.
Figure 6.34: Noman, *Verzameling van Nederlandsche tafereelen*, volume 4, 60–61; BC/UvA, 680 F 3.
Figure 6.35: Noman, *Verzameling van Nederlandsche tafereelen*, volume 4, 72–73; BC/UvA, 680 F 3.
Figure 6.36: painting attibuted to Josef Keller; Amsterdam Museum, SA 553.
Figure 6.37: Amsterdam Museum, Hl 12.
Figure 6.38: SAA/Bb 010097005168.
Figure 6.39: SAA/Bb 010094006953.
Figure 6.40: SAA/Bb 010094006826.
Figure 6.41: SAA, Atlas Dreesmann.
Figure 6.42: SAA, Atlas Dreesmann.
Figure 6.43: SAA/Bb 010094006787.

Topographical Index[1]

1 A page number followed by the letter m refers to a map.

For Product Safety Concerns and Information please contact our EU representative GPSR@taylorandfrancis.com Taylor & Francis Verlag GmbH, Kaufingerstraße 24, 80331 München, Germany

Batch number: 10722098

Printed by Printforce, the Netherlands